Law, Economics, and Philosophy

In this critical introduction to the rapidly growing "economic approach to law"—the application of economic methods of analysis to problems of legal interpretation—the editors have brought together the core literature on the subject and the most significant philosophical commentary upon that literature. The anthology is divided into two parts. The first focuses upon the economic approach in general: the Coase theorem, the role of efficiency considerations in the allocations of legal entitlements, and the case for and against wealth maximization as a norm. The second part consists of case studies featuring applications to the law of torts.

Law, Economics, and Philosophy: A Critical Introduction, with Applications to the Law of Torts

Edited by

Mark Kuperberg
and
Charles Beitz

Rowman & Allanheld
PUBLISHERS

ROWMAN & ALLANHELD

Published in the United States of America in 1983
by Rowman & Allanheld
(A division of Littlefield, Adams & Company)
81 Adams Drive, Totowa, New Jersey 07512

Library of Congress Cataloging in Publication Data
Main entry under title:

Law, economics, and philosophy.

   Includes bibliographical references and index.
   1. Law—Economic aspects. 2. Torts—Economic aspects.
I. Kuperberg, Mark, 1950– . II. Beitz, Charles R., 1949–
K487.E3L39 1983   338.4'734   83-9760
ISBN 0-8476-7288-3

83 84 85/ 10 9 8 7 6 5 4 3 2 1

Printed in the United States of America

Contents

Preface

In the last two decades, the "economic approach to law" has spread rapidly through the law schools and has increasingly engaged the attention of academic economists as well. Evidence of its influence today can be found in nearly every law review, and in the recent appointment of its most outspoken proponent (Richard Posner) to the federal bench.

This book is intended to provide the reader with a critical introduction to the literature in this area. It does not constitute a comprehensive survey of the field; however, taken together, the articles reprinted in this book introduce all of the central concepts of the normative economic analysis of law and consider the principal arguments for and against its adoption as a guide to judicial decisionmaking. As a result, the collection should serve the interests of those who simply wish to acquaint themselves with the principal controversies in the field as well as those who plan to explore the literature in greater depth.

The selections are divided into two parts. The first focuses on the analytical and philosophical foundations of the economic approach, with attention given to the Coase theorem and its relevance, the role of efficiency considerations in the allocation of legal entitlements, and arguments for and against wealth maximization as a norm. The second part takes up the law of torts as a case study of the economic approach in practice. This is the area of law in which the economic approach has been most fully developed and fruitfully applied. Detailed attention to this case not only allows the general considerations advanced earlier to be made concrete, but also gives an indication of how economists working within the general approach use its concepts to shed light on specific problems. In the Introductions to Part One and to Part Two, we discuss each of the selections separately and indicate what we regard as the leading questions that readers ought to consider as they proceed through the text.

PART ONE
Theoretical Foundations of the Economic Analysis of Law

Introduction to Part One

The economic approach to law is much more than a methodology for analyzing the consequences of judicial decisions. In addition to its methodological elements, the economic approach includes both positive and normative theses. The positive thesis is that the development of Anglo-American law can be understood as a continuing accommodation to changing social and economic circumstances by judges who interpret legal rules so as to produce economically efficient outcomes. The normative thesis is that this is as it should be.

The positive and normative theses of the economic approach are not necessarily linked. Even if we grant, for the sake of argument, that the development of Anglo-American law is, in fact, a process of promoting efficiency, we need not also agree that judges *ought* to decide cases on this basis.[1] On the other hand, we may think that the development of the law has been a haphazard process involving many different (and even conflicting) doctrinal and political currents, and yet think that judicial decisions should be justified partly or entirely in terms of their effects on efficiency.[2] The positive and normative theses of the economic approach, despite their outward similarity, are claims of very different kinds: the positive thesis is a thesis about judicial history, while the normative thesis is a thesis in political and legal philosophy. Neither thesis implies the other; each must stand or fall on its own merits.

The positive thesis raises interesting questions that are at the center of an active controversy among legal historians.[3] We shall not, however, pursue these questions in this book; instead, we will focus on the normative thesis, which is more directly related to the future evolution of the law and therefore more important for practicing lawyers and judges. It is worth pausing for a moment to see why.

In our legal system (as in any mature legal system), most of the cases that reach the courts are straightforward from a legal point of view. Well-established legal rules, based either on statute or precedent, point unambiguously to a decision for one or the other party in the case. There may, of course, be complex and controverted issues of fact for the court to resolve, but once the facts are determined, there is no difficulty in deciding how the law applies to them. Not all cases, however, are "easy cases" in this sense, for it may not be obvious, even to the informed and experienced judicial mind, which of several legal rules apply to the case, how conflicting rules should be compromised, or how a particular rule should be interpreted. Such "hard cases" raise the most perplexing question that any judge can be called upon to decide: what is the law?[4]

Much of traditional jurisprudence addresses this question. For example, the many variants of natural law theory hold that judges should resolve hard case in accordance with the requirements of natural justice or natural right.[5] Legal positivism, as represented by its most eminent contemporary exponent, H.L.A. Hart, holds that conscientious judges may have no alternative but to apply their own personal moral codes or political theories when the law is genuinely unsettled.[6] The importance of normative economic analysis of law is most obvious if the economic approach is regarded as a rival to each of these traditional schools of jurisprudence. For it instructs judges confronted with hard cases to give a central place—even, perhaps, an overriding place—in their deliberations to considerations of efficiency. How this idea can be formulated more exactly, whether one should accept it, and how, if accepted, it should be applied to cases are the chief issues explored in this volume.

Since most schools of legal thought develop from a variety of sources, it is usually difficult to identify any individual writer or work as the foundation of the school. The economic approach to law is an exception to this generalization, for its origins can be pinpointed exactly: they lie in Professor Ronald H. Coase's article, "The Problem of Social Cost," which appeared in 1960.

Coase's article examines the impact of the distribution of legal entitlements such as property rights on the production of certain costs known to economists as "externalities." An external cost is a cost generated by the activity of one economic agent that must be borne by another agent. As an illustration, consider the example discussed extensively by Coase himself. Imagine that a rancher and a farmer own adjacent tracts of land, and assume that there is no fence dividing them. The rancher's cattle are free to roam onto the farmer's property, where they will destroy (by trampling on) some of the farmer's crop. Every unit of crop destroyed by the cattle represents a potential loss to the farmer (since the farmer will be unable to sell that unit in the crop market). Since this loss is produced—inadvertently, although it might as well as be deliberately—by the rancher's cattle-raising activity, and since the loss will be borne by the farmer (in the absence of interference by the legal system), it is an *external* cost of ranching.

Economists have traditionally regarded externalities as a problem because there is no incentive for a self-interested agent whose activity produces these costs to take them into account in planning his activity.

An agent might act in a way that produces greater aggregate or society-wide costs than benefits because he is in a position to escape the costs while capturing the benefits. This is obviously a desirable situation from the point of view of the agent, but it might not be desirable from the point of view of society as a whole. More specifically, there might be another way of employing society's productive resources that would yield a greater overall balance of economic benefits and costs. The difficulty is that, if economic agents are not required to take external costs into account in planning their activities (to "internalize" their externalities), they may not act in ways that maximize the total value of the products derived from society's productive resources.

We will put aside temporarily the question of why one should be concerned with employing social resources so as to produce the greatest possible society-wide balance of economic benefits over costs. (We come back to this important question later.) For the moment, the point to make is that economists influenced by Pigou have thought that the only way to force agents to internalize their externalities was to put a tax on the production of externalities equal to the value of that portion of the external damage done by an activity that exceeds the socially optimal level.[7] In our example, a tax could be imposed on the rancher to equal the value of the damage his cattle do to the farmer's crop. (Or, what comes to the same thing in this case, the rancher could have legal liability imposed on him for this damage, so that the farmer could recover his losses by suing the rancher.) In this way, the rancher would be forced to equate the private costs of his activity—the costs to *him*—with its social cost.

Coase's article criticizes this approach as misguided. He argues that, under certain special circumstances, no governmental intervention (by way of a Pigouvian tax) is necessary to produce a socially optimal outcome. Moreover (and more importantly for our purposes), Coase argues that it makes no difference with regard to efficiency (again, under certain special conditions) how the law distributes property rights or liability. A more precise version of this proposition has come to be known as *Coase's theorem*: in a competitive economy with zero transaction costs and perfect information, the allocation of resources will be efficient however the law distributes initial entitlements.

The proof of this theorem in explained in detail in Coase's article. The essential idea is this: if two agents engage in productive activities that generate external costs, *someone* will suffer real or opportunity costs *however* the law distributes initial entitlements. In our example, if the law does not interfere (that is, if it leaves the liability for crop damage where it lies, on the farmer), then the *farmer* will bear a cost (the market value of the lost crop). On the other hand, if the law does interfere (by making the rancher liable for damage done by his cattle), then the *rancher* will suffer a cost (the amount that the law allows the farmer to recover from him, or the cost of fencing plus the reduced revenue from raising the smaller herd required by a decrease in available grazing land). Coase's insight is that, in either case, given the initial assumptions of zero transaction costs and perfect information, one of the parties, if he is a rational profit-maximizer, will try to buy the other's entitlement if he can do so for an amount less than the cost he would bear if there were no bargain between them. The other will sell his entitlement if he can realize more from doing so than the profit he could earn by retaining it. The result, Coase holds, will be an allocation of resources to productive uses that maximizes the aggregate market value of the two parties' joint product. In this sense—which is the standard sense in economics—the allocation of resources to productive uses will be efficient however the law distributes initial entitlements.

It is crucial to be clear about what Coase's theorem does *not* establish as well as about what it *does*. It does not establish that an allocatively efficient outcome will be reached when there are substantial transaction costs, which is to say, in many real-world cases. It also does not establish that the initial distribution of entitlements is indifferent to the ultimate allocation of *income* between the farmer and the rancher, as the reader can easily see by reconsidering the rancher/farmer example. (These points are discussed at some length in the article below by Jules Coleman.)

What, then, is the significance of Coase's theorem? There are two obvious answers, neither of which turns out to explain the theorem's influence in the subsequent literature. The obvious points are these. First, the theorem and its proof illustrate how the basic concepts of microeconomics can be employed to analyze the consequences for allocative efficiency of alternative legal rules, at least under the ideal conditions specified. Second, the theorem has normative significance (albeit in a somewhat attenuated sense) because it shows that the distribution of entitlements does not matter from the point of view of allocative efficiency, again under the conditions specified; so, under those conditions, a judge concerned only with allocative efficiency can do no wrong (so long as he leaves the parties free to bargain).

Most writers, however, have seen a third kind of significance in Coase's theorem. They have inferred from it a distinct principle of judicial decisionmaking that we may call *the efficiency principle*: when bargaining is difficult or impossible due to lack of information or high transaction costs, courts should assign entitlements so as to produce an efficient allocation of resources.[8] Or, as it is sometimes said, courts should "mimic the market." The fact that *this* is widely thought to be the upshot of Coase's pathbreaking article is more than a little strange. The efficiency principle does not follow logically from Coase's theorem at all. Indeed, the theorem is irrelevant to the efficiency principle. This is not only because the theorem is limited to a no-transaction-cost, perfect-information world, whereas the principle applies precisely when these limiting conditions are violated. The more basic point is that the efficiency principle is a principle of normative legal theory whereas the theorem is the conclusion of microeconomic analysis. Of course, this is not to say that the efficiency principle is incorrect, but only that the truth of the theorem (the explicit subject of Coase's article) provides no reason for accepting the principle. While Coase himself encourages readers to accept the efficiency principle, he offers no argument for it.

Consequently, if judges should follow the efficiency principle, the case for it still needs to be made.

With Coase and Judge Richard Posner (whose views we consider below), Professor Guido Calabresi of the Yale Law School is among the foremost exponents of the economic approach to law, although, as readers will appreciate from his two articles in this collection, Calabresi does not regard efficiency as the only goal that judges should try to pursue in their decisions. Calabresi's book, *The Costs of Accidents* (1970), remains a leading example of how the approach may be applied to a genuinely perplexing issue of tort doctrine—the allocation of liability for unintended harms. In the first of his articles reprinted here ("Property Rules, Liability Rules, and Inalienability: One View of the Cathedral"), Calabresi and his coauthor, A. Douglas Melamed, develop a unified framework for analyzing how the law enforces entitlements in the areas of property and torts. In the process, they illustrate the impressive analytical power of the economic approach. At the same time, they shed some light on the other goals, in addition to efficiency, that may be served by protecting entitlements (Calabresi and Melamed characterize these as "distributional goals" and "other justice considerations").

The analytical novelty of their essay lies in the perception that the property and tort laws have a common object but pursue them in different ways. The common object is the protection of entitlements. Roughly, these are legal rights not to be interfered with in the possession and use of a thing or in the exercise of various physical and mental capacities. The differences between property and torts are said to involve different legal instruments for protecting entitlements—property rules, in the first case, and liability rules, in the second. Indeed, at the end of their article, Calabresi and Melamed expand the scope of the analysis to cover the criminal law as well.

One reason for taking such a unified view of the legal protection of entitlements is that it enables us to give an abstract description of the kind of problem that judges often confront in hard cases in both property and torts. The problem is: what form of protection would it be best to extend to the entitlement in question? Should it be a property rule or a liability rule, and if the latter, should this be a rule of negligence or of strict liability? Calabresi and Melamed show how this type of problem might be solved by an appeal to efficiency (and perhaps other) considerations. (A detailed application of this solution to the tort law appears in the article by Calabresi and Hirschoff, also reprinted in this book.)

Several issues deserve attention in assessing the Calabresi and Melamed position. First, how do they interpret the efficiency norm? There is some confusion here. Calabresi and Melamed explicitly endorse the criterion of *Pareto efficiency*: one allocation of resources is preferable to another if, under the first allocation, at least one person is better off than under the second while no one else is worse off. But their discussion suggests that their real concern is a different idea, usually referred to as *Kaldor-Hicks efficiency* (or, the *hypothetical compensation* criterion): one allocation is preferable to another if, under the first allocation, some people are so much better off than they would be under the second that they could compensate those who would be better off under the second allocation and still come out ahead. (Note that, according to this conception, compensation need not *actually* be paid. Thus, Kaldor-Hicks efficiency might justify policies that Pareto efficiency would not.) Which conception do Calabresi and Melamed in fact accept? Clearly, it makes a difference.

Another issue concerns the relationship among the three classes of goals (efficiency, distribution, and "other justice considerations") that the authors appeal to in their discussion of the relative merits of the various ways of protecting entitlements. Can these goals conflict? If so, why and under what circumstances? When there is a conflict, is there any systematic method for resolving the conflict, or must judges rely on their moral intuitions?

Finally and most fundamentally, one must consider why efficiency should be given *any* independent weight in judicial decisionmaking. Calabresi and Melamed, in company with most economists, appear to think that efficiency is so obviously a virtue that it requires no very detailed justification. However, if only for the sake of philosophical completeness, one should ask the following question: assuming arguendo that it is possible fully to satisfy the requirements of distributive justice and "other justice considerations," why should a judge care if efficiency conflicts with them? Why not say, so much the worse for efficiency? (The question is not whether efficiency should matter *at all;* obviously, an efficient means of promoting equity and justice is better than an inefficient one. Our question, rather, is why one should care about efficiency *when it conflicts* with these other goals.)

In "The Economic Analysis of Law," Jules Coleman advances the discussion in several useful ways. First, he presents clear definitions of the rival conceptions of efficiency (Pareto and Kaldor-Hicks) to which we have already referred. He also calls attention to a distinction of great importance between two aspects of Pareto efficiency, which he calls *Pareto optimality* and *Pareto superiority.* Pareto optimality describes a state of affairs such that it is impossible by any reallocation of resources to make anyone better off without making someone else worse off. Pareto superiority, by contrast, describes a relation between two states of affairs, A and B, such that A is Pareto superior to B if and only if, in A, one person is better off than he or she would be in B, while no one else is worse off. (In that case, we may say that a shift from B to A is a "Pareto improvement.") The distinction may be clarified by considering that one state (A) may be Pareto superior to another (B) without being Pareto optimal: there might be another state (C) that is Pareto superior to A. One should also note that a Pareto suboptimal state (D) need not be Pareto inferior to a Pareto optimal state (E): it may not be possible to move from D to E without making someone worse off, even though, once E is attained, it will be impossible by any further reallocation of resources to confer additional benefits on anyone without imposing costs on someone else. These points, discussed in more detail by Coleman, are crucial. Inasmuch as the literature seems plagued with confusion about the meaning of efficiency, Coleman's distinctions deserve the reader's careful attention.[9]

A second helpful contribution is Coleman's discussion of the relationship of efficiency and utility. Many writers have thought that the answer to our earlier question about the normative significance of efficiency is to be found in utilitarian moral theory. The standard view is that efficiency is preferable to inefficiency because it yields greater social utility. Coleman points out two problems in this standard view. First, it is a controversial question whether social utility should be identified with market value. Philosophical utilitarianism regards utility as a function of happiness—the greater the happiness in a state of affairs, the greater its utility.[10] But the welfare economic concept of efficiency measures the value of a state of affairs by its place in people's preference ordering, which in turn is inferred from the amount of money that people are willing and able to pay for it—that is, from its market value. Obviously, therefore, utility and efficiency should not simply be identified with one another; they are not simply different names for the same thing. Of course, one might admit this but still maintain as a matter of fact that efficiency is a surrogate for utility. Since happiness itself is so notoriously difficult to measure and compare, this could seem to be an appealing maneuver. It is not clear, however, that market value is always a good proxy for utility. This depends on how income and wealth are distributed in a society, and perhaps on cultural and social background conditions as well.[11]

Another problem with the view that the value of efficiency can be explained in utilitarian terms is that efficiency itself is ambiguous. As Coleman points out, the utility properties of efficiency vary according to which conception of efficiency we adopt. Only judgments of Pareto superiority warrant judgments of social utility (for reasons explained by Coleman), and even this, he claims, is not enough to supply a utilitarian *justification* for promoting efficiency.

Finally, Coleman provides an analysis of the Coase theorem that clarifies the special conditions under which it holds and explores how (if at all) it might affect judicial reasoning when these conditions do not apply. In connection with the latter issue, Coleman develops the idea of an auction market for entitlements as a way of imagining how a judge might decide which distribution of entitlements would best "mimic the market." This idea gives structure to the theory implicit in the Calabresi and Melamed article discussed above, and suggests some criticisms of that theory that derive from Coleman's doubts about the connection of utility and efficiency.

If efficiency is not, in fact, an acceptable surrogate for utility, or if one is inclined in any event to distrust utilitarianism as a moral theory, then one must wonder if there are nonutilitarian reasons for valuing efficiency. One of the few economic analysts of law to have faced this issue straightforwardly is Judge Posner. Indeed, he has addressed it in at least two articles, giving two different justifications of the view that efficiency should be a judge's overriding consideration in hard cases. We include in this collection the more recent of these articles.[12]

The chief difficulty for readers of Posner's article will be to grasp the connection between his opening discussion of the virtues of Pareto efficiency and his concluding endorsement of the principle of wealth maximization (which he identifies with Kaldor-Hicks efficiency). We have already noted, as Posner clearly recognizes, that the two ideas of efficiency must not be confused with one another. Nevertheless, Posner contends that wealth maximization should be a judge's first concern for the same reasons that Pareto efficiency is (allegedly) morally appealing.

Posner begins from the observation that there is a prima facie case for any decision or policy that improves Pareto efficiency—which means, once again, that the decision or policy makes at least one person better off without making anyone else worse off. (Using Coleman's terminology, we may say that the result of such a policy is Pareto superior to the status quo.) The prima facie case rests on one of two suppositions (which Posner himself does not clearly distinguish). The first is that Pareto-improving moves are consensual from the points of view of all concerned, or at least, they do not require anyone to do what he or she does not want to do. The other supposition is that, under the circumstances, no one has any reason to complain; no one's position is worsened, and at least someone's position is improved. For both reasons, there is a presumption in favor of any Pareto-improving decision or policy. However, as Posner notes, the Pareto criterion is not very helpful in the real world, since even the most obviously desirable decisions sometimes impose costs on *someone;* the Pareto criterion would bar any such changes, and thus seems powerfully status quo-oriented.

Fortunately, Posner says, we need not settle for Pareto when we could have Kaldor-Hicks. All that is needed to justify the switch is an argument that the actual losses that some would suffer under Kaldor-Hicks would not be morally objectionable. (Recall that, under Kaldor-Hicks, while it must be *possible* for gainers to compensate losers and still come out ahead, actual payment of compensation is not required. If we interpret welfare as wealth, then Kaldor-Hicks is equivalent to what Posner calls the principle of wealth maximization: maximize overall social wealth, whatever the distributional consequences.) The pivot of Posner's argument to this effect is the notion of *ex ante compensation.* He holds that losses seemingly imposed on people without their consent have often been compensated in advance, which, he says, is tantamount to their having been consented to. For example, Posner considers the case of a factory that moves from city A to city B, thereby decreasing property values and thus causing losses to property owners in city A. He says that these losses have already been compensated since the initial purchase price of property in city A reflected the risk that the factory might close up and move away.

As Ronald Dworkin points out in his reply to Posner ("Why Efficiency?"), two different arguments seem to be combined here. One is that some losses can be said to have been consented to in advance by those who must bear them, and are therefore unobjectionable from a moral point of view. "Consent" is demonstrated in the willingness to pay a price that discounts the risk of loss. The other argument is that it is in the antecedent interest of most people that courts (and apparently other agencies of government) impose losses on some people when the effect is to maximize overall social wealth; thus, no one would be entitled to complain when it was his or her turn to suffer losses (since to complain would be special pleading).

Dworkin criticizes both arguments. Regarding the first, he claims that it is not true in most actual cases that people consent in advance to losses imposed upon them in the name of social wealth maximization. In the factory-moving case, even if the initial purchase price discounted the risk that the factory might close up and move, paying the price is not the same thing as agreeing to accept a loss. And in any event, Dworkin questions whether it is realistic to think that prices always accurately discount all of the risks of loss associated with ownership of the entitlement purchased.

With regard to the second argument, Dworkin notes that philosophical appeals to antecedent interest are deeply problematic, since it is not clear how a person's antecedent interests should be identified or why those interests should carry moral weight after the fact. It might have been in your interest yesterday to promise to buy your friend dinner tomorrow in return for some favor, but if you did not in fact make the promise yesterday, then you do not in fact owe your friend dinner tomorrow. Analogously, Dworkin objects that the supposed fact that wealth maximization is in almost everyone's interest before any decision is made does not imply that those on whom costs are imposed by a decision have any reason to regard the imposition as morally justified.

Readers seeking to resolve the dispute about efficiency as a norm in judicial decisionmaking will wish both to clarify the analytical confusions surrounding the meaning of efficiency and to consider the moral arguments advanced on both sides. However, we do not believe that this is sufficient for assessing the normative economic analysis of law. Indeed, in our view, the literature has too often stopped here and has therefore failed to explore analytical and moral issues that arise only in the context of economic analysis of particular branches of the law. Accordingly, we think it essential to consider in some detail the manner in which lawyers and economists have actually practiced economic analysis of law. In the next set of readings, we focus on key efforts to apply the economic approach to torts, where both the strengths and the shortcomings of the approach can be brought into relief.

Notes

1. The positive thesis is developed in Richard A. Posner, "Some Uses and Abuses of Economics in Law," *University of Chicago Law Review* 46, no. 2 (1979). See also Frank I. Michelman, "A Comment on 'Some Uses and Abuses of Economics in Law,'" *University of Chicago Law Review* 46, no. 2 (1979). For an effort to provide detailed documentation for the positive thesis as regards the tort law, see Richard A. Posner, "A Theory of Negligence," *Journal of Legal Studies* 1, no. 1 (1972).

2. A leading advocate of this position is Guido Calabresi. In addition to the articles

included below, see his important study, *The Costs of Accidents* (New Haven: Yale University Press, 1970).

3. See, for example, Lawrence M. Friedman, *A History of American Law* (New York: Simon & Schuster, 1974); Morton J. Horwitz, *The Transformation of American Law, 1780–1860* (Cambridge: Harvard University Press, 1977); and, for criticism of these approaches, Gary T. Schwartz, "Tort Law and the Economy in Nineteenth-Century America: A Reinterpretation," *Yale Law Journal* 90, no. 8 (1981).

4. See Ronald Dworkin, *Taking Rights Seriously* (Cambridge: Harvard University Press, 1977), pp. 81–130.

5. For an example, see J. N. Finnis, *Natural Law and Natural Rights* (Oxford: Clarendon Press, 1980).

6. H.L.A. Hart, *The Concept of Law* (Oxford: Clarendon Press, 1961), pp. 121–32.

7. A. C. Pigou, *The Economics of Welfare,* 4th ed. (London: Macmillan and Co., 1932). For a discussion, see Richard Musgrave and Peggy Musgrave, *Public Finance in Theory and Practice,* 3d ed. (New York: McGraw-Hill Inc., 1980), pp. 753–65.

8. Richard A. Posner, *Economic Analysis of Law,* 2d ed. (Boston: Little, Brown & Co., 1977), pp. 17–19.

9. There is a more extensive discussion of these distinctions in another paper by Coleman, "Efficiency, Exchange, and Auction: Philosophic Aspects of the Economic Approach to Law," *California Law Review* 68, no. 1 (1980).

10. For example, see J.J.C. Smart, "An Outline of a System of Utilitarian Ethics," in J.J.C. Smart and Bernard Williams, *Utilitarianism: For and Against* (New York: Cambridge University Press, 1973), pp. 3–74; and Richard B. Brandt, *A Theory of the Good and the Right* (New York: Oxford University Press, 1979), pp. 246–65.

11. For extended discussions of this point, see Hal R. Varian, "Distributive Justice, Welfare Economics, and the Theory of Fairness," *Philosophy and Public Affairs* 4, no. 3 (1975); and Ronald Dworkin, "Is Wealth a Value?" *Journal of Legal Studies* 9, no. 2 (1980).

12. The first is "Utilitarianism, Economics, and Legal Theory," *Journal of Legal Studies* 8, no. 1 (1979). For criticisms of Posner's argument, see Ronald Dworkin, "Is Wealth a Value?," *Journal of Legal Studies* 9, no. 2 (1980), and A. T. Kronman, "Wealth Maximization as a Normative Principle," *Journal of Legal Studies* 9, no. 2 (1980). Posner replies to both critics in "The Value of Wealth: A Reply to Dworkin and Kronman," *Journal of Legal Studies* 9, no. 2 (1980). Revised versions of both of Posner's defenses of efficiency appear as Chapters 3 and 4 in his *The Economics of Justice* (Cambridge: Harvard University Press, 1981).

THE PROBLEM OF SOCIAL COST

R. H. COASE
University of Virginia

I. The Problem To Be Examined[1]

THIS paper is concerned with those actions of business firms which have harmful effects on others. The standard example is that of a factory the smoke from which has harmful effects on those occupying neighbouring properties. The economic analysis of such a situation has usually proceeded in terms of a divergence between the private and social product of the factory, in which economists have largely followed the treatment of Pigou in *The Economics of Welfare*. The conclusions to which this kind of analysis seems to have led most economists is that it would be desirable to make the owner of the factory liable for the damage caused to those injured by the smoke, or alternatively, to place a tax on the factory owner varying with the amount of smoke produced and equivalent in money terms to the damage it would cause, or finally, to exclude the factory from residential districts (and presumably from other

---

[1] This article, although concerned with a technical problem of economic analysis, arose out of the study of the Political Economy of Broadcasting which I am now conducting. The argument of the present article was implicit in a previous article dealing with the problem of allocating radio and television frequencies (The Federal Communications Commission, 2 J. Law & Econ. [1959]) but comments which I have received seemed to suggest that it would be desirable to deal with the question in a more explicit.way and without reference to the original problem for the solution of which the analysis was developed.

areas in which the emission of smoke would have harmful effects on others).
It is my contention that the suggested courses of action are inappropriate, in
that they lead to results which are not necessarily, or even usually, desirable.

II. THE RECIPROCAL NATURE OF THE PROBLEM

The traditional approach has tended to obscure the nature of the choice
that has to be made. The question is commonly thought of as one in which A
inflicts harm on B and what has to be decided is: how should we restrain A?
But this is wrong. We are dealing with a problem of a reciprocal nature. To
avoid the harm to B would inflict harm on A. The real question that has to be
decided is: should A be allowed to harm B or should B be allowed to harm A?
The problem is to avoid the more serious harm. I instanced in my previous
article[2] the case of a confectioner the noise and vibrations from whose machinery disturbed a doctor in his work. To avoid harming the doctor would
inflict harm on the confectioner. The problem posed by this case was essentially whether it was worth while, as a result of restricting the methods of production which could be used by the confectioner, to secure more doctoring at the
cost of a reduced supply of confectionery products. Another example is
afforded by the problem of straying cattle which destroy crops on neighbouring land. If it is inevitable that some cattle will stray, an increase in the supply of meat can only be obtained at the expense of a decrease in the supply of
crops. The nature of the choice is clear: meat or crops. What answer should
be given is, of course, not clear unless we know the value of what is obtained
as well as the value of what is sacrificed to obtain it. To give another example,
Professor George J. Stigler instances the contamination of a stream.[3] If we
assume that the harmful effect of the pollution is that it kills the fish, the
question to be decided is: is the value of the fish lost greater or less than the
value of the product which the contamination of the stream makes possible.
It goes almost without saying that this problem has to be looked at in total
and at the margin.

III. THE PRICING SYSTEM WITH LIABILITY FOR DAMAGE

I propose to start my analysis by examining a case in which most economists would presumably agree that the problem would be solved in a completely satisfactory manner: when the damaging business has to pay for all
damage caused *and* the pricing system works smoothly (strictly this means
that the operation of a pricing system is without cost).

A good example of the problem under discussion is afforded by the case of
straying cattle which destroy crops growing on neighbouring land. Let us suppose that a farmer and a cattle-raiser are operating on neighbouring proper-

[2] Coase, The Federal Communications Commission, 2 J. Law & Econ. 26–27 (1959).

[3] G. J. Stigler, The Theory of Price 105 (1952).

ties. Let us further suppose that, without any fencing between the properties, an increase in the size of the cattle-raiser's herd increases the total damage to the farmer's crops. What happens to the marginal damage as the size of the herd increases is another matter. This depends on whether the cattle tend to follow one another or to roam side by side, on whether they tend to be more or less restless as the size of the herd increases and on other similar factors. For my immediate purpose, it is immaterial what assumption is made about marginal damage as the size of the herd increases.

To simplify the argument, I propose to use an arithmetical example. I shall assume that the annual cost of fencing the farmer's property is $9 and that the price of the crop is $1 per ton. Also, I assume that the relation between the number of cattle in the herd and the annual crop loss is as follows:

Number in Herd (Steers)	Annual Crop Loss (Tons)	Crop Loss per Additional Steer (Tons)
1	1	1
2	3	2
3	6	3
4	10	4

Given that the cattle-raiser is liable for the damage caused, the additional annual cost imposed on the cattle-raiser if he increased his herd from, say, 2 to 3 steers is $3 and in deciding on the size of the herd, he will take this into account along with his other costs. That is, he will not increase the size of the herd unless the value of the additional meat produced (assuming that the cattle-raiser slaughters the cattle), is greater than the additional costs that this will entail, including the value of the additional crops destroyed. Of course, if, by the employment of dogs, herdsmen, aeroplanes, mobile radio and other means, the amount of damage can be reduced, these means will be adopted when their cost is less than the value of the crop which they prevent being lost. Given that the annual cost of fencing is $9, the cattle-raiser who wished to have a herd with 4 steers or more would pay for fencing to be erected and maintained, assuming that other means of attaining the same end would not do so more cheaply. When the fence is erected, the marginal cost due to the liability for damage becomes zero, except to the extent that an increase in the size of the herd necessitates a stronger and therefore more expensive fence because more steers are liable to lean against it at the same time. But, of course, it may be cheaper for the cattle-raiser not to fence and to pay for the damaged crops, as in my arithmetical example, with 3 or fewer steers.

It might be thought that the fact that the cattle-raiser would pay for all crops damaged would lead the farmer to increase his planting if a cattle-raiser came to occupy the neighbouring property. But this is not so. If the crop was previously sold in conditions of perfect competition, marginal cost was equal to price for the amount of planting undertaken and any expansion would have reduced the profits of the farmer. In the new situation, the existence of crop damage would mean that the farmer would sell less on the open market but his receipts for a given production would remain the same, since the cattle-raiser would pay the market price for any crop damaged. Of course, if cattle-raising commonly involved the destruction of crops, the coming into existence of a cattle-raising industry might raise the price of the crops involved and farmers would then extend their planting. But I wish to confine my attention to the individual farmer.

I have said that the occupation of a neighbouring property by a cattle-raiser would not cause the amount of production, or perhaps more exactly the amount of planting, by the farmer to increase. In fact, if the cattle-raising has any effect, it will be to decrease the amount of planting. The reason for this is that, for any given tract of land, if the value of the crop damaged is so great that the receipts from the sale of the undamaged crop are less than the total costs of cultivating that tract of land, it will be profitable for the farmer and the cattle-raiser to make a bargain whereby that tract of land is left un-cultivated. This can be made clear by means of an arithmetical example. Assume initially that the value of the crop obtained from cultivating a given tract of land is $12 and that the cost incurred in cultivating this tract of land is $10, the net gain from cultivating the land being $2. I assume for purposes of simplicity that the farmer owns the land. Now assume that the cattle-raiser starts operations on the neighbouring property and that the value of the crops damaged is $1. In this case $11 is obtained by the farmer from sale on the market and $1 is obtained from the cattle-raiser for damage suffered and the net gain remains $2. Now suppose that the cattle-raiser finds it profitable to increase the size of his herd, even though the amount of damage rises to $3; which means that the value of the additional meat production is greater than the additional costs, including the additional $2 payment for damage. But the total payment for damage is now $3. The net gain to the farmer from cultivating the land is still $2. The cattle-raiser would be better off if the farmer would agree not to cultivate his land for any payment less than $3. The farmer would be agreeable to not cultivating the land for any payment greater than $2. There is clearly room for a mutually satisfactory bargain which would lead to the abandonment of cultivation.[4] But the same argument applies not only to the whole tract cultivated by the farmer but also to any

---

[4] The argument in the text has proceeded on the assumption that the alternative to cultivation of the crop is abandonment of cultivation altogether. But this need not be so. There may be crops which are less liable to damage by cattle but which would not be as profitable as the crop grown in the absence of damage. Thus, if the cultivation of a new crop would yield a return to the farmer of $1 instead of $2, and the size of the herd which would cause $3 damage with the old crop would cause $1 damage with the new crop, it would be profitable to the cattle-raiser to pay any sum less than $2 to induce the farmer

subdivision of it. Suppose, for example, that the cattle have a well-defined route, say, to a brook or to a shady area. In these circumstances, the amount of damage to the crop along the route may well be great and if so, it could be that the farmer and the cattle-raiser would find it profitable to make a bargain whereby the farmer would agree not to cultivate this strip of land.

But this raises a further possibility. Suppose that there is such a well-defined route. Suppose further that the value of the crop that would be obtained by cultivating this strip of land is $10 but that the cost of cultivation is $11. In the absence of the cattle-raiser, the land would not be cultivated. However, given the presence of the cattle-raiser, it could well be that if the strip was cultivated, the whole crop would be destroyed by the cattle. In which case, the cattle-raiser would be forced to pay $10 to the farmer. It is true that the farmer would lose $1. But the cattle-raiser would lose $10. Clearly this is a situation which is not likely to last indefinitely since neither party would want this to happen. The aim of the farmer would be to induce the cattle-raiser to make a payment in return for an agreement to leave this land uncultivated. The farmer would not be able to obtain a payment greater than the cost of fencing off this piece of land nor so high as to lead the cattle-raiser to abandon the use of the neighbouring property. What payment would in fact be made would depend on the shrewdness of the farmer and the cattle-raiser as bargainers. But as the payment would not be so high as to cause the cattle-raiser to abandon this location and as it would not vary with the size of the herd, such an agreement would not affect the allocation of resources but would merely alter the distribution of income and wealth as between the cattle-raiser and the farmer.

I think it is clear that if the cattle-raiser is liable for damage caused and the pricing system works smoothly, the reduction in the value of production elsewhere will be taken into account in computing the additional cost involved in increasing the size of the herd. This cost will be weighed against the value of the additional meat production and, given perfect competition in the cattle industry, the allocation of resources in cattle-raising will be optimal. What needs to be emphasized is that the fall in the value of production elsewhere which would be taken into account in the costs of the cattle-raiser may well be less than the damage which the cattle would cause to the crops in the ordinary course of events. This is because it is possible, as a result of market transactions, to discontinue cultivation of the land. This is desirable in all

---

to change his crop (since this would reduce damage liability from $3 to $1) and it would be profitable for the farmer to do so if the amount received was more than $1 (the reduction in his return caused by switching crops). In fact, there would be room for a mutually satisfactory bargain in all cases in which a change of crop would reduce the amount of damage by more than it reduces the value of the crop (excluding damage)—in all cases, that is, in which a change in the crop cultivated would lead to an increase in the value of production.

cases in which the damage that the cattle would cause, and for which the cattle-raiser would be willing to pay, exceeds the amount which the farmer would pay for use of the land. In conditions of perfect competition, the amount which the farmer would pay for the use of the land is equal to the difference between the value of the total production when the factors are employed on this land and the value of the additional product yielded in their next best use (which would be what the farmer would have to pay for the factors). If damage exceeds the amount the farmer would pay for the use of the land, the value of the additional product of the factors employed elsewhere would exceed the value of the total product in this use after damage is taken into account. It follows that it would be desirable to abandon cultivation of the land and to release the factors employed for production elsewhere. A procedure which merely provided for payment for damage to the crop caused by the cattle but which did not allow for the possibility of cultivation being discontinued would result in too small an employment of factors of production in cattle-raising and too large an employment of factors in cultivation of the crop. But given the possibility of market transactions, a situation in which damage to crops exceeded the rent of the land would not endure. Whether the cattle-raiser pays the farmer to leave the land uncultivated or himself rents the land by paying the land-owner an amount slightly greater than the farmer would pay (if the farmer was himself renting the land), the final result would be the same and would maximise the value of production. Even when the farmer is induced to plant crops which it would not be profitable to cultivate for sale on the market, this will be a purely short-term phenomenon and may be expected to lead to an agreement under which the planting will cease. The cattle-raiser will remain in that location and the marginal cost of meat production will be the same as before, thus having no long-run effect on the allocation of resources.

IV. THE PRICING SYSTEM WITH NO LIABILITY FOR DAMAGE

I now turn to the case in which, although the pricing system is assumed to work smoothly (that is, costlessly), the damaging business is not liable for any of the damage which it causes. This business does not have to make a payment to those damaged by its actions. I propose to show that the allocation of resources will be the same in this case as it was when the damaging business was liable for damage caused. As I showed in the previous case that the allocation of resources was optimal, it will not be necessary to repeat this part of the argument.

I return to the case of the farmer and the cattle-raiser. The farmer would suffer increased damage to his crop as the size of the herd increased. Suppose that the size of the cattle-raiser's herd is 3 steers (and that this is the size of the herd that would be maintained if crop damage was not taken into account). Then the farmer would be willing to pay up to $3 if the cattle-raiser would reduce his herd to 2 steers, up to $5 if the herd were reduced to 1 steer and would pay up to $6 if cattle-raising was abandoned. The cattle-raiser would therefore receive $3 from the farmer if he kept 2 steers instead of 3. This $3 foregone is therefore part of the cost incurred in keeping the third steer. Whether the $3 is a payment which the cattle-raiser has to make if he adds the third steer to his herd (which it would be if the cattle-raiser was liable to the farmer for damage caused to the crop) or whether it is a sum of money which he would have received if he did not keep a third steer (which it would be if the cattle-raiser was not liable to the farmer for damage caused to the crop) does not affect the final result. In both cases $3 is part of the cost of adding a third steer, to be included along with the other costs. If the increase in the value of production in cattle-raising through increasing the size of the herd from 2 to 3 is greater than the additional costs that have to be incurred (including the $3 damage to crops), the size of the herd will be increased. Otherwise, it will not. The size of the herd will be the same whether the cattle-raiser is liable for damage caused to the crop or not.

It may be argued that the assumed starting point—a herd of 3 steers—was arbitrary. And this is true. But the farmer would not wish to pay to avoid crop damage which the cattle-raiser would not be able to cause. For example, the maximum annual payment which the farmer could be induced to pay could not exceed $9, the annual cost of fencing. And the farmer would only be willing to pay this sum if it did not reduce his earnings to a level that would cause him to abandon cultivation of this particular tract of land. Furthermore, the farmer would only be willing to pay this amount if he believed that, in the absence of any payment by him, the size of the herd maintained by the cattle raiser would be 4 or more steers. Let us assume that this is the case. Then the farmer would be willing to pay up to $3 if the cattle raiser would reduce his herd to 3 steers, up to $6 if the herd were reduced to 2 steers, up to $8 if one steer only were kept and up to $9 if cattle-raising were abandoned. It will be noticed that the change in the starting point has not altered the amount which would accrue to the cattle-raiser if he reduced the size of his herd by any given amount. It is still true that the cattle-raiser could receive an additional $3 from the farmer if he agreed to reduce his herd from 3 steers to 2 and that the $3 represents the value of the crop that would be destroyed by adding the third steer to the herd. Although a different belief on the part of the farmer (whether justified or not) about the size of the herd that the cattle-raiser would maintain in the absence of payments from him may affect the total payment he can be induced to pay, it is not true that this different belief would have any effect on the size of the herd that the cattle-raiser will actually keep. This will be the same as it would be if the cattle-raiser had to pay for damage caused by his cattle, since a receipt foregone of a given amount is the equivalent of a payment of the same amount.

It might be thought that it would pay the cattle-raiser to increase his herd above the size that he would wish to maintain once a bargain had been made, in order to induce the farmer to make a larger total payment. And this may be true. It is similar in nature to the action of the farmer (when the cattle-raiser was liable for damage) in cultivating land on which, as a result of an agreement with the cattle-raiser, planting would subsequently be abandoned (including land which would not be cultivated at all in the absence of cattle-raising). But such manoeuvres are preliminaries to an agreement and do not affect the long-run equilibrium position, which is the same whether or not the cattle-raiser is held responsible for the crop damage brought about by his cattle.

It is necessary to know whether the damaging business is liable or not for damage caused since without the establishment of this initial delimitation of rights there can be no market transactions to transfer and recombine them. But the ultimate result (which maximises the value of production) is independent of the legal position if the pricing system is assumed to work without cost.

V. The Problem Illustrated Anew

The harmful effects of the activities of a business can assume a wide variety of forms. An early English case concerned a building which, by obstructing currents of air, hindered the operation of a windmill.[5] A recent case in Florida concerned a building which cast a shadow on the cabana, swimming pool and sunbathing areas of a neighbouring hotel.[6] The problem of straying cattle and the damaging of crops which was the subject of detailed examination in the two preceding sections, although it may have appeared to be rather a special case, is in fact but one example of a problem which arises in many different guises. To clarify the nature of my argument and to demonstrate its general applicability, I propose to illustrate it anew by reference to four actual cases.

Let us first reconsider the case of *Sturges v. Bridgman*[7] which I used as an illustration of the general problem in my article on "The Federal Communications Commission." In this case, a confectioner (in Wigmore Street) used two mortars and pestles in connection with his business (one had been in operation in the same position for more than 60 years and the other for more than 26 years). A doctor then came to occupy neighbouring premises (in Wimpole Street). The confectioner's machinery caused the doctor no harm until, eight years after he had first occupied the premises, he built a consulting room at the end of his garden right against the confectioner's kitchen. It was then found that the noise and vibration caused by the confectioner's machin-

[5] See Gale on Easements 237–39 (13th ed. M. Bowles 1959).

[6] See Fontainebleu Hotel Corp. v. Forty-Five Twenty-Five, Inc., 114 So. 2d 357 (1959).

[7] 11 Ch. D. 852 (1879).

ery made it difficult for the doctor to use his new consulting room. "In particular . . . the noise prevented him from examining his patients by auscultation[8] for diseases of the chest. He also found it impossible to engage with effect in any occupation which required thought and attention." The doctor therefore brought a legal action to force the confectioner to stop using his machinery. The courts had little difficulty in granting the doctor the injunction he sought. "Individual cases of hardship may occur in the strict carrying out of the principle upon which we found our judgment, but the negation of the principle would lead even more to individual hardship, and would at the same time produce a prejudicial effect upon the development of land for residential purposes."

The court's decision established that the doctor had the right to prevent the confectioner from using his machinery. But, of course, it would have been possible to modify the arrangements envisaged in the legal ruling by means of a bargain between the parties. The doctor would have been willing to waive his right and allow the machinery to continue in operation if the confectioner would have paid him a sum of money which was greater than the loss of income which he would suffer from having to move to a more costly or less convenient location or from having to curtail his activities at this location or, as was suggested as a possibility, from having to build a separate wall which would deaden the noise and vibration. The confectioner would have been willing to do this if the amount he would have to pay the doctor was less than the fall in income he would suffer if he had to change his mode of operation at this location, abandon his operation or move his confectionery business to some other location. The solution of the problem depends essentially on whether the continued use of the machinery adds more to the confectioner's income than it subtracts from the doctor's.[9] But now consider the situation if the confectioner had won the case. The confectioner would then have had the right to continue operating his noise and vibration-generating machinery without having to pay anything to the doctor. The boot would have been on the other foot: the doctor would have had to pay the confectioner to induce him to stop using the machinery. If the doctor's income would have fallen more through continuance of the use of this machinery than it added to the income of the confectioner, there would clearly be room for a bargain whereby the doctor paid the confectioner to stop using the machinery. That is to say, the circumstances in which it would not pay the confectioner to continue to use the machinery and to compensate the doctor for the losses that this would bring (if the doctor had the right to prevent the confectioner's using his

[8] Auscultation is the act of listening by ear or stethoscope in order to judge by sound the condition of the body.

[9] Note that what is taken into account is the change in income after allowing for alterations in methods of production, location, character of product, etc.

machinery) would be those in which it would be in the interest of the doctor to make a payment to the confectioner which would induce him to discontinue the use of the machinery (if the confectioner had the right to operate the machinery). The basic conditions are exactly the same in this case as they were in the example of the cattle which destroyed crops. With costless market transactions, the decision of the courts concerning liability for damage would be without effect on the allocation of resources. It was of course the view of the judges that they were affecting the working of the economic system— and in a desirable direction. Any other decision would have had "a prejudicial effect upon the development of land for residential purposes," an argument which was elaborated by examining the example of a forge operating on a barren moor, which was later developed for residual purposes. The judges' view that they were settling how the land was to be used would be true only in the case in which the costs of carrying out the necessary market transactions exceeded the gain which might be achieved by any rearrangement of rights. And it would be desirable to preserve the areas (Wimpole Street or the moor) for residential or professional use (by giving non-industrial users the right to stop the noise, vibration, smoke, etc., by injunction) only if the value of the additional residential facilities obtained was greater than the value of cakes or iron lost. But of this the judges seem to have been unaware.

Another example of the same problem is furnished by the case of *Cooke v. Forbes*.[10] One process in the weaving of cocoa-nut fibre matting was to immerse it in bleaching liquids after which it was hung out to dry. Fumes from a manufacturer of sulphate of ammonia had the effect of turning the matting from a bright to a dull and blackish colour. The reason for this was that the bleaching liquid contained chloride of tin, which, when affected by sulphuretted hydrogen, is turned to a darker colour. An injunction was sought to stop the manufacturer from emitting the fumes. The lawyers for the defendant argued that if the plaintiff "were not to use . . . a particular bleaching liquid, their fibre would not be affected; that their process is unusual, not according to the custom of the trade, and even damaging to their own fabrics." The judge commented: ". . . it appears to me quite plain that a person has a right to carry on upon his own property a manufacturing process in which he uses chloride of tin, or any sort of metallic dye, and that his neighbour is not at liberty to pour in gas which will interfere with his manufacture. If it can be traced to the neighbour, then, I apprehend, clearly he will have a right to come here and ask for relief." But in view of the fact that the damage was accidental and occasional, that careful precautions were taken and that there was no exceptional risk, an injunction was refused, leaving the plaintiff to bring an action for damages if he wished. What the subsequent developments

[10] L. R. 5 Eq. 166 (1867–1868).

were I do not know. But it is clear that the situation is essentially the same as that found in *Sturges v. Bridgman,* except that the cocoa-nut fibre matting manufacturer could not secure an injunction but would have to seek damages from the sulphate of ammonia manufacturer. The economic analysis of the situation is exactly the same as with the cattle which destroyed crops. To avoid the damage, the sulphate of ammonia manufacturer could increase his precautions or move to another location. Either course would presumably increase his costs. Alternatively he could pay for the damage. This he would do if the payments for damage were less than the additional costs that would have to be incurred to avoid the damage. The payments for damage would then become part of the cost of production of sulphate of ammonia. Of course, if, as was suggested in the legal proceedings, the amount of damage could be eliminated by changing the bleaching agent (which would presumably increase the costs of the matting manufacturer) and if the additional cost was less than the damage that would otherwise occur, it should be possible for the two manufacturers to make a mutually satisfactory bargain whereby the new bleaching agent was used. Had the court decided against the matting manufacturer, as a consequence of which he would have had to suffer the damage without compensation, the allocation of resources would not have been affected. It would pay the matting manufacturer to change his bleaching agent if the additional cost involved was less than the reduction in damage. And since the matting manufacturer would be willing to pay the sulphate of ammonia manufacturer an amount up to his loss of income (the increase in costs or the damage suffered) if he would cease his activities, this loss of income would remain a cost of production for the manufacturer of sulphate of ammonia. This case is indeed analytically exactly the same as the cattle example.

Bryant v. Lefever[11] raised the problem of the smoke nuisance in a novel form. The plaintiff and the defendants were occupiers of adjoining houses, which were of about the same height.

Before 1876 the plaintiff was able to light a fire in any room of his house without the chimneys smoking; the two houses had remained in the same condition some thirty or forty years. In 1876 the defendants took down their house, and began to rebuild it. They carried up a wall by the side of the plaintiff's chimneys much beyond its original height, and stacked timber on the roof of their house, and thereby caused the plaintiff's chimneys to smoke whenever he lighted fires.

The reason, of course, why the chimneys smoked was that the erection of the wall and the stacking of the timber prevented the free circulation of air. In a trial before a jury, the plaintiff was awarded damages of £40. The case then went to the Court of Appeals where the judgment was reversed. Bramwell, L.J., argued:

[11] 4 C.P.D. 172 (1878–1879).

. . . it is said, and the jury have found, that the defendants have done that which caused a nuisance to the plaintiff's house. We think there is no evidence of this. No doubt there is a nuisance, but it is not of the defendant's causing. They have done nothing in causing the nuisance. Their house and their timber are harmless enough. It is the plaintiff who causes the nuisance by lighting a coal fire in a place the chimney of which is placed so near the defendants' wall, that the smoke does not escape, but comes into the house. Let the plaintiff cease to light his fire, let him move his chimney, let him carry it higher, and there would be no nuisance. Who then, causes it? It would be very clear that the plaintiff did, if he had built his house or chimney after the defendants had put up the timber on theirs, and it is really the same though he did so before the timber was there. But (what is in truth the same answer), if the defendants cause the nuisance, they have a right to do so. If the plaintiff has not the right to the passage of air, except subject to the defendants' right to build or put timber on their house, then his right is subject to their right, and though a nuisance follows from the exercise of their right, they are not liable.

And Cotton, L.J., said:

Here it is found that the erection of the defendants' wall has sensibly and materially interfered with the comfort of human existence in the plaintiff's house, and it is said this is a nuisance for which the defendants are liable. Ordinarily this is so, but the defendants have done so, not by sending on to the plaintiff's property any smoke or noxious vapour, but by interrupting the egress of smoke from the plaintiff's house in a way to which . . . the plaintiff has no legal right. The plaintiff creates the smoke, which interferes with his comfort. Unless he has . . . a right to get rid of this in a particular way which has been interfered with by the defendants, he cannot sue the defendants, because the smoke made by himself, for which he has not provided any effectual means of escape, causes him annoyance. It is as if a man tried to get rid of liquid filth arising on his own land by a drain into his neighbour's land. Until a right had been acquired by user, the neighbour might stop the drain without incurring liability by so doing. No doubt great inconvenience would be caused to the owner of the property on which the liquid filth arises. But the act of his neighbour would be a lawful act, and he would not be liable for the consequences attributable to the fact that the man had accumulated filth without providing any effectual means of getting rid of it.

I do not propose to show that any subsequent modification of the situation, as a result of bargains between the parties (conditioned by the cost of stacking the timber elsewhere, the cost of extending the chimney higher, etc would have exactly the same result whatever decision the courts had come since this point has already been adequately dealt with in the discussion of the cattle example and the two previous cases. What I shall discuss is the argument of the judges in the Court of Appeals that the smoke nuisance was not caused by the man who erected the wall but by the man who lit the fires. The novelty of the situation is that the smoke nuisance was suffered by the man who lit the fires and not by some third person. The question is not a trivial one since it lies at the heart of the problem under discussion. Who caused the smoke nuisance? The answer seems fairly clear. The smoke nuisance was caused both by the man who built the wall *and* by the man who lit the fires. Given the fires, there would have been no smoke nuisance without the wall; given the wall, there would have been no smoke nuisance without the fires. Eliminate the wall *or* the fires and the smoke nuisance would disappear. On the marginal principle it is clear that *both* were responsible and *both* should be forced to include the loss of amenity due to the smoke as a cost in deciding whether to continue the activity which gives rise to the smoke. And given the possibility of market transactions, this is what would in fact happen. Although the wall-builder was not liable legally for the nuisance, as the man with the smoking chimneys would presumably be willing to pay a sum equal to the monetary worth to him of eliminating the smoke, this sum would therefore become for the wall-builder, a cost of continuing to have the high wall with the timber stacked on the roof.

The judges' contention that it was the man who lit the fires who alone caused the smoke nuisance is true only if we assume that the wall is the given factor. This is what the judges did by deciding that the man who erected the higher wall had a legal right to do so. The case would have been even more interesting if the smoke from the chimneys had injured the timber. Then it would have been the wall-builder who suffered the damage. The case would then have closely paralleled *Sturges v. Bridgman* and there can be little doubt that the man who lit the fires would have been liable for the ensuing damage to the timber, in spite of the fact that no damage had occurred until the high wall was built by the man who owned the timber.

Judges have to decide on legal liability but this should not confuse economists about the nature of the economic problem involved. In the case of the cattle and the crops, it is true that there would be no crop damage without the cattle. It is equally true that there would be no crop damage without the crops. The doctor's work would not have been disturbed if the confectioner had not worked his machinery; but the machinery would have disturbed no one if the doctor had not set up his consulting room in that particular place. The matting was blackened by the fumes from the sulphate of ammonia manufacturer; but no damage would have occurred if the matting manufacturer had not chosen to hang out his matting in a particular place and to use a particular bleaching agent. If we are to discuss the problem in terms of causation, both parties cause the damage. If we are to attain an optimum allocation of resources, it is therefore desirable that both parties should take the harmful effect (the nuisance) into account in deciding on their course of action. It is one of the beauties of a smoothly operating pricing system that, as has already been explained, the fall in the value of production due to the harmful effect would be a cost for both parties.

Bass v. Gregory[12] will serve as an excellent final illustration of the problem. The plaintiffs were the owners and tenant of a public house called the Jolly Anglers. The defendant was the owner of some cottages and a yard adjoining the Jolly Anglers. Under the public house was a cellar excavated in the rock. From the cellar, a hole or shaft had been cut into an old well situated in the defendant's yard. The well therefore became the ventilating shaft for the cellar. The cellar "had been used for a particular purpose in the process of brewing, which, without ventilation, could not be carried on." The cause of the action was that the defendant removed a grating from the mouth of the well, "so as to stop or prevent the free passage of air from [the] cellar upwards through the well. . . ." What caused the defendant to take this step is not clear from the report of the case. Perhaps "the air . . . impregnated by the brewing operations" which "passed up the well and out into the open air" was offensive to him. At any rate, he preferred to have the well in his yard stopped up. The court had first to determine whether the owners of the public house could have a legal right to a current of air. If they were to have such a right, this case would have to be distinguished from *Bryant v. Lefever* (already considered). This, however, presented no difficulty. In this case, the current of air was confined to "a strictly defined channel." In the case of *Bryant v. Lefever,* what was involved was "the general current of air common to all mankind." The judge therefore held that the owners of the public house could have the right to a current of air whereas the owner of the private house in *Bryant v. Lefever* could not. An economist might be tempted to add "but the air moved all the same." However, all that had been decided at this stage of the argument was that there could be a legal right, not that the owners of the public house possessed it. But evidence showed that the shaft from the cellar to the well had existed for over forty years and that the use of the well as a ventilating shaft must have been known to the owners of the yard since the air, when it emerged, smelt of the brewing operations. The judge therefore held that the public house had such a right by the "doctrine of lost grant." This doctrine states "that if a legal right is proved to have existed and been exercised for a number of years the law ought to presume that it had a legal origin."[13] So the owner of the cottages and yard had to unstop the well and endure the smell.

---

[12] 25 Q.B.D. 481 (1890).

[13] It may be asked why a lost grant could not also be presumed in the case of the confectioner who had operated one mortar for more than 60 years. The answer is that until the doctor built the consulting room at the end of his garden there was no nuisance. So the nuisance had not continued for many years. It is true that the confectioner in his affidavit referred to "an invalid lady who occupied the house upon one occasion, about thirty years before" who "requested him if possible to discontinue the use of the mortars before eight o'clock in the morning" and that there was some evidence that the garden wall had been subjected to vibration. But the court had little difficulty in disposing of this line of argument: ". . . this vibration, even if it existed at all, was so slight, and the com-

The reasoning employed by the courts in determining legal rights will often seem strange to an economist because many of the factors on which the decision turns are, to an economist, irrelevant. Because of this, situations which are, from an economic point of view, identical will be treated quite differently by the courts. The economic problem in all cases of harmful effects is how to maximise the value of production. In the case of *Bass v. Gregory* fresh air was drawn in through the well which facilitated the production of beer but foul air was expelled through the well which made life in the adjoining houses less pleasant. The economic problem was to decide which to choose: a lower cost of beer and worsened amenities in adjoining houses or a higher cost of beer and improved amenities. In deciding this question, the "doctrine of lost grant" is about as relevant as the colour of the judge's eyes. But it has to be remembered that the immediate question faced by the courts is *not* what shall be done by whom *but* who has the legal right to do what. It is always possible to modify by transactions on the market the initial legal delimitation of rights. And, of course, if such market transactions are costless, such a rearrangement of rights will always take place if it would lead to an increase in the value of production.

VI. The Cost of Market Transactions Taken into Account

The argument has proceeded up to this point on the assumption (explicit in Sections III and IV and tacit in Section V) that there were no costs involved in carrying out market transactions. This is, of course, a very unrealistic assumption. In order to carry out a market transaction it is necessary to discover who it is that one wishes to deal with, to inform people that one wishes to deal and on what terms, to conduct negotiations leading up to a bargain, to draw up the contract, to undertake the inspection needed to make sure that the terms of the contract are being observed, and so on. These operations are often extremely costly, sufficiently costly at any rate to prevent many transactions that would be carried out in a world in which the pricing system worked without cost.

In earlier sections, when dealing with the problem of the rearrangement of legal rights through the market, it was argued that such a rearrangement would be made through the market whenever this would lead to an increase in the value of production. But this assumed costless market transactions. Once the costs of carrying out market transactions are taken into account it is clear that such a rearrangement of rights will only be undertaken when the increase in the value of production consequent upon the rearrangement

---

plaint, if it can be called a complaint, of the invalid lady . . . was of so trifling a character, that . . . the Defendant's acts would not have given rise to any proceeding either at law or in equity" (11 Ch.D. 863). That is, the confectioner had not committed a nuisance until the doctor built his consulting room.

is greater than the costs which would be involved in bringing it about. When it is less, the granting of an injunction (or the knowledge that it would be granted) or the liability to pay damages may result in an activity being discontinued (or may prevent its being started) which would be undertaken if market transactions were costless. In these conditions the initial delimitation of legal rights does have an effect on the efficiency with which the economic system operates. One arrangement of rights may bring about a greater value of production than any other. But unless this is the arrangement of rights established by the legal system, the costs of reaching the same result by altering and combining rights through the market may be so great that this optimal arrangement of rights, and the greater value of production which it would bring, may never be achieved. The part played by economic considerations in the process of delimiting legal rights will be discussed in the next section. In this section, I will take the initial delimitation of rights and the costs of carrying out market transactions as given.

It is clear that an alternative form of economic organisation which could achieve the same result at less cost than would be incurred by using the market would enable the value of production to be raised. As I explained many years ago, the firm represents such an alternative to organising production through market transactions.[14] Within the firm individual bargains between the various cooperating factors of production are eliminated and for a market transaction is substituted an administrative decision. The rearrangement of production then takes place without the need for bargains between the owners of the factors of production. A landowner who has control of a large tract of land may devote his land to various uses taking into account the effect that the interrelations of the various activities will have on the net return of the land, thus rendering unnecessary bargains between those undertaking the various activities. Owners of a large building or of several adjoining properties in a given area may act in much the same way. In effect, using our earlier terminology, the firm would acquire the legal rights of all the parties and the rearrangement of activities would not follow on a rearrangement of rights by contract, but as a result of an administrative decision as to how the rights should be used.

It does not, of course, follow that the administrative costs of organising a transaction through a firm are inevitably less than the costs of the market transactions which are superseded. But where contracts are peculiarly difficult to draw up and an attempt to describe what the parties have agreed to do or not to do (e.g. the amount and kind of a smell or noise that they may make or will not make) would necessitate a lengthy and highly involved document, and, where, as is probable, a long-term contract would be desir-

---

[14] See Coase, The Nature of the Firm, 4 Economica, New Series, 386 (1937). Reprinted in Readings in Price Theory, 331 (1952).

able;[15] it would be hardly surprising if the emergence of a firm or the extension of the activities of an existing firm was not the solution adopted on many occasions to deal with the problem of harmful effects. This solution would be adopted whenever the administrative costs of the firm were less than the costs of the market transactions that it supersedes and the gains which would result from the rearrangement of activities greater than the firm's costs of organising them. I do not need to examine in great detail the character of this solution since I have explained what is involved in my earlier article.

But the firm is not the only possible answer to this problem. The administrative costs of organising transactions within the firm may also be high, and particularly so when many diverse activities are brought within the control of a single organisation. In the standard case of a smoke nuisance, which may affect a vast number of people engaged in a wide variety of activities, the administrative costs might well be so high as to make any attempt to deal with the problem within the confines of a single firm impossible. An alternative solution is direct Government regulation. Instead of instituting a legal system of rights which can be modified by transactions on the market, the government may impose regulations which state what people must or must not do and which have to be obeyed. Thus, the government (by statute or perhaps more likely through an administrative agency) may, to deal with the problem of smoke nuisance, decree that certain methods of production should or should not be used (e.g. that smoke preventing devices should be installed or that coal or oil should not be burned) or may confine certain types of business to certain districts (zoning regulations).

The government is, in a sense, a super-firm (but of a very special kind) since it is able to influence the use of factors of production by administrative decision. But the ordinary firm is subject to checks in its operations because of the competition of other firms, which might administer the same activities at lower cost and also because there is always the alternative of market transactions as against organisation within the firm if the administrative costs become too great. The government is able, if it wishes, to avoid the market altogether, which a firm can never do. The firm has to make market agreements with the owners of the factors of production that it uses. Just as the government can conscript or seize property, so it can decree that factors of production should only be used in such-and-such a way. Such authoritarian methods save a lot of trouble (for those doing the organising). Furthermore, the government has at its disposal the police and the other law enforcement agencies to make sure that its regulations are carried out.

It is clear that the government has powers which might enable it to get some things done at a lower cost than could a private organisation (or at any

[15] For reasons explained in my earlier article, see Readings in Price Theory, n. 14 at 337.

rate one without special governmental powers). But the governmental administrative machine is not itself costless. It can, in fact, on occasion be extremely costly. Furthermore, there is no reason to suppose that the restrictive and zoning regulations, made by a fallible administration subject to political pressures and operating without any competitive check, will necessarily always be those which increase the efficiency with which the economic system operates. Furthermore, such general regulations which must apply to a wide variety of cases will be enforced in some cases in which they are clearly inappropriate. From these considerations it follows that direct governmental regulation will not necessarily give better results than leaving the problem to be solved by the market or the firm. But equally there is no reason why, on occasion, such governmental administrative regulation should not lead to an improvement in economic efficiency. This would seem particularly likely when, as is normally the case with the smoke nuisance, a large number of people are involved and in which therefore the costs of handling the problem through the market or the firm may be high.

There is, of course, a further alternative, which is to do nothing about the problem at all. And given that the costs involved in solving the problem by regulations issued by the governmental administrative machine will often be heavy (particularly if the costs are interpreted to include all the consequences which follow from the Government engaging in this kind of activity), it will no doubt be commonly the case that the gain which would come from regulating the actions which give rise to the harmful effects will be less than the costs involved in Government regulation.

The discussion of the problem of harmful effects in this section (when the costs of market transactions are taken into account) is extremely inadequate. But at least it has made clear that the problem is one of choosing the appropriate social arrangement for dealing with the harmful effects. All solutions have costs and there is no reason to suppose that government regulation is called for simply because the problem is not well handled by the market or the firm. Satisfactory views on policy can only come from a patient study of how, in practice, the market, firms and governments handle the problem of harmful effects. Economists need to study the work of the broker in bringing parties together, the effectiveness of restrictive covenants, the problems of the large-scale real-estate development company, the operation of Government zoning and other regulating activities. It is my belief that economists, and policy-makers generally, have tended to over-estimate the advantages which come from governmental regulation. But this belief, even if justified, does not do more than suggest that government regulation should be curtailed. It does not tell us where the boundary line should be drawn. This, it seems to me, has to come from a detailed investigation of the actual results of handling the problem in different ways. But it would be unfortunate if this investigation were undertaken with the aid of a faulty economic analysis. The aim of this article is to indicate what the economic approach to the problem should be.

VII. THE LEGAL DELIMITATION OF RIGHTS AND THE ECONOMIC PROBLEM

The discussion in Section V not only served to illustrate the argument but also afforded a glimpse at the legal approach to the problem of harmful effects. The cases considered were all English but a similar selection of American cases could easily be made and the character of the reasoning would have been the same. Of course, if market transactions were costless, all that matters (questions of equity apart) is that the rights of the various parties should be well-defined and the results of legal actions easy to forecast. But as we have seen, the situation is quite different when market transactions are so costly as to make it difficult to change the arrangement of rights established by the law. In such cases, the courts directly influence economic activity. It would therefore seem desirable that the courts should understand the economic consequences of their decisions and should, insofar as this is possible without creating too much uncertainty about the legal position itself, take these consequences into account when making their decisions. Even when it is possible to change the legal delimitation of rights through market transactions, it is obviously desirable to reduce the need for such transactions and thus reduce the employment of resources in carrying them out.

A thorough examination of the presuppositions of the courts in trying such cases would be of great interest but I have not been able to attempt it. Nevertheless it is clear from a cursory study that the courts have often recognized the economic implications of their decisions and are aware (as many economists are not) of the reciprocal nature of the problem. Furthermore, from time to time, they take these economic implications into account, along with other factors, in arriving at their decisions. The American writers on this subject refer to the question in a more explicit fashion than do the British. Thus, to quote Prosser on Torts, a person may

make use of his own property or . . . conduct his own affairs at the expense of some harm to his neighbors. He may operate a factory whose noise and smoke cause some discomfort to others, so long as he keeps within reasonable bounds. It is only when his conduct is unreasonable, *in the light of its utility and the harm which results* [italics added], that it becomes a nuisance. . . . . As it was said in an ancient case in regard to candle-making in a town, "Le utility del chose excusera le noisomeness del stink."

The world must have factories, smelters, oil refineries, noisy machinery and blasting, even at the expense of some inconvenience to those in the vicinity and the plaintiff may be required to accept some not unreasonable discomfort for the general good.[16]

The standard British writers do not state as explicitly as this that a comparison between the utility and harm produced is an element in deciding whether a harmful effect should be considered a nuisance. But similar views, if less strongly expressed, are to be found.[17] The doctrine that the harmful effect must be substantial before the court will act is, no doubt, in part a reflection of the fact that there will almost always be some gain to offset the harm. And in the reports of individual cases, it is clear that the judges have had in mind what would be lost as well as what would be gained in deciding whether to grant an injunction or award damages. Thus, in refusing to prevent the destruction of a prospect by a new building, the judge stated:

I know no general rule of common law, which . . . says, that building so as to stop another's prospect is a nuisance. Was that the case, there could be no great towns; and I must grant injunctions to all the new buildings in this town. . . .[18]

In *Webb v. Bird*[19] it was decided that it was not a nuisance to build a schoolhouse so near a windmill as to obstruct currents of air and hinder the working of the mill. An early case seems to have been decided in an opposite direction. Gale commented:

In old maps of London a row of windmills appears on the heights to the north of London. Probably in the time of King James it was thought an alarming circumstance, as affecting the supply of food to the city, that anyone should build so near them as to take the wind out from their sails.[20]

In one of the cases discussed in section V, *Sturges v. Bridgman,* it seems clear that the judges were thinking of the economic consequences of alternative decisions. To the argument that if the principle that they seemed to be following

[16] See W. L. Prosser, The Law of Torts 398–99, 412 (2d ed. 1955). The quotation about the ancient case concerning candle-making is taken from Sir James Fitzjames Stephen, A General View of the Criminal Law of England 106 (1890). Sir James Stephen gives no reference. He perhaps had in mind *Rex. v. Ronkett,* included in Seavey, Keeton and Thurston, Cases on Torts 604 (1950). A similar view to that expressed by Prosser is to be found in F. V. Harper and F. James, The Law of Torts 67–74 (1956); Restatement, Torts §§826, 827 and 828.

[17] See Winfield on Torts 541–48 (6th ed. T. E. Lewis 1954); Salmond on the Law of Torts 181–90 (12th ed. R.F.V. Heuston 1957); H. Street, The Law of Torts 221–29 (1959).

[18] Attorney General v. Doughty, 2 Ves. Sen. 453, 28 Eng. Rep. 290 (Ch. 1752). Compare in this connection the statement of an American judge, quoted in Prosser, op. cit. supra n. 16 at 413 n. 54: "Without smoke, Pittsburgh would have remained a very pretty village," Musmanno, J., in Versailles Borough v. McKeesport Coal & Coke Co., 1935, 83 Pitts. Leg. J. 379, 385.

[19] 10 C.B. (N.S.) 268, 142 Eng. Rep. 445 (1861); 13 C.B. (N.S.) 841, 143 Eng. Rep. 332 (1863).

[20] See Gale on Easements 238, n. 6 (13th ed. M. Bowles 1959).

were carried out to its logical consequences, it would result in the most serious practical inconveniences, for a man might go—say into the midst of the tanneries of *Bermondsey,* or into any other locality devoted to any particular trade or manufacture of a noisy or unsavoury character, and by building a private residence upon a vacant piece of land put a stop to such trade or manufacture altogether,

the judges answered that

whether anything is a nuisance or not is a question to be determined, not merely by an abstract consideration of the thing itself, but in reference to its circumstances; What would be a nuisance in *Belgrave Square* would not necessarily be so in *Bermondsey;* and where a locality is devoted to a particular trade or manufacture carried on by the traders or manufacturers in a particular and established manner not constituting a public nuisance, Judges and juries would be justified in finding, and may be trusted to find, that the trade or manufacture so carried on in that locality is not a private or actionable wrong.[21]

That the character of the neighborhood is relevant in deciding whether something is, or is not, a nuisance, is definitely established.

He who dislikes the noise of traffic must not set up his abode in the heart of a great city. He who loves peace and quiet must not live in a locality devoted to the business of making boilers or steamships.[22]

What has emerged has been described as "planning and zoning by the judiciary."[23] Of course there are sometimes considerable difficulties in applying the criteria.[24]

An interesting example of the problem is found in *Adams v. Ursell*[25] in which a fried fish shop in a predominantly working-class district was set up near houses of "a much better character." England without fish-and-chips is a contradiction in terms and the case was clearly one of high importance. The judge commented:

It was urged that an injunction would cause great hardship to the defendant and to the poor people who get food at his shop. The answer to that is that it does not follow that the defendant cannot carry on his business in another more suitable place somewhere in the neighbourhood. It by no means follows that because a fried fish shop is a nuisance in one place it is a nuisance in another.

In fact, the injunction which restrained Mr. Ursell from running his shop did not even extend to the whole street. So he was presumably able to move to other premises near houses of "a much worse character," the inhabitants

[21] 11 Ch.D. 865 (1879).

[22] Salmond on the Law of Torts 182 (12th ed. R.F.V. Heuston 1957).

[23] C. M. Haar, Land-Use Planning, A Casebook on the Use, Misuse, and Re-use of Urban Land 95 (1959).

[24] See, for example, Rushmer v. Polsue and Alfieri, Ltd. [1906] 1 Ch. 234, which deals with the case of a house in a quiet situation in a noisy district.

[25] [1913] 1 Ch. 269.

of which would no doubt consider the availability of fish-and-chips to out-weigh the pervading odour and "fog or mist" so graphically described by the plaintiff. Had there been no other "more suitable place in the neighbour-hood," the case would have been more difficult and the decision might have been different. What would "the poor people" have had for food? No English judge would have said: "Let them eat cake."

The courts do not always refer very clearly to the economic problem posed by the cases brought before them but it seems probable that in the interpre-tation of words and phrases like "reasonable" or "common or ordinary use" there is some recognition, perhaps largely unconscious and certainly not very explicit, of the economic aspects of the questions at issue. A good example of this would seem to be the judgment in the Court of Appeals in *Andreae v. Selfridge and Company Ltd.*[26] In this case, a hotel (in Wigmore Street) was situated on part of an island site. The remainder of the site was acquired by Selfridges which demolished the existing buildings in order to erect another in their place. The hotel suffered a loss of custom in consequence of the noise and dust caused by the demolition. The owner of the hotel brought an action against Selfridges for damages. In the lower court, the hotel was awarded £4,500 damages. The case was then taken on appeal.

The judge who had found for the hotel proprietor in the lower court said:

I cannot regard what the defendants did on the site of the first operation as having been commonly done in the ordinary use and occupation of land or houses. It is neither usual nor common, in this country, for people to excavate a site to a depth of 60 feet and then to erect upon that site a steel framework and fasten the steel frames together with rivets. . . . Nor is it, I think, a common or ordinary use of land, in this country, to act as the defendants did when they were dealing with the site of their second operation—namely, to demolish all the houses that they had to demolish, five or six of them I think, if not more, and to use for the purpose of demolishing them pneumatic hammers.

Sir Wilfred Greene, M.R., speaking for the Court of Appeals, first noted

that when one is dealing with temporary operations, such as demolition and re-build-ing, everybody has to put up with a certain amount of discomfort, because operations of that kind cannot be carried on at all without a certain amount of noise and a certain amount of dust. Therefore, the rule with regard to interference must be read subject to this qualification. . . .

He then referred to the previous judgment:

With great respect to the learned judge, I take the view that he has not approached this matter from the correct angle. It seems to me that it is not possible to say . . . that the type of demolition, excavation and construction in which the defendant company was engaged in the course of these operations was of such an abnormal and unusual nature as to prevent the qualification to which I have referred coming

[26] [1938] 1 Ch. 1.

into operation. It seems to me that, when the rule speaks of the common or ordinary use of land, it does not mean that the methods of using land and building on it are in some way to be stabilised for ever. As time goes on new inventions or new methods enable land to be more profitably used, either by digging down into the earth or by mounting up into the skies. Whether, from other points of view, that is a matter which is desirable for humanity is neither here nor there; but it is part of the normal use of land, to make use upon your land, in the matter of construction, of what particular type and what particular depth of foundations and particular height of building may be reasonable, in the circumstances, and in view of the developments of the day. . . . Guests at hotels are very easily upset. People coming to this hotel, who were accustomed to a quiet outlook at the back, coming back and finding demolition and building going on, may very well have taken the view that the particular merit of this hotel no longer existed. That would be a misfortune for the plaintiff; but assuming that there was nothing wrong in the defendant company's works, assuming the defendant company was carrying on the demolition and its building, productive of noise though it might be, with all reasonable skill, and taking all reasonable precautions not to cause annoyance to its neighbors, then the planitiff might lose all her clients in the hotel because they have lost the amenities of an open and quiet place behind, but she would have no cause of complaint. . . . [But those] who say that their interference with the comfort of their neighbors is justified because their operations are normal and usual and conducted with proper care and skill are under a specific duty . . . to use that reasonable and proper care and skill. It is not a correct attitude to take to say: 'We will go on and do what we like until somebody complains!' . . . Their duty is to take proper precautions and to see that the nuisance is reduced to a minimum. It is no answer for them to say: 'But this would mean that we should have to do the work more slowly than we would like to do it, or it would involve putting us to some extra expense.' All these questions are matters of common sense and degree, and quite clearly it would be unreasonable to expect people to conduct their work so slowly or so expensively, for the purpose of preventing a transient inconvenience, that the cost and trouble would be prohibitive. . . . In this case, the defendant company's attitude seems to have been to go on until somebody complained, and, further, that its desire to hurry its work and conduct it according to its own ideas and its own convenience was to prevail if there was a real conflict between it and the comfort of its neighbors. That . . . is not carrying out the obligation of using reasonable care and skill. . . . The effect comes to this . . . the plaintiff suffered an actionable nuisance; . . . she is entitled, not to a nominal sum, but to a substantial sum, based upon those principles . . . but in arriving at the sum . . . I have discounted any loss of custom . . . which might be due to the general loss of amenities owing to what was going on at the back. . . .

The upshot was that the damages awarded were reduced from £4,500 to £1,000.

The discussion in this section has, up to this point, been concerned with court decisions arising out of the common law relating to nuisance. Delimitation of rights in this area also comes about because of statutory enactments. Most economists would appear to assume that the aim of governmental action in this field is to extend the scope of the law of nuisance by designating as nuisances activities which would not be recognized as such by the common law. And there can be no doubt that some statutes, for example, the Public Health Acts, have had this effect. But not all Government enactments are of this kind. The effect of much of the legislation in this area is to protect businesses from the claims of those they have harmed by their actions. There is a long list of legalized nuisances.

The position has been summarized in *Halsbury's Laws of England* as follows:

Where the legislature directs that a thing shall in all events be done or authorises certain works at a particular place for a specific purposes or grants powers with the intention that they shall be exercised, although leaving some discretion as to the mode of exercise, no action will lie at common law for nuisance or damage which is the inevitable result of carrying out the statutory powers so conferred. This is so whether the act causing the damage is authorised for public purposes or private profit. Acts done under powers granted by persons to whom Parliament has delegated authority to grant such powers, for example, under provisional orders of the Board of Trade, are regarded as having been done under statutory authority. In the absence of negligence it seems that a body exercising statutory powers will not be liable to an action merely because it might, by acting in a different way, have minimised an injury.

Instances are next given of freedom from liability for acts authorized:

An action has been held not to be against a body exercising its statutory powers without negligence in respect of the flooding of land by water escaping from watercourses, from water pipes, from drains, or from a canal; the escape of fumes from sewers; the escape of sewage: the subsidence of a road over a sewer; vibration or noise caused by a railway; fires caused by authorised acts; the pollution of a stream where statutory requirements to use the best known method of purifying before discharging the effluent have been satisfied; interference with a telephone or telegraph system by an elctric tramway; the insertion of poles for tramways in the subsoil; annoyance caused by things reasonably necessary for the excavation of authorised works; accidental damage caused by the placing of a grating in a roadway; the escape of tar acid; or interference with the access of a frontager by a street shelter or safety railings on the edge of a pavement.[27]

The legal position in the United States would seem to be essentially the same as in England, except that the power of the legislatures to authorize what would otherwise be nuisances under the common law, at least without giving compensation to the person harmed, is somewhat more limited, as it is subject to constitutional restrictions.[28] Nonetheless, the power is there and cases more or less identical with the English cases can be found. The

[27] See 30 Halsbury, Law of England 690–91 (3d ed. 1960), Article on Public Authorities and Public Officers.

[28] See Prosser, op. cit. supra n. 16 at 421; Harper and James, op. cit. supra n. 16 at 86–87.

R. H. Coase / 37

question has arisen in an acute form in connection with airports and the operation of aeroplanes. The case of *Delta Air Corporation v. Kersey, Kersey v. City of Atlanta*[29] is a good example. Mr. Kersey bought land and built a house on it. Some years later the City of Atlanta constructed an airport on land immediately adjoining that of Mr. Kersey. It was explained that his property was "a quiet, peaceful and proper location for a home before the airport was built, but dust, noises and low flying of airplanes caused by the operation of the airport have rendered his property unsuitable as a home," a state of affairs which was described in the report of the case with a wealth of distressing detail. The judge first referred to an earlier case, *Thrasher v. City of Atlanta*[30] in which it was noted that the City of Atlanta had been expressly authorized to operate an airport.

By this franchise aviation was recognised as a lawful business and also as an enterprise affected with a public interest . . . all persons using [the airport] in the manner contemplated by law are within the protection and immunity of the franchise granted by the municipality. An airport is not a nuisance per se, although it might become such from the manner of its construction or operation.

Since aviation was a lawful business affected with a public interest and the construction of the airport was autorized by statute, the judge next referred to *Georgia Railroad and Banking Co. v. Maddox*[31] in which it was said:

Where a railroad terminal yard is located and its construction authorized, under statutory powers, if it be constructed and operated in a proper manner, it cannot be adjudged a nuisance. Accordingly, injuries and inconveniences to persons residing near such a yard, from noises of locomotives, rumbling of cars, vibrations produced thereby, and smoke, cinders, soot and the like, which result from the ordinary and necessary, therefore proper, use and operation of such a yard, are not nuisances, but are the necessary concomitants of the franchise granted.

In view of this, the judge decided that the noise and dust complained of by Mr. Kersey "may be deemed to be incidental to the proper operation of an airport, and as such they cannot be said to constitute a nuisance." But the complaint against low flying was different:

. . . can it be said that flights . . . at such a low height [25 to 50 feet above Mr. Kersey's house] as to be imminently dangerous to . . . life and health . . . are a necessary concomitant of an airport? We do not think this question can be answered in the affirmative. No reason appears why the city could not obtain lands of an area [sufficiently large] . . . as not to require such low flights. . . . For the sake of public convenience adjoining-property owners must suffer such inconvenience from noise and dust as result from the usual and proper operation of an airport, but their private rights are entitled to preference in the eyes of the law where the inconvenience is not one demanded by a properly constructed and operated airport.

[29] Supreme Court of Georgia. 193 Ga. 862, 20 S.E. 2d 245 (1942).

[30] 178 Ga. 514, 173 S.E. 817 (1934).   [31] 116 Ga. 64, 42 S.E. 315 (1902).

Of course this assumed that the City of Atlanta could prevent the low flying and continue to operate the airport. The judge therefore added:

From all that appears, the conditions causing the low flying may be remedied; but if on the trial it should appear that it is indispensable to the public interest that the airport should continue to be operated in its present condition, it may be said that the petitioner should be denied injunctive relief.

In the course of another aviation case, *Smith v. New England Aircraft Co.,*[32] the court surveyed the law in the United States regarding the legalizing of nuisances and it is apparent that, in the broad, it is very similar to that found in England:

It is the proper function of the legislative department of government in the exercise of the police power to consider the problems and risks that arise from the use of new inventions and endeavor to adjust private rights and harmonize conflicting interests by comprehensive statutes for the public welfare. . . . There are . . . analogies where the invasion of the airspace over underlying land by noise, smoke, vibration, dust and disagreeable odors, having been authorized by the legislative department of government and not being in effect a condemnation of the property although in some measure depreciating its market value, must be borne by the landowner without compensation or remedy. Legislative sanction makes that lawful which otherwise might be a nuisance. Examples of this are damages to adjacent land arising from smoke, vibration and noise in the operation of a railroad . . . ; the noise of ringing factory bells . . . ; the abatement of nuisances . . . ; the erection of steam engines and furnaces . . . ; unpleasant odors connected with sewers, oil refining and storage of naphtha. . . .

Most economists seem to be unaware of all this. When they are prevented from sleeping at night by the roar of jet planes overhead (publicly authorized and perhaps publicly operated), are unable to think (or rest) in the day because of the noise and vibration from passing trains (publicly authorized and perhaps publicly operated), find it difficult to breathe because of the odour from a local sewage farm (publicly authorized and perhaps publicly operated) and are unable to escape because their driveways are blocked by a road obstruction (without any doubt, publicly devised), their nerves frayed and mental balance disturbed, they proceed to declaim about the disadvantages of private enterprise and the need for Government regulation.

While most economists seem to be under a misapprehension concerning the character of the situation with which they are dealing, it is also the case that the activities which they would like to see stopped or curtailed may well be socially justified. It is all a question of weighing up the gains that would accrue from eliminating these harmful effects against the gains that accrue from allowing them to continue. Of course, it is likely that an extension of Government economic activity will often lead to this protection against

[32] 270 Mass. 511, 523, 170 N.E. 385, 390 (1930).

action for nuisance being pushed further than is desirable. For one thing, the Government is likely to look with a benevolent eye on enterprises which it is itself promoting. For another, it is possible to describe the committing of a nuisance by public enterprise in a much more pleasant way than when the same thing is done by private enterprise. In the words of Lord Justice Sir Alfred Denning:

. . . the significance of the social revolution of today is that, whereas in the past the balance was much too heavily in favor of the rights of property and freedom of contract, Parliament has repeatedly intervened so as to give the public good its proper place.[33]

There can be little doubt that the Welfare State is likely to bring an extension of that immunity from liability for damage, which economists have been in the habit of condemning (although they have tended to assume that this immunity was a sign of too little Government intervention in the economic system). For example, in Britain, the powers of local authorities are regarded as being either absolute or conditional. In the first category, the local authority has no discretion in exercising the power conferred on it. "The absolute power may be said to cover all the necessary consequences of its direct operation even if such consequences amount to nuisance." On the other hand, a conditional power may only be exercised in such a way that the consequences do not constitute a nuisance.

It is the intention of the legislature which determines whether a power is absolute or conditional. . . . [As] there is the possibility that the social policy of the legislature may change from time to time, a power which in one era would be construed as being conditional, might in another era be interpreted as being absolute in order to further the policy of the Welfare State. This point is one which should be borne in mind when considering some of the older cases upon this aspect of the law of nuisance.[34]

It would seem desirable to summarize the burden of this long section. The problem which we face in dealing with actions which have harmful effects is not simply one of restraining those responsible for them. What has to be decided is whether the gain from preventing the harm is greater than the loss which would be suffered elsewhere as a result of stopping the action which produces the harm. In a world in which there are costs of rearranging the rights established by the legal system, the courts, in cases relating to nuisance, are, in effect, making a decision on the economic problem and determining how resources are to be employed. It was argued that the courts are conscious of this and that they often make, although not always in a very explicit fashion, a comparison between what would be gained and what lost by preventing

[33] See Sir Alfred Denning, Freedom Under the Law 71 (1949).
[34] M. B. Cairns, The Law of Tort in Local Government 28–32 (1954).

actions which have harmful effects. But the delimitation of rights is also the result of statutory enactments. Here we also find evidence of an appreciation of the reciprocal nature of the problem. While statutory enactments add to the list of nuisances, action is also taken to legalize what would otherwise be nuisances under the common law. The kind of situation which economists are prone to consider as requiring corrective Government action is, in fact, often the result of Government action. Such action is not necessarily unwise. But there is a real danger that extensive Government intervention in the economic system may lead to the protection of those responsible for harmful effects being carried too far.

PROPERTY RULES, LIABILITY RULES, AND INALIENABILITY: ONE VIEW OF THE CATHEDRAL

Guido Calabresi * *and A. Douglas Melamed* **

Professor Calabresi and Mr. Melamed develop a framework for legal analysis which they believe serves to integrate various legal relationships which are traditionally analyzed in separate subject areas such as Property and Torts. By using their model to suggest solutions to the pollution problem that have been overlooked by writers in the field, and by applying the model to the question of criminal sanctions, they demonstrate the utility of such an integrated approach.

I. INTRODUCTION

ONLY rarely are Property and Torts approached from a unified perspective. Recent writings by lawyers concerned with economics and by economists concerned with law suggest, however, that an attempt at integrating the various legal relationships treated by these subjects would be useful both for the beginning student and the sophisticated scholar.[1] By articulating a concept of "entitlements" which are protected by property, liability, or inalienability rules, we present one framework for such an approach.[2] We then analyze aspects of the pollution problem and of

* John Thomas Smith Professor of Law, Yale University. B.S. Yale, 1953; B.A. Oxford, 1955; LL.B. Yale, 1958; M.A. Oxford, 1959.

** Member of the District of Columbia Bar. B.A. Yale University, 1967; J.D. Harvard University, 1970.

[1] *See, e.g.,* Michelman, *Pollution as a Tort: A Non-Accidental Perspective on Calabresi's* Costs, 80 YALE L.J. 647 (1971) (analysis of three alternative rules in pollution problems); Demsetz, *Toward a Theory of Property Rights*, 57 AM. ECON. REV. 347 (1967) (Vol. 2 — Papers and Proceedings) (analysis of property as a means of cost internalization which ignores liability rule alternatives).

[2] Since a fully integrated approach is probably impossible, it should be emphasized that this article concerns only one possible way of looking at and analyzing legal problems. Thus we shall not address ourselves to those fundamental legal questions which center on what institutions and what procedures are most suitable for making what decisions, except insofar as these relate directly to the problems of selecting the initial entitlements and the modes of protecting these entitlements. While we do not underrate the importance, indeed perhaps the primacy, of legal process considerations, *see* pp. 1116–17 *infra*, we are merely interested in the light

criminal sanctions in order to demonstrate how the model enables us to perceive relationships which have been ignored by writers in those fields.

The first issue which must be faced by any legal system is one we call the problem of "entitlement." Whenever a state is presented with the conflicting interests of two or more people, or two or more groups of people, it must decide which side to favor. Absent such a decision, access to goods, services, and life itself will be decided on the basis of "might makes right" — whoever is stronger or shrewder will win.[3] Hence the fundamental thing that law does is to decide which of the conflicting parties will be entitled to prevail. The entitlement to make noise versus the entitlement to have silence, the entitlement to pollute versus the entitlement to breathe clean air, the entitlement to have children versus the entitlement to forbid them — these are the first order of legal decisions.

Having made its initial choice, society must enforce that choice. Simply setting the entitlement does not avoid the problem of "might makes right"; a minimum of state intervention is always necessary.[4] Our conventional notions make this easy to compre-

---

that a rather different approach may shed on problems frequently looked at primarily from a legal process point of view.

As Professor Harry Wellington is fond of saying about many discussions of law, this article is meant to be only *one* of Monet's paintings of the Cathedral at Rouen. To understand the Cathedral one must see all of them. *See* G. HAMILTON, CLAUDE MONET'S PAINTINGS OF ROUEN CATHEDRAL 4–5, 19–20, 27 (1960).

[3] One could of course look at the state as simply a larger coalition of friends designed to enforce rules which merely accomplish the dominant coalition's desires. Rules of law would then be no more than "might makes right" writ large. Such a view does not strike us as plausible if for no other reason than that the state decides too many issues in response to too many different coalitions. This fact, by itself, would require a different form of analysis from that which would suffice to explain entitlements resulting from more direct and decentralized uses of "might makes right."

[4] For an excellent presentation of this general point by an economist, see Samuels, *Interrelations Between Legal and Economic Processes*, 14 J. LAW & ECON. 435 (1971).

We do not intend to imply that the state relies on force to enforce all or most entitlements. Nor do we imply that absent state intervention only force would win. The use by the state of feelings of obligation and rules of morality as means of enforcing most entitlements is not only crucial but terribly efficient. Conversely, absent the state, individuals would probably agree on rules of behavior which would govern entitlements in whole series of situations on the basis of criteria other than "might makes right." That these rules might themselves reflect the same types of considerations we will analyze as bases for legal entitlements is, of course, neither here nor there. What is important is that these "social compacts" would, no less than legal entitlements, give rise to what may be called obligations. These obligations in turn would cause people to behave in accordance with the compact in particular cases regardless of the existence of a predominant force. In this article

hend with respect to private property. If Taney owns a cabbage patch and Marshall, who is bigger, wants a cabbage, he will get it unless the state intervenes.[5] But it is not so obvious that the state must also intervene if it chooses the opposite entitlement, communal property. If large Marshall has grown some communal cabbages and chooses to deny them to small Taney, it will take state action to enforce Taney's entitlement to the communal cabbages. The same symmetry applies with respect to bodily integrity. Consider the plight of the unwilling ninety-eight-pound weakling in a state which nominally entitles him to bodily integrity but will not intervene to enforce the entitlement against a lustful Juno. Consider then the plight — absent state intervention — of the ninety-eight-pounder who desires an unwilling Juno in a state which nominally entitles everyone to use everyone else's body. The need for intervention applies in a slightly more complicated way to injuries. When a loss is left where it falls in an auto accident, it is not because God so ordained it. Rather it is because the state has granted the injurer an entitlement to be free of liability and will intervene to prevent the victim's friends, if they are stronger, from taking compensation from the injurer.[6] The loss is shifted in other cases because the state has granted an entitlement to compensation and will intervene to prevent the stronger injurer from rebuffing the victim's requests for compensation.

---

we are not concerned as much with the workings of such obligations as with the reasons which may explain the rules which themselves give rise to the obligations.

[5] "Bigger" obviously does not refer simply to size, but to the sum of an individual's resources. If Marshall's gang possesses superior brain and brawn to that of Taney, Marshall's gang will get the cabbages.

[6] Different cultures deal with the problem in different ways. Witness the following account:

"Life Insurance" Fee is 4 Bulls and $1200. Port Moresby, New Guinea. Peter Howard proved that he values his life more than four bulls and $1200. But he wants $24 and one pig in change.

Mr. Howard gave the money and livestock to members of the Jiga tribe, which had threatened to kill him because he killed a tribe member in an auto accident last October 29.

The police approved the extortion agreement after telling the 38 year old Mr. Howard they could not protect him from the sworn vengeance of the tribe, which lives at Mt. Hagen, about 350 miles Northeast of Port Moresby.

Mr. Howard, of Cambridge, England, was attacked and badly beaten by the tribesmen after the accident.

They said he would be killed unless the payment of money and bulls was made according to the tribal traditions. It was the first time a white man in New Guinea had been forced to bow to tribal laws.

After making the payment, Mr. Howard demanded to be compensated for the assault on him by the tribesmen. He said he wanted $24 and one pig. A Jiga spokesman told him the tribe would "think about it." New York Times, Feb. 16, 1972, at 17, col. 6.

The state not only has to decide whom to entitle, but it must also simultaneously make a series of equally difficult second order decisions. These decisions go to the manner in which entitlements are protected and to whether an individual is allowed to sell or trade the entitlement. In any given dispute, for example, the state must decide not only which side wins but also the kind of protection to grant. It is with the latter decisions, decisions which shape the subsequent relationship between the winner and the loser, that this article is primarily concerned. We shall consider three types of entitlements — entitlements protected by property rules, entitlements protected by liability rules, and inalienable entitlements. The categories are not, of course, absolutely distinct; but the categorization is useful since it reveals some of the reasons which lead us to protect certain entitlements in certain ways.

An entitlement is protected by a property rule to the extent that someone who wishes to remove the entitlement from its holder must buy it from him in a voluntary transaction in which the value of the entitlement is agreed upon by the seller. It is the form of entitlement which gives rise to the least amount of state intervention: once the original entitlement is decided upon, the state does not try to decide its value.[7] It lets each of the parties say how much the entitlement is worth to him, and gives the seller a veto if the buyer does not offer enough. Property rules involve a collective decision as to who is to be given an initial entitlement but not as to the value of the entitlement.

Whenever someone may destroy the initial entitlement if he is willing to pay an objectively determined value for it, an entitlement is protected by a liability rule. This value may be what it is thought the original holder of the entitlement would have sold it for. But the holder's complaint that he would have demanded more will not avail him once the objectively determined value is set. Obviously, liability rules involve an additional stage of state intervention: not only are entitlements protected, but their transfer or destruction is allowed on the basis of a value determined by some organ of the state rather than by the parties themselves.

An entitlement is inalienable to the extent that its transfer is not permitted between a willing buyer and a willing seller. The state intervenes not only to determine who is initially entitled and to determine the compensation that must be paid if the en-

---

[7] A property rule requires less state intervention only in the sense that intervention is needed to decide upon and enforce the initial entitlement but not for the separate problem of determining the value of the entitlement. Thus, if a particular property entitlement is especially difficult to enforce — for example, the right to personal security in urban areas — the actual amount of state intervention can be very high and could, perhaps, exceed that needed for some entitlements protected by easily administered liability rules.

titlement is taken or destroyed, but also to forbid its sale under some or all circumstances. Inalienability rules are thus quite different from property and liability rules. Unlike those rules, rules of inalienability not only "protect" the entitlement; they may also be viewed as limiting or regulating the grant of the entitlement itself.

It should be clear that most entitlements to most goods are mixed. Taney's house may be protected by a property rule in situations where Marshall wishes to purchase it, by a liability rule where the government decides to take it by eminent domain, and by a rule of inalienability in situations where Taney is drunk or incompetent. This article will explore two primary questions: (1) In what circumstances should we grant a particular entitlement? and (2) In what circumstances should we decide to protect that entitlement by using a property, liability, or inalienability rule?

II. THE SETTING OF ENTITLEMENTS

What are the reasons for deciding to entitle people to pollute or to entitle people to forbid pollution, to have children freely or to limit procreation, to own property or to share property? They can be grouped under three headings: economic efficiency, distributional preferences, and other justice considerations.[8]

A. Economic Efficiency

Perhaps the simplest reason for a particular entitlement is to minimize the administrative costs of enforcement. This was the reason Holmes gave for letting the costs lie where they fall in accidents unless some clear societal benefit is achieved by shifting them.[9] By itself this reason will never justify any result except that of letting the stronger win, for obviously that result minimizes enforcement costs. Nevertheless, administrative efficiency may be relevant to choosing entitlements when other reasons are taken into account. This may occur when the reasons accepted are indifferent between conflicting entitlements and one entitlement is cheaper to enforce than the others. It may also occur when the reasons are not indifferent but lead us only slightly to prefer one over another and the first is considerably more expensive to enforce than the second.

But administrative efficiency is just one aspect of the broader
. concept of economic efficiency. Economic efficiency asks that we

---

[8] *See generally* G. CALABRESI, THE COSTS OF ACCIDENTS 24–33 (1970) [hereinafter cited as COSTS].

[9] *See* O.W. HOLMES, JR., THE COMMON LAW 76–77 (Howe ed. 1963). For a criticism of the justification as applied to accidents today, see COSTS 261–63. *But cf.* Posner, *A Theory of Negligence,* 1 J. LEGAL STUD. 29 (1972).

choose the set of entitlements which would lead to that allocation of resources which could not be improved in the sense that a further change would not so improve the condition of those who gained by it that they could compensate those who lost from it and still be better off than before. This is often called Pareto optimality.[10] To give two examples, economic efficiency asks for that combination of entitlements to engage in risky activities and to be free from harm from risky activities which will most likely lead to the lowest sum of accident costs and of costs of avoiding accidents.[11] It asks for that form of property, private or communal, which leads to the highest product for the effort of producing.

Recently it has been argued that on certain assumptions, usually termed the absence of transaction costs, Pareto optimality or economic efficiency will occur regardless of the initial entitlement.[12] For this to hold, "no transaction costs" must be under-

---

[10] We are not here concerned with the many definitional variations which encircle the concept of Pareto optimality. Many of these variations stem from the fact that unless compensation actually occurs after a change (and this itself assumes a preexisting set of entitlements from which one makes a change to a Pareto optimal arrangement), the redistribution of wealth implicit in the change may well make a return to the prior position also seem Pareto optimal. There are any number of variations on this theme which economists have studied at length. Since in the world in which lawyers must live, anything close to Pareto efficiency, even if desirable, is not attainable, these refinements need not detain us even though they are crucial to a full understanding of the concept.

Most versions of Pareto optimality are based on the premise that individuals know best what is best for them. Hence they assume that to determine whether those who gain from a change could compensate those who lose, one must look to the values the individuals themselves give to the gains and losses. Economic efficiency may, however, present a broader notion which does not depend upon this individualistic premise. It may be that the state, for paternalistic reasons, *see* pp. 1113–14 *infra*, is better able to determine whether the total gain of the winners is greater than the total loss of the losers.

[11] The word "costs" is here used in a broad way to include all the disutilities resulting from an accident and its avoidance. As such it is not limited to monetary costs, or even to those which could in some sense be "monetizable," but rather includes disutilities or "costs" — for instance, the loss to an individual of his leg — the very expression of which in monetary terms would seem callous. One of the consequences of not being able to put monetary values on some disutilities or "costs" is that the market is of little use in gauging their worth, and this in turn gives rise to one of the reasons why liability, or inalienability rules, rather than property rules may be used.

[12] This proposition was first established in Coase's classic article, *The Problem of Social Cost*, 3 J. LAW & ECON. 1 (1960), and has been refined in subsequent literature. *See, e.g.*, Calabresi, *Transaction Costs, Resource Allocation and Liability Rules — A Comment*, 11 J. LAW & ECON. 67 (1968); Nutter, *The Coase Theorem on Social Cost: A Footnote*, 11 J. LAW & ECON. 503 (1968). *See also* G. STIGLER, THE THEORY OF PRICE 113 (3d ed. 1966); Mishan, *Pareto Optimality and the Law*, 19 OXFORD ECON. PAPERS 255 (1967).

stood extremely broadly as involving both perfect knowledge and the absence of any impediments or costs of negotiating. Negotiation costs include, for example, the cost of excluding would-be freeloaders from the fruits of market bargains.[13] In such a frictionless society, transactions would occur until no one could be made better off as a result of further transactions without making someone else worse off. This, we would suggest, is a necessary, indeed a tautological, result of the definitions of Pareto optimality and of transaction costs which we have given.

Such a result would not mean, however, that the *same* allocation of resources would exist regardless of the initial set of entitlements. Taney's willingness to pay for the right to make noise may depend on how rich he is; Marshall's willingness to pay for silence may depend on his wealth. In a society which entitles Taney to make noise and which forces Marshall to buy silence from Taney, Taney is wealthier and Marshall poorer than each would be in a society which had the converse set of entitlements. Depending on how Marshall's desire for silence and Taney's for noise vary with their wealth, an entitlement to noise will result in negotiations which will lead to a different quantum of noise than would an entitlement to silence.[14] This variation in the quantity

---

[13] The freeloader is the person who refuses to be inoculated against smallpox because, given the fact that almost everyone else is inoculated, the risk of smallpox to him is less than the risk of harm from the inoculation. He is the person who refuses to pay for a common park, though he wants it, because he believes that others will put in enough money to make the park available to him. *See* Costs 137 n.4. The costs of excluding the freeloader from the benefits for which he refused to pay may well be considerable as the two above examples should suggest. This is especially so since these costs may include the inefficiency of pricing a good, like the park once it exists, above its marginal cost in order to force the freeloader to disclose his true desire to use it — thus enabling us to charge him part of the cost of establishing it initially.

It is the capacity of the market to induce disclosure of individual preferences which makes it theoretically possible for the market to bring about exchanges leading to Pareto optimality. But the freeloader situation is just one of many where no such disclosure is achieved by the market. If we assume perfect knowledge, defined more broadly than is normally done to include knowledge of individual preferences, then such situations pose no problem. This definition of perfect knowledge, though perhaps implicit in the concept of no transaction costs, would not only make reaching Pareto optimality easy through the market, it would make it equally easy to establish a similar result by collective fiat.

For a further discussion of what is implied by a broad definition of no transaction costs, see note 59 *infra*. For a discussion of other devices which may induce individuals to disclose their preferences, see note 38 *infra*.

[14] *See* Mishan, *Pareto Optimality and the Law*, 19 Oxford Econ. Papers 255 (1967). Unless Taney's and Marshall's desires for noise and silence are totally unaffected by their wealth, that is, their desires are totally income inelastic, a change in their wealth will alter the value each places on noise and silence and hence will alter the outcome of their negotiations.

of noise and silence can be viewed as no more than an instance of the well accepted proposition that what is a Pareto optimal, or economically efficient, solution varies with the starting distribution of wealth. Pareto optimality is optimal *given* a distribution of wealth, but different distributions of wealth imply their own Pareto optimal allocation of resources.[15]

All this suggests why distributions of wealth may affect a society's choice of entitlements. It does not suggest why *economic efficiency* should affect the choice, if we assume an absence of any transaction costs. But no one makes an assumption of no transaction costs in practice. Like the physicist's assumption of no friction or Say's law in macro-economics, the assumption of no transaction costs may be a useful starting point, a device which helps us see how, as different elements which may be termed transaction costs become important, the goal of economic efficiency starts to prefer one allocation of entitlements over another.[16]

Since one of us has written at length on how in the presence of various types of transaction costs a society would go about deciding on a set of entitlements in the field of accident law,[17] it is enough to say here: (1) that economic efficiency standing alone would dictate that set of entitlements which favors knowledgeable choices between social benefits and the social costs of obtaining them, and between social costs and the social costs of avoiding them; (2) that this implies, in the absence of certainty as to whether a benefit is worth its costs to society, that the cost should be put on the party or activity best located to make such a cost-benefit analysis; (3) that in particular contexts like accidents or pollution this suggests putting costs on the party or activity which

---

[15] There should be no implication that a Pareto optimal solution is in some sense better than a non-Pareto optimal solution which results in a different wealth distribution. The implication is only that given the *same* wealth distribution Pareto optimal is in some meaningful sense preferable to non-Pareto optimal.

[16] *See* Demsetz, *When Does the Rule of Liability Matter?*, 1 J. LEGAL STUD. 13, 25–28 (1972); Stigler, *The Law and Economics of Public Policy: A Plea to the Scholars*, 1 J. LEGAL STUD. 1, 11–12 (1972).

The trouble with a term like "no transaction costs" is that it covers a multitude of market failures. The appropriate collective response, if the aim is to approach Pareto optimality, will vary depending on what the actual impediments to full bargaining are in any given cases. Occasionally the appropriate response may be to ignore the impediments. If the impediments are merely the administrative costs of establishing a market, it may be that doing nothing is preferable to attempting to correct for these costs because the administrative costs of collective action may be even greater. Similarly, if the impediments are due to a failure of the market to cause an accurate disclosure of freeloaders' preferences it may be that the collective can do no better.

[17] *See* COSTS 135–97.

can most cheaply avoid them; (4) that in the absence of certainty as to who that party or activity is, the costs should be put on the party or activity which can with the lowest transaction costs act in the market to correct an error in entitlements by inducing the party who can avoid social costs most cheaply to do so; [18] and (5) that since we are in an area where by hypothesis markets do not work perfectly — there are transaction costs — a decision will often have to be made on whether market transactions or collective fiat is most likely to bring us closer to the Pareto optimal result the "perfect" market would reach.[19]

Complex though this summary may suggest the entitlement choice to be, in practice the criteria it represents will frequently indicate which allocations of entitlements are most likely to lead to optimal market judgments between having an extra car or taking a train, getting an extra cabbage and spending less time working in the hot sun, and having more widgets and breathing the pollution that widget production implies. Economic efficiency is not, however, the sole reason which induces a society to select a

---

[18] In *The Costs of Accidents*, the criteria here summarized are discussed at length and broken down into subcriteria which deal with the avoidance of different types of externalization and with the finding of the "best briber." Such detailed analysis is necessary to the application of the criteria to any specific area of law. At the level of generality of this article it did not seem to us necessary.

[19] In accident law this election takes the form of a choice between general or market deterrence and specific deterrence, in which the permitted level and manner of accident causing activities is determined collectively. For example, society may decide to grant an entitlement to drive and an entitlement to be compensated for accidents resulting from driving, and allow decisions by individual parties to determine the level and manner of driving. But a greater degree of specific deterrence could be achieved by selecting a different set of initial entitlements in order to accord with a collective cost-benefit analysis — by, for example, prohibiting cars of more than a certain horsepower.

The primary disadvantage of specific deterrence, as compared with general deterrence, is that it requires the central decisionmaker not only to determine the costs of any given activity, but also to measure its benefits, in order to determine the optimum level of activity. It is exceedingly difficult and exceedingly costly for any centralized decisionmaker to be fully informed of the costs and benefits of a wide range of activities. The irony is that collective fiat functions best in a world of costless perfect information; yet in a world of costless transactions, including costless information, the optimum allocation would be reached by market transactions, and the need to consider the alternative of collective fiat would not arise. One could, however, view the irony conversely, and say that the market works best under assumptions of perfect knowledge where collective fiat would work perfectly, rendering the market unnecessary. The fact that both market and collective determinations face difficulties in achieving the Pareto optimal result which perfect knowledge and no transaction costs would permit does not mean that the same difficulties are always as great for the two approaches. Thus, there are many situations in which we can assume fairly confidently that the market will do better than a collective decider, and there are situations where we can assume the opposite to be true. *See* Costs 103–13.

set of entitlements. Wealth distribution preferences are another, and thus it is to distributional grounds for different entitlements to which we must now turn.

B. Distributional Goals

There are, we would suggest, at least two types of distributional concerns which may affect the choice of entitlements. These involve distribution of wealth itself and distribution of certain specific goods, which have sometimes been called merit goods.

All societies have wealth distribution preferences. They are, nonetheless, harder to talk about than are efficiency goals. For efficiency goals can be discussed in terms of a general concept like Pareto optimality to which exceptions — like paternalism — can be noted.[20] Distributional preferences, on the other hand, cannot usefully be discussed in a single conceptual framework. There are some fairly broadly accepted preferences — caste preferences in one society, more rather than less equality in another society. There are also preferences which are linked to dynamic efficiency concepts — producers ought to be rewarded since they will cause everyone to be better off in the end. Finally, there are a myriad of highly individualized preferences as to who should be richer and who poorer which need not have anything to do with either equality or efficiency — silence lovers should be richer than noise lovers because they are worthier.[21]

Difficult as wealth distribution preferences are to analyze, it should be obvious that they play a crucial role in the setting of entitlements. For the placement of entitlements has a fundamental effect on a society's distribution of wealth. It is not enough, if a society wishes absolute equality, to start everyone off with the same amount of money. A financially egalitarian society which gives individuals the right to make noise immediately makes the would-be noisemaker richer than the silence

---

[20] For a discussion of paternalism, see pp. 1113–14 infra.

[21] The first group of preferences roughly coincides with those notions which writers like Fletcher, following Aristotle, term distributive justice. The second and third groups, instead, presumably deal with Fletcher's "corrective" justice — rewards based on what people do rather than what they are. See Fletcher, Fairness and Utility in Tort Theory, 85 HARV. L. REV. 537, 547 n.40 (1972).

Within the "corrective" justice category our second and third groupings distinguish those preferences which are transparently linked to efficiency notions from those whose roots are less obvious. If there were a generally accepted theory of desserts, one could speak in general terms about the role the third group plays just as one tends to speak about the role of either the first or second group. We do not believe that an adequate theory of desserts — even if possible — is currently available. See also pp. 1102–05 infra.

loving hermit.[22] Similarly, a society which entitles the person with brains to keep what his shrewdness gains him implies a different distribution of wealth from a society which demands from each according to his relative ability but gives to each according to his relative desire. One can go further and consider that a beautiful woman or handsome man is better off in a society which entitles individuals to bodily integrity than in one which gives everybody use of all the beauty available.

The consequence of this is that it is very difficult to imagine a society in which there is complete equality of wealth. Such a society either would have to consist of people who were all precisely the same, or it would have to compensate for differences in wealth caused by a given set of entitlements. The former is, of course, ridiculous, even granting cloning. And the latter would be very difficult; it would involve knowing what everyone's tastes were and taxing every holder of an entitlement at a rate sufficient to make up for the benefits the entitlement gave him. For example, it would involve taxing everyone with an entitlement to private use of his beauty or brains sufficiently to compensate those less favorably endowed but who nonetheless desired what beauty or brains could get.

If perfect equality is impossible, a society must choose what entitlements it wishes to have on the basis of criteria other than perfect equality. In doing this, a society often has a choice of methods, and the method chosen will have important distributional implications. Society can, for instance, give an entitlement away free and then, by paying the holders of the entitlement to limit their use of it, protect those who are injured by the free entitlement. Conversely, it can allow people to do a given thing only if they buy the right from the government. Thus a society can decide whether to entitle people to have children and then induce them to exercise control in procreating, or to require people to buy the right to have children in the first place. A society can also decide whether to entitle people to be free of military service and then induce them to join up, or to require all to serve but enable each to buy his way out. Which entitlement a society decides to sell, and which it decides to give away, will likely depend in part on which determination promotes the wealth distribution that society favors.[23]

---

[22] This assumes that there is not enough space for the noisemaker and the silence lover to coexist without intruding upon one another. In other words, this assumes that we are dealing with a problem of allocation of scarce resources; if we were not, there would be no need to set the initial entitlement. *See generally* Mishan, *supra* note 12.

[23] Any entitlement given away free implies a converse which must be paid for. For all those who like children, there are those who are disturbed by children;

If the choice of entitlements affects wealth distribution generally, it also affects the chances that people will obtain what have sometimes been called merit goods.[24] Whenever a society wishes to maximize the chances that individuals will have at least a minimum endowment of certain particular goods — education, clothes, bodily integrity — the society is likely to begin by giving the individuals an entitlement to them. If the society deems such an endowment to be essential regardless of individual desires, it will, of course, make the entitlement inalienable.[25] Why, however, would a society entitle individuals to specific goods rather than to money with which they can buy what they wish, unless it deems that it can decide better than the individuals what benefits them and society; unless, in other words, it wishes to make the entitlement inalienable?

We have seen that an entitlement to a good or to its converse is essentially inevitable.[26] We either are entitled to have silence or entitled to make noise in a given set of circumstances. We either have the right to our own property or body or the right to share others' property or bodies. We may buy or sell our-

for all those who detest armies, there are those who want what armies accomplish. Otherwise, we would have no scarce resource problem and hence no entitlement problem. Therefore, one cannot simply say that giving away an entitlement free is progressive while selling it is regressive. It is true that the more "free" goods there are the less inequality of wealth there is, if everything else has stayed the same. But if a free entitlement implies a costly converse, entitlements are *not* in this sense free goods. And the issue of their progressivity and regressivity must depend on the relative desire for the entitlement as against its converse on the part of the rich and the poor.

Strictly speaking, even this is true only if the money needed to finance the alternative plans, or made available to the government as a result of the plans, is raised and spent in a way that is precisely neutral with respect to wealth distribution. The point is simply this: even a highly regressive tax will aid wealth equality if the money it raises is all spent to benefit the poorest citizens. And even a system of outdoor relief for the idle rich aids wealth equality if the funds it requires are raised by taxing only the wealthiest of the wealthy. Thus whenever one speaks of a taxing program, spending program, or a system of entitlements as progressive or regressive, one must be assuming that the way the money is spent (if it is a tax) or the way it is raised (if it is a spending program) does not counter the distributive effect of the program itself.

[24] *Cf.* R. MUSGRAVE, THE THEORY OF PUBLIC FINANCE 13–14 (1959).

[25] The commonly given reasons why a society may choose to do this are discussed *infra* at pp. 1111–15. All of them are, of course, reasons which explain why such goods are often categorized as merit goods. When a society subsidizes a good it makes a similar decision based on similar grounds. Presumably, however, in such cases the grounds only justify making possession of the good less costly than would be the case without government intervention, rather than making possession of the good inevitable.

[26] This is true unless we are prepared to let the parties settle the matter on the basis of might makes right, which itself may also be viewed as a form of entitlement.

selves into the opposite position, but we must start somewhere. Under these circumstances, a society which prefers people to have silence, or own property, or have bodily integrity, but which does not hold the grounds for its preference to be sufficiently strong to justify overriding contrary preferences by individuals, will give such entitlements according to the collective preference, even though it will allow them to be sold thereafter.

Whenever transactions to sell or buy entitlements are very expensive, such an initial entitlement decision will be nearly as effective in assuring that individuals will have the merit good as would be making the entitlement inalienable. Since coercion is inherent because of the fact that a good cannot practically be bought or sold, a society can choose only whether to make an individual have the good, by giving it to him, or to prevent him from getting it by giving him money instead.[27] In such circumstances society will pick the entitlement it deems favorable to the general welfare and not worry about coercion or alienability; it has increased the chances that individuals will have a particular good without increasing the degree of coercion imposed on individuals.[28] A common example of this may occur where the good involved is the present certainty of being able to buy a future benefit and where a futures market in that good is too expensive to be feasible.[29]

[27] For a discussion of this inevitable, and therefore irrelevant degree of coercion in the accident context, see Costs 50–55, 161–73.

[28] The situation is analogous to that which involves choosing between systems of allocation of accident costs which minimize rapid changes in wealth, through spreading, and those that do not. Indeed, if the avoidance of rapid changes in wealth is, itself, viewed as a merit good, the analogy is complete. In the accident field a great deal of attention has been devoted to the problem of rapid changes in wealth. *See, e.g.,* Morris & Paul, *The Financial Impact of Automobile Accidents,* 110 U. PA. L. REV. 913, 924 (1962). *But see* W. BLUM & H. KALVEN, PUBLIC LAW PERSPECTIVES ON A PRIVATE LAW PROBLEM — AUTO COMPENSATION PLANS (1965).

[29] A full discussion of this justification for the giving of goods in "kind" is well beyond the scope of this article. An indication of what is involved may be in order, however. One of the many reasons why the right to vote is given in kind instead of giving individuals that amount of money which would assure them, in a voteless society, of all the benefits which having the vote gives them, is that at any given time the price of those benefits in the future is totally uncertain and, therefore, virtually no amount of money would assure individuals of having those future benefits. This would not be the case if an entrepreneur could be counted on to guarantee those future benefits in exchange for a present money payment. That is what happens in a futures market for, say, sow's bellies. The degree of uncertainty in the cost of the future benefits of the vote is such, however, that a futures market is either not feasible, or, what is the same thing, much too costly to be worthwhile. In such circumstances the nonmarket alternative of giving of the good in kind seems more efficient. Many of the merit goods which are, in fact, given in kind in our society — for example, education — share this character-

C. Other Justice Reasons

The final reasons for a society's choice of initial entitlements we termed other justice reasons, and we may as well admit that it is hard to know what content can be poured into that term, at least given the very broad definitions of economic efficiency and distributional goals that we have used. Is there, in other words, a reason which would influence a society's choice of initial entitlements that cannot be comprehended in terms of efficiency and distribution? A couple of examples will indicate the problem.

Taney likes noise; Marshall likes silence. They are, let us assume, inevitably neighbors. Let us also assume there are no transaction costs which may impede negotiations between them. Let us assume finally that we do not know Taney's and Marshall's wealth or, indeed, anything else about them. Under these circumstances we know that Pareto optimality — economic efficiency — will be reached whether we choose an entitlement to make noise or to have silence. We also are indifferent, from a general wealth distribution point of view, as to what the initial entitlement is because we do not know whether it will lead to greater equality or inequality. This leaves us with only two reasons on which to base our choice of entitlement. The first is the relative worthiness of silence lovers and noise lovers. The second is the consistency of the choice, or its apparent consistency, with other entitlements in the society.

The first sounds appealing, and it sounds like justice. But it is hard to deal with. Why, unless our choice affects other people, should we prefer one to another? [30] To say that we wish, for

---

istic of involving present rights to future benefits in circumstances where a futures market does not exist and at first glance seems very difficult to organize cheaply. We do not suggest that this is the sole explanation for the way voting is handled in our society. For instance, it does not explain why the vote cannot be sold. (An explanation for that may be found in the fact that Taney's benefit from the vote may depend on Marshall's not having more of it than he.) It does, however, add another, not frequently given, explanation for the occasional allocation of goods rather than money to individuals.

[30] The usual answer is religious or transcendental reasons. But this answer presents problems. If it means that Chase, a third party, suffers if the noise-maker is preferred, because Chase's faith deems silence worthier than noise, then third parties *are* affected by the choice. Chase suffers; there is an external effect. But that possibility was excluded in our hypothetical. In practice such external effects, often called moralisms, are extremely common and greatly complicate the reaching of Pareto optimality. *See* pp. 1112–13 *infra.*

Religious or transcendental reasons may, however, be of another kind. Chase may prefer silence not because he himself cares, not because he suffers if noise-makers get the best of it when his faith deems silence lovers to be worthier, but because he believes God suffers if such a choice is made. No amount of compensation will help Chase in this situation since he suffers nothing which can be

instance, to make the silence lover relatively wealthier because we prefer silence is no answer, for that is simply a restatement of the question. Of course, if the choice does affect people other than Marshall and Taney, then we have a valid basis for decision. But the fact that such external effects are extremely common and greatly influence our choices does not help us much. It does suggest that the reaching of Pareto optimality is, in practice, a very complex matter precisely because of the existence of many external effects which markets find hard to deal with. And it also suggests that there often are general distributional considerations between Taney-Marshall and the rest of the world which affect the choice of entitlement. It in no way suggests, however, that there is more to the choice between Taney-Marshall than Pareto optimality and distributional concerns. In other words, if the assumptions of no transaction costs and indifference as to distributional considerations, made as between Taney and Marshall (where they are unlikely), could be made as to the world as a whole (where they are impossible), the fact that the choice between Taney's noise or Marshall's silence might affect other people would give us no guidance. Thus what sounds like a justice standard is simply a handy way of importing efficiency and distributional notions too diverse and general in their effect to be analyzed fully in the decision of a specific case.

The second sounds appealing in a different way since it sounds like "treating like cases alike." If the entitlement to make noise in other people's ears for one's pleasure is viewed by society as closely akin to the entitlement to beat up people for one's pleasure, and if good efficiency and distributional reasons exist for not allowing people to beat up others for sheer pleasure, then there may be a good reason for preferring an entitlement to silence rather than noise in the Taney-Marshall case. Because the two entitlements are apparently consistent, the entitlement to silence strengthens the entitlement to be free from gratuitous beatings which we assumed was based on good efficiency and distributional reasons.[31] It does so by lowering the enforcement costs of the entitlement to be free from gratuitous beatings; the entitlement to silence reiterates and reinforces the values protected by the entitlement to be free from gratuitous beatings and reduces the number of discriminations people must make between one activity and another, thus simplifying the task of obedience.

compensated, and compensating God for the wrong choice is not feasible. Such a reason for a choice is, we would suggest, a true nonefficiency, nondistribution reason. Whether it actually ever plays a role may well be another matter.

[31] The opposite would be true if noisemaking were thought to be akin to industry, and drive and silence to lethargy and laziness, and we had good efficiency or distributional reasons for preferring industry to lethargy.

The problem with this rationale for the choice is that it too comes down to efficiency and distributional reasons. We prefer the silence maker because *that* entitlement, even though it does not of itself affect the desired wealth distribution or lead us away from efficiency in the Taney-Marshall case, helps us to reach those goals in other situations where there are transaction costs or where we do have distributional preferences. It does this because people do not realize that the consistency is only apparent. If we could explain to them, both rationally and emotionally, the efficiency and distributional reasons why gratuitous beating up of people was inefficient or led to undesirable wealth distribution, and if we could also explain to them why an entitlement to noise rather than silence in the Taney-Marshall case would not lead to either inefficiency or maldistribution, then the secondary undermining of the entitlement to bodily integrity would not occur. It is only because it is expensive, even if feasible, to point out the difference between the two situations that the apparent similarity between them remains. And avoiding this kind of needless expense, while a very good reason for making choices, is clearly no more than a part of the economic efficiency goal.[32]

Still we should admit that explaining entitlements solely in terms of efficiency and distribution, in even their broadest terms, does not seem wholly satisfactory. The reasons for this are worth at least passing mention. The reason that we have so far explained entitlements simply in terms of efficiency and distribution is ultimately tautological. We defined distribution as covering *all* the reasons, other than efficiency, on the basis of which we might prefer to make Taney *wealthier* than Marshall. So defined, there obviously was no room for any other reasons. Distributional grounds covered broadly accepted ideas like "equality" or, in some societies, "caste preference," and highly specific ones like "favoring the silence lover." We used this definition because there is a utility in lumping together all those reasons for preferring Taney to Marshall which cannot be explained in terms of a desire to make everyone better off, and in contrasting them with efficiency reasons, whether Paretian or not, which can be so explained.

Lumping them together, however, has some analytical dis-

---

[32] We do not mean to underestimate the importance of apparent consistency as a ground for entitlements. Far from it, it is likely that a society often prefers an entitlement which even leads to mild inefficiencies or maldistribution of wealth between, say, Taney and Marshall, because that entitlement tends to support other entitlements which are crucial in terms of efficiency or wealth distribution in the society at large and because the cost of convincing people that the situations are, in fact, different is not worth the gain which would be obtained in the Taney-Marshall case.

advantages. It seems to assume that we cannot say any more about the reasons for some distributional preferences than about others. For instance, it seems to assume a similar universality of support for recognizing silence lovers as relatively worthier as there is for recognizing the relative desirability of equality. And that, surely, is a dangerous assumption. To avoid this danger the term "distribution" is often limited to relatively few broad reasons, like equality. And those preferences which cannot be easily explained in terms of these relatively few broadly accepted distributional preferences, or in terms of efficiency, are termed justice reasons. The difficulty with this locution is that it sometimes is taken to imply that the moral gloss of justice is reserved for these residual preferences and does not apply to the broader distributional preferences or to efficiency based preferences. And surely this is wrong, for many entitlements that properly are described as based on justice in our society can easily be explained in terms either of broad distributional preferences like equality or of efficiency or of both.

By using the term "*other* justice reasons" we hope to avoid this difficulty and emphasize that justice notions adhere to efficiency and broad distributional preferences as well as to other more idiosyncratic ones. To the extent that one is concerned with contrasting the difference between efficiency and other reasons for certain entitlements, the bipolar efficiency-distribution locution is all that is needed. To the extent that one wishes to delve either into reasons which, though possibly originally linked to efficiency, have now a life of their own, or into reasons which, though distributional, cannot be described in terms of broad principles like equality, then a locution which allows for "other justice reasons" seems more useful.[33]

III. RULES FOR PROTECTING AND REGULATING ENTITLEMENTS

Whenever society chooses an initial entitlement it must also determine whether to protect the entitlement by property rules, by liability rules, or by rules of inalienability. In our framework, much of what is generally called private property can be viewed as an entitlement which is protected by a property rule. No one can take the entitlement to private property from the holder unless the holder sells it willingly and at the price at which he subjectively values the property. Yet a nuisance with sufficient public utility to avoid injunction has, in effect, the right to take property with compensation. In such a circumstance the entitlement to the property is protected only by what we call a liability rule:

---

[33] *But see* Fletcher, *supra* note 21, at 547 n.40.

an external, objective standard of value is used to facilitate the transfer of the entitlement from the holder to the nuisance.[34] Finally, in some instances we will not allow the sale of the property at all, that is, we will occasionally make the entitlement inalienable.

This section will consider the circumstances in which society will employ these three rules to solve situations of conflict. Because the property rule and the liability rule are closely related and depend for their application on the shortcomings of each other, we treat them together. We discuss inalienability separately.

A. Property and Liability Rules

Why cannot a society simply decide on the basis of the already mentioned criteria who should receive any given entitlement, and then let its transfer occur only through a voluntary negotiation? Why, in other words, cannot society limit itself to the property rule? To do this it would need only to protect and enforce the initial entitlements from all attacks, perhaps through criminal sanctions,[35] and to enforce voluntary contracts for their transfer. Why do we need liability rules at all?

In terms of economic efficiency the reason is easy enough to see. Often the cost of establishing the value of an initial entitlement by negotiation is so great that even though a transfer of the entitlement would benefit all concerned, such a transfer will not occur. If a collective determination of the value were available instead, the beneficial transfer would quickly come about.

Eminent domain is a good example. A park where Guidacres, a tract of land owned by 1,000 owners in 1,000 parcels, now sits would, let us assume, benefit a neighboring town enough so that the 100,000 citizens of the town would each be willing to pay an average of $100 to have it. The park is Pareto desirable if the owners of the tracts of land in Guidacres actually value their entitlements at less than $10,000,000 or an average of $10,000 a tract. Let us assume that in fact the parcels are all the same and all the owners value them at $8,000. On this assumption, the park is, in economic efficiency terms, desirable — in values foregone it costs $8,000,000 and is worth $10,000,000 to the buyers. And yet it may well not be established. If enough of the owners hold-out for more than $10,000 in order to get a share of the $2,000,000 that they guess the buyers are willing to pay over the

---

[34] *See, e.g.*, Boomer v. Atlantic Cement Co., 26 N.Y.2d 219, 309 N.Y.S.2d 312, 257 N.E.2d 870 (1970) (avoidance of injunction conditioned on payment of permanent damages to plaintiffs).

[35] The relationship between criminal sanctions and property entitlements will be examined *infra* pp. 1124–27.

value which the sellers in actuality attach, the price demanded will be more than $10,000,000 and no park will result. The sellers have an incentive to hide their true valuation and the market will not succeed in establishing it.

An equally valid example could be made on the buying side. Suppose the sellers of Guidacres have agreed to a sales price of $8,000,000 (they are all relatives and at a family banquet decided that trying to hold-out would leave them all losers). It does not follow that the buyers can raise that much even though each of 100,000 citizens *in fact* values the park at $100. Some citizens may try to free-load and say the park is only worth $50 or even nothing to them, hoping that enough others will admit to a higher desire and make up the $8,000,000 price. Again there is no reason to believe that a market, a decentralized system of valuing, will cause people to express their true valuations and hence yield results which all would *in fact* agree are desirable.

Whenever this is the case an argument can readily be made for moving from a property rule to a liability rule. If society can remove from the market the valuation of each tract of land, decide the value collectively, and impose it, then the holdout problem is gone. Similarly, if society can value collectively each individual citizen's desire to have a park and charge him a "benefits" tax based upon it, the freeloader problem is gone. If the sum of the taxes is greater than the sum of the compensation awards, the park will result.

Of course, one can conceive of situations where it might be cheap to exclude all the freeloaders from the park, or to ration the park's use in accordance with original willingness to pay. In such cases the incentive to free-load might be eliminated. But such exclusions, even if possible, are usually not cheap. And the same may be the case for market methods which might avoid the holdout problem on the seller side.

Moreover, even if holdout and freeloader problems can be met feasibly by the market, an argument may remain for employing a liability rule. Assume that in our hypothetical, freeloaders can be excluded at the cost of $1,000,000 and that all owners of tracts in Guidacres can be convinced, by the use of $500,000 worth of advertising and cocktail parties, that a sale will only occur if they reveal their true land valuations. Since $8,000,000 plus $1,500,000 is less than $10,000,000, the park will be established. But if collective valuation of the tracts and of the benefits of the prospective park would have cost less than $1,500,000, it would have been inefficient to establish the park through the market — a market which was not worth having would have been paid for.[36]

---

[36] It may be argued that, given imperfect knowledge, the market is preferable because it places a limit — the cost of establishing a market — on the size of the

Of course, the problems with liability rules are equally real. We cannot be at all sure that landowner Taney is lying or holding out when he says his land is worth $12,000 to him. The fact that several neighbors sold identical tracts for $10,000 does not help us very much; Taney may be sentimentally attached to his land. As a result, eminent domain may grossly undervalue what Taney would actually sell for, even if it sought to give him his true valuation of his tract. In practice, it is so hard to determine Taney's true valuation that eminent domain simply gives him what the land is worth "objectively," in the full knowledge that this may result in over or under compensation. The same is true on the buyer side. "Benefits" taxes rarely attempt, let alone succeed, in gauging the individual citizen's relative desire for the alleged benefit. They are justified because, even if they do not accurately measure each individual's desire for the benefit, the market alternative seems worse. For example, fifty different households may place different values on a new sidewalk that is to abut all the properties. Nevertheless, because it is too difficult, even if possible, to gauge each household's valuation, we usually tax each household an equal amount.

The example of eminent domain is simply one of numerous instances in which society uses liability rules. Accidents is another. If we were to give victims a property entitlement not to be accidentally injured we would have to require all who engage in activities that may injure individuals to negotiate with them before an accident, and to buy the right to knock off an arm or a leg.[37] Such pre-accident negotiations would be extremely ex-

---

possible loss, while the costs of coercion cannot be defined and may be infinite. This may be true in some situations but need not always be the case. If, for example, we know that the holdouts would sell for $500,000 more than is offered, because they recently offered the land at that higher price, coercing them to sell at an objectively determined price between the seller's offer and the purchaser's offer cannot result in more than $500,000 in harm. Thus, the costs of coercion would also not be infinite. Nor is it an answer to say that the man who would sell for a higher price but is coerced for a lower one suffers an indefinite nonmonetary cost in addition to the price differential simply because he is coerced and resents it. For while this may well be true, the same nonmonetary resentment may also exist in those who desire the park and do not get it because the market is unable to pay off those who are holding out for a greater than actual value. In other words, unascertainable resentment costs may exist as a result of either coercion or market failure.

[37] Even if it were possible, it should be clear that the good which would be sold would not be the same as the good actually taken. If Taney waives for $1,000 the right to recover for the loss of a leg, should he ever lose it, he is negotiating for a joint product which can be described as his "desire or aversion to gamble" and "his desire to have a leg." The product actually taken, however, is the leg. That the two goods are different can be seen from the fact that a man who demands $1,000 for a 1 in a 1,000 chance of losing a leg may well demand more

pensive, often prohibitively so.[38] To require them would thus preclude many activities that might, in fact, be worth having. And, after an accident, the loser of the arm or leg can always very plausibly deny that he would have sold it at the price the buyer would have offered. Indeed, where negotiations after an accident do occur — for instance pretrial settlements — it is largely because the alternative is the collective valuation of the damages.

It is not our object here to outline all the theoretical, let alone the practical, situations where markets may be too expensive or fail and where collective valuations seem more desirable. Economic literature has many times surrounded the issue if it has not

---

than $100,000 for a 1 in 10 chance of losing it, and more than $1,000,000 for the sale of his leg to someone who needs it for a transplant. *See generally* COSTS 88–94. This does not mean that the result of such transactions, if feasible, would *necessarily* be worse than the result of collective valuations. It simply means that the situation, even if feasible, is different from the one in which Taney sells his house for a given price.

[38] Such preaccident negotiations between potential injurers and victims are at times not too costly. Thus in a typical products liability situation the cost of negotiation over a potential injury need not be prohibitive. The seller of a rotary lawn mower may offer to sell at a reduced price if the buyer agrees not to sue should he be injured. Nevertheless, society often forbids such negotiations because it deems them undesirable. This may occur because of the reasons suggested in note 37 *supra*, or for any of the other reasons which cause us to make some entitlements wholly or partly inalienable, *see infra* pp. 1111–15.

Attempts have been made to deal with situations where ex ante negotiations are not feasible by fiscal devices designed to cause people to reveal their preferences. One of these contemplates requiring individuals to declare a value on their properties, or even limbs, and paying a tax on the self assessed value. That value would be the value of the good if it were taken in an accident or by eminent domain. *See generally* N. Tideman, Three Approaches to Improving Urban Land Use, ch. III (1969) (unpublished Ph.D. dissertation submitted to U. of Chicago Economics Department, on file in Yale Law Library). Of course, if the good is only taken as a result of an accident or eminent domain, the problem of gambling described in note 37 *supra* would remain. If, instead, the property or limb could be taken at will at the self assessed value, serious problems would arise from the fact that there are enormous nonmonetizable, as well as monetizable, costs involved in making people put money values on all their belongings and limbs.

An additional, though perhaps solvable, problem with self assessed taxes is the fact that the taking price would exclude any consumer surplus. This may have no significance in terms of economic efficiency, but if the existence of consumer surplus in many market transactions is thought to have, on the whole, a favorable wealth distribution effect, it might well be a reason why self assessed taxes are viewed with skepticism. *Cf.* Little, Self-Assessed Valuations: A Critique (1972) (unpublished paper, on file in Harvard Law School Library). The reader might reasonably wonder why many individuals who view self assessed taxes with skepticism show no similar concerns for what may be a very similar device, optional first party insurance covering pain and suffering damages in automobile injuries. *See, e.g.*, Calabresi, *The New York Plan: A Free Choice Modification*, 71 COLUM. L. REV. 267, 268 n.6 (1971).

always zeroed in on it in ways intelligible to lawyers.[39] It is enough for our purposes to note that a very common reason, perhaps the most common one, for employing a liability rule rather than a property rule to protect an entitlement is that market valuation of the entitlement is deemed inefficient, that is, it is either unavailable or too expensive compared to a collective valuation.

We should also recognize that efficiency is not the sole ground for employing liability rules rather than property rules. Just as the initial entitlement is often decided upon for distributional reasons, so too the choice of a liability rule is often made because it facilitates a combination of efficiency and distributive results which would be difficult to achieve under a property rule. As we shall see in the pollution context, use of a liability rule may allow us to accomplish a measure of redistribution that could only be attained at a prohibitive sacrifice of efficiency if we employed a corresponding property rule.

More often, once a liability rule is decided upon, perhaps for efficiency reasons, it is then employed to favor distributive goals as well. Again accidents and eminent domain are good examples. In both of these areas the compensation given has clearly varied with society's distributive goals, and cannot be readily explained in terms of giving the victim, as nearly as possible, an objectively determined equivalent of the price at which he would have sold what was taken from him.

It should not be surprising that this is often so, even if the original reason for a liability rule is an efficiency one. For distributional goals are expensive and difficult to achieve, and the collective valuation involved in liability rules readily lends itself to promoting distributional goals.[40] This does not mean that distributional goals are always well served in this way. Ad hoc decision-making is always troublesome, and the difficulties are especially acute when the settlement of conflicts between parties is used as a vehicle for the solution of more widespread distributional problems. Nevertheless, distributional objectives may be better attained in this way than otherwise.[41]

---

[39] For a good discussion of market failure which is intelligible to lawyers, see Bator, *The Anatomy of Market Failure*, 72 Q. J. ECON. 351 (1958).

[40] Collective valuation of costs also makes it easier to value the costs at what the society thinks they should be valued by the victim instead of at what the victim would value them in a free market if such a market were feasible. The former kind of valuation is, of course, paternalism. This does not mean it is undesirable; the danger is that paternalism which is not desirable will enter mindlessly into the cost valuation because the valuation is necessarily done collectively. *See* pp. 1113–14 *infra*.

[41] For suggestions that at times systematic distributional programs may cause

B. Inalienable Entitlements

Thus far we have focused on the questions of when society should protect an entitlement by property or liability rules. However, there remain many entitlements which involve a still greater degree of societal intervention: the law not only decides who is to own something and what price is to be paid for it if it is taken or destroyed, but also regulates its sale — by, for example, prescribing preconditions for a valid sale or forbidding a sale altogether. Although these rules of inalienability are substantially different from the property and liability rules, their use can be analyzed in terms of the same efficiency and distributional goals that underlie the use of the other two rules.

While at first glance efficiency objectives may seem undermined by limitations on the ability to engage in transactions, closer analysis suggests that there are instances, perhaps many, in which economic efficiency is more closely approximated by such limitations. This might occur when a transaction would create significant externalities — costs to third parties.

For instance, if Taney were allowed to sell his land to Chase, a polluter, he would injure his neighbor Marshall by lowering the value of Marshall's land. Conceivably, Marshall could pay Taney not to sell his land; but, because there are many injured Marshalls, freeloader and information costs make such transactions practically impossible. The state could protect the Marshalls and yet facilitate the sale of the land by giving the Marshalls an entitlement to prevent Taney's sale to Chase but only protecting the entitlement by a liability rule. It might, for instance, charge an excise tax on all sales of land to polluters equal to its estimate of the external cost to the Marshalls of the sale. But where there are so many injured Marshalls that the price required under the liability rule is likely to be high enough so that no one would be willing to pay it, then setting up the machinery for collective valuation will be wasteful. Barring the sale to polluters will be the most efficient result because it is clear that avoiding pollution is cheaper than paying its costs — including its costs to the Marshalls.

Another instance in which external costs may justify inalienability occurs when external costs do not lend themselves to collective measurement which is acceptably objective and nonarbitrary. This nonmonetizability is characteristic of one category of external costs which, as a practical matter, seems frequently to lead us to rules of inalienability. Such external costs are often called moralisms.

If Taney is allowed to sell himself into slavery, or to take undue risks of becoming penniless, or to sell a kidney, Marshall may be harmed, simply because Marshall is a sensitive man who is made unhappy by seeing slaves, paupers, or persons who die because they have sold a kidney. Again Marshall could pay Taney not to sell his freedom to Chase the slaveowner; but again, because Marshall is not one but many individuals, freeloader and information costs make such transactions practically impossible. Again, it might seem that the state could intervene by objectively valuing the external cost to Marshall and requiring Chase to pay that cost. But since the external cost to Marshall does not lend itself to an acceptable objective measurement, such liability rules are not appropriate.

In the case of Taney selling land to Chase, the polluter, they were inappropriate because we *knew* that the costs to Taney and the Marshalls exceeded the benefits to Chase. Here, though we are not certain of how a cost-benefit analysis would come out, liability rules are inappropriate because any monetization is, by hypothesis, out of the question. The state must, therefore, either ignore the external costs to Marshall, or if it judges them great enough, forbid the transaction that gave rise to them by making Taney's freedom inalienable.[42]

Obviously we will not always value the external harm of a moralism enough to prohibit the sale.[43] And obviously also, external costs other than moralisms may be sufficiently hard to value to make rules of inalienability appropriate in certain circumstances; this reason for rules of inalienability, however, does seem most often germane in situations where moralisms are involved.[44]

---

[42] Granting Taney an inalienable right to be free is in many respects the same as granting most of the people a property entitlement to keep Taney free. The people may bargain and decide to surrender their entitlement, *i.e.*, to change the law, but there are limits on the feasibility of transactions of this sort which make the public's entitlements virtually inalienable.

[43] For example, I am allowed to buy and read whatever books I like, or to sell my house to whomever I choose, regardless of whether my doing so makes my neighbors unhappy. These entitlements could be a form of self paternalism on the part of the neighbors who fear a different rule would harm them more in the long run, or they could be selected because they strengthen seemingly similar entitlements. *See* pp. 1103–04 *supra*. But they may also reflect a judgment that the injury suffered by my neighbors results from a moralism shared by them but not so widespread as to make more efficient their being given an entitlement to prevent my transaction. In other words, people who are hurt by my transaction are the cheapest cost avoiders, *i.e.*, the cost to them of my being allowed to transact freely is less than the cost to me and others similarly situated of a converse entitlement.

[44] The fact that society may make an entitlement inalienable does not, of

There are two other efficiency reasons for forbidding the sale of entitlements under certain circumstances: self paternalism and true paternalism. Examples of the first are Ulysses tying himself to the mast or individuals passing a bill of rights so that they will be prevented from yielding to momentary temptations which they deem harmful to themselves. This type of limitation is not in any real sense paternalism. It is fully consistent with Pareto efficiency criteria, based on the notion that over the mass of cases no one knows better than the individual what is best for him or her. It merely allows the individual to choose what is best in the long run rather than in the short run, even though that choice entails giving up some short run freedom of choice. Self paternalism may cause us to require certain conditions to exist before we allow a sale of an entitlement; and it may help explain many situations of inalienability, like the invalidity of contracts entered into when drunk, or under undue influence or coercion. But it probably does not fully explain even these.[45]

True paternalism brings us a step further toward explaining such prohibitions and those of broader kinds — for example the prohibitions on a whole range of activities by minors. Paternalism is based on the notion that at least in some situations the Marshalls know better than Taney what will make Taney better off.[46] Here we are not talking about the offense to Marshall from Taney's choosing to read pornography, or selling himself into slavery, but rather the judgment that Taney was not in the position to choose best for himself when he made the choice for erotica or servitude.[47]

---

course, mean that there will be no compensation to the holder of the entitlement if it is taken from him. Thus even if a society forbids the sale of one's kidneys it will still probably compensate the person whose kidney is destroyed in an auto accident. The situations are distinct and the kidney is protected by different rules according to which situation we are speaking of.

[45] As a practical matter, since it is frequently impossible to limit the effect of an inalienable rule to those who desire it for self paternalistic reasons, self paternalism would lead to some restraints on those who would desire to sell their entitlements. This does not make self paternalism any less consistent with the premises of Pareto optimality; it is only another recognition that in an imperfect world, Pareto optimality can be approached more closely by systems which involve some coercion than by a system of totally free bargains.

[46] This locution leaves open the question whether Taney's future well-being will ultimately be decided by Taney himself or the many Marshalls. The latter implies a further departure from Paretian premises. The former, which may be typical of paternalism towards minors, implies simply that the minors do not know enough to exercise self paternalism.

[47] Sometimes the term paternalism is used to explain use of a rule of inalienability in situations where inalienability will not make the many Marshalls or the coerced Taney any better off. Inalienability is said to be imposed because the many Marshalls believe that making the entitlement inalienable is doing God's

The first concept we called a moralism and is a frequent and important ground for inalienability. But it is consistent with the premises of Pareto optimality. The second, paternalism, is also an important economic efficiency reason for inalienability, but it is not consistent with the premises of Pareto optimality: the most efficient pie is no longer that which costless bargains would achieve, because a person may be better off if he is prohibited from bargaining.

Finally, just as efficiency goals sometimes dictate the use of rules of inalienability, so, of course, do distributional goals. Whether an entitlement may be sold or not often affects directly who is richer and who is poorer. Prohibiting the sale of babies makes poorer those who can cheaply produce babies and richer those who through some nonmarket device get free an "unwanted" baby.[48] Prohibiting exculpatory clauses in product sales makes richer those who were injured by a product defect and poorer those who were not injured and who paid more for the product because the exculpatory clause was forbidden.[49] Favoring the specific group that has benefited may or may not have been the reason for the prohibition on bargaining. What is important is that, regardless of the reason for barring a contract, a group did gain from the prohibition.

This should suffice to put us on guard, for it suggests that direct distributional motives may lie behind asserted nondistributional grounds for inalienability, whether they be paternalism, self paternalism, or externalities.[50] This does not mean that giving

---

will, that is, that a sale or transfer of the entitlement would injure God. Assuming this situation exists in practice, we would not term it paternalism, because that word implies looking after the interests of the coerced party. *See* note 30 *supra*.

[48] This assumes that a prohibition on the sale of unwanted babies can be effectively enforced. If it can, then those unwanted babies which are produced are of no financial benefit to their natural parents and bring an increase in well-being to those who are allowed to adopt them free and as a result of a nonmarket allocation. Should the prohibition on sales of babies be only partially enforceable, the distributional result would be more complex. It would be unchanged for those who could obtain babies for adoption legally, *i.e.*, for those who received them without paying bribes, as it would for the natural parents who obeyed the law, since they would still receive no compensation. On the other hand, the illegal purchaser would probably pay, and the illegal seller receive, a higher price than if the sale of babies were legal. This would cause a greater distributive effect within the group of illegal sellers and buyers than would exist if such sales were permitted.

[49] *See* note 37 *supra*.

[50] As a practical matter, it is often impossible to tell whether an entitlement has been made partially inalienable for any of the several efficiency grounds mentioned or for distributional grounds. Do we bar people from selling their bodies for paternalistic, self paternalistic, or moralistic cost reasons? On what basis do we prohibit an individual from taking, for a high price, one chance in three of having

weight to distributional goals is undesirable. It clearly is desirable where on efficiency grounds society is indifferent between an alienable and an inalienable entitlement and distributional goals favor one approach or the other. It may well be desirable even when distributional goals are achieved at some efficiency costs. The danger may be, however, that what is justified on, for example, paternalism grounds is really a hidden way of accruing distributional benefits for a group whom we would not otherwise wish to benefit. For example, we may use certain types of zoning to preserve open spaces on the grounds that the poor will be happier, though they do not know it now. And open spaces may indeed make the poor happier in the long run. But the zoning that preserves open space also makes housing in the suburbs more expensive and it may be that the whole plan is aimed at securing distributional benefits to the suburban dweller regardless of the poor's happiness.[51]

IV. The Framework and Pollution Control Rules

Nuisance or pollution is one of the most interesting areas where the question of who will be given an entitlement, and how it will be protected, is in frequent issue.[52] Traditionally, and very ably in the recent article by Professor Michelman, the nuisance-pollution problem is viewed in terms of three rules.[53] First, Taney

---

to give his heart to a wealthy man who needs a transplant? Do we try to avoid a market in scarce medical resources for distributional or for some or all of the efficiency reasons discussed?

[51] There is another set of reasons which causes us to prohibit sales of some entitlements and which is sometimes termed distributional; this set of reasons causes us to prohibit sales of some entitlements because the underlying distribution of wealth seems to us undesirable. These reasons, we would suggest, are not true distributional grounds. They are, rather, efficiency grounds which become valid because of the original maldistribution. As such they can once again be categorized as due to externalities, self paternalism, and pure paternalism: (1) Marshall is offended because Taney, due to poverty, sells a kidney, and therefore Marshall votes to bar such sales (a moralism); (2) Taney, seeking to avoid temporary temptation due to his poverty, votes to bar such sales (self paternalism); and (3) the law prohibits Taney from the same sale because, regardless of what Taney believes, a majority thinks Taney will be better off later if he is barred from selling than if he is free to do so while influenced by his own poverty (pure paternalism). We do not mean to minimize these reasons by noting that they are not strictly distributional. We call them nondistributional simply to distinguish them from the more direct way in which distributional considerations affect the alienability of entitlements.

[52] It should be clear that the pollution problem we discuss here is really only a part of a broader problem, that of land use planning in general. Much of this analysis may therefore be relevant to other land use issues, for example exclusionary zoning, restrictive covenants, and ecological easements. See note 58 infra.

[53] Michelman, supra note 1, at 670. See also RESTATEMENT (SECOND) OF TORTS

may not pollute unless his neighbor (his only neighbor let us assume), Marshall, allows it (Marshall may enjoin Taney's nuisance).[54] Second, Taney may pollute but must compensate Marshall for damages caused (nuisance is found but the remedy is limited to damages).[55] Third, Taney may pollute at will and can only be stopped by Marshall if Marshall pays him off (Taney's pollution is not held to be a nuisance to Marshall).[56] In our terminology rules one and two (nuisance with injunction, and with damages only) are entitlements to Marshall. The first is an entitlement to be free from pollution and is protected by a property rule; the second is also an entitlement to be free from pollution but is protected only by a liability rule. Rule three (no nuisance) is instead an entitlement to Taney protected by a property rule, for only by buying Taney out at Taney's price can Marshall end the pollution.

The very statement of these rules in the context of our framework suggests that something is missing. Missing is a fourth rule representing an entitlement in Taney to pollute, but an entitlement which is protected only by a liability rule. The fourth rule, really a kind of partial eminent domain coupled with a benefits tax, can be stated as follows: Marshall may stop Taney from polluting, but if he does he must compensate Taney.

As a practical matter it will be easy to see why even legal writers as astute as Professor Michelman have ignored this rule. Unlike the first three it does not often lend itself to judicial imposition for a number of good legal process reasons. For example, even if Taney's injuries could practicably be measured, apportionment of the duty of compensation among many Marshalls would present problems for which courts are not well suited. If only those Marshalls who voluntarily asserted the right to enjoin Taney's pollution were required to pay the compensation, there would be insuperable freeloader problems. If, on the other

---

§§ 157–215 (1965). Michelman also discusses the possibility of inalienability. Michelman, *supra*, at 684. For a discussion of the use of rules of inalienability in the pollution context, see pp. 1123–24 *infra*.

[54] *See, e.g.*, Department of Health & Mental Hygiene v. Galaxy Chem. Co., 1 ENVIR. REP. 1660 (Md. Cir. Ct. 1970) (chemical smells enjoined); Ensign v. Walls, 323 Mich. 49, 34 N.W. 2d 549 (1948) (dog raising in residential neighborhood enjoined).

[55] *See, e.g.*, Boomer v. Atlantic Cement Co., 26 N.Y. 2d 219, 309 N.Y.S. 2d 312, 257 N.E.2d 870 (1970) (avoidance of injunction conditioned on payment of permanent damages to plaintiffs).

[56] *See, e.g.*, Francisco v. Department of Institutions & Agencies, 13 N.J. Misc. 663, 180 A. 843 (Ct. Ch. 1935) (plaintiffs not entitled to enjoin noise and odors of adjacent sanitarium); Rose v. Socony-Vacuum Corp., 54 R.I. 411, 173 A. 627 (1934) (pollution of percolating waters not enjoinable in absence of negligence).

hand, the liability rule entitled one of the Marshalls alone to enjoin the pollution and required all the benefited Marshalls to pay their share of the compensation, the courts would be faced with the immensely difficult task of determining who was benefited how much and imposing a benefits tax accordingly, all the while observing procedural limits within which courts are expected to function.[57]

The fourth rule is thus not part of the cases legal scholars read when they study nuisance law, and is therefore easily ignored by them. But it is available, and may sometimes make more sense than any of the three competing approaches. Indeed, in one form or another, it may well be the most frequent device employed.[58] To appreciate the utility of the fourth rule and to com-

---

[57] This task is much more difficult than that which arises under rule two, in which the many Marshalls would be compensated for their pollution injuries. Under rule two, each victim may act as an individual, either in seeking compensation in the first instance or in electing whether to be a part of a class seeking compensation. If he wishes to and is able to convince the court (by some accepted objective standard) that he has been injured, he may be compensated. Such individual action is expensive, and thus may be wasteful, but it presents no special problems in terms of the traditional workings of the courts. But where the class in question consists, not of those with a right to enjoin, but of those who must pay to enjoin, freeloader problems require the court to determine that an unwilling Marshall has been benefited and should be required to pay. The basic difficulty is that if we begin with the premise which usually underlies our notion of efficiency — namely, that individuals know what is best for them — we are faced with the anomaly of compelling compensation from one who denies he has incurred a benefit but whom we require to pay because *the court* thinks he has been benefited.

This problem is analogous to the difficulties presented by quasi-contracts. In terms of the theory of our economic efficiency goal, the case for requiring compensation for unbargained for (often accidental) benefits is similar to the argument for compensating tort victims. Yet courts as a general rule require compensation in quasi-contract only where there is both an indisputable benefit (usually of a pecuniary or economic nature) and some affirmative acknowledgment of subjective benefit (usually a subsequent promise to pay). See A. CORBIN, CONTRACTS §§ 231–34 (1963). This hesitancy suggests that courts lack confidence in their ability to distinguish real benefits from illusions. Perhaps even more importantly, it suggests that the courts recognize that what may clearly be an objective "benefit" may, to the putative beneficiary, not be a subjective benefit — if for no other reason than that unintended changes from the status quo often exact psychological costs. If that is the case, there has been no benefit at all in terms of our efficiency criterion.

[58] See A. KNEESE & B. BOWER, MANAGING WATER QUALITY: ECONOMICS, TECHNOLOGY, INSTITUTIONS 98–109 (1968); Krier, *The Pollution Problem and Legal Institutions: A Conceptual Overview*, 18 U.C.L.A.L. REV. 429, 467–75 (1971).

Virtually all eminent domain takings of a nonconforming use seem to be examples of this approach. Ecological easements may be another prime example. A local zoning ordinance may require a developer to contribute a portion of his land for purposes of parkland or school construction. In compensation for taking

pare it with the other three rules, we will examine why we might choose any of the given rules.

We would employ rule one (entitlement to be free from pollution protected by a property rule) from an economic efficiency point of view if we believed that the polluter, Taney, could avoid or reduce the costs of pollution more cheaply than the pollutee, Marshall. Or to put it another way, Taney would be enjoinable if he were in a better position to balance the costs of polluting against the costs of not polluting. We would employ rule three (entitlement to pollute protected by a property rule) again solely from an economic efficiency standpoint, if we made the converse judgment on who could best balance the harm of pollution against its avoidance costs. If we were wrong in our judgments and if transactions between Marshall and Taney were costless or even very cheap, the entitlement under rules one or three would be traded and an economically efficient result would occur in either case.[59] If we entitled Taney to pollute and Marshall valued clean air more than Taney valued the pollution, Marshall would pay Taney to stop polluting even though no nuisance was found. If we entitled Marshall to enjoin the pollution and the right to pollute was worth more to Taney than freedom from pollution was to Marshall, Taney would pay Marshall not to seek an injunction or would buy Marshall's land and sell it to someone who would agree not to seek an injunction. As we have assumed no one else was hurt by the pollution, Taney could now pollute even though the initial entitlement, based on a wrong guess of who was the cheapest avoider of the costs involved, allowed the pollution to be enjoined. Wherever transactions between Taney and Marshall are easy, and wherever economic efficiency is our goal, we could employ entitlements protected by property rules even though we would not be sure that the entitlement chosen was the right one. Transactions as described above would cure the error. While the entitlement might have important distributional effects, it would not substantially undercut economic efficiency.

the developer's entitlement, the locality will pay the developer "damages": it will allow him to increase the normal rate of density in his remaining property. The question of damage assessment involved in ecological easements raises similar problems to those raised in the benefit assessment involved in the question of quasi-contract. *See* note 57 *supra*.

[59] For a discussion of whether efficiency would be achieved in the long, as well as the short, run, see Coase, *supra* note 12; Calabresi, *supra* note 12 (pointing out that if "no transaction costs" means no impediments to bargaining in the short or long run, and if Pareto optimality means an allocation of resources which cannot be improved by bargains, assumptions of no transaction costs and rationality necessarily imply Pareto optimality); Nutter, *supra* note 12 (a technical demonstration of the applicability of the Coase theorem to long run problems). *See also* Demsetz, *supra* note 16, at 19–22.

The moment we assume, however, that transactions are not cheap, the situation changes dramatically. Assume we enjoin Taney and there are 10,000 injured Marshalls. Now *even if* the right to pollute is worth more to Taney than the right to be free from pollution is to the sum of the Marshalls, the injunction will probably stand. The cost of buying out all the Marshalls, given holdout problems, is likely to be too great, and an equivalent of eminent domain in Taney would be needed to alter the initial injunction. Conversely, if we denied a nuisance remedy, the 10,000 Marshalls could only with enormous difficulty, given free-loader problems, get together to buy out even one Taney and prevent the pollution. This would be so even if the pollution harm was greater than the value to Taney of the right to pollute.

If, however, transaction costs are not symmetrical, we may still be able to use the property rule. Assume that Taney can buy the Marshalls' entitlements easily because holdouts are for some reason absent, but that the Marshalls have great freeloader problems in buying out Taney. In this situation the entitlement should be granted to the Marshalls unless we are sure the Marshalls are the cheapest avoiders of pollution costs. Where we do not know the identity of the cheapest cost avoider it is better to entitle the Marshalls to be free of pollution because, even if we are wrong in our initial placement of the entitlement, that is, even if the Marshalls are the cheapest cost avoiders, Taney will buy out the Marshalls and economic efficiency will be achieved. Had we chosen the converse entitlement and been wrong, the Marshalls could not have bought out Taney. Unfortunately, transaction costs are often high on both sides and an initial entitlement, though incorrect in terms of economic efficiency, will not be altered in the market place.

Under these circumstances — and they are normal ones in the pollution area — we are likely to turn to liability rules whenever we are uncertain whether the polluter or the pollutees can most cheaply avoid the cost of pollution. We are only likely to use liability rules where we are uncertain because, if we are certain, the costs of liability rules — essentially the costs of collectively valuing the damages to all concerned plus the cost in coercion to those who would not sell at the collectively determined figure — are unnecessary. They are unnecessary because transaction costs and bargaining barriers become irrelevant when we are certain who is the cheapest cost avoider; economic efficiency will be attained without transactions by making the correct initial entitlement.

As a practical matter we often are uncertain who the cheapest cost avoider is. In such cases, traditional legal doctrine tends to find a nuisance but imposes only damages on Taney payable to the Marshalls.[60] This way, if the amount of damages Taney is made to pay is close to the injury caused, economic efficiency will have had its due; if he cannot make a go of it, the nuisance was not worth its costs. The entitlement to the Marshalls to be free from pollution unless compensated, however, will have been given *not* because it was thought that polluting was probably worth less to Taney than freedom from pollution was worth to the Marshalls, nor even because on some distributional basis we preferred to charge the cost to Taney rather than to the Marshalls. It was so placed *simply because we did not know* whether Taney desired to pollute more than the Marshalls desired to be free from pollution, and the only way we thought we could test out the value of the pollution was by the only liability rule we thought we had. This was rule two, the imposition of nuisance damages on Taney. At least this would be the position of a court concerned with economic efficiency which believed itself limited to rules one, two, and three.

Rule four gives at least the possibility that the opposite entitlement may also lead to economic efficiency in a situation of uncertainty. Suppose for the moment that a mechanism exists for collectively assessing the damage resulting to Taney from being stopped from polluting by the Marshalls, and a mechanism also exists for collectively assessing the benefit to each of the Marshalls from such cessation. Then — assuming the same degree of accuracy in collective valuation as exists in rule two (the nuisance damage rule) — the Marshalls would stop the pollution if it harmed them more than it benefited Taney. If this is possible, then even if we thought it necessary to use a liability rule, we would still be free to give the entitlement to Taney or Marshall for whatever reasons, efficiency or distributional, we desired.

Actually, the issue is still somewhat more complicated. For just as transaction costs are not necessarily symmetrical under the two converse property rule entitlements, so also the liability rule equivalents of transaction costs — the cost of valuing collectively and of coercing compliance with that valuation — may not be symmetrical under the two converse liability rules. Nuisance damages may be very hard to value, and the costs of informing all the injured of their rights and getting them into court may be prohibitive. Instead, the assessment of the objective damage to Taney from foregoing his pollution may be cheap and so might the as-

---

[60] *See, e.g.,* City of Harrisonville v. W.S. Dickey Clay Mfg. Co., 289 U.S. 334 (1933) (damages appropriate remedy where injunction would prejudice important public interest); Madison v. Ducktown Sulphur, Copper & Iron Co., 113 Tenn. 331, 83 S.W. 658 (1904) (damages appropriate because of plaintiff's ten year delay in seeking to enjoin fumes).

sessment of the relative benefits to all Marshalls of such freedom from pollution. But the opposite may also be the case. As a result, just as the choice of which property entitlement may be based on the asymmetry of transaction costs and hence on the greater amenability of one property entitlement to market corrections, so might the choice between liability entitlements be based on the asymmetry of the costs of collective determination.

The introduction of distributional considerations makes the existence of the fourth possibility even more significant. One does not need to go into all the permutations of the possible tradeoffs between efficiency and distributional goals under the four rules to show this. A simple example should suffice. Assume a factory which, by using cheap coal, pollutes a very wealthy section of town and employs many low income workers to produce a product purchased primarily by the poor; assume also a distributional goal that favors equality of wealth. Rule one — enjoin the nuisance — would possibly have desirable economic efficiency results (if the pollution hurt the homeowners more than it saved the factory in coal costs), but it would have disastrous distribution effects. It would also have undesirable efficiency effects if the initial judgment on costs of avoidance had been wrong and transaction costs were high. Rule two — nuisance damages — would allow a testing of the economic efficiency of eliminating the pollution, even in the presence of high transaction costs, but would quite possibly put the factory out of business or diminish output and thus have the same income distribution effects as rule one. Rule three — no nuisance — would have favorable distributional effects since it might protect the income of the workers. But if the pollution harm was greater to the homeowners than the cost of avoiding it by using a better coal, and if transaction costs — holdout problems — were such that homeowners could not unite to pay the factory to use better coal, rule three would have unsatisfactory efficiency effects. Rule four — payment of damages to the factory after allowing the homeowners to compel it to use better coal, and assessment of the cost of these damages to the homeowners — would be the only one which would accomplish both the distributional and efficiency goals.[61]

An equally good hypothetical for any of the rules can be constructed. Moreover, the problems of coercion may as a

---

[61] Either of the liability rules may also be used in another manner to achieve distributional goals. For example, if victims of pollution were poor, and if society desired a more equal distribution of wealth, it might intentionally increase "objective" damage awards if rule two were used; conversely, it might decrease the compensation to the factory owners, without any regard for economic efficiency if rule four were chosen. There are obvious disadvantages to this ad hoc method of achieving distributional goals. *See* p. 1110 *supra*.

practical matter be extremely severe under rule four. How do the homeowners decide to stop the factory's use of low grade coal? How do we assess the damages and their proportional allocation in terms of benefits to the homeowners? But equivalent problems may often be as great for rule two. How do we value the damages to each of the many homeowners? How do we inform the homeowners of their rights to damages? How do we evaluate and limit the administrative expenses of the court actions this solution implies?

The seriousness of the problem depends under each of the liability rules on the number of people whose "benefits" or "damages" one is assessing and the expense and likelihood of error in such assessment. A judgment on these questions is necessary to an evaluation of the possible economic efficiency benefits of employing one rule rather than another. The relative ease of making such assessments through different institutions may explain why we often employ the courts for rule two and get to rule four — when we do get there — only through political bodies which may, for example, prohibit pollution, or "take" the entitlement to build a supersonic plane by a kind of eminent domain, paying compensation to those injured by these decisions.[62] But

---

[62] Of course, variants of the other rules may be administered through political institutions as well. Rule three, granting a property entitlement to a polluter, may be effectuated by tax credits or other incentives such as subsidization of nonpolluting fuels offered for voluntary pollution abatement. In such schemes, as with rule four, political institutions are used to effect comprehensive benefit assessment and overcome freeloader problems which would be encountered in a more decentralized market solution. However, this centralization — to the extent that it replaces voluntary payments by individual pollution victims with collective payments not unanimously agreed upon — is a hybrid solution. The polluter must assent to the sale of his entitlement, but the amount of pollution abatement sought and the price paid by each pollution victim is not subjectively determined and voluntarily assented to by each.

The relationship of hybrids like the above to the four basic rules can be stated more generally. The buyer of an entitlement, whether the entitlement is protected by property or liability rules, may be viewed as owning what is in effect a property right not to buy the entitlement. But when freeloader problems abound, that property right may instead be given to a class of potential buyers. This "class" may be a municipality, a sewer authority, or any other body which can decide to buy an entitlement and compel those benefited to pay an objective price. When this is done, the individuals within the class have themselves only an entitlement not to purchase the seller's entitlement protected by a liability rule.

As we have already seen, the holder of an entitlement may be permitted to sell it at his own price or be compelled to sell it at an objective price: he may have an entitlement protected by a property or liability rule. Since, therefore, in any transaction the buyer may have a property or liability entitlement not to buy and the seller may have a property or a liability entitlement not to sell, there are, in effect, four combinations of rules for each possible original location of the enall this does not, in any sense, diminish the importance of the fact that an awareness of the possibility of an entitlement to pollute, but one protected only by a liability rule, may in some instances allow us best to combine our distributional and efficiency goals.

We have said that we would say little about justice, and so we shall. But it should be clear that if rule four might enable us best to combine efficiency goals with distributional goals, it might also enable us best to combine those same efficiency goals with other goals that are often described in justice language. For example, assume that the factory in our hypothetical was using cheap coal *before* any of the wealthy houses were built. In these circumstances, rule four will not only achieve the desirable efficiency and distributional results mentioned above, but it will also accord with any "justice" significance which is attached to being there first. And this is so whether we view this justice significance as part of a distributional goal, as part of a long run efficiency goal based on protecting expectancies, or as part of an independent concept of justice.

Thus far in this section we have ignored the possibility of employing rules of inalienability to solve pollution problems. A general policy of barring pollution does seem unrealistic.[63] But rules of inalienability can appropriately be used to limit the levels of pollution and to control the levels of activities which cause pollution.[64]

One argument for inalienability may be the widespread exist-

---

titlement: voluntary seller and voluntary buyer; voluntary seller and compelled buyer; compelled seller and voluntary buyer; compelled seller and compelled buyer. Moreover, since the entitlement to that which is being bought or sold could have been originally given to the opposite party, there are, in effect, eight possible rules rather than four.

We do not mean by the above to suggest that political institutions are used only to allocate collectively held property rights. Quite the contrary, rule two, for instance, gives pollution victims an entitlement protected by a liability rule to be free from pollution. This rule could be administered by decentralized damage assessment as in litigation, or it could be effected by techniques like effluent fees charged to polluters. The latter type of collective intervention may be preferred where large numbers are involved and the costs of decentralized injury valuation are high. Still, under either system the "sale price" is collectively determined, so the basic character of the victims' entitlement is not changed.

[63] *See* Michelman, *supra* note 1, at 667.

[64] This is the exact analogue of specific deterrence of accident causing activities. *See* COSTS at 95–129.

Although it may seem fanciful to us, there is of course the possibility that a state might wish to grant a converse entitlement — an inalienable entitlement to pollute in some instances. This might happen where the state believed that in the long run everyone would be better off by allowing the polluting producers to make their products, regardless of whether the polluter thought it advantageous to accept compensation for stopping his pollution.

ence of moralisms against pollution. Thus it may hurt the
Marshalls — gentleman farmers — to see Taney, a smoke-choked
city dweller, sell his entitlement to be free of pollution. A different
kind of externality or moralism may be even more important. The
Marshalls may be hurt by the expectation that, while the present
generation might withstand present pollution levels with no serious
health dangers, future generations may well face a despoiled,
hazardous environmental condition which they are powerless to
reverse.[65] And this ground for inalienability might be strength-
ened if a similar conclusion were reached on grounds of self paternalism. Finally, society might restrict alienability on paternalistic
grounds. The Marshalls might feel that although Taney himself
does not know it, Taney will be better off if he really can see the
stars at night, or if he can breathe smogless air.

Whatever the grounds for inalienability, we should reemphasize that distributional effects should be carefully evaluated in
making the choice for or against inalienability. Thus the citizens
of a town may be granted an entitlement to be free of water pollution caused by the waste discharges of a chemical factory; and
the entitlement might be made inalienable on the grounds that
the town's citizens really would be better off in the long run to
have access to clean beaches. But the entitlement might also be
made inalienable to assure the maintenance of a beautiful resort
area for the very wealthy, at the same time putting the town's
citizens out of work.[66]

V. THE FRAMEWORK AND CRIMINAL SANCTIONS

Obviously we cannot canvass the relevance of our approach
through many areas of the law. But we do think it beneficial to
examine one further area, that of crimes against property and
bodily integrity. The application of the framework to the use of
criminal sanctions in cases of theft or violations of bodily integrity
is useful in that it may aid in understanding the previous material,
especially as it helps us to distinguish different kinds of legal
problems and to identify the different modes of resolving those
problems.

Beginning students, when first acquainted with economic
efficiency notions, sometimes ask why ought not a robber be simply
charged with the value of the thing robbed. And the same question

---

[65] See Michelman, *supra* note 1, at 684.

[66] *Cf.* Frady, *The View from Hilton Head*, HARPER'S, May, 1970, at 103–112
(conflict over proposed establishment of chemical factory that would pollute the
area's beaches in economically depressed South Carolina community; environmental
groups that opposed factory backed by developers of wealthy resorts in the area,
proponents of factory supported by representatives of unemployed town citizens).

is sometimes posed by legal philosophers.[67] If it is worth more to the robber than to the owner, is not economic efficiency served by such a penalty? Our answers to such a question tend to move quickly into very high sounding and undoubtedly relevant moral considerations. But these considerations are often not very helpful to the questioner because they depend on the existence of obligations on individuals not to rob for a fixed price and the original question was why we should impose such obligations at all.

One simple answer to the question would be that thieves do not get caught every time they rob and therefore the costs to the thief must at least take the unlikelihood of capture into account.[68] But that would not fully answer the problem, for even if thieves were caught every time, the penalty we would wish to impose would be greater than the objective damages to the person robbed.

A possible broader explanation lies in a consideration of the difference between property entitlements and liability entitlements. For us to charge the thief with a penalty equal to an objectively determined value of the property stolen would be to convert all property rule entitlements into liability rule entitlements.

The question remains, however, why *not* convert all property rules into liability rules? The answer is, of course, obvious. Liability rules represent only an approximation of the value of the object to its original owner and willingness to pay such an approximate value is no indication that it is worth more to the thief than to the owner. In other words, quite apart from the expense of arriving collectively at such an objective valuation, it is no guarantee of the economic efficiency of the transfer.[69] If this is so with property, it is all the more so with bodily integrity, and we would not presume collectively and objectively to value the cost of a rape to the victim against the benefit to the rapist even if economic efficiency is our sole motive. Indeed when we approach bodily integrity we are getting close to areas where we do not let the entitlement be sold at all and where economic efficiency enters

---

[67] One of the last articles by Professor Giorgio Del Vecchio came close to asking this question. *See* Del Vecchio, *Equality and Inequality in Relation to Justice*, 11 Nat. Law Forum 36, 43–45 (1966).

[68] *See, e.g.*, Becker, *Crime and Punishment: An Economic Approach*, 76 J. Pol. Econ. 169 (1968).

[69] One might also point out that very often a thief will not have the money to meet the objectively determined price of the stolen object; indeed, his lack of resources is probably his main motivation for the theft. In such cases society, if it insists on a liability rule, will have to compensate the initial entitlement holder from the general societal coffers. When this happens the thief will not feel the impact of the liability rule and hence will not be sufficiently deterred from engaging in similar activity in the future. *Cf.* Costs at 147–48.

in, if at all, in a more complex way. But even where the items taken or destroyed are things we do allow to be sold, we will not without special reasons impose an objective selling price on the vendor.

Once we reach the conclusion that we will not simply have liability rules, but that often, even just on economic efficiency grounds, property rules are desirable, an answer to the beginning student's question becomes clear. The thief not only harms the victim, he undermines rules and distinctions of significance beyond the specific case. Thus even if in a given case we can be sure that the value of the item stolen was no more than X dollars, and even if the thief has been caught and is prepared to compensate, we would not be content simply to charge the thief X dollars. Since in the majority of cases we cannot be sure of the economic efficiency of the transfer by theft, we must add to each case an undefinable kicker which represents society's need to keep all property rules from being changed at will into liability rules.[70] In other words, we impose criminal sanctions as a means of deterring future attempts to convert property rules into liability rules.[71]

The first year student might push on, however, and ask why we treat the thief or the rapist differently from the injurer in an auto

---

[70] If we were not interested in the integrity of property rules and hence we were not using an indefinable kicker, we would still presumably try to adjust the amount of damages charged to the thief in order to reflect the fact that only a percentage of thieves are caught; that is, we would fix a price-penalty which reflected the value of the good and the risk of capture.

[71] A problem related to criminal sanctions is that of punitive damages in intentional torts. If Taney sets a spring gun with the purpose of killing or maiming anyone who trespasses on his property, Taney has knowledge of what he is doing and of the risks involved which is more akin to the criminal than the negligent driver. But because Taney does not know precisely which one of many Marshalls will be the victim of his actions, ex ante negotiations seem difficult. How then do we justify the use of criminal sanctions and of more than compensatory damages? Probably the answer lies in the fact that we assume that the benefits of Taney's act are not worth the harm they entail if that harm were fully valued. Believing that this fact, in contrast with what is involved in a simple negligence case, should be, and in a sense can be, made known to the actor at the time he acts, we pile on extra damages. Our judgment is that most would act differently if a true cost-benefit burden could be placed. Given that judgment and given the impossibility of imposing a true cost-benefit burden by collective valuations — because of inadequate knowledge — we make sure that if we err we will err on the side of overestimating the cost.

There may be an additional dimension. Unlike fines or other criminal sanctions, punitive damages provide an extra compensation for the victim. This may not be pure windfall. Once the judgment is made that injuries classified as intentional torts are less desirable than nonintentional harms — either because they are expected to be less efficient or because there is less justification for the tortfeasor's not having purchased the entitlement in an ex ante bargain — then it may be that the actual, subjective injury to the victim from the tort is enhanced. One

accident or the polluter in a nuisance case. Why do we allow liability rules there? In a sense, we have already answered the question. The only level at which, before the accident, the driver can negotiate for the value of what he might take from his potential victim is one at which transactions are too costly. The thief or rapist, on the other hand, could have negotiated without undue expense (at least if the good was one which we allowed to be sold at all) because we assume he knew what he was going to do and to whom he would do it. The case of the accident is different because knowledge exists only at the level of deciding to drive or perhaps to drive fast, and at that level negotiations with potential victims are usually not feasible.

The case of nuisance seems different, however. There the polluter knows what he will do and, often, whom it will hurt. But as we have already pointed out, freeloader or holdout problems may often preclude any successful negotiations between the polluter and the victims of pollution; additionally, we are often uncertain who is the cheapest avoider of pollution costs. In these circumstances a liability rule, which at least allowed the economic efficiency of a proposed transfer of entitlements to be tested, seemed appropriate, even though it permitted the non-accidental and unconsented taking of an entitlement. It should be emphasized, however, that where transaction costs do not bar negotiations between polluter and victim, or where we are sufficiently certain who the cheapest cost avoider is, there are no efficiency reasons for allowing intentional takings, and property rules, supported by injunctions or criminal sanctions, are appropriate.[72]

VI. Conclusion

This article has attempted to demonstrate how a wide variety of legal problems can usefully be approached in terms of a specific framework. Framework or model building has two shortcomings.

---

whose automobile is destroyed accidentally suffers from the loss of his car; one whose automobile is destroyed intentionally suffers from the loss of the car, and his injury is made greater by the knowledge that the loss was intentional, wilful, or otherwise avoidable.

[72] *Cf.* pp 1111–13.

We have not discussed distributional goals as they relate to criminal sanctions. In part this is because we have assumed the location of the initial entitlement — we have assumed the victim of a crime was entitled to the good stolen or to his bodily integrity. There is, however, another aspect of distributional goals which relates to the particular rule we choose to protect the initial entitlement. For example, one might raise the question of linking the severity of criminal sanctions to the wealth of the criminal or the victim. While this aspect of distributional goals would certainly be a fruitful area of discussion, it is beyond the scope of the present article.

The first is that models can be mistaken for the total view of phenomena, like legal relationships, which are too complex to be painted in any one picture. The second is that models generate boxes into which one then feels compelled to force situations which do not truly fit. There are, however, compensating advantages. Legal scholars, precisely because they have tended to eschew model building, have often proceeded in an ad hoc way, looking at cases and seeing what categories emerged. But this approach also affords only one view of the Cathedral. It may neglect some relationships among the problems involved in the cases which model building can perceive, precisely because it does generate boxes, or categories. The framework we have employed may be applied in many different areas of the law. We think its application facilitated perceiving and defining an additional resolution of the problem of pollution. As such we believe the painting to be well worth the oils.

THE ETHICAL AND POLITICAL BASIS OF THE EFFICIENCY NORM IN COMMON LAW ADJUDICATION

Richard A. Posner*

In a recent article I argued that a society which aims at maximizing wealth, unlike a society which aims at maximizing utility (happiness), will produce an ethically attractive combination of happiness, of rights (to liberty and property), and of sharing with the less fortunate members of society.[1] Evidently, I did not explain adequately why this combination was ethically attractive.[2] The present Article began as an attempt to extend the argument of the last one by considering this question in greater depth. But as the paper took shape, it became both narrower and broader than the original conception. It narrowed as my interest shifted to showing that wealth maximization was an ethically attractive objective to guide common law adjudication, rather than social choice generally.[3] It broadened as I began to see that the same considerations which made wealth maximization an ethically attractive norm in common law adjudication might help to explain why it has played an important role in shaping the substantive rules and procedures of the common law.[4]

---

* Lee and Brena Freeman Professor of Law, University of Chicago. I want to thank Lea Brilmayer, Dennis Carlton, John Keenan, William Landes, Mitchell Polinsky, Steven Shavell, George Stigler, and participants in the Faculty Colloquium on Law, Economics, and Society at New York University for helpful comments and suggestions. This Article appears, in revised form, as chapter 4 of my book *The Economics of Justice*, forthcoming from Harvard University Press. Anyone interested in my views on wealth maximization should read chapters 3 and 4 of that book.

1. Posner, *Utilitarianism, Economics, and Legal Theory*, 8 J. LEGAL STUD. 103 (1979).

2. *See* Dworkin, *Is Wealth a Value?*, 9 J. LEGAL STUD. 191 (1980); Kronman, *Wealth Maximization as a Normative Principle*, 9 J. LEGAL STUD. 227 (1980). I reply to these critics in Posner, *The Value of Wealth: A Reply to Dworkin and Kronman*, 9 J. LEGAL STUD. 243 (1980).

3. I consider it an attractive objective to guide social choice generally, but do not pursue the argument for that position in this Article.

4. For a recent statement of the "efficiency theory" of the common law, see Posner, *Some Uses and Abuses of Economics in Law*, 46 U. CHI. L. REV. 281, 288-95 (1979).

The main ethical argument of this Article, developed in the first section, is that wealth maximization, especially in the common law setting, derives support from the principle of consent that can also be regarded as underlying the otherwise quite different approach of Pareto ethics. The second section shifts the focus from normative to positive. I argue that the political counterpart of consent—consensus—explains the role of wealth maximization in shaping the common law. The principle of consent supports the wealth-maximization norm in the common law setting precisely because common law judges deal with problems, and by methods, in which redistributive considerations are not salient. This means that consent to efficient solutions can be presumed; but it also means that politically influential groups can do no better, in general, than to support efficient policies. Such policies maximize aggregate wealth in a setting where, by hypothesis, altering the shares (redistribution) is not a feasible means by which a group can increase its wealth. I also briefly discuss whether the common law is utilitarian or wealth maximizing.

THE CONSENSUAL BASIS OF EFFICIENCY

From Pareto to Kaldor-Hicks

Pareto superiority is the principle that one allocation of resources is superior to another if at least one person is better off under the first allocation than under the second and no one is worse off.[5] Pareto invented the principle as an answer to the traditional problem of practical utilitarianism, that of measuring happiness across persons for purposes of determining the effect of a policy on total utility.[6] The change to a Pareto-superior allocation must yield a net increase in utility, since no one is made worse off and at least one person is made better off by the change, even though the *amount* by which total utility has been increased may not be measurable.

But, as is well known,[7] the solution is apparent rather than real. Because of the impossibility of measuring utility directly, the

---

5. For a lucid discussion of Pareto ethics by a philosopher, see Coleman, *Efficiency, Exchange, and Auction: Philosophic Aspects of the Economic Approach to Law*, 68 CAL. L. REV. 221 (1980). And for a good recent textbook treatment by an economist, see C. PRICE, WELFARE ECONOMICS IN THEORY AND PRACTICE (1977).

6. *See* V. TARASCIO, PARETO'S METHODOLOGICAL APPROACH TO ECONOMICS 79-84 (1968).

7. *See, e.g.*, G. CALABRESI & P. BOBBITT, TRAGIC CHOICES 83-85 (1978).

only way to demonstrate that a change in the allocation of resources is Pareto superior is to show that everyone affected by the change consented to it. If A sells a tomato to B for \$2 and no one else is affected by the transaction, we can be sure that the utility to A of \$2 is greater than the utility of the tomato to A, and vice versa for B, even though we do not know how much A's and B's utility has been increased by the transaction. But because the crucial assumption in this example, the absence of third-party effects, is not satisfied with regard to *classes* of transactions, the Pareto-superiority criterion is useless for most policy questions. For example, if the question is not whether, given a free market in tomatoes, A's sale to B is a Pareto-superior change, but whether a free market in tomatoes is Pareto superior to a market in which there is a ceiling on the price of tomatoes, the concept of Pareto superiority is unhelpful. The price ceiling will result in a lower market price, a lower quantity produced, lower rents to land specialized to the growing of tomatoes, and other differences from the results of a free market in tomatoes. It would be impossible to identify, let alone negotiate for the consent of, everyone affected by a move from a price-regulated to a free tomato-market, so the criterion of Pareto superiority cannot be satisfied. Stating this conclusion differently, one cannot say that the movement to a free market would increase total utility or, conversely, that if we had a free market in tomatoes, imposing a price ceiling would reduce total utility.[8]

I have been speaking thus far of Pareto ethics and specifically of the concept of Pareto superiority as an answer, though not a practical one, to the utilitarian's problem of the interpersonal comparison of utilities. But it is also possible to locate Pareto ethics in a different philosophical tradition from the utilitarian, in the tradition, broadly Kantian, which attaches a value over and above the

---

8. The revealed-preference approach, *see generally* P. SAMUELSON, FOUNDA-TIONS OF ECONOMIC ANALYSIS 146-56 (1947), offers a method, unfortunately not very practical either, of determining whether a change is Pareto superior that does not require express consent. Imagine that C is a third party affected by the transaction between A and B in the example in the text. Before the transaction, C's income is X and he uses it to purchase commodities $a \ldots n$. The transaction may affect C's income, as well as the prices of $a \ldots n$. If, however, after the transaction C's income, now Y, is large enough to enable him to purchase $a \ldots n$ at their current prices, then we may say (without having to consult C) that the transaction between A and B did not make him worse off. But the information necessary to apply this approach is rarely available, in part because some of the commodities that C buys may not be priced in any market (love, respect, etc.) and his ability to obtain them may be adversely affected by the transaction between A and B.

utilitarian to individual autonomy. One ethical criterion of change that is highly congenial to the Kantian emphasis on autonomy is consent. And consent is the operational basis of the concept of Pareto superiority. It is not the theoretical basis, at least if Pareto superiority is viewed as a tool of utilitarian ethics, because if the utilitarian could devise a practical utility-metric he could dispense with the consensual or transactional method of determining whether an allocation of resources was Pareto superior; indeed, he could dispense with the concept of Pareto superiority itself.

Suppose we consider consent an ethically attractive basis for permitting changes in the allocation of resources, on Kantian grounds unrelated to the fact that a consensual transaction is likely to increase the happiness at least of the immediate parties to it. We are then led, in the manner of Nozick and Epstein,[9] to an ethical defense of market transactions that is unrelated to their effect in promoting efficiency either in the Pareto sense or in the sense of wealth maximization.

In the setting of a market free from third-party effects, it is clear that forbidding transactions would reduce both the wealth of society and personal autonomy, so that the goals of maximizing wealth and of protecting autonomy coincide. But the setting is a special one. For example, suppose that a company decides to close a factory in town A and open a new one in B, and that in neither location are there significant pollution, congestion, or other technological externalities from the plant. The move may still lower property values in A and raise them in B, making landowners in A worse off and those in B better off. The parties to the move will not take account of these effects and their failure to do so makes it impossible for the plant's move to satisfy the criterion of a Pareto-superior move.[10]

That the third-party effects are merely "pecuniary" externalities, meaning that they result simply from a change in demand rather than from the consumption of some scarce resource (e.g., clean air, in the case of pollution, which is a technological externality), or, stated otherwise, that they have no net effect on the wealth of the society, is irrelevant from the standpoint of Pareto superiority. Not only is it impossible to say that no one will be

---

9. See R. NOZICK, ANARCHY, STATE, AND UTOPIA (1974); Epstein, *Causation and Corrective Justice: A Reply to Two Critics*, 8 J. LEGAL STUD. 477, 487-88 (1979).
10. I ignore for the moment the possibility of ex ante compensation of the affected landowners. *See* p. 492 *infra*.

made worse off by the plant move, but it is in fact certain that some people will be made worse off—the landowners in A and others, such as workers in A who have skills specialized to the plant that is being closed and positive costs of relocating in B. By the same token—and here the relationship of the Pareto-superiority criterion to utilitarian thought is clear—one cannot be sure that the move will increase total utility.[11] The disutility to the losers from the move may exceed the utility to the winners, even though, by the assumption that only pecuniary externalities are involved, the total wealth of the people affected by, but not party to, the transaction is unchanged, so that the transaction is wealth maximizing.

In a case such as the one I have put, the wealth-maximization criterion elaborated in my previous Article indicates that the transaction should be allowed. So, equivalently, as Jules Coleman has pointed out, does the Kaldor-Hicks criterion (sometimes called "Potential Pareto Superiority"), which requires, not that no one be made worse off by the move, but only that the increase in value be sufficiently large that the losers could be fully compensated.[12] Since the decrease in land values in A is matched by the increase in B, in principle (i.e., ignoring transfer costs) the landowners in A could be compensated and then no one would be worse off. But neither the Pareto criterion itself nor the utilitarian imperative underlying the Pareto criterion—to maximize utility—would be satisfied, because there is no way of knowing whether the utility to the winners of not having to pay compensation will exceed the disutility to the losers of not receiving compensation. Suppose the landowners in A incurred a loss of 100 utiles (an arbitrary measure of utility) because of the $1 million decrease in property values in A resulting from the move of the plant, while the landowners in B obtained only 80 utiles from the $1 million increase in their property values. The Kaldor-Hicks criterion would be satisfied but the Pareto-superiority criterion would not be.

Wealth Maximization and the Principle of Consent

I want to defend the Kaldor-Hicks or wealth-maximization approach, not by reference to Pareto superiority as such or its utili-

---

11. The externalities could be internalized by the cities' offering tax inducements to the plant's owner. But that would not make the plant's moving (or remaining) Pareto superior, since those people who paid the higher taxes necessary to finance these inducements would be worse off.

12. See Coleman, *supra* note 5, at 239-42.

tarian premise, but by reference to the idea of consent that I have said provides an alternative basis to utilitarianism for the Pareto criterion. The notion of consent used here is what economists call ex ante compensation.[13] I contend, I hope uncontroversially, that if you buy a lottery ticket and lose the lottery, then, so long as there is no question of fraud or duress, you have consented to the loss. Many of the involuntary, uncompensated losses experienced in the market, or tolerated by the institutions that take the place of the market where the market cannot be made to work effectively, are fully compensated ex ante and hence are consented to. Suppose some entrepreneur loses money because a competitor develops a superior product. Since the return to entrepreneurial activity will include a premium to cover the risk of losses due to competition, the entrepreneur is compensated for those losses ex ante. Similarly, the landowners in A, in my previous example, were compensated when they bought the land. The probability that the plant would move was discounted in the purchase price that they paid.[14]

The concept of ex ante compensation provides an answer to the argument that the wealth-maximization criterion, applied unflinchingly in market settings such as my plant-relocation example, would violate the principle of consent. A more difficult question is raised, however, by the similar attempt to ground nonmarket, but arguably wealth-maximizing institutions, such as the embattled negligence system of automobile accident liability, in the principle of consent. In what sense may the driver injured by another driver in an accident in which neither was at fault be said to have consented to the injury, so as not to be entitled, under a negligence system, to compensation?

To answer this question, we must consider the effect on the

---

13. The argument that follows is sketched in Posner, *Epstein's Tort Theory: A Critique*, 8 J. LEGAL STUD. 457, 460, 464 (1979). A similar argument is made independently in Michelman, *Constitutions, Statutes, and the Theory of Efficient Adjudication*, 9 J. LEGAL STUD. 431, 438-40 (1980). Both arguments resemble a position taken by many welfare economists: that the Kaldor-Hicks criterion for deciding whether to undertake a public project satisfies the Pareto-superiority criterion provided that there is a sufficient probability that an individual will benefit in the long run from such projects, though he may be a loser from a particular one. *See* Polinsky, *Probabilistic Compensation Criteria*, 86 Q.J. ECON. 407 (1972), and references cited therein.

14. A parallel, but because of possible information costs more difficult, case is that of the worker who loses his job and incurs positive relocation costs when the demand for his services collapses as a result of the development of a superior substitute product.

costs of driving of insisting on ex post compensation, as under a system of strict liability. By hypothesis they would be higher; otherwise the negligence system would not be the wealth-maximizing system and no issue of justifying wealth maximization by reference to the principle of consent would arise. Would drivers be willing to incur higher costs of driving in order to preserve the principle of ex post compensation? They would not. Any driver who wanted to be assured of compensation in the event of an accident regardless of whether he was at fault need only buy first-party, or accident, insurance, by hypothesis at lower cost than he could obtain compensation ex post through a system of strict liability.

This can be most easily visualized by imagining that everyone involved in a traffic accident is identical—everyone is the same age, drives the same amount, and so on. In these circumstances everyone will pay the same rate for both liability insurance and accident insurance. The difference between negligence and strict liability will be that under negligence, liability-insurance rates will be lower and accident insurance rates higher, because fewer accidents will give rise to liability, while under strict liability the reverse will be true. But if, as I am assuming, negligence is the more efficient system, the *sum* of the liability and accident insurance premiums will be lower under negligence,[15] and everyone will prefer this.

All this assumes, of course, that people are identical; the implications of relaxing that assumption will be considered later. It also depends on my initial assumption that negligence is a cheaper system of automobile accident liability than strict liability would be. But that assumption is immaterial to my basic point, which is that an institution predicated on wealth maximization may be justifiable by reference to the consent of those affected by it even though the institution authorizes certain takings, such as the taking of life, health, or property of an individual injured in an accident in which neither party is negligent, without requiring compensation ex post.

I have used the example of negligence versus strict liability because it has been used to argue that the wealth-maximization approach is inconsistent with an approach consistent with notions of

---

15. This assumes that all accident costs are reflected in insurance rates. Most accident-prevention costs (*e.g.*, the value of time lost in driving more slowly) are not. Presumably these costs would also be higher under strict liability if that is indeed the less efficient liability rule.

personal autonomy or, in the terminology of this Article, consent.[16] Other examples could be offered, but it is not the purpose of this Article to deduce the institutional structure implied by wealth maximization; it is to show that social institutions that maximize wealth without requiring ex post compensation need not on that account be viewed as inconsistent with an ethical system premised on the principle of consent.

Some may object to the above analysis on the ground that the consent on the basis of which I am prepared, in principle at least, to justify institutions such as the negligence system is fictitious because no one has given his *express* consent. It would indeed be naïve to regard the political survival of negligence in the automobile accident arena as evidence of such consent; the radical imperfections of the political system in registering preferences are the subject of a vast literature in social choice and in the economic theory of legislation.[17] Nevertheless, the objection founders, in my opinion, precisely on the unavailability of a practical method of eliciting express consent, not so much to individual market transactions—though even there the consent of third parties affected by those transactions often cannot feasibly be elicited[18]—as to *institutions*, such as the negligence system or indeed the market itself. If there is no reliable mechanism for eliciting express consent, it follows, not that we must abandon the principle of consent, but rather that we should look for implied consent, as by trying to answer the hypothetical question whether, if transaction costs were zero, the affected parties would have agreed to the institution. This procedure[19] resembles a judge's imputing the intent of parties to a contract that fails to provide expressly for some contingency. Although the task of imputation is easier in the contract case, that case is still significant in showing that implicit consent is a meaningful form of consent. The absence of an underlying contract is relevant to the confidence with which an inference of implicit consent can be drawn rather than to the propriety of drawing such inferences.

---

16. See Epstein, *A Theory of Strict Liability*, 2 J. LEGAL STUD. 151 (1973).

17. For further discussion of the economic theory of legislation, see pp. 502-06 *infra*.

18. See p. 489 *supra*.

19. One, incidentally, that many economists use to make judgments of Pareto efficiency. For a recent example see S. Shavell, Accidents, Liability, and Insurance 5-7 (June 1979) (Harv. Inst. Econ. Research, Discussion Paper No. 685).

To be sure, "[a] proposal is not legislation simply because all the members of the legislature are in favor of it."[20] But this is because there is a mechanism by which legislators can express actual consent to a proposal. Sometimes the mechanism is inoperative, as when a question arises as to the scope or meaning of a past legislative enactment, and then we allow the courts to infer the legislative intent. This is an example of implicit but meaningful consent.

Another objection to using consent to justify institutions which maximize wealth is that the consent will rarely be unanimous. Contrary to my earlier assumption, people are not identical ex ante. Even if the costs of driving would be higher under a system of strict liability than under a negligence system, why should nondrivers prefer the negligence system? To the extent that groups of this sort could actually be identified, one might grant them the protection of a strict liability system if one placed a high value on autonomy.[21] But this may not be required by the principle of consent. Most people who do not drive do not stay at home either; they use other modes of transportation—taxis, buses, or subways, to name a few—whose costs would by assumption be higher under a system of strict liability. Those costs, or a large fraction of them at least, would be borne by the users. Even the nondrivers might therefore consent to a negligence system of liability for transport accidents if it were cheaper than a system of strict liability.[22] No institution, of course, will command the implicit consent of everyone. But only a fanatic would insist that absolute unanimity is required to legitimize a social institution such as the negligence system.

To summarize, the wealth-maximization or Kaldor-Hicks criterion can sometimes be applied without violating the principle of consent. While Kaldor-Hicks is not a Pareto criterion as such, it will sometimes function as a tolerable and, more to the point, administrable approximation of the Pareto-superiority criterion. To attempt to defend wealth maximization on Pareto grounds, however, is to raise the following question: why should not the principle that guides society be the protection and enhancement of personal autonomy, the value that underlies the principle of consent, rather

20. Epstein, *supra* note 9, at 496.

21. As suggested in Fletcher, *Fairness and Utility in Tort Theory*, 85 HARV. L. REV. 537, 543-51 (1972). *But see* p. 496 *infra*.

22. This leaves open the possibility of further subdividing the transport industry for liability purposes, and of having one rule for buses, another for autos, etc.

than the maximization of wealth? One objection to using autonomy directly as an ethical norm, an objection well illustrated by the choice between strict liability and negligence, is that it requires an arbitrary initial assignment of rights. I assumed that the victim of an accident had some kind of moral claim to compensation, ex post or ex ante, even though the injurer was not at fault. One could equally well assume that people have a right not to be hampered in their activities by being held liable for accidents that they could not have prevented at reasonable cost. No liability denies the autonomy of the victim, and strict liability the autonomy of the injurer. To differentiate the two *when neither is at fault* is no simple task.[23]

Another objection to building an ethical system directly on the idea of autonomy is that, just as literal adherence to the Pareto-superiority criterion could be paralyzing, so the ethics of personal autonomy, interpreted and applied without regard for the consequences for human welfare, would lead to a great deal of misery. This is conceded by the adherents to the ethics of personal autonomy in modern jurisprudential thought, such as Charles Fried and Richard Epstein.[24] Wealth maximization as an ethical norm has the property of giving weight both to preferences, though less heavily than utilitarianism does, and to consent, though less heavily than Kant himself would have done. Also, as explained in my previous article, it gives weight to the human impulse, apparently genetically based, to share wealth with people who are less effective in producing it.[25]

---

23. For the divergent view of Kantian philosophers on this question, see Posner, *supra* note 1, at 115 n.43.

24. *See* C. FRIED, RIGHT AND WRONG 9-10 (1978); Epstein, *Nuisance Law: Corrective Justice and Its Utilitarian Constraints*, 8 J. LEGAL STUD. 49, 74-75, 79 (1979).

25. *See* Posner, *supra* note 1, at 123, 129 n.80, arguing that the producer puts more into society than he takes out, because he cannot (barring perfect price discrimination) appropriate the entire consumer surplus generated by his production. It is true that the marginal producer creates no consumer surplus—he takes out exactly what he puts in—and so if each producer is the marginal producer none would reduce the wealth of other people by withdrawing from the market. However, not every producer is marginal; we may be reasonably confident that the American people would have been poorer if Henry Ford had decided to become a Trappist monk rather than an automobile manufacturer. More important, even in an industry where each producer is marginal and his withdrawal from the industry would not reduce consumer surplus, the withdrawal of a group of producers would. Each producer's contribution to consumer surplus is negligible but the sum of their contributions is not.

These characteristics of wealth maximization are not, as Professor Dworkin has suggested, accidental.[26] The perfectly free market, in which there are no third-party effects, is paradigmatic of how utility is promoted noncoercively, through the voluntary transactions of autonomous, utility-seeking individuals. The system of wealth maximization consists of institutions that facilitate, or where that is infeasible approximate, the operations of a free market and thus maximize autonomous, utility-seeking behavior. Because utility seeking in a market requires inducing others to enter into transactions advantageous to them, wealth is automatically transferred to those who have productive assets, whether goods or time. By the same token, those who have no productive assets have no ethical claim on the assets of others. This is not necessarily a result that maximizes utility; it is of course uncongenial to those who believe that the individual is separable from his endowments of skill, energy, and character. It is consistent, however, with a desire, rooted in the principles of autonomy and consent, to minimize coercion.

The system of wealth maximization outlined in this and my previous Article could be viewed as one of constrained utilitarianism. The constraint, which is not ad hoc but is supplied by the principle of consent, is that people may seek to promote their utility only through the market or institutions modeled on the market. As I have been at pains to stress, transactions that are consensual between the immediate parties may be coercive as to third parties. But as the negligence example showed, the amount of coercion in a system of wealth maximization is easily exaggerated; where it is wealth maximizing to deny compensation ex post, ex ante the potentially affected parties may prefer that such compensation be denied.

Comparison to Rawls' Approach

My discussion of the choice that the individual is assumed to make between negligence and strict liability systems before an accident occurs—a choice under uncertainty from which consent to a social institution is then inferred—may seem derivative of Rawls' analysis of justice.[27] In fact, both Rawls' analysis and the analysis in this Article have common roots. The "original position" approach was apparently first used by economists seeking to establish the

---

26. *See* Dworkin, *supra* note 2.
27. *See* J. RAWLS, A THEORY OF JUSTICE 17-22 (1971).

consensual foundations of utility maximization in a somewhat similar fashion to what I have done here.[28] As Kenneth Arrow has explained, they

> start[ed] from the position . . . that choice under risky conditions can be described as the maximization of expected utility. In the original position, each individual may with equal probability be any member of the society. If there are n members of the society and if the ith member will have utility u_i under some given allocation decision, then the value of that allocation to any individual is Σu_i $(1/n)$, since $1/n$ is the probability of being individual i. Thus, in choosing among alternative allocations of goods, each individual in the original position will want to maximize this expectation, or, what is the same thing for a given population, maximize the sum of utilities.[29]

The twist that Rawls gave to choice in the original position was to argue that people would choose to maximize, not expected utility, but the utility of the worst outcomes in the distribution.[30] Again in the words of Arrow:

> It has, however, long been remarked that the maximin theory has some implications that seem hardly acceptable. It implies that any benefit, no matter how small, to the worst-off member of society, will outweigh any loss to a better-off individual, provided it does not reduce the second below the level of the first. Thus, there can easily exist medical procedures which serve to keep people barely alive but with little satisfaction and which are yet so expensive as to reduce the rest of the population to poverty. A maximin principle would apparently imply that such procedures be adopted.[31]

If, with Arrow, one finds expected utility a more plausible maximand than maximin is, one will be driven to the startling conclusion that utilitarianism has a firmer basis in the principle of consent than Rawls' "justice as fairness." But any theory of consent that is based on choice in the original position is unsatisfactory, not only because of the well-known difficulties of describing the preference functions of people in that position, but also because the original-position approach opens the door to the claims of the unpro-

---

28. *See* Arrow, *Some Ordinalist-Utilitarian Notes on Rawls's Theory of Justice,* 70 J. PHILOSOPHY 245, 250 (1973).
29. *Id.*
30. J. RAWLS, *supra* note 27, at 150-61.
31. Arrow, *supra* note 28, at 251.

ductive. In the original position, no one knows whether he has productive capabilities, so choices made in that position will presumably reflect some probability that the individual making the choice will turn out not to be endowed with any such capabilities. In effect, the choices of the unproductive are weighted equally with those of the productive. This result obscures the important moral distinction, between capacity to enjoy and capacity to produce for others, that distinguishes utility from wealth.[32] I prefer therefore to imagine actual people, deploying actual endowments of skill and energy and character, making choices under uncertainty. I prefer, that is, to imagine choice under conditions of natural ignorance to choice under the artificial ignorance of the original position.

Limitations of Wealth Maximization as an Ethical Norm Founded on Consent

The domain within which the principle of consent can supply an ethical justification for social institutions that maximize wealth is limited in at least two principal respects.

1. Where the distributive impact of a wealth-maximizing policy is substantial and nonrandom, broad consent will be difficult to elicit or impute without actual compensation. I mentioned this possibility in connection with the choice between negligence and strict liability to govern traffic accidents but it seemed unimportant there. Suppose, however, the issue was whether to substitute a proportionate income tax for the current progressive one. The substitution would increase the wealth of society if the increase in output (counting both work and leisure as output) by upper bracket taxpayers, whose marginal-tax rate would be lowered by the substitution, exceeded the reduction in output caused by raising the marginal tax rate of lower bracket taxpayers. However, unless the net increase in output was sufficiently great to result in an increase in the after-tax incomes even of those taxpayers who would be paying

---

32. My concept of wealth includes, as noted in the previous article, Posner, *supra* note 1, at 105 n. 11, the dollar value (or cost) that people who are not risk-neutral attach to uncertain outcomes. Thus, my concept is similar to what most economists mean when they say expected utility. I avoid the latter word, however, because utilitarian philosophers (and perhaps implicitly therefore those economists who think of themselves as applied utilitarians) do not differentiate between preferences backed by willingness to pay and preferences backed simply by desire. In my analysis, only the former preferences enter into a determination as to which choices are wealth maximizing.

higher taxes under a proportionate than under a progressive income tax—and let us assume it was not—the lower bracket taxpayers could hardly be assumed to consent to the tax change, even though it would be wealth maximizing.

I was first stimulated to investigate the ethical foundations of wealth maximization by the suggestion that it was too unappealing a value to ascribe to common law judges.[33] Yet it is precisely in the context of common law adjudication, as contrasted with the redistributive statutory domain illustrated by my tax example, that a consensual basis for wealth maximization is most plausible. The rules that govern the acquisition and transfer of property rights, the making and enforcement of contracts, and liability for accidents and the kinds of naked aggression that were made crimes at common law are supported by a broad consensus and distribute their benefits very widely. For example, only a naïve analysis of the economic consequences of refusing to enforce the leases that poor people sign with presumably wealthier landlords would conclude that the poor would be better off under such a regime. Landlords would either charge higher rentals because of the greater risk of loss or shift their property into alternative uses, so that the low-income housing supply would be smaller and its price higher.[34] If we can generalize from this example that the choice between common law rules usually does not have systematic distributive consequences, then it is reasonable to suppose that there is—or would be, if it paid people to inform themselves in these matters—general consent to those common law rules that maximize wealth. If so, a common law judge guided by the wealth-maximization criterion will at the same time be promoting personal autonomy.

2. Another area in which the principle of consent and the principle of wealth maximization are potentially in conflict, aside from redistributive policies such as those embodied in the progressive income tax, is in the initial assignment of property rights, the starting point for a market system.

What if A's labor is worth more to B than to A? Then it would be efficient to make A the slave of B but this result would hardly comport with the principle of consent. Such cases must be very rare. Not only will A probably have a better idea than anyone else

---

33. For a recent statement of this argument, see Michelman, A *Comment on Some Uses and Abuses of Economics in Law*, 46 U. CHI. L. REV. 307, 308 (1979).

34. Komesar, *Return to Slumville: A Critique of the Ackerman Analysis of Housing Code Enforcement and the Poor*, 82 YALE L.J. 1175, 1187-91 (1973).

where he could be most productively employed, but the costs of overcoming A's disincentive to work hard when the benefits of his hard work would enure exclusively to another are likely to make the net value of his labor less than if he owned it himself. If there are cases where the costs of physical coercion are so low relative to the costs of administering contracts as to make slavery a more efficient method of organizing production than any voluntary system, they either arise under such different social conditions from our own as to make ethical comparison difficult,[35] or involve highly unusual circumstances (*e.g.*, military discipline) to which the term slavery is not attached.

A related problem is that where large allocative questions are involved, as in the initial assignment of rights, the very concept of wealth maximization becomes problematic. Since the wealth of society is the output of all tangible and intangible commodities multiplied by their market values, it is difficult to compare the wealth of two states of society in which prices are different. The prices in a social order in which one person owned all the other members of society might be different from the prices in a social order where everyone was his own master. But even here guesses may be possible. For example, if we started with a society where one person owned all the others, soon most of the others would have bought their freedom from that person because their output would be greater as free individuals than as slaves, enabling them to pay more for the right to their labor than that right was worth to the slave owner.[36] It would be clear, then, that the slave society was inefficient, even though the prices in a slave and free society might be different for many commodities.

Consider the following example of how the initial assignment of rights might appear to have such an effect on prices that the wealth of society under alternative assignments could not be compared.[37] Imagine that A, if a free man, would derive a lifetime market income of 100 in present value from working and a nonmarket income of 50 from leisure, for a total income of 150, but that if A is B's slave, A will be forced to produce an output having a market value of 110 and will obtain zero nonpecuniary income.

---

35. On the costs of monitoring economic activity in primitive societies, see Posner, A *Theory of Primitive Society, with Special Reference to Law*, 23 J.L. & ECON. 1 (1980).

36. The slave would borrow against his future earnings to finance the purchase of his freedom.

37. A similar example is analyzed in Dworkin, *supra* note 2, at 208-10.

A's wealth is higher in the free than in the slave state (150 versus zero), so that if he has the right to his labor he will not sell that right to B. Freedom is therefore wealth maximizing if A is free to begin with. But if B owns the right to A's labor, then it may seem that A will not be able to buy it back from B. How can A pay more than 100 since that is the value of his output as a free man? A's output is worth 110 to B, and A cannot use his nonpecuniary income in the free state to buy his freedom because his leisure has no value to anyone else.[38] Therefore, it seems that slavery is wealth maximizing if the initial assignment of rights is to make A the slave of B.

But this analysis overlooks the possibility of converting non-pecuniary into pecuniary income. A's preferred mixture of work and leisure is such as to yield 100 in market income and 50 in nonpecuniary income from leisure, but A could work harder, as he does for B. Suppose by working harder (but not all the time), A could earn a market income of 120 and leisure income of 10. A could then buy his freedom from B. It is true that, having done so, A would be worse off than if he had had the right to his labor in the first place. The point of the analysis, however, is that freedom is indeed more efficient than slavery, because by giving A his freedom in the first place we obviate the need for a transaction whereby A buys his freedom from B.

Thus, while the theoretical possibility exists that efficiency might dictate slavery or some other monstrous rights assignment, it is difficult to give examples where this would actually happen. I conclude that it is possible to deduce a structure of rights congruent with our ethical intuitions from the wealth-maximization premise.

SOME IMPLICATIONS FOR THE POSITIVE ECONOMIC ANALYSIS OF LAW

Why the Common Law Is Efficient

Scholars like myself who have argued that the common law is best explained as an effort, however inarticulate, to promote efficiency have lacked a good reason why this should be so—making them seem, perhaps, the naïve adherents of the outmoded "public interest" theory of the state.[39] This is the theory that the state op-

---

38. A's leisure might have value to another, but let us assume that it does not.
39. For a review of the rival theories of government discussed in this part of

erates, albeit imperfectly, to promote widely shared social goals—
of which wealth maximization is surely one, regardless of how
important a goal it may be. The state promotes efficiency by ar-
ranging for the provision of "public goods," that is, goods that
confer benefits not limited to those who pay for them and hence
that are produced in suboptimal amounts by private markets. One
of these public goods is a legal system that corrects sources of market failure such as externalities.

The public-interest theory of the state has been under severe
attack from the proponents of the "interest group" or, more nar-
rowly, the "producer protection" theory of the governmental process.[40] This theory assigns primary importance to redistribution as
an object of public policy. The redistributive emphasis stems from
treating governmental action as a commodity, much like other
commodities, that is allocated in accordance with the forces of supply and demand. The focus of research has been on demand. The
characteristics that enable an industry or other group to overcome
free-rider problems and thereby outbid rival claimants for governmental protection and largesse have been studied, and the conclusion has been reached that compact groups will generally outbid
diffuse ones for government favor.

The interest-group theory is an economic theory because it
links governmental action to utility maximization by the people
seeking such action. The public-interest theory is a description,
rather than an economic theory, of the political process because it
does not show how utility maximizing by individuals results in governmental action that promotes the interest of such diffuse groups
as the "public," consumers, or taxpayers. The implication of the interest group theory that diffuse groups are likely to lose out in
competition with more compact groups for government protection
undermines the plausibility of the public-interest theory even as
description.

However, common law doctrines that satisfy the Pareto-
superiority criterion in the "principle of consent" form in which I
have cast it in this Article (no common law doctrine would satisfy a
literal interpretation of the Pareto criterion) are plausible candi-

---

the Article, see Posner, *Theories of Economic Regulation*, 5 BELL J. ECON. & MGT.
SCI. 335 (1974).

40. The seminal article in the economic theory of interest-group politics (as
distinct from the earlier political-science theory) is Stigler, *The Theory of Economic
Regulation*, 2 BELL J. ECON. & MGT. SCI. 3 (1971).

dates for survival even in a political system otherwise devoted to redistribution. The reason is that a rule or institution that satisfies the principle of consent cannot readily be altered, at least not by the remedies available to common law judges, in a way that will redistribute wealth toward some politically effective interest group. This is particularly clear in cases, such as the landlord-tenant case discussed earlier,[41] where the parties to litigation have a pre-existing voluntary relationship. In effect, the court would be changing only one term of a contract, and the parties could alter the other contract terms in the future.[42] This is not an effective method of redistributing wealth. Even if the dispute does not arise from a contract, the parties may be interrelated in a way that to-tally or largely cancels any wealth effects from a change in the rule of liability. For example, since farmers were the major customers of railroads in the nineteenth century, it would not have made much sense to try to transfer wealth from railroads to farmers or vice versa simply by increasing or decreasing the liability of rail-roads for damage caused to crops growing along railroad rights of way.

The potential for using the common law to redistribute wealth is not great even in cases involving complete strangers. Consider again the negligence system of automobile-accident liability. It is hard to see how moving to a system of strict liability would in-crease the wealth of a compact, readily identifiable, and easily or-ganizable group in the society. The principal effect would simply be to increase or decrease most people's wealth a small amount, depending upon whether strict liability is more or less efficient than negligence in the automobile setting.

There is a literature that contends that the common law has been biased in favor of the rich—has served, that is, systematic and perverse redistributive ends.[43] The above analysis makes this an implausible contention, though it would carry me too far afield

---

41. See p. 500 supra.

42. It is noteworthy that Professor Ackerman, a leading advocate of using tort law to force landlords to increase the quality of slum housing, couples this with a proposal for a public subsidy to prevent tort liability from leading to a reduction in the supply of housing for the poor. See Ackerman, Regulating Slum Housing Markets on Behalf of the Poor: Of Housing Codes, Housing Subsidies, and Income Redistribution Policy, 80 YALE L.J. 1093 (1971).

43. See, e.g., M. HORWITZ, THE TRANSFORMATION OF AMERICAN LAW, 1780-1860, ch. III (1977).

to attempt to refute it in detail here.[44] If I am correct that the common law is not an effective method of redistributing wealth,[45] whether from rich or poor, farmers or railroads, tenants or landlords, or between any reasonably well defined, plausibly effective interest groups, then there is no reason to expect the common law to be dominated by redistributive concerns even if legislatures are.

To say what the common law is not is not to say what it is, but that too can be derived from the preceding analysis. There are numerous politically effective groups in the society; the question is what their rational objectives are likely to be in areas regulated by common law methods. Probably their self-interest is promoted by supporting the efficiency norm in those areas. By doing so they increase the wealth of the society; they will get a share of that increased wealth; and there is no alternative norm that would yield a larger share. To be sure, none of them will devote substantial resources to promoting the efficiency norm in the common law, because the benefits that each group derives will be small and because each will be tempted to take a free ride on the others. But few resources have to be devoted to promoting the efficiency norm for it to survive: its distributive neutrality operates to reduce potential opposition as well as support.

This analysis implicitly treats judges simply as agents of the government and hence does not confront the difficulties that judicial independence from political control poses for any self-interest theory of judicial behavior. That is a problem in the economics of agency. The utility of the analysis is in relating the efficiency theory of the common law to the redistributive theory of the state, albeit some of the links in the chain are obscure. Notice that it is an implication of the theory that where legislatures legislate within the area of common law regulation—as with respect to rights and remedies in torts, contracts, property, and related fields—they too will be trying to promote efficiency. For, in this view, it is not the nature of the regulating institution,[46] but the subjects and methods

---

44. For some criticism of the literature, see R. POSNER, ECONOMIC ANALYSIS OF LAW § 8.2 (2d ed. 1977).

45. As also argued on theoretical grounds in S. Shavell, A Note on Efficiency vs. Equity in Legal Rulemaking: Should Equity Matter, Given Optimal Income Taxation? (1979) (unpublished paper Harv. Univ. Dep't of Econ.).

46. In this analysis, the features of the judicial process that I have argued elsewhere tend to suppress distributive considerations, *see, e.g.,* R. POSNER, *supra* note 44, § 19.2, are thus viewed as effects rather than as causes of the judicial emphasis on efficiency.

of regulation, that determine whether the government will promote efficiency or redistribute wealth.

The relationship of the above political analysis to the ethical
discussion in the earlier parts of the Article should now be clear.
The principle of consent that I extracted from the Pareto-superiority criterion was another name for an absence of systematic distributive effects. The probabilistic compensation discussed in connection with the negligence system of automobile accident liability
made it possible to ignore ex post distributive effects in evaluating
that system. By the same token, no group can hope to benefit ex
ante from a change in the system, assuming the system is the most
efficient one possible, and those few and scattered parties who lose
out ex post are a diffuse and therefore ineffective interest group. If
this example can be generalized to the common law as a whole, it
provides a reason for believing that the political forces in the society will converge in seeking efficiency in common law adjudication.
In this instance what is ethical is also politic.

Is the Common Law Efficient or Utilitarian?

I want to consider finally and very briefly whether it is possible to distinguish empirically between the efficiency theory of the
common law and a theory that says that in the heyday of the common law the judges subscribed to the dominant utilitarian ideology
of the nineteenth century. My previous article noted that some influential figures in legal scholarship described the common law as
utilitarian.[47] Did they mean utilitarian in contradistinction to economic? I think not, for I can think of no instances in which utilitarian deviates from economic teaching where the common law followed the utilitarian approach. For example, income equality,
protection of animals, and prohibition of begging are all policies
that were advocated by Bentham,[48] the most thoroughgoing utilitarian, yet no traces of these policies can be found in the common
law. Bentham also believed in imposing a legal duty to be a good
Samaritan, but the common law, perhaps on economic grounds, rejected such a duty.[49] There is also no trace in the common law of
sympathy for thieves, rapists, or other criminals who seek to de-

---

47.   *See* Posner, *supra* note 1, at 106.
48.   *See* Posner, *Blackstone and Bentham*, 19 J.L. & ECON. 569, 590-600 (1976).
49.   *Compare* J. BENTHAM, THEORY OF LEGISLATION 189-90 (R. Hildreth ed.
1864), *with* Landes & Posner, *Salvors, Finders, Good Samaritans, and Other Rescuers: An Economic Study of Law and Altruism*, 7 J. LEGAL STUD. 83, 119-27 (1978).

fend their crimes on the ground that they derived more pleasure from the act than the pain suffered by their victims. Of course utilitarianism is a flexible enough philosophy to accommodate arguments as to why allowing a criminal such a defense would not really maximize happiness over the long term. But this is just to say that enlightened utilitarianism will incorporate the sorts of constraints that makes wealth maximization an appealing ethical norm.

THE ECONOMIC ANALYSIS OF LAW

JULES L. COLEMAN*

Proponents of the economic approach to law find in welfare economics a framework for both understanding large bodies of the common law and developing new law—through the legislative, judical, and administrative processes. The unifying principle of both analytic and normative law and economics is the principle of efficiency. The economic approach to law involves three efficiency related notions: Pareto optimality, Pareto superiority, and Kaldor-Hicks efficiency. I propose to analyze these notions and to develop the analytic relations among them. In addition, I shall explore aspects of their alleged connection to utilitarian moral theory and discuss critically their respective roles in the prevailing normative economic theories of law.

I. PARETO AND KALDOR-HICKS

When a proponent of economic analysis maintains that a change in legal rules or in the market is warranted or required because it is efficient, his claim is ambiguous. He or she may be understood to mean either that the proposed rule is Pareto optimal, whereas the existing order of affairs is not; or that his proposal constitutes a Pareto improvement, that is, is Pareto superior to the existing state of affairs; or that the envisaged change constitutes a Kaldor-Hicks improvement over the existing distribution of resources.[1]

Resources are allocated in a Pareto optimal fashion if and only if any further reallocation can make one person better off only at the expense of another. An allocation of resources, S^1, is Pareto superior to an alternative allocation, S, provided no one is made worse off in going from S to S^1, and the welfare of at least one person is enhanced. A Pareto optimal distribution has no distributions Pareto superior to it. In addition, Pareto optimal distributions are Pareto noncomparable, that is, the Pareto superior standard cannot be employed to choose among them. Another way of putting this last point is to say that the choice among Pareto optimal distributions must be made on grounds other than efficiency.

One distribution of resources, S^1, is Kaldor-Hicks efficient to another distribution, S, if and only if in going from S to S^1 the winners could compensate the losers with a net gain in welfare. Because Kaldor-Hicks requires that winners *could* compensate losers, not that they must, a Kaldor-Hicks improvement, unlike a Pareto improvement, produces losers as well as winners. Were compensation costless and actually paid, a Kaldor-Hicks improvement would become a Pareto improvement. Because the Kaldor-Hicks standard does not require compensation, it is often referred to as "the hypothetical compensation principle," or simply, "the compensation principle." Furthermore, because under the conditions of costless compensation, a Kaldor-Hicks improvement could be transformed into a Pareto improvement, it is sometimes referred to as the "Potential Pareto test."[2]

This last way of characterizing Kaldor-Hicks is misleading, however. It suggests that a Kaldor-Hicks improvement is just a Pareto improvement waiting for compensation to be paid. That would be a mistake. Not every Kaldor-Hicks improvement corresponds to a Pareto one. Whenever the transaction costs of rendering compensation exceed the difference between the amount of compensation losers demand and the gain to the winners, requiring gainers to compensate losers will make the gainers worse off than they were under the original distribution. This just emphasizes the importance of the distinction between the *hypothetical* compensation required by the Kaldor-Hicks test and the *actual* compensation required by the Pareto superior test.

II. EFFICIENCY AND UTILITY[3]

The claim that a change in the market or in the legal order is desirable or warranted because it would be efficient is a normative one that requires the proponent of economic analysis to relate the conceptions of efficiency to standards of value and right conduct, which in turn impart moral significance to the notions of efficiency. To this end, proponents of economic analysis have relied on an alleged connection between at least the Pareto standards and classical utilitarian moral theory.

According to classical utilitarianism, an individual is obligated to perform that action among the set of possible actions open to him at a given time that is most likely to produce the greatest net balance of utility over disutility. This formulation of the principle of utility calls for interpersonal comparison of utilities, a requirement that, according to the prevailing wisdom, cannot adequately be met. Since a Pareto superior redistribution of resources improves the welfare of at least one person without adversely affecting the welfare of another, the standard of Pareto superiority may be used to bypass the interpersonal comparability problem of classical utilitarianism. In other words, because a Pareto improvement produces winners but no losers, no need exists to compare the relative gains and losses of respective winners and losers to determine if a course of conduct increases total utility. If a course of conduct is Pareto superior, total utility increases, though there may be increases in total utility that are not the result of Pareto improvements.[4]

Not every net gain in utility constitutes a Pareto improvement; and the use of the Pareto superior standard will not enable us to determine by how much net utility has increased.[5] For these reasons, the Pareto standard resolves the interpersonal utility problem in a limited way. Still, the fact that the Pareto standard enables one to determine in a reliable way whether a policy increases total utility makes it easy to see why one might be led to consider utilitarianism to be the normative basis of at least the Pareto superior criterion.

The argument that Pareto optimality is connected to utilitarianism is more difficult. Since not every move to a Pareto optimal distribution of resources involves a Pareto improvement, one can *not* infer from the fact that an existing state of affairs is Pareto optimal that the move to it increases total utility. Moreover, because the set of Pareto optimal states of affairs is Pareto noncomparable, no judgments concerning the relative total utility contained in them are warranted.[6]

On the other hand, from the fact that a state of affairs is Pareto optimal, one can infer that it contains more total utility than the set of distributions that may be represented by points to the southwest of it within the utility / possibility frontier. That is because every distribution represented by a point on the utility / possibility frontier, that is, a Pareto optimal distribution, is *Pareto superior* to those distributions represented by points within the frontier to its southwest. Moreover, the net utility contained in any Pareto optimal distribution *cannot* be increased by a Pareto improvement. This feature of Pareto optimality follows from its conceptual connection to Pareto superiority; namely, a Pareto optimal distribution has no distributions Pareto superior to it.

Every utility judgment warranted by the Pareto optimality standard is a logical consequence of its analytic relation to Pareto superiority. No independent argument for the claim that Pareto optimality is rooted in utilitarian moral theory is possible. Whether Pareto optimality can be defended on utilitarian grounds will depend on whether Pareto superiority can be. Moreover, even if Pareto superiority can be defended on utilitarian grounds, it will not follow that Pareto optimality can, since not every Pareto optimal state of affairs need be the result of a Pareto improvement.

The problem of constructing a utilitarian account of Kaldor-Hicks efficiency runs even deeper. Under the Kaldor-Hicks test, winners are not required to compensate losers; all that is required is the *capacity* to render full compensation. Consequently, in order to infer a net increase in utility from the fact that the Kaldor-Hicks requirement has been satisfied, we have to know that winners have won more in utility than losers have lost in utility. Such a judgment requires interpersonal cardinal comparability, which the Pareto superior criterion was originally introduced to avoid. Satisfaction of the Kaldor-Hicks test does *not* require comparability; using the Kaldor-Hicks test as an index of utility *does*.

Second, the Kaldor-Hicks test is subject to the Scitovsky Paradox. The Scitovsky Paradox is the result that two states of affairs, S and S^1, can be Kaldor-Hicks efficient to one another. The proof is simple enough. Assume a two-person (X, Y), two-commodity (a, b) universe and the preference orderings for the distributions of a and b between X and Y shown in the accompanying illustration. Consider the states of affairs S and S^1. The distribution of a and b between X and Y in S and S^1 is given by the accompanying matrix.

PoX a b	PoY a b
1,1	1,1
2,0	0,2
1,0	0,1

		a	b
S	X	2	0
	Y	0	1

		a	b
S^1	X	1	0
	Y	0	2

Here, S^1 is Kaldor-Hicks efficient to S since Y (the winner) could compensate X (the loser) one unit of b. Having done so, X would be in his most preferred state; Y would then be no worse off than in S.

Also, S is Kaldor-Hicks efficient to S^1, since X (the winner) could compensate Y (the loser) one unit of a. Having done so, Y would be in his most preferred state; X would be no worse off than in S^1.

In short, satisfaction of the Kaldor-Hicks criterion cannot entail a net gain in utility because, without appealing to any particular standard of interpersonal comparison, one can determine if Kaldor-Hicks has been satisfied; but one cannot determine if utility has been increased by a Kaldor-Hicks improvement in which there are both winners and losers without appealing to such a standard; and S^1 can be Kaldor-Hicks efficient to S and S Kaldor-Hicks efficient to S^1, though S^1 cannot have more total utility than S while S has more total utility than S^1. Because satisfaction of the Kaldor-Hicks test does not entail an increase in utility, the justification, if there is one, for pursuing Kaldor-Hicks improvements cannot be utilitarian.[7]

On the other hand, even though satisfaction of the Pareto superior standard *does* entail an increase in utility, it will not follow that the justification for *its* use is utilitarian. There is an important distinction between the claim that Pareto superiority *warrants* a utility judgment and the claim that it is this connection to utilitarianism that justifies pursuing Pareto improvements. I have elsewhere discussed at length alternatives to the utilitarian justification for Pareto superiority, so I will only summarily discuss one of them here.

The empirical content of Pareto superiority judgments is given in terms of their relation to individual preference theories, not to total utility theories. Pareto superiority is defined in terms of preference orderings: S^1 is Pareto superior to S if and only if at least one individual in S^1 is further along his preference ranking than he is in S, and no individual is any worse off with respect to hers in S^1 than she is in S. Suppose that judgments made in terms of individual preference orderings could not be made into judgments regarding total utility. In such a case, the notion of total utility would be meaningless, and the standard of Pareto superiority could not serve as an index of total utility. Nevertheless, the concept of Pareto superiority would be meaningful; and a claim that S^1 is Pareto superior to S would have empirical content. Under such circumstances, one could not *ex hypothesi* purport to justify a Pareto improvement on the ground that it increases total utility. (Remember, we are assuming that the notion of total utility is meaningless.) It would not follow, however, that a Pareto improvement or policies in pursuit thereof could not be justified. One possible justification is this: because a Pareto improvement makes at least one individual better off and no one worse off, no rational person would object to it. That is, rational individuals would choose to pursue Pareto superior policies, not because they increase utility, but because they improve the well-being of some without adversely affecting the well-being of others. This is an argument from consent, not utility.

In short, the argument for identifying the Pareto criteria with utilitarian moral theory is problematic in two ways. First, only Pareto superiority judgments entail judgments cast in terms of total or net utility. Second, the fact that a Pareto judgment of any sort warrants a utility judgment is inadequate to establish the proposition that the justification for pursuing Pareto improvements is utilitarian.

III. THE COASE THEOREM

The most influential discussion of the relation of economic efficiency to law is Ronald Coase's "The Problem of Social Cost."[8] Whenever reference is made to this article, visions of the Coase Theorem spring to mind. Often overlooked is the fact that Coase's purpose was *not* to develop a theorem about the relation of law to efficiency; his intention was to criticize and provide an alternative to the Pigouvian approach to externalities.[9]

The Pigouvian approach to externalities involves three steps. First, an appropriate civil authority identifies an activity as the source or cause of the externality. Next, the authority determines how much of the external by-product of the "offending" party is optimal or efficient. Then the requisite body imposes on the offending party a per unit tax equal to the marginal damage caused by each "unit" of the offending activity beyond the optimal level. The Pigouvian approach requires first a judgment of causal responsibility for damage, then a determination of efficient resource use, and finally the imposition of a tax in order to reduce the output of the offending party to the efficient level. The per unit tax reduces output by requiring the offending party to pay not only the *private* but the *social costs* of its activity.

An example may be helpful. Suppose no fence separates adjacent plots of land owned by a rancher and a farmer, respectively. Because cows wander, each cow the rancher raises results in damage to the farm crop. If the rancher's decision about how many cows to raise does not require him to take into account the costs of ranching on farming, he will raise cows as if no corn were being farmed. He will cease raising additional cows only when his marginal profit in doing so is equaled by his marginal *private* costs.

In the Pigouvian approach to externalities, the appropriate authority determines first that the rancher's cattle adversely affect the level of corn and beef production, so that the price of beef is too low and the price of corn too high. When the rancher's activity does not reflect its effect on corn, too much beef and too little corn are produced.

The next step in the Pigouvian analysis requires determining how much of each activity is optimal or efficient. One way of doing this is to imagine that both activites and plots of land are owned by the same person, Mr. R. F. (rancher/farmer). The question R. F. would pose to himself is this: "Given this land and the fact that it can be used for raising both cows and corn, how much of my resources should be devoted to each?" His answer, of course, will depend on what he wants to do with the land. Let's simplify matters by assuming that R. F. desires to use his resources at their optimal productive level; he wants, in other words, to maximize his revenue from the land. In order to maximize revenue from his enterprises, R. F. must consider, not only the private costs of ranching and farming, but the costs of ranching *on* farming and that of farming *on* ranching as well. His strategy will be to choose that level of each activity such that any further increase in either will mean forgoing a greater benefit that could be secured by devoting those resources to the other activity. So if the next cow is worth X, whereas the damage to the corn crop it will cause exceeds X, then R. F. will forgo *that* cow in favor of the corn crop. In general, R. F. will decide on that level of ranching and farming such that any further ranching is more costly than farming (in terms of forgone farming opportunities) and any further farming is more costly than ranching (in terms of forgone ranching opportunities). No more ranching or farming can be undertaken without imposing a marginal loss. The levels of ranching and farming R. F. decides upon are in this sense efficient.

Once the efficient levels of ranching and farming are determined, the requisite authority imposes a per unit tax on the rancher equal to the marginal damage to corn crops of each additional cow.[10] As a result of the tax, the rancher gains nothing by raising any cow beyond the number represented by R. F.'s decision. The Pigouvian tax forces the rancher to internalize into his decisions the effects of his ranching on the farmer's farming. Because the true costs of ranching are now reflected in the sum of private and social costs, the prices of beef and corn are accurate, and consumers' decisions concerning how much corn and beef they want are based on accurate relative prices.

"The Problem of Social Cost" presents an alternative to the Pigouvian approach to internalizing externalities. The Coasian method relies on private exchange rather than on public taxation. The argument that externalities can be internalized by private exchange assumes that the relevant parties have substantial knowledge of their preferences, are rational, and that transactions between (or among) them are costless (i.e., that they exhibit cooperative behavior), or that these costs are trivial. Under these conditions, Coase argues, the relevant parties will negotiate to the efficient level of the respective activities.

Suppose the rancher is not required to take into account the costs of raising cows on corn. He will raise cows as if no corn was being grown on the adjacent land. Suppose the rancher will raise one hundred cows, where R. F. would have raised only fifty. To say that R. F. would have raised only fifty cows is just to say that each cow beyond the fiftieth causes more damage to the corn crop than it produces in ranching profits. Whatever the value of each cow between the fifty-first and the one hundreth is to the rancher, the value to the farmer of the associated corn crop damage exceeds it. The farmer therefore has an incentive to pursue an accord with the rancher that will prohibit the rancher from raising any more than fifty cows in return for which the farmer will pay the rancher an amount equal to or greater than the value of each additional cow but less than the crop damage associated with each cow. The rancher will accept some such offer, since he gains at least as much from the farmer's offer as he would from actually raising the cow. The rancher and farmer will continue to negotiate until the efficient level of ranching and farming—that is, that level R. F. would have chosen—is reached.

The same outcome is secured if we begin by assuming that

the farmer would grow corn as if no raising of cattle took place on the adjacent land. This scenario requires that we assume that the rancher begins by raising no cows; otherwise it is impossible even to conceive of the farmer growing corn as if no cows were within trampling distance. Suppose, then, that the rancher begins by raising no cows at all. By hypothesis, the marginal value of each of the first fifty cows to the rancher is greater than the marginal value of the associated corn crop to the farmer. Consequently, the rancher has an incentive to purchase from the farmer the right to raise each cow up to the fiftieth one. The farmer will accept any offer that exceeds the marginal benefit to him of each unit of corn the rancher's cows require him to forgo. The rancher is prepared to make such an offer; again the two will negotiate to the efficient level of ranching and farming.

Whether negotiations begin with too much or too little ranching, that is, with ranching imposing inefficient external costs on farming or with farming imposing inefficient external costs on ranching, the result of negotiations will be the same. The rancher and farmer will negotiate to that level of ranching and farming represented by R. F.'s decision about how to allocate his ranching and farming resources. In the absence of transaction costs the externalities of ranching on farming will be internalized by private exchange.

Not only is the Pigouvian tax just one way of controlling externalities, as long as the parties remain free to negotiate after the tax is imposed, imposing the tax may lead to inefficient levels of production. Moreover, unlike the Pigouvian approach that requires identifying one activity as the source of an externality, the Coasian approach reveals an underlying *reciprocity* between activities:[11] too much farming means too little ranching even if corn doesn't harm cows in the way in which meandering cows harm corn.

Commentators have seen in Coase's argument the basis of a formal or analytic claim about the relation between the goal of economic efficiency and the assignment of legal rights as an instrument in its pursuit. This is the Coase Theorem. There are as many ways of stating the theorem as there are illustrations of it and controversies arising from it. I prefer to state it as follows: if we assume that the relevant parties to negotiations are rational, that they have substantial knowledge of their own and one another's preferences, that transactions between them are costless, that the state will enforce contracts between them, that their negotiations are not affected by their relative wealth (no income effects), that the prices on the basis of which they bid against one another are given to them rather than established by their negotiations (the partial equilibrium model), the assignment of property rights by the state to either party will be irrelevant to the goal of efficiency, provided of course that the rights are divisible and negotiable.

I state the theorem with all these qualifications, partly for effect, and partly because so much confusion arises in its application simply because commentators either ignore or are unfamiliar with all the initial conditions that must be satisfied. The basic idea is really quite simple, however. As long as two people, A and B, can negotiate with one another, it won't matter from the point of view of efficiency whether the state gives B the right to prevent A from acting in a way that adversely affects B, or A the right to act in a way that harms B. As long as transactions are costless, A and B will negotiate to an efficient level of their respective activities through the process of mutual gain *via* trade, though there is no guarantee that they will negotiate to the *same* efficient distribution.[12]

In efficiency terms, the argument is this. The initial assignment of entitlements will either be efficient, that is, Pareto optimal, or not. If it *is* efficient, no negotiations will occur. Rational parties will not negotiate away from an efficient distribution, since doing so must make one of them worse off; that is just another way of saying that there are no Pareto superior moves from Pareto optimal states of affairs. On the other hand, if the initial assignment is inefficient, a Pareto superior redistribution exists; and rational parties will reach an agreement that is Pareto superior to their current relative positions. This process of mutual gain through trade, that is, Pareto improvements through exchange, continues until further trade is unrewarding for either or both parties.

Immediately upon stating the Coase Theorem—that the assignment of entitlements is irrelevant to the goal of efficiency—analysts go on to point out that the assignment of rights does make a difference from the point of view of the distribution of wealth between the relevant parties. That is, the party who is not assigned the entitlement must purchase it from the party who is assigned it. This effects a wealth transfer between them. So if the farmer is entitled to prohibit all cows, there will be fifty cows in the end, but the rancher will have had to pay the farmer for the privilege of ranching fifty cows; whereas if the rancher was entitled to ranch one hundred cows, there will be fifty in the end, but the rancher will be compensated by the farmer for each cow he forgoes.

I have become persuaded that this way of characterizing the wealth redistributive effects of the assignment of entitlements is mistaken. For it seems to me that what the farmer would be willing to pay for the farmland in the first place would depend on his future liabilities and, in particular, on whether he will have to *bribe* the rancher to reduce the level of ranching. Certainly, he would pay less for the right to farm the land if he is not assigned as well the right to prohibit cows on the adjacent property. Concern for his liability to the farmer would also effect what the rancher is willing to pay for the right to ranch. The financial gains and losses in relative wealth between rancher and farmer associated with the right either to raise or prohibit cows appears to be discounted in the purchase price of the *prior* rights.[13] Generally, the standard understanding of the redistributive effect of the assignment of entitlements looks at individual right assignments in isolation, piecemeal. The piecemeal approach misses the crucial point that the value of any right to a person depends on associative rights, on clusters or bundles of rights. When the respective bundles of rights and liabilities of the rancher and farmer are taken into account, it may well be that the relative wealth of the parties is not affected by any *particular* assignment.

IV. AUCTIONING ENTITLEMENTS

Having expressed my skepticism concerning the universally accepted understanding of the redistributive aspects of the Coase Theorem, I want to move on to the application of the theorem to law when the conditions necessary for its satisfaction are not met; in particular, when transaction costs are not insignificant. In many cases the existence of transaction costs may make it impossible for the relevant parties to reach an accord that will improve their well-being. For example, if the cost of the transaction exceeds the difference between what the rancher values adding another cow at and what the farmer values the corn he will lose at, the rancher will not purchase from the farmer the right to that cow (assuming the farmer is initially assigned the right to prohibit it). Because no transaction occurs, the farmer maintains the entitlement, though his doing so is inefficient; that is, Pareto superior redistributions exists. Failures of this sort are called market failures.

Where transaction costs create market failures, the initial assignment of entitlements makes a difference from the point of view of efficiency. Consequently, the essential question for economists concerns how externalities are to be internalized (or controlled) when transaction costs threaten the capacity of the market to promote efficiency through private exchange.

In the economic theory of law, the failure of private exchange to promote efficiency calls for some sort of public intervention. One form of intervention, which was briefly discussed earlier, would involve taxing the inefficient activity—for example, ranching—thus requiring the adverse effects of ranching on farming, to be reflected in its total costs. Another form of intervention, subsidy, would involve subsidizing the inefficient activity for each reduction in inefficient levels of its activity undertaken.

Neither the tax nor the subsidy policy involves a claim concerning the legal rights of the respective parties. Presumably the farmer would be entitled to farm as much as he would like to, and the rancher would be free to raise cows as he pleases. The tax or subsidy is intended simply to make it economically more feasible for the farmer and rancher to engage in their activities at the efficient levels.

In contrast, externalities or inefficiences may be controlled through the legal process by the imposition of either a *liability* or a *property* rule.[14] Both the liability and property rule techniques involve two steps. The first is assignment of a legal right to one or the other activity to act in a particular way; the second step involves a means for protecting the right once assigned. The alternatives differ with respect to the vehicles for protecting legal rights. A property rule protects an entitlement by enjoining others from interfering with the right bearer's exercise of the right except insofar as the right bearer may choose to forgo his liberty at an acceptable "price." A liability rule affords protection by entitling the right bearer to compensation should the liberty secured by the entitlement be abridged by others. In other words, the nonentitled party may reduce the value of the entitlement without securing the consent of the entitled party, provided he pays damages. Under liability rules, damages are set by a court and need not reflect the price the originally entitled party would have been willing to accept for the reduction in the value of his entitlement. While liability rules in effect permit nonentitled parties to bring about nonconsented to transfers of entitlements at prices set by third parties, property rules prohibit such transfers in the absence of mutual agreement.[15] If my right to my house is protected by a property rule, you may not do anything to it except as I permit you to. If, however, my right to my house is protected by a liability rule, you may do as you wish with it, provided you adequately compensate me for the infringements. We can further distinguish among liability rules. Some require compensation only if the infringement involves some kind of *fault*; others require compensation without regard to the injurer's fault.

Both the liability and the property rule assume that entitlements to efficient resource use have been assigned. They differ with respect to the vehicles employed for maintaining an efficient distribution of rights to resource uses under the dynamics of human interaction. Considerations of efficiency enter into the analysis of legal rights at two levels: first with respect to the efficient allocation of legal rights; then with respect to efficiency in the enforcement or protection of these rights. I want to confine the discussion to the common element in economic analysis of legal rights: the question of efficiency in allocating entitlements.

Richard Posner has advanced the following rule to guide the law in promoting efficient resource use in the absence of efficient private exchanges:

Assign the relevant entitlements to that party who would have purchased it in an exchange market in which the conditions of the Coase Theorem were satisfied.

The idea is simple enough. Economic analysis relies on competitive market models of efficiency. Where efficient outcomes cannot be obtained and the law must intervene, entitlements are to be conferred to produce the result an efficient market would have. In an efficienct market, the relevant right would eventually have worked its way to the party who would have paid the most for it. The general principle, then, is to assign entitlements by simulating or mimicking the market.

The rationale for the principle is straightforward. The Coase Theorem demonstrates that, in the absence of transaction costs, any assignment of rights will be efficient. Resources will be traded to their highest value; that is, ultimately the person willing to pay the most for a resource will get it. Such a result would be efficient in the sense that no mutually advantageous trades could then be made, since an individual willing to pay any less for the entitlement would be incapable of rendering compensation sufficient to induce the high bidder to agree to part with the entitlement. When the market is incapable of securing the efficient outcome through exchanges, Posner's principle tells authorities to secure the efficient outcome *directly* by conferring the relevant legal right on the "high bidder," that is, that individual who would have purchased the entitlement in the market.

Posner's intention is to translate into the law so far as possible the implications of the Coase Theorem. But Posner's principle for assigning entitlements, what I have called the "auction principle,"[16] fails to duplicate crucial features of Coase's analysis. Most important, whereas the Coase argument relies on the model of exchange, on freely consented to Pareto superior moves to efficient or Pareto optimal outcomes, Posner's principle abandons Pareto superiority in favor of the Kaldor-Hicks standard. Assigning an entitlement to the person who ultimately would have purchased it in an exchange market is to assign it to a party who *could* have compensated the other party; that is, if he could purchase the entitlement at price, P, then he could compensate someone willing to pay less than P. For example, under Posner's rule, instead of the rancher purchasing the right to the fiftieth cow from the farmer and thereby compensating the farmer for the crop damage, the state entitles the rancher to the fiftieth cow, and the farmer goes uncompensated. The rancher *could* have compensated the farmer because he would have been able to purchase the right from the farmer—had the farmer initially been entitled to prohibit the cow. Consequently, the Kaldor-Hicks test is satisfied. Because the rancher does not compensate the farmer, and because wandering cows damage crops, assigning the right to the rancher makes him better off and the farmer worse off. Consequently, the Pareto superiority standard is *not* satisfied. To the extent the Posner principle replaces the Pareto test by the Kaldor-Hicks standard, it deviates from that aspect of the Coase argument.

Moreover, because of information problems, it is doubtful whether following Posner's rule can guarantee that the assignment of entitlements will be Pareto optimal; that is, it is doubtful that Posner's rule will duplicate the efficient outcome aspect of costless voluntary exchange. Suppose two individuals are vying for a right to use a plot of land in different, indeed incompatible ways. Following Posner's rule we are supposed to assign the use to the high bidder—as the market eventually would have done. In following Posner we abandon the market in an effort to mimic its outcome. Once we abandon the market, however, how are we to gather the pertinent information regarding the respective parties' willingness to pay? On the other hand, if a market exists, or can be established to determine relative willingness to pay, Posner's rule becomes otiose, since all the relevant ingredients of an exchange market are present. Posner's rule may be either otiose or unworkable.

Information problems also arise in determining the efficient level of activities. The efficient level of activities depends on the preferences of individuals who engage in them. For example, if we assume that R. F. desires to maximize revenue from ranching and farming, then, given the relevant prices, we can determine that he will raise fifty cows. If he had as well an aesthetic preference of cows to corn, then he would raise more than fifty cows. How many more would depend on a variety of factors. The traditional way of determining how many cows he would raise would be for him to reveal his preferences through market behavior. In following Posner we abandon the market in an effort to simulate its outcomes. But in this sort of case, where preferences are complex, we need the market to reveal the relevant preferences and to enable us to determine the efficient level of the relevant activities. This problem is further exacerbated by income effects.[17]

In short, if we follow Posner in assigning rights, we cannot be certain that we have duplicated the market in producing efficient levels of resource use; and, if we are fortunate enough to have done so, we would have achieved the Pareto optimal outcome by a Kaldor-Hicks rather than by a Pareto superior move. To that extent Posner's rule fails to replicate in law the special insight of the Coase Theorem.

In *theory* an efficiency-related intervention in the market might be justified because it constitutes either a Pareto improvement or a Kaldor-Hicks improvement, or because the effect of the redistribution of resources is Pareto optimal. In fact, however, almost no interventions involve actual Pareto improvements. Certainly interventions that follow Posner's rule do not. They involve the Kaldor-Hicks criterion.

The Kaldor-Hicks criterion is subject to the Scitovsky reversal problem. Consequently, the Kaldor-Hicks criterion does not provide an adequate linear ordering of states of affairs. It will not follow, therefore, that satisfaction of the Kaldor-Hicks criterion is adequate to justify preferring one state of affairs to another. Moreover, Kaldor-Hicks is not an index of utility. So an intervention in the market following Posner's rule would not be justifiable on utilitarian grounds. The fact that Posner's rule satisfies the Kaldor-Hicks test would therefore be inadequate to justify it.

Suppose we shift gears. Instead of arguing that the assignment of legal rights on the model of mimicking markets is justified because doing so constitutes Kaldor-Hicks improvements, a proponent of economic analysis would argue that the effect of such interventions is to produce Pareto optimal outcomes; and that interventions that follow the principle of mimicking markets are justified for that reason. This justification of assigning entitlements by mimicking markets relies, not on the efficiency of the *process*, but on efficiency of the outcome instead.

There are of course enormous information cost problems that suggest that in fact applying Posner's rule rarely results in Pareto optimal states of affairs. The problems with this defense of the auction rule go much deeper, however. We can understand the claim that the auction rule is justified because it produces Pareto optimal outcomes in two ways, depending upon the justification for pursuing Pareto optimal outcomes. If we understand the claim to be that the Pareto optimal outcome is justified on utilitarian grounds, that is, as the assertion that the optimal outcome maximizes utility, then the claim must be mistaken, since not every Pareto optimal outcome is utility maximizing. (This follows from the fact discussed above that one can achieve Pareto optimal results in a number of ways.[18])

If, however, we understand the claim to be that the intervention is justified because it is efficient, whereas the existing state of affairs is not, the argument turns on the proposition that every Pareto optimal state of affairs is, on efficiency grounds, preferable to every non-Pareto optimal one. That claim, however, is false.

Posner's rule comes into play when the market *cannot* reach a Pareto optimal outcome via exchange. At that point, the distribution is a non-Pareto optimal one. If we set aside information problems involved in applying Posner's rule, then when resources are redistributed in virtue of the assignment of rights, they are done so efficiently.[19] From an efficiency standpoint the optimal distribution is *necessarily* preferable to the nonoptimal one *only if* every Pareto optimal distribution is preferable to every non-Pareto optimal one. But as every welfare economist knows, only the set of points on the frontier that are to the northeast of points within the frontier constitute distributions preferable on efficiency grounds. So unless Posner's rule assigns entitlements that produce distributions to the northeast of the inefficient market situation, there is no efficiency-related reason for preferring the efficient outcome of the Posner rule to the inefficient market. And since Posner's principle satisfies the Kaldor-Hicks but not necessarily the Pareto superiority test, we have no way of knowing a priori that Posner's rule guarantees such assignments.

Current thinking about normative law and economics seems to me to face the following problem. On the one hand it tells us to design policy to promote efficiency. When asked why, the answer is that efficiency is ethically rooted in utilitarianism: that efficiency analysis is utility analysis without the problems of interpersonal comparability. As it turns out, however, of the various efficiency notions bandied about in economic analysis, only one, Pareto superiority, is connected to utility in a way that *might* be justificatory in nature. Unfortunately, the prevailing normative economic approach to law does not rely on the Pareto superiority standard—as indeed it cannot, since that standard, as is well known, is unworkable.[20] Instead, it relies on the one efficiency standard that logically *cannot* be an index of utility, namely Kaldor-Hicks. Moreover, to the extent that economic analysis relies on neither Pareto superiority nor Kaldor-Hicks, but on Pareto optimality instead, it afford us no utilitarian defense, since whatever claims about total utility one can make from Pareto optimality follow from its analytic connection to Pareto superiority. What is worse, any alleged justification of market interventionism that relies entirely on the optimality of the outcome is committed to the mistaken proposition that every Pareto optimal distribution is preferable (on economic grounds only) to every non-Pareto optimal one.[21]

NOTES

* Research for this paper was undertaken during a leave of absence financed by an N.E.H. research fellowship. I am grateful to participants in the law and economics workshop at Stanford University and at the University of Southern California for their helpful comments on earlier drafts of this paper.

1. For a more complete analysis of efficiency notions, see Coleman, "Efficiency, Exchange and Auction: Philosophic Aspects of the Economic Approach to Law," 68 *Calif. L. Rev.* 2, (hereafter cited as "Philosophic Aspects").
2. Here I am following Guido Calabresi and Phillip Bobbitt's means of characterizing the Kaldor-Hicks criterion in *Tragic Choices* (New York: Norton, 1977).
3. For a more complete discussion of the relationship of efficiency to moral theory, see Coleman, "Efficiency, Utility and Wealth Maximization" 8 *Hofstra L. Rev.*, 509 (1980).
4. There may be ways of increasing overall utility by making some people worse off. Determining which redistributions increase overall utility by making some people worse off and others better off, unlike the Pareto test, requires interpersonal comparability.
5. Still, the Pareto test enables us to linear-order states of affairs in terms of their utility. In other words, while we could not determine by how much total utility increases in going from S to either S^1 or S^2, and therefore determine on those grounds which is most preferable to S, provided that S^1 and S^2 are Pareto comparable,

we could linear-order by use of the Pareto standard S^1 and S^2 and determine on that basis which is most preferable to S.

6. Provided, of course, that we rule out interpersonal comparability.
7. The following utility/possibility graph illustrates the relationship among various efficiency distributions of resources:

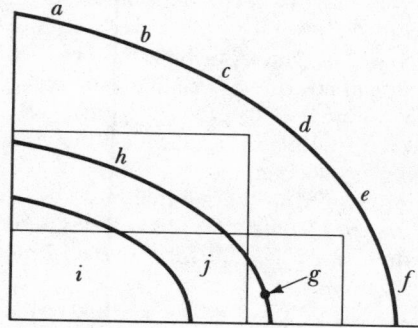

the utility/possibility frontier representing the set of all Pareto optimal distributions — e.g., distributions — a, b, c, d, e, and f.

(i) because c and e represents P.O. distributions they are Pareto noncomparable.

(ii) c is P.S. to all points to its southwest, including h and i, but not g, with which it is Pareto noncomparable.

(iii) e is P.S. to g and i, but not h. It is Pareto noncomparable.

(iv) h and g are Pareto noncomparable; both are Pareto superior to i, but not to j, with which they are both Pareto noncomparable.

8. Ronald Coase, "The Problem of Social Cost," 3 *J. Law & Econ* 1 (1960).

9. Externalities are by-products of engaging in an activity that adversely affect the levels of production of other activities or the well-being of other individuals.

10. This argument relies on the assumption that there are currently too many cows being raised.

11. Proponents of economic analysis tend to make too much of this underlying reciprocity; critics of economic analysis make too little of it. See Coleman, "Philosophic Aspects," esp. sec. II.

12. That is, there are instances in which assigning the relevant entitlement to either A or B will preclude further negotiations, since neither will part with entitlement at any price the other is willing to pay. This happens most often with tragically scarce resources, e.g., a bucket of water in the desert. Either distribution will be efficient in such cases.

13. The idea is simple enough. Suppose I am interested in purchasing and then farming a plot of land you own. When we discuss purchase price, one question I ask you is who lives next door—Is

he a rancher or a farmer? If you answer "rancher," then I want to know whether his cows roam on the property. If you again answer in the affirmative, I want next to know whether he or I is liable for the losses to crops his cows cause. If you say he is, I offer you $X for the land; but if the loss lies where it falls, I offer you $(X − Y)$, where Y represents the costs of anticipated crop damage. If I want to increase my crop to the level it would have been had he, not I, been liable for the damages, I must bribe him to reduce his ranching accordingly. That will cost me $Y, so I am no worse off than before. And he no doubt had to pay an equivalently greater price for his ranch in the first place, because it came with the right to let his cows graze neighboring land.

14. These terms were originally introduced in the seminal piece by G. Calabresi and Malamed, "Liability Rules, Property Rules and Inalienability: One View of the Cathedral," 85 *Harv. L. Rev.* 1089 (1972).

15. The claim that the level of protection afforded by a liability rule cannot be reduced except by agreement depends on the rights being otherwise protected, for example, by criminal sanction.

16. Coleman "Philosophic Aspects," esp. sec. III.

17. "Income effects" describe the impact of one's relative wealth on one's willingness to pay to satisfy a particular preference.

18. See the discussion on pp. 85 and 86 above.

19. But it is unlikely that employing Posner's rule to assign entitlements produces a Pareto optimal outcome, since that supposes that once rights and duties are in place no gains can be obtained by further negotiations. Posner himself would argue that one purpose of his principle is to assign entitlements so as to facilitate *further* exchange.

20. This point has been made by Calabresi and Bobbitt in *Tragic Choices*, note 2, *supra*, and by Posner himself in "The Ethical and Political Basis of the Efficiency Norm in Common Law Adjudication," 8 *Hofstra L. Rev.* 487 (1980). See note 3, *supra*.

21. Whether it is time for lawyers enamored of the normative economic approach to law to abandon ship depends in part on whether these objections can be met. I consider this matter in "Strategies in Defence of Normative Economic Analysis of Law: Why They Fail," (unpublished manuscript).

WHY EFFICIENCY?

A Response to Professors Calabresi and Posner

*Ronald Dworkin**

POSNER'S WRONG START

Professor Posner believes that agencies of government, and particularly courts, should make political decisions in such a way as to maximize social wealth.[11] In the present article[12] he narrows his claim and offers a new argument. He wishes to show, not as before why society as a whole should seek wealth maximization in every political decision, but only why common law judges should decide cases so as to maximize wealth. He offers two arguments meant to be connected (or perhaps even to be only one argument).[13] First, everyone (or at least almost everyone) may be deemed to have consented in advance to the principles or rules that judges who seek to maximize wealth will apply. Second, the enforcement of these principles and rules is in fact in the interest of everyone (or almost everyone) including those who thereby lose law suits. The first—the argument from consent—is supposed to introduce the idea of autonomy (and therefore a strain of Kant) to the case for wealth. The second—the argument from universal interest—insists in the continuing relevance of welfare to justice, and therefore is

---

11. Posner, *Utilitarianism, Economics, and Legal Theory*, 8 J. LEGAL STUD. 103 (1979).
12. Posner, *supra* note 3.
13. *Id.* at 491-97.

supposed to add a dose of utilitarianism. The combined arguments, Posner suggests, show that wealth maximization—at least by judges —provides the best of both these traditional theories of political morality and avoids their famous problems.

Posner illustrates the second claim by showing why, if negligence rules are superior from the standpoint of wealth maximization to rules of strict liability, it follows that all those who benefit from reduced driving costs—almost everyone—would be better off under a regime of negligence than a regime of strict liability.[14] The first claim—about consent—is then supposed to follow directly: If it is in fact true that almost everyone would be better off under a regime of negligence than strict liability, then it is fair to assume that almost everyone would have chosen negligence if offered the choice between these two regimes at a suitably early time, and therefore fair to deem almost everyone to have consented to negligence even though, of course, no one has actually done so.

The Argument from Consent

In fact both these arguments are more complex and I think more confused than first appears. (I discussed them both at length several years ago.[15]) It is important to remember, first, that consent and self-interest are independent concepts that have independent roles in political justification. If I have consented in advance to governance by a certain rule, then this counts as some reason for enforcing against me the rule to which I have consented. Of course, in determining how much reason my actual consent provides we must look to the circumstances of my consent, in particular to see whether it was informed and uncoerced. In this latter investigation the question of whether it was in my self-interest to have consented may figure only as evidence: if it was plainly not in my self-interest, this might suggest, though it does not prove, that my consent was either uninformed or coerced. But the bare fact that my consent was against my own interest provides no argument in itself against enforcing my consent against my later wishes.

Conversely, the fact that it would have been in my self-interest to have consented to something is sometimes evidence that I did in fact consent, if the question of whether I did actually consent is for some reason in doubt. But only evidence: the fact of self-interest, of course, in no way constitutes an actual consent. In

---

14. *Id.*
15. R. DWORKIN, *supra* note 8, at ch. 6.

some circumstances, however, the fact of self-interest is good evidence for what we might call a counterfactual consent: that is, the proposition that I would have consented had I been asked. But a counterfactual consent provides no reason in itself for enforcing against me that to which I would have (but did not) consent. Perhaps the fact of my earlier self-interest does provide an argument for enforcing the principle against me now. I shall consider that later. But the counterfactual consent, of which the self-interest is evidence, can provide no further argument beyond whatever argument the self-interest itself provides. Since Posner's argument from consent depends entirely on counterfactual consent, and since counterfactual consent is in itself irrelevant to political justification, the argument from consent wholly fails. Posner's appeal to "autonomy"—and his associated claim to have captured what is most worthwhile in "Kantian" theories—is wholly spurious.

Autonomy is, I agree, a different concept from consent. It contemplates what is sometimes called—perhaps misleadingly—authentic consent, meaning the consent of the true or genuine person. That dark idea is often elaborated as a kind of hypothetical or counterfactual consent. But then the authenticity is provided by—and everything turns on—the way the conditions of the counterfactual consent are specified. Kant himself deployed a complex metaphysical psychology to identify the consent of the genuine person counterfactually. Rawls constructs an elaborate "original position" for an arguably similar purpose. But Posner's argument lacks any comparable structure, and so provides no reason to think that the counterfactual consent he describes has more claim to authenticity—and hence to autonomy—than any other choice people might have, but did not, make.

Why has Posner confused self-interest and consent in this apparently elementary way? His present article[16] provides a variety of clues. Consider the following extraordinary passage:

> The notion of consent used here is what economists call ex ante compensation. I contend, I hope uncontroversially, that if you buy a lottery ticket and lose the lottery . . . you have consented to the loss. Many of the involuntary, uncompensated losses experienced in the market, or tolerated by the institutions that take the place of the market where the market cannot be made to work effectively, are fully compensated ex ante and hence are consented to.[17]

---

16. Posner, *supra* note 3.
17. *Id.* at 492 (footnote omitted).

This passage confuses two questions: Is it fair that someone should bear some loss? Has he consented to bear that loss? If I buy a lottery ticket knowing the odds, and was uncoerced, it is perhaps fair that I bear the loss that follows, because I received a benefit ("compensation") for assuming the risk. But it hardly follows, nor is it true, that I have consented to that loss. What, indeed, would that mean? (Perhaps that I agreed that the game should be rigged so that I must lose.)

In some circumstances it may be said that I consented to the *risk* of loss, which is different, though even this stretches a point and in many cases is just false. Suppose (with no question of fraud or duress) I wildly overestimated my chance of winning—perhaps I thought it a sure thing. It may nevertheless be fair that I lose, if the ticket was in fact fairly priced, even though I would not have bet if I had accurately assessed my chances of winning. All this— the importance of distinguishing between fairness and consent—is even clearer in the case of the "entrepreneurial risks" Posner discusses.[18] He imagines a case in which someone buys land which then falls in value when the biggest plant in town unexpectedly moves. He says that the loss was compensated ex ante (and hence "consented to") because "[t]he probability that the plant would move was discounted in the purchase price that they paid."[19] The latter suggestion is mysterious. Does it assume that the price was lower because both parties to the sale expected the move? But then the plant's move would not have been unexpected. Or does it mean simply that anyone buying or selling anything knows that the unexpected may happen? In either case the argument begs the question even as an argument that it is fair that the buyer bear the loss. For it assumes that it has already been established and understood by the parties that the buyer must bear the loss—otherwise the price would not have reflected just the risk that the plant would move, but also the risk that the buyer would be required to bear the loss if it did move.

But in any event it is just wrong to say, in either case, that the buyer consented to the loss. Perhaps, though the buyer knew that the plant would very likely move and that he was getting a bargain price because the seller expected that the buyer would bear the loss if the plant did move, the buyer hoped that he might be able to persuade some court to rescind the sale if the feared

---

18. *Id.* at 491-92.
19. *Id.* at 492 (footnote omitted).

move did take place or to persuade some legislature to bail him out. It would be fair, in these circumstances, for the court to refuse rescission, but dead wrong to say that the buyer had consented to bear the loss. The argument of fairness must stand on its own, that is, and gains nothing from any supposition about consent. Autonomy is simply not a concept here in play.

So Posner may have conflated interest and consent because he has conflated consent more generally with the grounds of fairness. A second clue is provided by his remarks about what he calls "implied consent."[20] He acknowledges that plaintiffs in negligence suits cannot be said to have consented expressly to rules of negligence rather than strict liability—even in the way he believes buyers of lottery tickets have consented to losing. But he says that courts can *impute* consent to such plaintiffs the way courts impute intentions to parties to a contract who have not spelled out every term, or to legislatures whose statutes are dark with ambiguity. Once again Posner's analogy betrays a confusion; in this case it is a confusion between unexpressed and counterfactual consent.

Lawyers disagree about how best to describe contractual or statutory interpretation. According to one theory, the court takes what the parties or the legislators say expressly as evidence—as clues to the existence of some individual or group psychological state which is an actual intention, though one that is never expressed formally in the requisite document. According to the competing theory, the court does not purport to discover such a hidden psychological state, but rather uses the fiction of an unexpressed psychological state as a vehicle for some argument about what the parties or the legislature would have done (or, perhaps, should have done) if they had attended to the issue now in question. These are different and competing theories of constructive intention, precisely because they describe very different justifications for a judicial decision. If a judge really has discovered a hidden but actual psychological state—some common understanding of parties to a contract or of members of a legislative group— then the fact of that common understanding provides a direct argument for his decision. But if the putative psychological state is fiction only, then the fiction can of course provide no argument in itself. In that case it is the arguments the judge himself deploys, about what the parties or the legislature would or should have

---

20. *Id.* at 494-95.

done, that do all the work, and the idea of consent plays no role whatsoever. When Posner says that the courts might impute consent to plaintiffs in automobile-accident cases, there can be no doubt which kind of description he means to suggest. He does not suppose that plaintiffs have really but secretly consented to negligence rules, taking a silent vow to that effect each morning before breakfast. He means that the imputed consent would be a fiction. He has in mind only counterfactual, not unexpressed, consent. But a counterfactual consent is not some pale form of consent. It is no consent at all.

The third clue Posner offers us is more interesting. He notices that Rawls (and Harsanyi and other economists) have built elaborate arguments for theories of justice that are based on counterfactual consent.[21] He means to make the same sort of argument, though, as he makes plain, he has in mind a different basis for counterfactual consent and a different theory of justice. He asks himself, not what parties to some original position would consent to under conditions of radical uncertainty, but what actual people, each of whom knows his particular situation in full detail, would consent to in the fullness of that understanding. He answers that they would consent, not to principles seeking maximin over wealth or even average utility, but to just those rules that common law judges concerned about maximizing social wealth would employ.

But Posner ignores the fact that Rawls' (and Harsanyi's) arguments have whatever force they do have just because the questions they describe must be answered under conditions of radical uncertainty. Indeed (as I have tried to make plain elsewhere[22]) Rawls' original position is a powerful mechanic for thinking about justice because the design of that position embodies and enforces the theory of deep equality described in the last part of this essay. It embodies that theory precisely through the stipulation that parties consent to principles of justice with no knowledge of any qualities or attributes that give them advantages over others, and with no knowledge of what conception of the good they hold as distinct from others.

Posner says that his own arguments improve on Rawls because Posner is concerned with actual people making choices under what he calls "natural" ignorance—he means, I suppose, ignorance about

---

21. *Id.* at 497-99.
22. R. DWORKIN, *supra* note 8, at ch. 6.

whether they will actually be unlucky—rather than under what he calls Rawls' "artificial" and more radical ignorance.[23] But this "improvement" is fatal. Posner does not contemplate, as we saw, actual consent. If he did, then the degree of "natural" ignorance to attribute to the choosers (or, what comes to the same thing, the date at which to define that ignorance) would be given. It would be the date of the actual, historical choice. But since Posner has in mind a counterfactual rather than an actual choice, any selection of a degree or date of ignorance must be wholly arbitrary, and different selections would dictate very different rules as fair. It would plainly be arbitrary, for example, to construct "natural" ignorance so that no one knew whether he was one of the few inveterate pedestrians whose expected welfare would be improved by strict liability rather than negligence rules for automobile accidents. But if natural ignorance does not exclude such self-knowledge, then Posner cannot claim that even the counterfactual consent would be unanimous. It must be a matter of the counterfactual choice of most people and that provides, as we shall see, not an improved version of a Rawlsian argument, but a utilitarian argument only.

In fact, the situation is worse even than that. For if only "natural" ignorance is in play, then there is no nonarbitrary reason to exclude the knowledge of those who know that they have already been unlucky—that is, the plaintiffs of the particular law suits the judge is asked to decide by imposing a wealth-maximizing rule. After all, at any moment, some people are in that position, and their consent will not be forthcoming then, even counterfactually. Posner plainly wants to invite consent under what turns out to be, not natural ignorance, but a tailored ignorance that is even more artifical than Rawls' original position. For any particular plaintiff, he wants to invite consent at some time after that person's driving habits are sufficiently well formed so that he is a gainer from reduced driving costs, but before the time he has suffered an uninsured nonnegligence accident. What time is that? Why is that time decisive? Rawls chose his original position, with its radical ignorance, for reasons of political morality: the original position, so defined, is a device for enforcing a theory of deep equality. Posner seems to be able to define his conditions of counterfactual choice only so as to reach the results he wants.

---

23. Posner, *supra* note 3, at 497-99.

The Argument from Interest

Posner's second main argument, as I said earlier, is an argument from the self-interest of most people. He offers to show that it is in the interest of almost everyone that judges decide common law cases by enforcing those rules that maximize social wealth. Even those people who do not drive, he notices, use motor vehicles—they take buses or are driven by others—and so gain from reduced driving costs. If a regime of negligence rules, rather than rules of strict liability, would reduce driving costs, and if nearly everyone would benefit overall from that reduction, then something very like a Pareto justification on the welfare space is available for negligence. Almost everyone is better off and almost no one is worse off. Of course not absolutely everyone will be better off—we can imagine someone who is always a pedestrian and never even a passenger—but "only a fanatic" would insist on complete unanimity when a Pareto justification is in play.[24]

This is Posner's argument from nonfanatical Paretianism, shorn of its autonomy or consent claims. What are we to make of it? We must first of all try to become clearer about whom the "almost everyone" proviso leaves out. Suppose I am an automobile driver who benefits steadily over my whole life from the reduced driving costs made possible by the institution of negligence. One day I am run down (on one of my rare walks around the block) by a nonnegligent driver, and I suffer medical and other costs far in excess of the amount I formerly saved from reduced driving costs, and will save from reduced ambulance charges and motorized wheelchair costs in the future. In what sense do I benefit from a regime of negligence, which denies me recovery, over a regime of strict liability? Only in the sense of what might be called my antecedent self-interest. I was better off under the system of negligence before I was run down, at least on the reasonable assumption that I had no more chance of being run down than any one else. After all (by hypothesis) I could have bought insurance against being run down with part of what I saved, as a motorist, from the lower driving costs. But of course *after* the accident (if I have not in fact bought such insurance) I would be better off under a system of strict liability. The difference can also be expressed not temporally, but as a difference in expected welfare under different states of knowledge. When I do not know that it is I who will be run down, my expected welfare is higher under negligence. When I do know that,

---

24. *Id*. at 495.

my expected welfare is higher under strict liability.

But what is the appropriate point (expressed either temporally or as a function of knowledge) at which to calculate my expected welfare? Suppose my case is a hard case at law because it has not yet been decided in my jurisdiction whether negligence or strict liability governs cases like mine. (It is, after all, just in such hard cases that we need a theory of adjudication like the one Posner proposes.) Now the fact that I would have been better off, before my accident, under a system of negligence seems irrelevant. I did not in fact have the benefits of a negligence rule. In such a case the question—under which rule will everyone be better off—must look to the future only. And I, for one, will not be better off under negligence. I will be better off under strict liability.

But suppose it is said that at least everyone else—or everyone else except the few who walk and never drive or are driven—will be better off. Only I and these inveterate pedestrians will be worse off. Is that true? It is true that (ignoring these inveterate pedestrians) everyone else's expected welfare, fixed at the time of my lawsuit, will be improved. But it is not true that everyone's actual welfare will be improved. For there will be some who will not, in fact, take out the appropriate insurance, and who will be unlucky. They will suffer so much uncompensated loss from nonnegligent accidents that they would have been better off, ex post, had the court laid down a regime of strict liability in my case, even when their reduced driving costs in the meantime, and their reduced ambulance costs thereafter, have been taken into account. Suppose you are one of these unlucky people. You sue. You cannot say that you have had no benefit from the system of negligence, but you nevertheless suggest that the system of negligence be abandoned now and strict liability instituted, starting with your case.

It cannot be said, as a reason for refusing your request, that you in fact gained more than you lost from the decision in my case. You did not—you lost more than you gained. But suppose it were true that you gained more than you lost. Let me change the facts once again so that that is so. Suppose that your present accident arises near the end of your expected life and that you did arrange insurance after the decision in my case so that you will now suffer only a short-lived increase in your premium if you lose your case. You have gained more in reduced driving costs in the meantime than you will lose even if you lose your case. Nevertheless it is not true that you will gain more *in the future* if the judge in your case refuses your request and maintains the system of negligence. Even under the new set of facts you will gain more if strict liability is now instituted, starting with your case. Otherwise (being rational) you would not have made the request that you did.

I hope the point is now clear. If we set out to justify any particular common law decisions on Pareto grounds, then the class of exceptions—the class of those worse off through the decision—must include, at a minimum, those who lose the lawsuit and others in like cases. It does not improve the Pareto justification that the rule now imposed would have increased the expected welfare of the loser had it been imposed earlier. Nor that the rule was in fact imposed earlier so that his expected welfare was in fact increased at some earlier date. Nor that, because the rule was in fact imposed earlier, the loser in the present suit gained more from that past rule than he now loses. Each of these is irrelevant because a Pareto justification is a forward-looking, not a backward-looking, justification. It proposes that a decision is right because no one is worse off through *that* decision being taken. But then all those who are worse off from a forward-looking point of view must stand as counter examples to a proposed Pareto justification. Of course these different *backward*-looking considerations might well be relevant to a different kind of justification of a judicial decision. They might, in particular, be relevant to a familiar sort of argument from fairness. (I shall, in fact, consider that argument later.) But they are not relevant to a Pareto justification, which justification Posner is at pains to supply.

Is Posner saved here by his caveat, that only a fanatic would insist on absolute unanimity? Perhaps it does sound fanatical to insist that every last person must benefit—or at least not lose—before any social decision is taken. If we accepted that constraint almost no social decision would be justified. Nevertheless that is exactly what the Pareto criterion requires. It insists that no one be worse off, and if any one is, then the Pareto justification is not simply weakened; it is destroyed. Pareto is all or nothing, like pregnancy and legal death.

Why? Because unless the Pareto criterion is treated as all or nothing, as fanatical in this way, it simply collapses into the utilitarian criterion. In particular, it assumes the burden of both the conceptual and the moral defects of utilitarian theories. Suppose we state the Pareto criterion in the following, nonfanatical way: "A political (including a judicial) decision is justified if it will make the vast bulk of people better off and only a relatively few people worse off." Surely we must interpret this test so as to take account of the quantity of welfare gained or lost as well as the numbers who gain or lose. Otherwise it might justify devastating losses to a few in exchange for such trivial gains to the many that the sum of the latter, on any reckoning, falls short of the sum of the former. But when we do introduce the dimension of quantity of welfare gained and lost we also introduce the familiar problems of interpersonal comparisons of utility. One important claim for the Pareto criterion is that it avoids such comparisons; if it turns out not to avoid them after all, then this claim must be withdrawn.

A second claim for the Pareto criterion is a claim of political morality. Utilitarianism faces the problem of explaining to someone who loses in a Benthamite calculation why it is fair to make him suffer simply so that others may prosper. Critics of utilitarianism hold that any Benthamite justification offered to him will commit what I have called the ambiguous sin of ignoring the difference between people.[25] Now if a fanatical Pareto justification is available for a given political decision, then this problem—explaining why someone must be worse off in order that others be better off—is avoided. I do not mean that Pareto justifications are wholly unproblematical. Someone who holds a deep-egalitarian theory of absolute equality of welfare will object to a decision that makes some better off and no one worse off if that decision destroys a preexisting absolute equality of welfare. But fanatical Pareto justifications do avoid the obviously more serious problem of justifying losses to some so that others may gain.

It is important to see, moreover, that this is not a problem of the numbers of who lose. Suppose only one person loses in a Benthamite calculation. If the fact that the gain to others outweighs, in total, the loss to that one person provides a justification for the loss to him, then that same justification must obviously be available when the number of losers increases to any number, provided, of course, that the aggregate gain still exceeds the aggregate loss. The issue of principle is raised, decisively, in the individual case. That is the eye of the needle; if utility can pass through that eye it gains heaven. So our relaxed Pareto criterion can have no advantage of political morality over straightforward Benthamism. Nonfanatical Paretianism is utilitarianism merely.

It is time for a reckoning. Posner is pleased to claim that wealth maximization combines the most appealing features of both the Kantian concern with autonomy and the utilitarian concern with individual preferences, while avoiding the excesses of either of these traditional theories. His argument from counterfactual consent is meant to supply the Kantian features. But this is spuri-

---

25. See R. DWORKIN, supra note 8, at 233.

ous: In fact the idea of consent does no work at all in the theory and the appeal to autonomy is therefore a facade. His argument from the common interest is meant to supply the utilitarian features. But it does this too well. He cannot claim a genuine Pareto justification for common law decisions, in either hard or easy cases. His relaxed version of Paretianism is simply utilitarianism with all the warts. The voyage of his present essay ends in the one traditional theory he was formerly most anxious to disown.

Beyond Consent and Interest

Can we discover, in Posner's various discussions, some more attractive argument of fairness than those he makes explicitly? The following general principle (we may call it the antecedent-interest principle) seems somehow in play. If a rule is in everyone's antecedent interest at the time it is enacted, then it is fair to enforce that rule even against those who turn out, in the event, to lose by its adoption, provided that they were, in advance, no more likely to lose by it than others were. That is not, as we have seen, the Pareto criterion, nor will everyone agree that it is, in fact, a fair principle. Indeed I shall provide reasons to doubt it. But it has enough initial appeal for us to ask whether it provides a base for Posner's arguments for wealth maximization in adjudication.

The antecedent-interest principle cannot, of course, be used directly in favor of any particular wealth-maximizing rule a judge might adopt, for the first time, in a hard case. For any particular rule will fail the test the principle provides: It will not be in the interest of the party against whom it is used at the time of its adoption, because the time of its adoption is just the time at which it is used against him. But the antecedent-interest principle does seem to support a *meta*-rule of adjudication (call it alpha) which provides that in a hard case judges should choose and apply that rule, if any, that is in the then antecedent interests of the vast bulk of people though not in the interests of the party who then loses. Once alpha has been in force in a community for some time, at least, alpha itself meets the antecedent-interest-principle test. For each individual, alpha may unhappily make it more likely that some rule will be adopted that will work against his interests. For inveterate pedestrians, for example, alpha may make it more likely that the negligence rule will be adopted. But since each individual will gain through the adoption of other rules in virtue of alpha—inveterate pedestrians will gain through all manner of common law rules that work in their benefit as well as the benefit of most others—it may plausibly be said that alpha *itself* is in the antecedent interest of

absolutely everyone. But even if it turns out that this is wrong—
that a certain economic or other minority exists such that that minority characteristically loses by a wide range of particular rules
meeting the test of alpha—then alpha can be suitably amended.
Let us therefore restate alpha this way: In a hard case, judges
should choose that rule, if any, that is in the then antecedent interests of the vast bulk of people and not against the interests of the
worst-off economic group or any other group that would be generally and antecedently disadvantaged, as a group, by the enforcement of this principle without this qualification.

Now Posner believes that alpha (taken hereafter to be amended
in this way) would require judges to adopt a wealth-maximizing
test for common law adjudication, at least in general. If this is so,
then the combination of the antecedent-interest rule and alpha
might seem to provide an argument of fairness in favor of (at least
general) wealth-maximizing adjudication at common law. That
would be an important conclusion and, in my opinion, a clear advance over previous attempts to justify wealth maximization as a
standard for adjudication. It is more convincing to argue that, under the conditions of common law adjudication, wealth-maximizing
rules are fair, than to say either that wealth is good in itself or that
it is causally related to other, independently stated, goods in such
a way as to justify instrumentally the doctrine that society should
single-mindedly pursue wealth.

So we have good reason to ask whether the antecedent-
interest principle is fair. We should notice that if that principle
could be sensibly applied by the parties to Rawls' original position,
and if they chose to apply it, then they would select the principle
of average utility as the fundamental principle of justice rather than
the principles Rawls says they would select, (Harsanyi and others,
as Posner reminds us, have argued for average utility in just this
way.) We can immediately see one reason, however, why parties to
the original position, under one description of their interests,
would not accept the antecedent-interest principle. If they were
conservative about risks and adopted a maximin strategy for that
reason, they would avoid the principle, because it works against
those who in one way or another have very bad luck.

We have already seen why this is so. Suppose alpha has been
in force for generations. But the question of whether negligence or
strict liability holds for automobile accidents has never been settled. Some person who is injured by a nonnegligent driver, and is
uninsured, finds that a court, responding to alpha, chooses a negligence rule, and he is therefore ruined by medical expenses. He ar-

gues that this is unfair. It is not an appealing reply that the economic group to which he belongs gains along with everyone else under a regime of negligence. He loses. Nor is it necessarily true that, as things turned out, he gained more than he lost from alpha being accepted in his community. It is hard to guess at how much he gained. We should have to ask what other arguments were in favor of the rules that were adopted earlier in virtue of alpha in order to decide whether the same rules would have been adopted even if alpha had been rejected from the outset. But if he is absolutely ruined by his uncompensated accident he might well be better off, ex post, had alpha never been recognized.

Suppose we say to him, in reply to his complaint, that he should have known that alpha would settle any case testing negligence against strict liability for accidents, should have calculated that alpha required negligence, and should have purchased appropriate insurance against nonnegligent injury. He will answer, with some force, that we have begged every important question. First, it does not follow, from the fact that alpha in fact recommends negligence, that the argument that it does was, in the appropriate sense, publicly available. That argument might rest on reasonably recondite economic analysis developed and worked through for the first time in connection with this litigation. Second, our reply assumes that alpha is fair, so that he should have made provisions for insurance in its light, though that is just what he questions. He did not, of course, consent to alpha just because it was in his antecedent interest when established—that claim simply repeats Posner's initial mistake. Nor does he accept that it is fair to impose some standard on him just because he has had some benefit from it in the past, particularly if he had no choice whether to accept that benefit.[26] We must show that the principle of antecedent interest is fair, not just assume it.

We shall clarify these objections, I think, if we construct a different principle (call it beta). Beta is not, in its basic formulation, a principle for adjudication, as alpha is, but it furnishes one. Beta is basically a theory of social responsibility. We might formulate it in its most abstract form this way. People should take responsibility for such costs of accidents (defined, as elsewhere in this Article, broadly) if responsibility for such costs would be assigned to them by legislation in an ideal community in which everyone acted and voted with a sense of justice and with mutual and equal concern

---

26. *See* Simmons, *The Principle of Fair Play*, 8 PHILOSOPHY & PUB. AFF. 307 (1979).

and respect, based on information that is also easily, publicly, and reliably available to the actor. Beta (stated at that level of abstraction) might well be said to be only a schema for a principle of responsibility not a principle itself. Reasonable people who accept it will nevertheless disagree about what it requires because they disagree about how just people would act and vote. (Beta, we might say, admits of different interpretations or conceptions.) But even put so abstractly beta is far from empty. On the contrary, it is very demanding—perhaps too demanding—because it proposes to enforce legislation that would be adopted in certain unlikely circumstances but in fact has not yet been. Beta is a strong theory of responsibility because it is a theory of natural responsibility tied to counterfactual propositions about legislation. Someone might intelligibly believe that beta requires people to take responsibility themselves for the costs of nonnegligent accidents, and yet deny that they should do so until and unless the legislation described in beta is actually in force. He accepts, that is, that beta requires some particular assumption of responsibility, but rejects beta.

Though beta is a theory of natural responsibility, it furnishes a recommendation for adjudication, particularly against the background of a general theory of adjudication, which argues that, in principle, natural rights and duties should be enforced in court. Suppose someone now says, however, that beta is in fact nothing but alpha. Or (perhaps a bit more plausibly) that alpha is one interpretation or conception of beta. Either would be a mistake, and a serious confusion. For alpha will, under certain circumstances all too familiar, recommend judicial decisions that no plausible interpretation of beta could countenance. Suppose, as we just imagined, that a particular rule will in fact meet the requirements of alpha, but for reasons that are neither familiar nor generally available but are developed in adjudication in just the way in which recondite economic data or analysis might properly be developed looking towards legislation. Alpha will insist that that rule must be applied to someone who, even though aware of alpha, could not reliably have anticipated the rule. Beta, of course, will not eliminate all surprises: If people disagree radically about what it requires, because they disagree about the underlying moral issues, then someone may indeed be surprised by its application. But the grounds and incidents of this surprise differ greatly between the two principles.

A second difference seems to me more important. Consider the following familiar argument about the consequences of a principle like alpha. Suppose considerations of fairness recommend that members of some group—the poor, for example, or the uneducated—should have certain contractual privileges or immunities, either through special rules or through general rules that will have special importance for people in their situation. But if a court adopts such a rule members of that group will in fact suffer in the long run, because merchants or other contractors will be less likely to contract with them, or will insist on compensatory price increases or other conditions, or will in some other way thwart the purpose of the rule in question. Alpha now argues against the immediately protective rule. If alpha is followed, someone loses in the present case who is told that, although fairness would justify a decision for him if his case could be considered on its own merits, he must lose in order to protect others in his economic class in the future. Beta, on the other hand, argues the other way. It regards the fact that others would act so as to undermine the requirements of fairness as irrelevant to the question of natural responsibility, and so irrelevant to the question put for adjudication. The merchants who will ignore the claims of the disadvantaged group, claims we assume *arguendo* to be required by justice, are not behaving as they would in the counterfactual conditions stipulated for fixing natural responsibility.

Legislators would be wiser, no doubt, to consider the real world rather than these counterfactual conditions, and so to prefer alpha to beta as a guide for forward-looking legislation about contractual immunities, responsibility for accidents, and so forth. Some people might think that judges deciding hard cases at law should also prefer alpha to beta, though others, perhaps more sensitive to the differences between the questions put to the two instituitions, will disagree. My present point is only that beta is different from alpha, both in what it requires and in its philosophical basis.

But beta will in fact require much of what alpha requires. If Posner is right about the fact and the distribution of the cost savings under a negligence rule, for example, both beta and alpha will recommend a regime of negligence rather than strict liability over a certain range of cases. Under even more plausible assumptions beta as well as alpha will recommend some version of the Hand test[27] as the basis for computing negligence. Perhaps beta as well as alpha would characteristically recommend wealth-maximizing rules for the sorts of disputes that come to adjudication under common law. (Perhaps beta would recommend the wealth-maximizing rule in more of such cases than alpha would.)

---

27. *See* United States v. Carroll Towing Co., 159 F.2d 169, 173 (2d Cir. 1947).

What conclusions should we draw? Beta seems to me inherently more attractive as a guide to adjudication than alpha does. Beta is itself a principle about natural responsibility, and so, as a guide for adjudication, unites adjuducation and private morality and permits the claim that a decision in a hard case, assigning responsibility to some party, simply recognizes that party's moral responsibility. Alpha is not itself a principle of responsibility at all, but only a guide to wise forward-looking legislation. It must rely on the antecedent-interest principle to supply an argument of fairness in adjuducation, and that principle (as we noticed in considering the complaints of someone who loses when alpha is applied) is seriously flawed.

In any case, however, there is a fatal objection to relying on the combination of alpha and the antecedent-interest principle to justify wealth-maximizing decisions in our own legal system. I skirted over this problem in explaining the argument for alpha, but must confront it now. The antecedent-interest principle could never justify introducing alpha itself in a hard case, for if some member of the then community loses who would not otherwise have lost—either the losing party in that case or someone else— then the antecedent-interest principle is violated. It is only after alpha has been in force for some time that it could be in the antecedent interests of every *then* member of the community to ̂nave introduced it. It can never be fair to introduce alpha for the first time (if the fairness of doing so depends on the antecedent-interest principle) though the unfairness of having introduced it may disappear over time.

Is this a boring technical point, calling attention only to some presumed unfairness in a past long dead, or something of practical importance? That depends on what is taken to be the adoption of alpha. Can we say that alpha has already been adopted as a principle of adjudication within a legal system when the decisions the courts have reached (or tended to reach) are the same as the decisions that alpha would have required had it been expressly adopted? Or only when alpha has in fact been expressly adopted and relied on in reaching those decisions? The antecedent-interest principle supports alpha only after alpha has been adopted in the second sense. That principle supposes a moment at which people's antecedent or expected welfare is improved by a social decision to adjudicate in a certain way, and that moment is not supplied simply by a set of decisions that would have been reached by an institution that had taken that decision. For no one's expected welfare would be improved in the way alpha promises simply by a course of decisions, however consistent with alpha, that did not carry a commitment to enforce alpha generally, and this is true even if that course of decisions worked to enforce alpha not by coincidence, but through some invisible hand, or even by the subconscious motivation of judges. What is essential is a commitment, and that can be achieved only by adoption in the second sense.

But since that is so, alpha has never been adopted in our own legal system in the pertinent sense, even if the positive claims of Posner and others about the explanatory power of wealth maximization are accepted in full. So we cannot rely on alpha to show that wealth-maximizing decisions in the past were fair through some combination of alpha and the antecedent-interest principle. Nor can we rely on that combination to justify any wealth-maximizing decisions in the future. On a more careful look, that is, alpha drops away as a candidate for the basis of a normative theory of wealth maximization.

We might well be left with beta. Beta does not, of course, rely on the antecedent-interest principle in the way alpha did. Beta is itself a principle of fairness—it is, as I said, a principle of natural responsibility—and though it will seem to some too demanding, it requires no help from the antecedent-interest principle to count as an argument of fairness in adjudication. So it is irrelevant that beta has never been expressly recognized as a commitment of our legal system. It carries, as it were, its own claims to be a principle of fairness. If it can be shown that past decisions were those that beta would have justified, that does count as an argument that these decisions were fair. If the same can be shown for future decisions, that, without more, recommends these decisions as fair.

So it would be well to carry further than I have here the possibility that beta requires common law decisions that (at least over a certain range of cases) are just those decisions that maximize wealth. If beta does have that consequence, then a Kantian justification of wealth maximization may indeed be available. Posner's long search for a philosophical basis for his normative theory of adjudication may therefore end in what seemed, at the beginning, unlikely territory for him. For the roots of Kantian morality (as beta practically shouts) are deeply egalitarian. Incidentally, at the close of his letter Calabresi seems to use "policy" as I use "principle." So it appears we do agree about the role of principle in adjudication though perhaps still disagree about what principle requires.

PART TWO
Economic Analysis Applied:
The Law of Torts

Introduction to Part Two

In this anthology, we have decided to devote a large section to the economic analysis of tort law. There are several reasons for concentrating on this particular area of the law to the exclusion of others. First, torts are actions that are often legitimate in themselves but nevertheless have harmful consequences that are generally unintended.[1] The tortfeasor, therefore, is usually seen as being less culpable than the criminal. As a consequence, the moral quality of a tortious act is sufficiently ambiguous to make economic efficiency a potentially persuasive justification for regulating the activity. A second and no doubt related point is that the explicit use of economic analysis in judicial decisions in tort cases has a long history, dating back at least to the Hand Rule. It is reasonable, then, to expect that the recent outpouring of academic writing concerning the economic analysis of law will have its greatest impact on torts. Therefore, if the legal practitioner is to study only one area in the new literature, torts is the appropriate choice.

More important for our purposes, however, is the fact that economic analysis has been rigorously applied to torts so that the strengths and weaknesses of the method are clearly visible. In contrast, much of economic analysis in other areas of the law is at a level of generality that would justify almost any assertion about the "efficiency" of various legal rules. The readings reprinted in this anthology are, we believe, the best in the existing literature. Unfortunately, some are rather technical, but the mathematical analysis is invoked only when necessary to do the job correctly. We feel that only such an in-depth treatment can provide a true understanding of both the particular subject and the general method of economic analysis. Clearly, such an understanding requires more work on the reader's part, and the purpose of this introduction is to help the reader along.

Almost all analysts agree that tort law has two main purposes: (1) the regulation of tort-producing activity, and (2) the distribution of accident losses. The economic analysis of tort law defines each of these purposes in terms of the achievement of a particular goal. The goal of regulation is the minimization of total accident costs, which are generally defined to include the accident losses of victims and the prevention costs of injurers. The goal of distribution is the minimization of the welfare loss that results from insufficient risk spreading. In this introduction, we will occasionally adopt Guido Calabresi's shorthand terminology for these costs:[2] for future reference, total accident costs are equivalent to Calabresi's primary accident costs, and the welfare loss due to insufficient risk spreading is equivalent to Calabresi's secondary accident costs.

In economic analysis, tort law is conceived of as providing two instruments for the achievement of these goals: a due care standard and a liability rule. The due care standard specifies a level of care and defines parties who take less care to be at fault. There are, then, four possible combinations of victim and injurer fault. A liability rule is applied to these combinations in order to determine whether compensation should be paid and remuneration exacted. The tort dilemma is that it is not always possible through the use of these two instruments to achieve both goals. This is true whether the goals are defined as in economic analysis or by some alternative system.

Our readings begin with an article by Guido Calabresi and Jon Hirschoff that can be viewed as providing an agenda for the research carried out in the next three papers. In this article the authors introduce four concepts that will form the basis for this introduction:

1. the Hand Rule as a due care standard
2. the concept of least-cost avoider
3. the concept of reverse- or mirror-image liability rules, and
4. the appropriate liability rule under imperfect information.

The articles by John Brown and Steven Shavell that follow either clarify or amend the Calabresi-Hirschoff analysis of these concepts. This introduction will discuss each idea in turn, referring to the articles as necessary.

The Hand Rule implicitly specifies a due care standard that defines a party to be at fault if expected accident losses are greater than the prevention costs that the party has undertaken. Expected accident losses are defined as the probability of an accident occurring multiplied by the size of the accident loss when it occurs. Calabresi and Hirschoff note that such a due care standard will not in general produce an efficient outcome, but they do not explain why the standard is flawed. The problem is that the standard is based on the total costs and benefits of taking care and not on the marginal costs and benefits. Brown's article makes this clear in the distinction between the "Literal Learned Hand Standard" and the "Full Information Incremental Standard" where the latter is based on marginal costs and benefits. Obedience to the Literal Hand Standard will in general result in too much care being taken because in order to be faultless, each party must take care up to the point that the next increment of care results in total prevention costs greater than or equal to total benefits. To be faultless, then, implies that so much care is being taken that the social benefit of care has fallen to zero. The *efficient* last unit of care, on the other hand, is the unit whose *own* cost equals its benefit in accident reduction; it is not the unit whose benefit is so low in comparison to its cost that it negates all of the net benefit that has been accumulated by all previous units of care.

Calabresi and Hirschoff then proceed to define the least-cost avoider as the party "in the best position to make the cost-benefit analysis between accident costs and accident avoidance costs and to act on that decision once it is made."[3] This definition introduces two components of least-cost avoidance that for the moment it is useful to separate: knowledge and the ability to act. Concentrating on the second, a more precise definition of the least-cost avoider is given by Brown as the party who, by taking an *extra* unit of care, more effectively reduces accident losses per dollar expended on care. This definition differs from Calabresi and Hirschoff's only in the sense that it uses the correct marginal concept of the benefits and costs of taking care, and not the total concept embodied in the Hand Rule.

After developing their concept of least-cost avoider, Calabresi and Hirschoff suggest that strict liability be applied to that party—this procedure has been termed the Calabresi-Hirschoff Rule. In order to make the Rule comparable to traditional tort concepts, one can think of it as a symmetric negligence rule where fault is determined on the basis of the Calabresi-Hirschoff definition of least-cost avoider. The rule is symmetric in the sense that either the injurer or the victim could be found at fault and have liability imposed upon him. It is a negligence rule in the sense that this liability cannot be reversed by the behavior of the other party—that is, the defense of contributory negligence is not available. Since strict liability is conventionally only applied to injurers, we find this alternative terminology preferable even if, in practice, injurers tend to be the least-cost avoiders.

Viewed in this way, the Calabresi-Hirschoff Rule is very similar to Brown's Relative Negligence Rule. The Rule, in either form, would be very useful if: (1) it were easier to define liability on the basis of relative avoidance ability than it is to define efficient due care standards, and (2) the parties responded to the Rule by taking the efficient amount of care. Here, however, the Rule runs afoul of a subtle interdependency between the care taken by each party. It is usual and reasonable to assume that in terms of reducing accident probabilities, the care taken by one party is a partial substitute for the care taken by the other. In other words, the less care taken by one party, the more "productive" is the care taken by the other, and alternatively, the more care taken by one party, the less "productive" is its own care in comparison to the care taken by the other. This interdependency implies that no one party is in general the least-cost avoider for all care levels. A potential solution is to evaluate relative abilities to take care at a fixed point such as the efficient levels of care for both parties, but the information required to make this determination is identical to the information needed to calculate the efficient due care standards themselves.

An alternative solution seems to be to announce that liability will be imposed on the least-cost avoider where that determination is made on the basis of the care observed at the time of the accident. Unfortunately, both Brown and Calabresi-Hirschoff are in error in believing that the parties will respond to this Rule by taking the efficient amount of care. The problem, once again, is the interdependency of care. At the efficient-care levels, the incentive exists for each party to take more care, cease being the least-cost avoider, and thereby impose liability on the other. The Rule, then, is not operational in the sense that either it requires as much information as conventional tort regimes or it does not create the correct incentives. There seems to be no alternative to the courts actually defining the efficient due care standard for each party and using that level of care in the determination of fault.

But, if the courts set the due care standard at the efficient level, then Brown's results translate into the statement that *all* fault-related liability rules are efficient. In other words, every liability rule, with the exception of strict liability, results in the minimization of primary accident costs. This is the first important result of the mathematical literature, and it should be contrasted with many of the verbal answers given to the problem. For example, it has been argued that negligence with a defense of contributory negligence is superior in terms of efficiency to simple negligence because the defense of contributory negligence gives the victim an incentive to take care. On the other hand, it has been argued that the defense is inefficient because it reduces the incentive of the injurer to take care since it introduces the possibility of escaping liability if the victim is also at fault. What the Brown paper proves is that with full information all of these arguments are irrelevant: *all fault-related liability rules are efficient.* The choice between liability rules can then be made solely on equity grounds.

Calabresi and Hirschoff also introduce the concept of reverse- or mirror-image liability rules. For someone who has not studied tort law extensively, their description of these rules is fairly difficult to follow. Brown, however, provides a graphical analysis of the differing concepts that should greatly aid the reader. For ease of comparison, Calabresi and Hirschoff's Reverse Hand Rule is equivalent to Brown's Strict Liability with Contributory Negligence and their Reverse Hand Rule with a Defense of Contributory Negligence is equivalent to Brown's Strict Liability with Dual Contributory Negligence.

Both of the contributions by Steven Shavell deserve the reader's serious attention because they illustrate in a dramatic way the sensitivity of results in this field to the underlying assumptions about the accident technology and the environment within which accidents occur. By "accident technology," we mean the physical circumstances that affect the probability and severity of accidents. In the first paper, Shavell considers two pairs of alternative technologies: (1) accidents where the care taken by one or both parties matters for the probability of the accident (that is, unilateral versus bilateral accidents), and (2) accidents where the level at which the parties pursue the tort-producing activity does or does not affect the number of accidents in a given period of time. We already know from Brown that, with full information, all fault-related liability rules are efficient. Yet, when one adds the possibility that the intensity of tort-producing activity affects accident probabilities, *none of the liability rules are efficient.* This is because tort law only regulates the level of care and not the intensity of use. For example, tort law investigates the care a party takes prior to a given automobile accident but does not ask how many miles the party has driven in the past month. Unfortunately, it is *very* difficult to think of accidents where the level at which the activity is pursued does not, for any given level of care, influence the number of accidents per unit of time. Tort law is, consequently, a very imperfect system through which to attempt to achieve efficiency.

By "the environment within which accidents occur," we mean the social institutions that surround the accident. In the first paper, Shavell considers the issue of whether the accident occurs in the process of a market transaction, such as in product liability; in the second paper, he considers the issue of whether there exists first-party and/or liability insurance. The question of asymmetric information arises in both environments: in the first with respect to the consumer's knowledge of the quality, or inherent safety, of the product he is buying, and in the second with respect to an insurer's knowledge of the safety precautions being taken by the insured.

The first type of asymmetry relates directly to Calabresi and Hirschoff's concept of the least-cost avoider as the party with the most knowledge and therefore in the best position to make the cost-benefit analysis. Tables 1, 2, and 3 in Shavell's first paper indicate how the efficiency of various liability rules changes as the assumed level of consumer information deteriorates. Table 1 analyzes the case of unilateral accidents and supports Calabresi and Hirschoff's contention that strict liability is the appropriate rule. This case, however, is weighted in favor of that outcome because in unilateral accidents consumers have no influence on accident probabilities. Recalling the Calabresi-Hirschoff concept of least-cost avoider, there is in such cases no conflict between knowledge and the ability to take action. Table 2 extends the analysis to the case where consumers can influence the probability of accidents by taking care and concludes that strict liability with a defense of contributory negligence is efficient, but strict liability by itself is not. The reason, of course, is that the defense of contributory negligence serves to regulate the consumer's behavior while simple strict liability does not. In such cases, therefore, it is wrong to conclude, as Calabresi and Hirschoff do, that the courts have chosen strict liability over the Reverse Hand Rule (i.e., strict liability with contributory negligence) because they favor efficient outcomes as opposed to simply favoring victims. Quite the opposite seems to be the case.

Finally, Table 3 analyzes the case where victim activity levels as well as care levels influence accident probabilities. Under full information, negligence and no liability are the efficient rules despite the fact that we previously stated that when activity levels are considered there are, in general, no efficient rules. The reason for this seeming inconsistency is that Table 3 only considers accidents that occur in the process of market transactions. Liability rules are not the only form of social regulation; markets also regulate behavior. Competitive markets, however, place more constraints on producers than on consumers and therefore regulate behavior asymmetrically. It is sometimes thought that producers can create any kind of shoddy or unsafe product and somehow convince consumers to buy it. But, if consumers have correct information about the product, producers of products with the efficient amount of safety will be able to make the highest profits becaue the efficiently safe product has the lowest "true" cost. The "true" cost equals the stated price of the product plus the cost to the consumer of the product's inherent danger. While the market thereby constrains producer behavior, consumers remain free to take what care they wish. Therefore, rules such as no liability and negligence, which place much of the burden on consumers, are more attractive in terms of efficiency. As consumer information deteriorates, however, the concern that faulty products will be marketed increases, and rules that place more liability on producers become more attractive. This is the spirit of the Calabresi-Hirschoff Rule, but one must always balance these incentives for producer care against the disincentives for consumer care: there is no totally efficient liability rule in such cases.

In his second paper, Shavell presents a systematic discussion of how competitive insurance markets deal with the second goal of tort law—the distribution of accident losses. From an efficiency standpoint, this goal reduces to a desire to minimize the secondary accident costs that result from insufficient risk spreading. The difficulty is that in the process of distributing losses incentives are changed, so that while moving toward the goal of minimizing secondary accident costs, one may be increasing primary accident costs. Shavell studies the particular case of unilateral accidents and compares strict liability with negligence. Concentrating on unilateral accidents simplifies the problem because the victim's care level is no longer relevant; unfortunately, as the reader will discover, the analysis remains fairly difficult. In order to make the discussion manageable, we will divide the paper into four parts:

1. the totally efficient, or first-best, solution (Proposition 1)
2. feasible, or second-best, solutions without insurance (Propositions 2 and 3)
3. feasible, and totally efficient, solutions in an insurance market with full information (Propositions 4 and 5), and
4. feasible solutions in an insurance market with imperfect information (Propositions 4 and 5).

The totally efficient solution involves injurers taking the efficient amount of care and both parties completely insured in the sense that their welfare is independent of whether or not an accident occurs.

Shavell then discusses the possibility of achieving this solution without insurance markets. Since insurance markets exist precisely to even out an individual's welfare across favorable and unfavorable events, a totally efficient solution without these markets is usually not attainable.[4] Shavell labels the attainable solutions "Pareto efficient," but this usage of the term "efficient" should be *carefully* distinguished from the usage of the term throughout this introduction *and* throughout most of the law and economics literature. As previously applied, the term "efficient" has referred to totally efficient, or "first-best," solutions. Shavell's solutions are the most efficient *given* that insurance markets are either imperfect or nonexistent; they are what economists call "second-best" solutions.

Given that the lack of insurance markets implies that a totally efficient solution does not exist, the choice between strict liability and negligence involves a decision as to which party one is more interested in insuring through the tort system, combined with a consideration of the adverse incentives with respect to primary accident costs that such insurance creates. Specifically, under strict liability the best feasible outcome involves injurers paying only a portion of the victim's accident losses. *A priori,* one cannot determine whether injurers will take the efficient level of care in these circumstances. If injurers were risk neutral, the requirement that they only pay partial compensation would certainly induce them to take less than the first-best level of care. For risk averse injurers, however, the outcome is ambiguous because they have a greater incentive to reduce the probability of accidents for which they are required to pay even partial damages. While we cannot, on a theoretical basis, predict whether too many or too few accidents will occur, the first-best is certainly not achieved because neither victims nor injurers are fully insulated from the costs of the accidents that do occur. Secondary accident costs are not minimized, and it is unlikely, though possible, that primary accident costs are minimized.

Against the second-best losses under strict liability, one must weigh the losses associated with a negligence rule where the optimal due care standard is set higher than the first-best level. If the due care standard were set at the first-best level, then injurers would obey it and minimize primary accident costs, but victims would be left to bear the burden of all accidents that occurred. Contrary to statements that one may find in the literature, this solution is not the best *in terms of efficiency* even though it minimizes the sum of accident losses and prevention costs. A better solution is to raise the due care standard and provide victims with partial insurance in the form of a reduced number of accidents, even at the cost of "excessive" prevention activity.

The existence of insurance markets where insurers have complete information about the care taken by injurers results in a first-best solution with *either* liability rule. Under strict liability, injurers buy full-coverage liability insurance with premiums dependent upon the care they take. Given this dependence, injurers are induced to take the first-best level of care so as to minimize their premiums. Under negligence, the due care standard is set at the first-best level; injurers obey the standard and remain nonnegligent and victims buy full-coverage, first-party insurance. In this case, the choice between liability rules can be based solely on equity considerations with regard to which party should bear the actuarial cost of accidents.

If insurers do not have complete information about the care taken by injurers, then the problem returns to the world of the second best. Under strict liability, injurers will be forced to pay full compensation and will buy incomplete liability insurance coverage in order to help pay off claims against them. Insurance companies must offer incomplete coverage in order to induce injurers to take care since the companies cannot directly monitor care and make premiums dependent upon it. The level of care taken by injurers under this system is subject to two opposing forces: the nonobservability of care discovrages accident prevention activity, while partial insurance encourages it. *A priori,* one cannot predict what level of care will be the outcome of these opposing forces. The careful reader may be interested in knowing that the reason for this ambiguity is identical to the one noted previously. Shavell shows that the result under strict liability and incomplete insurance is identical to a result under strict liability where the state prohibits liability insurance but requires injurers to pay only partial compensation. This second alternative, however, is precisely the first ambiguous case analyzed above.

Under negligence, injurers have a choice of either taking sufficient care so as not to be found negligent or taking insufficient care and buying liability insurance. Since insurance companies will have to adjust their premiums for the fact that they cannot observe care, these imperfect insurance contracts will necessarily be less attractive to injurers than self-insurance (i.e., taking care equal to the legal standard). Injurers will, therefore, choose to take sufficient care because this is cheaper than buying imperfect insurance. If the legal standard is set so as to minimize primary accident costs, victims will buy full-coverage, first-party insurance and a first-best solution is achieved. Given imperfect insurance markets, it appears that negligence is a more attractive rule, but this result depends in part on the assumption that first-party insurance is perfect (since the company can observe the victim's injuries) while liability insurance is not.

These results differ substantially from what are many times thought to be the implications of liability insurance. One must admit that, on the face of it, the system looks somewhat absurd, The law defines a due care standard that individuals are expected to obey and *then* allows those individuals to insure themselves against the penalty imposed for not obeying the standard. Economic analysis, however, serves to rationalize the system. The definition of a due care standard provides the basis upon which premiums are determined and individuals gauge the cost and benefit of being found at fault. With perfect insurance markets, the combined tort-insurance system is capable of achieving both goals of tort law—someting that was not possible in the absence of these markets. Furthermore, if the due care standard is set appropriately, the negligence system is efficient for unilateral accidents even when insurers cannot make premiums dependent upon care levels.

Unfortunately, this is not the case for strict liability and imperfect insurance markets. The relevant policy issue in all cases, however, is whether the outcome with liability insurance is superior to the outcome without it, and Shavell has shown that under reasonable assumptions the liability-insurance outcome cannot be improved upon. But, it should be noted that for bilateral accidents, which are not analyzed in Shavell's paper, outcomes where liability insurance is prohibited may be superior.

Our readings end with a paper by George Fletcher, which should be viewed as a critique of the approach taken in the four previous articles and a criticism of the entire economic analysis of tort law. Fletcher places that literature in what he terms the paradigm of reasonableness and distinguishes it from the paradigm of reciprocity. This is a very rich article and should be read by anyone who wishes to create a distinctively legal alternative to the economic analysis of tort law.

Fletcher argues that the paradigm of reasonableness is instrumental in the sense that it neglects any consideration of the particular circumstances of an accident in order to achieve the social goals of accident avoidance and risk spreading. Fletcher is certainly correct on this point, and it is important to realize the full extent to which the law is made the handservant of efficiency in the economic analysis. The concept of least-cost avoider makes a determination of responsibility for fault on the basis of marginal ability to avoid accidents per dollars expended. Parties who find themselves relatively more able to prevent accidents are at fault whether or not this is because other parties are very inept or because they themselves are very able. No determination is ever made of what one might *rightfully* expect of parties in paticular circumstances.

This is especially true for accidents where the level at which an activity is pursued influences the probability of its occurrence per unit time. For such accidents, efficiency demands that the activity level also be regulated. Automobile drivers, therefore, should be penalized not only for how they drive but also for how much they drive. Tort law, of course, does not regulate activity levels and consequently does not generally result in an efficient outcome. But if due care standards did consider activity levels, then two drivers taking identical care prior to an accident would bear different liability depending upon how much they had driven previously. In this regard, tort law is clearly closer to the paradigm of reciprocity in the sense that it defines an expected level of care but does not feel justified in restricting usage by individuals exercising that level of care.

In contrast to economic analysis, the paradigm of reciprocity takes explicit consideration of the context within which the particular accident occurs. Compensation is paid to victims and remuneration exacted from injurers on the basis of what the community can reasonably expect of individuals. We will attempt to express this paradigm in terms of the two goals of tort law and hope, in doing so, not to distort severely Feltcher's ideas. The paradigm of reciprocity imposes a due care standard based on some definition of acceptable moral behavior. Victims who fall below this standard are not entitled to compensation, as in the defense of contributory negligence. Injurers whose behavior is above the standard are not required to pay remuneration, as in negligence. This we take to be the significance of Fletcher's attempt to excuse injurers who involuntarily impose extreme risks upon victims. As Fletcher recognizes, the tort system cannot completely satisfy such a moral standard because there will be instances when the injurer is faultless and the victim is entitled to compensation and alternatively instances when the injurer is at fault and the victim is not entitled to compensation.

With respect to the second goal of tort law, Fletcher states that victims are entitled to compensation if they are exposed to risks that are greater than the background risks that each of us is required to bear in daily life. As the statement stands, it is circular in the sense that it can be translated into "victims are entitled to compensation for those risks that they are not required to bear." Fletcher's concept, however, can provide a criterion for how accident costs should be distributed if background risks can be *independently* differentiated from all other risks. In principle, there seems to be no reason why this could not be done. But, as with the efficiency standard, there can be conflicts between the two goals. One can for example easily imagine a case where the victim has suffered an extraordinary loss (a non-background risk) that is in large part due to his own inappropriate behavior. It is not clear how Fletcher would resolve such cases.

Finally, Fletcher argues that the paradigm of reasonableness, unlike the paradigm of reciprocity, cannot distinguish the right to receive compensation from the obligation to pay remuneration. This, we believe, is more a deficiency of tort law itself than of the economic analysis of it. Minimization of secondary accident costs involves complete risk spreading for both injurers and victims, which cannot be achieved through tort law alone. Ideally, the economic method *desires* to uncouple regulation of behavior from payment of compensation. What makes tort law difficult from an efficiency standpoint and the first-best unattainable *is* the fact that this uncoupling is not always possible. Both paradigms, therefore, face a similar problem in that there will be instances when the victim should be compensated but the injurer excused. *Neither* paradigm can be completely satisfied by tort law because the tort system is a mechanism for private compensation between the two parties directly involved in the accident. Without some other mechanism appended to it (such as outside insurance markets), tort law can only compensate the victim at the expense of the injurer. The two paradigms differ in terms of what they expect from individuals and how these expectations are formulated, but it is an indictment of the law of torts as a means of dealing with risk that it cannot satisfy either paradigm.

Notes

1. There never has been, and probably never will be, a completely satisfactory definition of a tort. William Prosser, in *The Law of Torts* (St. Paul, Minn.: West Publishing Co., 1971) has written, "The numerous attempts which have been made to define the term have succeeded only in achieving language so broad that it includes other matters than

torts, or else so narrow that it leaves out some torts themselves" (pp. 1–2). The definition used in the text is designed to focus attention on the kinds of torts studied by economists. This definition excludes intentional torts which are many times identical to crimes and are perhaps only defined as torts so as to provide the victim with an avenue through which to obtain compensation. As the text indicates, we are concerned with activities where the tortfeasor bears a lesser degree of guilt.

2. Guido Calabresi, *The Costs of Accidents* (New Haven: Yale University Press, 1970).

3. Guido Calabresi and Jon T. Hirschoff, "Toward a Test for Strict Liability in Torts," *The Yale Law Journal* 81, no. 6 (1972): 1060.

4. Shavell in his paper considers cases in which the injurer and/or the victim are risk neutral. The assumption of a risk neutral agent is a useful device because all of the risk that results from accidents can be heaped on the risk neutral agent without *any* loss in welfare. Risk neutral agents, therefore, increase the possibility of totally efficient outcomes. Clearly, this is a very special case in that the second goal of tort law is effectively disconnected with respect to those agents assumed to be risk neutral. In the text, we have ignored this possibility and assumed that both the injurer and the victim are averse to risk.

Toward a Test for Strict Liability in Torts

Guido Calabresi[†] and Jon T. Hirschoff[‡]

I. Introduction

The fifteen years since Fleming James addressed the question of whether manufacturers should be liable without negligence[1] have seen a remarkable expansion in the scope of strict liability in the law of torts, yet the very courts which have been the leaders in this trend have been consistently troubled by the question of how far strict liability should extend within the areas in which it is being applied.[2] While strict liability of the manufacturer for product defects, for example, has been announced in jurisdiction after jurisdiction,[3] in many jurisdictions this has simply led to a morass of questions regarding the *definition* of "defect" and how liability for a defect relates to (a) adequacy of warnings, (b) unexpected or improper use, (c) assumption of risk, and even (d) contributory negligence.[4] Nor is this at all surprising.

† John Thomas Smith Professor of Law, Yale Law School. B.S. 1953, LL.B. 1958, Yale University; M.A. 1959, Oxford University.

‡ Assistant Professor of Law, Indiana University School of Law. A.B. 1963, Stanford University; J.D. 1967, Yale University.

1. James, *General Products—Should Manufacturers Be Liable Without Negligence?*, 24 TENN. L. REV. 923, 924 (1957). *See also* James, *Products Liability*, 34 TEXAS L. REV. 44, 192 (1955).

2. *See, e.g.,* Wasik v. Borg, 423 F.2d 44 (2d Cir. 1970); Lamendola v. Mizell, 115 N.J. Super. 514, 280 A.2d 241 (1971); Foster v. Preston Mill Co., 44 Wash.2d 440, 268 P.2d 645 (1954). *See also* James, *The Future of Negligence in Accident Law*, 53 VA. L. REV. 911 (1967); Kalven, *Torts: The Quest for Appropriate Standards*, 53 CALIF. L. REV. 189 (1965); and Prosser, *The Fall of the Citadel—Strict Liability to the Consumer*, 50 MINN. L. REV. 791 (1966).

Since writing this article, we have read Professor Franklin's excellent article analyzing the application of various theories of liability in cases of patient claims for hepatitis resulting from blood transfusions. Franklin, *Tort Liability for Hepatitis: An Analysis and a Proposal*, 24 STAN. L. REV. 439 (1972). The test for strict liability which we suggest in this article looks to the same kinds of practical considerations, by and large, as those which Professor Franklin takes into account in concluding that hospitals and blood banks should be strictly liable for transfusion related hepatitis.

3. *See* L. FRUMER & M. FRIEDMAN, PRODUCTS LIABILITY, § 16A[3], n.2 (1970).

4. *See, e.g.,* as to adequacy of warning, Alman Brothers Farms & Feed Mill, Inc. v. Diamond Laboratories, Inc., 437 F.2d 1295, 1303 (5th Cir. 1971); Davis v. Wyeth Laboratories, Inc., 399 F.2d 121 (9th Cir. 1968); Wright v. Carter Products, Inc., 244 F.2d 53, at 56-59 (2d Cir. 1957); as to unexpected or improper use, Hardy v. Hull Corporation, 446 F.2d 34 (9th Cir. 1971); Schemel v. General Motors Corporation, 384 F.2d 802 (7th Cir. 1967); Johnson v. Standard Brands Paint Co., 274 Cal. App. 2d 331, 79 Cal. Rptr. 194 (1969); as to assumption of risk, Greco v. Bucciconi Engineering Co., 407 F.2d 87 (3d Cir. 1969); Sperling v. Hatch, 10 Cal. App. 3d 54, 88 Cal. Rptr. 704 (1970); Bartkewich

Strict liability has never meant that the party held strictly liable is to be a general insurer for the victim no matter how or where the victim comes to grief. General insurance was not the rule in classical instances of strict liability, such as ultrahazardous activities, or in legislatively mandated instances, such as workmen's compensation, and it is not the rule in the recent instances of application such as products liability.[5] The questions which the courts now find themselves asking (and being asked) in the new areas of application, such as products liability, involve the same basic issue as did equally difficult questions faced in traditional areas of strict liability, which were couched in words such as "natural or unnatural use" and "arising out of and in the course of employment." The issue is just where strict liability should stop.

Despite the courts' recognition that strict liability must be limited, they have seldom been very confident in trying to describe the limits. Indeed, their efforts at answering the questions posed in strict liability cases seem in many cases to degenerate into either meaningless semantic disputes or attempts at balancing the costs of the accident against the costs of avoiding it;[6] yet the latter approach sounds devilishly like the very calculus of negligence, or Learned Hand's test for fault, which strict liability was meant to replace.

Strict liability's limits can, however, be defined in a meaningful way. The questions the courts have been asking are often highly relevant to those limits, and strict liability so limited is very different from the negligence calculus, or Learned Hand's test for fault. Analysis of strict liability's limits together with a suggested test for strict liability will, we believe, give insight into both the negligence calculus and its growing disfavor.

II.   The Learned Hand Test Considered

Learned Hand's test for fault defines the defendant's duty of care as a function of three variables: (1) the probability that the accident will

---

v. Billinger, 432 Pa. 351, 247 A.2d 603 (1968); and as to contributory negligence, Friedman v. General Motors Corp., 411 F.2d 533 (3d Cir. 1969); Matthias v. Lehn & Fink Products Corp., 70 Wash.2d 541, 424 P.2d 284 (1967).

5.   *See* as to ultrahazardous activities, W. PROSSER, THE LAW OF TORTS 517 (4th ed. 1971); as to workmen's compensation, S. HARPER, THE LAW OF WORKMEN'S COMPENSATION 470 (2d ed. 1920); and as to products liability, *e.g.*, Suvada v. White Motor Co., 32 Ill.2d 612, 210 N.E.2d 182 (1965); Elliott v. Lachance, 109 N.H. 481, 256 A.2d 153, 156 (1969); Dippel v. Sciano, 37 Wis.2d 443, 451, 155 N.W.2d 55 (1967).

6.   *See* Pike v. Frank G. Hough Co., 2 Cal.3d 465, 467 P.2d 229, 85 Cal. Rptr. 629 (1970); Christofferson v. Kaiser Foundation Hospitals, 15 Cal. App. 3d 75, 92 Cal. Rptr. 825 (1971); Dunham v. Vaughan & Bushnell Mfg. Co., 86 Ill. App. 2d 315, 327, 229 N.E.2d 684, 690 (1967); *cf.* Sanders v. Western Auto Supply Co., 183 S.E.2d 321 (S.Car. 1971). *See also* Wade, *Strict Tort Liability of Manufacturers*, 19 Sw. L.J. 5 (1965).

occur, (2) the gravity of the injury which will be suffered if the accident does occur, and (3) the burden of precautions adequate to prevent such accidents.[7] If the cost to the defendant of avoiding the accident would have been less than the cost of the accident, discounted by the probability of its occurrence, the defendant's failure to avoid the accident is termed negligence.[8]

For the purpose of the first parts of this discussion, we will assume that the traditional test for fault, as given expression in Learned Hand's formula, was designed to do what Professor Posner says it was designed to do,[9] namely to minimize the sum of accident costs and the costs of accident avoidance.[10] The Learned Hand test would seem to accomplish this objective in theory, because *if it were applied perfectly*, it would put the costs of the accident on the injurer when and only when it was cheaper for him to avoid the accident costs by appropriate safety measures than to pay those costs. *Assuming injurers had the requisite foresight*, this would cause potential injurers to avoid all accidents worth avoiding, *i.e.*, those where avoidance costs less than the accident, and to have only those accidents not worth avoiding.[11]

The application of the traditional rule of contributory negligence would make some difference, but not much. Using the rubric of the test, contributory negligence would exist when the victim, too, could have avoided the accident at a cost lower than the cost generated by the accident. Since under the traditional rule contributory negligence is a complete defense, the cost would remain on the victim despite the negligence of the injurer, *even if avoidance by the injurer would have*

7. Conway v. O'Brien, 111 F.2d 611, 612 (2d Cir. 1940), *rev'd on other grounds,* 312 U.S. 492; United States v. Carroll Towing Co., 159 F.2d 169 (2d Cir. 1947).

8. Perhaps anticipating what others would do in the name of his test, Judge Hand cautioned that "[the three elements of the test] are practically not susceptible of any quantitative estimate, and the second two are generally not so, even theoretically." Conway v. O'Brien, 111 F.2d 611, 612 (2d Cir. 1940). *See also* Moisan v. Loftus, 178 F.2d 148 (2d Cir. 1949).

9. Posner, *A Theory of Negligence,* 1 J. LEGAL STUD. 29 (1972) [hereinafter cited as Posner].

10. Our assumption, more precisely, is that the object is optimization of primary accident costs. *See* G. CALABRESI, THE COST OF ACCIDENTS 26-31 (1970) [hereinafter cited as COSTS]. But the statement in text is sufficiently accurate for purposes of this article.

11. The goal, strictly speaking, is accident cost avoidance rather than accident avoidance. It may be, for example, that minimization of the sum of automobile accident costs and avoidance costs would come about by measures designed to make automobiles "crashproof" rather than by measures directed at the avoidance of automobile accidents altogether.

In determining whether an accident cost is worth avoiding, the test would look not to the entire cost of the safety measure which would avoid it, but to the cost of that safety measure discounted appropriately to take account of all of the other accident costs that same measure would avoid. Thus the cost of avoiding a given accident is ten dollars if a 100 dollar safety device would also avoid nine other accidents of equal severity.

There are numerous other assumptions implicit in the application of any test of this kind, but this is not the place to discuss them. See COSTS, *supra* note 10, *passim.*

cost less than avoidance by the victim. Thus, even in the wonderful, let us freely admit, fantastic world of Professor Posner, in which none of the costs of an accident are borne by third parties other than the injurer and victim, and in which there is perfect foresight, the rule of contributory negligence would prevent the negligence calculus from optimizing primary accident cost reduction. The potential injurer who could avoid a $100 accident at a cost of $5, knowing that the victim could do so at a cost of $50, might well not undertake the $5 safety measure because of his knowledge that the victim will either avoid the accident or be held contributorily negligent. Given adequate foresight, one would expect the accident to be avoided, but at a cost $45 higher than necessary.[12]

A Learned Hand test for injurer liability with the defense of contributory negligence removed, however, would also fail to optimize accident costs, and for exactly the same reason. Under such a rule, there would be instances in which the victim who could avoid an accident more cheaply than could the injurer would fail to do so, because he would know that the injurer would nonetheless be held liable. Thus the *correct* optimizing rule, under the Learned Hand test, would be to have a doctrine of contributory negligence, but to apply it only where the cost of injurer avoidance exceeds the cost of victim avoidance.[13]

Whatever defects the Learned Hand test may have, given the existence of an absolute defense of contributory negligence, it can at least be said that if the test worked, all the accidents worth avoiding would be avoided. If they were occasionally avoided at somewhat greater expense than necessary, that would not be a matter of great consequence. At the same time, it must be recognized that all the costs of all the accidents not worth avoiding would fall on the victim, raising distributional or justice issues. We will, however, postpone consideration of those issues to a later section of this article, and limit our discussion here to primary accident cost reduction.[14]

If we make the assumptions under which the Learned Hand test would work adequately, the fascinating thing is that as good a result in terms of reducing primary accident costs could be achieved by a liability rule which is the exact reverse of the Learned Hand test. Un-

12. The $45 excess cost would be avoided only in the yet more wonderful world of Professor Coase, where transaction costs are nonexistent, and a pre-accident "bribe" of the injurer by the victim would result in the injurer taking the $5 safety measure. See Coase, *The Problem of Social Costs,* 3 J. LAW & ECON. 1 (1960), Calabresi, *Transaction Costs, Resource Allocation and Liability Rules—A Comment,* 11 J. LAW & ECON. 67 (1968), and COSTS, *supra* note 10, at 135-40.

13. Professor Posner realizes this, and adds that this refinement, though not explicit in the cases, may be implicit in them. Posner, *supra* note 9, at 33.

14. *See* part VI, *infra.*

der such a "reverse Learned Hand test," the costs of an accident would be borne by the *injurer* unless accident avoidance on the part of the victim would have cost less than the accident. If a reverse contributory negligence test were added, the victim would bear the accident costs only if the injurer could not also have avoided the accident at less cost than the accident entailed. A reverse Learned Hand test, in other words, which always made the injurer liable without fault unless the victim were negligent, and even then held the injurer liable if he also were negligent, would do for primary accident cost avoidance just what the actual Learned Hand test with contributory negligence is said to do. The only difference between the tests is distributional. Under the Learned Hand test, the costs of all accidents *not* worth avoiding are borne by victims, whereas under the reverse Learned Hand test they would be borne by injurers.[15]

In focusing on the reverse Learned Hand test, we are not simply playing with mirrors. The point is that a perfect world with perfect foresight is a prerequisite to optimization of primary accident cost reduction under *either* Learned Hand type test, and that given such a world, any number of other devices would also accomplish that goal.[16] To the extent that we are concerned with the practical minimization of accident costs, the choice among these devices will depend not on their *theoretical* ability to optimize accident costs given certain assumptions, but on the degree to which the particular assumptions required by each device actually do obtain.[17] We will suggest a test which we think is much more likely than either Learned Hand type test to accomplish a satisfactory job of primary accident cost optimization. We also think that application of the proposed test requires asking questions which are closely related to those questions courts have always asked in strict liability cases. That is why we believe the proposed test is an appropriate one for defining the limits of strict liability.

---

15. As our subsequent discussion indicates, the practical implications of the two tests are also very different. It may be, for example, that one test would result in more disputes over the shifting of losses than would the other, and thus in greater administrative costs. This practical consideration was, in Holmes' view, an overriding one. *See* O. HOLMES, THE COMMON LAW (Howe ed. 1963) 76-77. *But cf.* COSTS, *supra* note 10, at 261-62.

16. Consider, for example, a test pursuant to which an all-knowing accident prevention agency issues an accident avoidance order to the appropriate party whenever an accident is worth avoiding, with a sanction sufficiently severe to guarantee that the order will be followed. *Compare* COSTS, *supra* note 10, at 111-13. *See* note 73 *infra*.

17. These assumptions relate, *inter alia*, to the cost of information to each party, the absence of psychological or other impediments to acting on the basis of available information, the administrative costs of shifting losses, and the extent to which parties actually bear the costs which the particular tests impose upon them. These are, in economists' terms, principally assumptions relating to transaction costs and externalization. *See generally* COSTS, *supra* note 10, at 55-64, 143-50, 178-86, 244-50.

III. The Strict Liability Test Defined

When a case comes to judgment under either of the two Learned Hand type tests, a cost-benefit analysis is made by an outside governmental institution (a judge or a jury) as to the relative costs of the accident and of accident avoidance.[18] Liability would be placed on the party initially free of responsibility only if the *decider* found the benefits of avoidance (*i.e.,* not incurring the cost of the accident) to be greater than the costs of such avoidance to that party. The strict liability test we suggest does not require that a governmental institution make such a cost-benefit analysis. It requires of such an institution only a decision as to which of the parties to the accident *is in the best position to make the cost-benefit analysis between accident costs and accident avoidance costs and to act on that decision once it is made.* The question for the court reduces to a search for the cheapest cost avoider.[19]

So stated, the strict liability test sounds deceptively simple to apply. Instead of requiring a judgment as to whether an injurer *should* have avoided the accident costs because the costs of avoidance were less than the foreseeable accident costs as the Learned Hand test does, the strict liability test would simply require a decision as to whether the injurer or the victim was in the better position both to judge whether avoidance costs would exceed foreseeable accident costs and to act on that judgment.[20] The issue becomes not *whether* avoidance is worth it, but

18. The decision may also be made by the legislature, as it sometimes is through the application of the "negligence per se" concept. See 2 F. HARPER & F. JAMES, THE LAW OF TORTS, § 17.6 (1956). The history of the respective roles of judges and juries in the making of the analysis can be seen in cases such as Grand Trunk Ry. v. Ives, 144 U.S. 408 (1892); Baltimore & O.R.R. v. Goodman, 275 U.S. 66 (1927); Pokora v. Wabash Ry., 292 U.S. 98 (1934) (limiting *Goodman*); Lorenzo v. Wirth, 170 Mass. 596, 49 N.E. 1010 (1897); and Sylvester v. Shea, 280 Mass. 508, 182 N.E. 916 (1932). *See also* Nixon, *Changing Rules of Liability in Automobile Accident Litigation,* 3 LAW & CONTEMP. PROB. 476 (1936).

19. The cheapest cost avoider has been elsewhere defined as the party "an arbitrary initial bearer of accident costs would (in the absence of transaction and information costs) find it most worthwhile to 'bribe' in order to obtain that modification of behavior which would lessen accident costs most." COSTS, *supra* note 10, at 135. This definition, unlike the terminology we have been using in this article, includes the costs of accident avoidance within the term "accident costs." It should be clear upon reflection that the most "worthwhile" bribe would be one to the party who is in the best position both to determine what accident cost avoidance measures will result in the minimal sum of avoidance costs and accident costs (*i.e.,* to make the cost-benefit analysis) and to act upon that determination. We do not mean to suggest that the party in the best position to make the cost-benefit analysis is always in the best position to act upon it; where that is not the case, the decision requires weighing comparative advantages.

The imposition of accident costs on the cheapest cost avoider will, of course, have its own set of distributional consequences, and these may well differ from those resulting from applications of the Learned Hand or reverse Learned Hand tests.

20. We are assuming for purposes of the discussion in text that accident costs and avoidance costs are not only ascertainable but also fungible, so that the cost-benefit analysis involves only a comparison of relative costs. We would guess that in practice the judge or jury making the cost-benefit analysis under the Learned Hand test would

which of the parties is relatively more likely to find out whether avoidance is worth it. This judgment is by no means an easy one, but we would suggest that in practice it is usually easier to make correctly than is the judgment required under either the Learned Hand test or its reverse.[21] It also implies a lesser degree of governmental intervention than does either of the Hand type tests.[22]

As a first step toward seeing what is implied in such a strict liability test, we propose to examine how the issues raised by courts in various areas of strict liability relate to the proposed test. We will do this first in an oversimplified context, treating accidents as though they involved only the injurer and the victim. Subsequently, we will examine what is implied for the test in considering accidents as events involving whole categories of victims, injurers and affected third parties.

In strict products liability cases, the first question asked is, "was there a defect?" A defect may be defined to mean simply that something went wrong. All that in turn means, however, is that a safer product might have been designed, and this would mean that there is a defect whenever there is an accident. If, instead, existence of a defect is defined to mean a failure of a product to meet levels deemed customary in the trade, then strict liability would be even less successful in achieving optimal reduction of primary accident costs than is the Learned Hand test and would be far narrower than fault.[23] It is not surprising, therefore, that courts have tended to reject both of these extremes.[24]

be significantly affected by considerations other than the relative costs of accidents and accident avoidance, though this is expressly denied by Professor Posner. Posner, *supra* note 9, at 31-32, 33-34. These other considerations, involving the collectively determined worth of the parties or the activities they are engaged in, are in fact of crucial importance in determining the type and level of accident cost causing activities a society wishes to permit. The manner in which we would introduce them into the decision is discussed under the heading of "specific deterrence" in Costs, *supra* note 10, at 95-129, 174-98. *See also* notes 72 & 73 *infra* and accompanying text.

21. It is an easier judgment because it looks to questions such as which party is better informed as to risks and alternatives instead of to questions requiring the weighing of accident costs and avoidance costs, both of which must be subjectively determined by the trier of fact.

22. *See* pp. 1074-75 *infra*.

23. The Learned Hand test asks whether an accident avoidance measure would cost less than it would save in accident costs, and this has very little to do with custom. *See* Posner, *supra* note 9, at 39. Custom has not generally been a defense under the fault system, although it may be admissible as relevant to what is proper conduct under the circumstances. 2 F. HARPER & F. JAMES, THE LAW OF TORTS § 17.3.

24. As to rejection of custom as an absolute defense in strict products liability cases, *see, e.g.,* Williams v. Brown Mfg. Co., 93 Ill. App. 2d 334, 236 N.E.2d 125, 138 (1968); Badorek v. General Motors Corp., 11 Cal. App. 3d 902, 935, 90 Cal. Rptr. 305, 328 (1970) (dictum), both citing Judge Hand's famous opinion in The T. J. Hooper, 60 F.2d 737 (2d Cir. 1932), *cert. denied sub nom.* Eastern Transportation Co. v. Northern Barge Co., 287 U.S. 662. Rejection of the other extreme is implicit in rejection of the notion that a manufacturer is liable without exception for accidents arising out of the use of his products. *See, e.g.,* the products liability cases cited in note 5 *supra*.

The courts have instead tended to determine whether a defect exists by asking a series of secondary questions relating to (a) the adequacy of warning and (b) the use to which the product was put. They have also noted that assumption of risk on the part of the victim might serve either to negate the existence of a defect or to be a defense to it.[25] In fact, the defense of assumption of risk may be viewed as broad enough to encompass adequacy of warning and appropriateness of product use, which are in turn appropriate ways of raising some of the questions implicit in the strict liability test we have offered.

Let us look first to adequacy of warning. Suppose that a product occasionally causes the user's leg to fall off. Failure to warn the potential user that this may happen in .0001 per cent of the cases will normally result in manufacturer liability.[26] But even such a warning is not likely to allow the user to make an intelligent cost-benefit analysis between accident and avoidance costs. Unless the user has reason to believe himself to be in the dangerous category and unless a close substitute exists which at some cost avoids the danger, the user is hardly in a position to evaluate the benefits of the product as against its costs. The producer may seem to be no better suited, but if we move from a static to a dynamic situation, this will not be the case. The producer is in a position to compare the existing accident costs with the costs of avoiding this type of accident by developing either a new product or a test which would serve to identify the risky .0001 per cent. The consumer, in practice, cannot make this comparison. Relatively, the producer is the cheapest cost avoider, the party best suited to make the cost-benefit analysis and to act upon it.

Should a patch test be developed which enables the consumer to identify himself as an especially risky user, the situation may well be changed. The existence of the patch test, sold together with the product and coupled with a warning, may be enough to make the consumer the party best able to avoid the costs of mishap.[27] This will depend in part, but only in part, on the nature of the warning and the adequacy (including ease of use) of the patch test. Even if the warning is unmistakably clear and the patch test 100 per cent accurate, however, the manufacturer may still be in the best position to make the cost-benefit analysis. For the analysis depends not only on the adequacy of the warning and the likelihood that a risky user will be able to identify him-

---

25. *See* note 4 *supra*.
26. *See, e.g.,* Davis v. Wyeth Laboratories, Inc., 399 F.2d 121 (9th Cir. 1968); Basko v. Sterling Drug, Inc., 416 F.2d 417, 430 (2d Cir. 1969).
27. *See, e.g.,* Matthis v. Lehn & Fink Products Corp., 70 Wash.2d 541, 424 P.2d 284 (1967).

self, but also on the availability of alternatives to the product.[28] If the product is a cosmetic with many reasonably close substitutes, identifying and clearly warning the risky group will very likely put the user in the best position to choose. If instead the product is a medicine, the use of which is the only way of saving the user's life, identifying and warning the risky users probably would not suffice to make the users the better choosers.[29] The manufacturer would in those circumstances be best suited to compare the cost of the occasional lost leg with the *cost of further research* designed to give rise to an adequate substitute entailing fewer risks, or equivalent risks but to another definable group.[30]

We do not mean to suggest that these examples resolve the issue, but they should serve to indicate why, when courts ask about adequacy of warning in attempting to determine whether a defect exists, they are often on the right track. The examples also demonstrate why mere clarity of warning or mere percentages of likelihood of harm may not by themselves resolve the issue. For these are only factors going to the basic question of who is in the best position to make the cost-benefit analysis and act upon it, and must be considered together with other factors such as availability of substitutes and the nature of the user's use of the product in order to determine liability.

The relevance of the use to which the product is put has seemed especially troublesome for the courts.[31] The fact that a lawn mower was not designed to protect its driver should he care to drive it on the throughway ought not to be viewed as a design defect making the man-

28. Alternatives include not only alternative products, but also non-use of the product.
29. This is because the cheapest cost avoider must be able to make the required analysis and act upon it, and the only meaningful action is one which would reduce the risk. Where the product is the only medicine which will save the user's life, it is meaningless to say that the user is in a position to act upon the basis of the analysis.
The cost of action by the manufacturer in such a situation (*i.e.*, research for alternative products) may have an undesirable effect in the long run. Charging the manufacturer may unduly reduce the number or output of drug companies. Whether the long run effect, if it exists, is sufficiently adverse to negate the short run effect depends on the relative ability of the users as against the manufacturers to avoid the accident costs in the long run, that is, on which is the cheapest cost avoider in the long run. In this example it is hard to see what the user could do in the long run. In other situations, however, the long run issue may turn on the relative merits of more output in different industries.
Undesirable long run effects may, of course, be dealt with through governmental subsidies funded by lump sum taxes on the long run cheapest cost avoider; this seems to us to be a better solution by and large than denying liability. For a more detailed treatment of the problems of long versus short run cost avoidance, *see* Calabresi, note 12 *supra.*
30. The discussion in text over-simplifies the alternatives. The manufacturer may, for example, decide to identify the high risk users and sell the product to them at a higher price. *See* Costs, *supra* note 10, at 170-71. If he is allowed to do this, and if doing it is economically feasible, the long run consequences of imposing liability on him referred to in note 28, *supra,* may be avoided. *See id.* at 162, 168-72.
31. *See, e.g.,* Brown v. General Motors Corporation, 355 F.2d 814 (4th Cir. 1966); Helene Curtis Industries, Inc. v. Pruitt, 385 F.2d 841 (5th Cir. 1967).

ufacturer liable either to users or to rescuers. But neither should a warning that the lawn mower ought not to be used where there are rocks *preclude* manufacturer's liability to passers-by hit by rocks or even to the user himself. Again, the issue is who can best make a cost-benefit analysis and act on it, viewed in realistic terms. Many uses of a product, though forbidden by the producer, are actually not unexpected. Other uses, though not forbidden, are in fact so unusual as to make the user more suited to make the cost-benefit analysis than the manufacturer.

Moreover, the question whether the manufacturer could sufficiently anticipate the use[32] as to be in a good position to make the cost-benefit analysis has little to do with whether society deems the use worth its costs. In other words, it is logically distinct from the question of whether the user was contributorily negligent. Thus a user may have an excellent reason for driving down the throughway on a lawn mower (the benefits of the use outweigh the costs), in which case the collective decider in a negligence/contributory negligence regime ought not to deem his conduct to be contributorily negligent. Yet such a user would in all probability be a better evaluator than the manufacturer of the costs and benefits involved. As a consequence, his strict liability suit against the manufacturer for injuries resulting from such driving would fail.[33] Conversely, the fact that a use of the product is deemed contributorily negligent does not necessarily mean that the manufacturer is not in a better position than the user to evaluate the costs and benefits. To take an example from a different area of strict liability, a worker may negligently use a piece of equipment, but his employer may nonetheless be in a better position to evaluate the relevant costs and benefits. That is, he may know the propensity to negligent use and be better able to evaluate a substitute piece of equipment which cannot readily be negligently used. This explains why contributory negligence has not been an inevitable defense to an action based on strict liability.[34]

We hope that the foregoing discussion of adequacy of warning and appropriateness of use has caused the reader to think that what we have

32. *See, e.g.*, Higgins v. Paul Hardeman, Inc., 457 S.W.2d 943 (Mo. App., 1970); and Dunham v. Vaughan & Bushnell Mfg. Co., 86 Ill. App. 2d 315, 229 N.E.2d 684 (1967), holding that an abnormal use of a product relieves the defendant from liability only if such use is not reasonably foreseeable.

33. *See, e.g.*, Greeno v. Clark Equipment Co., 237 F. Supp. 427, 429 (D.Ind. 1965), where the court stated that although contributory negligence is not a defense to strict products liability, "misuse" is a defense.

34. *See, e.g.*, Bachner v. Pearson, 479 P.2d 319 (Alaska, 1970); Barth v. B.F. Goodrich Tire Co., 265 Cal. App. 2d 228, 71 Cal. Rptr. 306 (1968).

been talking about sounds strangely like assumption of risk, not in its secondary, and technically improper, sense of contributory negligence, but in its original sense.[35] The doctrine of assumption of risk—though grossly misapplied by courts which have not looked realistically to whether the plaintiff in practice had the requisite knowledge and possibility of choice the doctrine implied—is essential to an understanding of a non-fault world.[36] It is, and always has been, a kind of plaintiff's strict liability—the other side of the coin of defendant's strict liability. It may even go to negate defendant's negligence, by expressing a judgment that although the defendant's conduct was not worth its costs (*i.e.*, was negligent), the plaintiff was in a better position than the defendant to evaluate the costs and benefits involved (*i.e.*, the plaintiff assumed the risk). Just as the employer may be in the better position to evaluate the costs and benefits of a piece of equipment given the likelihood of occasional employee negligence (defendant's strict liability), so a spectator at a baseball game may be best suited to evaluate the desirability of sitting in an unscreened bleacher given the likelihood of occasional negligent wild throws by the players during the game which may result in the spectator's being hit on the head (plaintiff's strict liability, or assumption of risk).[37] In both these situations, the conclusion as to whether an accident cost should be shifted depends not on whether a party was negligent, but rather on a judgment as to which party was in a better position to make the cost-benefit analysis irrespective of the other's negligence.[38] In each situation, strict liability (whether defendant's or plaintiff's) is imposed regardless of whether the other party "ought" to have done what he did.

35. In its original, or "primary" sense, assumption of risk bars recovery by a plaintiff who voluntarily and reasonably chooses to encounter a known risk. *See* 2 F. HARPER & F. JAMES, THE LAW OF TORTS, § 21.1 (1956).

36. *Cf.* Kalven, *Torts: The Quest for Appropriate Standards*, 53 CALIF. L. REV. 189, 206 (1965), suggesting that there is a "haunting analogy" between Chief Justice Traynor's emphasis on the inability of the consumer to detect defects in the goods he buys (*i.e.*, to avoid the risks) and the distinction drawn in terms of assumption of risk between traffic accidents and "accidents" between adjoining landowners by Blackburn, J., in Fletcher v. Rylands, L.R. 1 Exch. 265, 287 (1866), *aff'd sub nom.* Rylands v. Fletcher L.R. 3 H.L. 330 (1868).

Another interesting analogy is that between Chief Justice Traynor's emphasis on distributional considerations (*see, e.g.,* Escola v. Coca Cola Bottling Co. of Fresno, 24 Cal.2d 453, 150 P.2d 436 (1944) (concurring opinion)) and Bohlen's suggestion that the judges who wrote the opinions in Fletcher v. Rylands sought to protect the landed gentry against the encroachments of industry. Bohlen, *The Rule in Rylands v. Fletcher*, 59 U. PA. L. REV. 298 (1911). *See generally* part VI, *infra.*

37. *Cf.* Kavafian v. Seattle Baseball Club Ass'n, 105 Wash. 215, 177 P. 776, 181 P. 679 (1919).

38. Thus strict liability cannot be explained as the "reverse" of negligence, or as a reverse Learned Hand test, for if it did it would have to take into account the negligence of the injurer, *i.e.*, reverse contributory negligence (*see* pp. 1058-59 *supra*) in determining whether to shift the cost from injurer to victim because of the victim's conduct.

The doctrine of assumption of risk, properly interpreted, not only encompasses the questions the courts are now asking about adequacy of warning and appropriateness of use, but also can be viewed as covering much of the traditional rubric by which the classical forms of strict liability were limited. These forms of liability, whether for animals, ultrahazardous activities, *Fletcher v. Rylands* situations[39] or even workmen's compensation, were limited in two general ways. The first limit was usually put in terms of whether the injury stemmed from the risk whose presence was the reason for making the activity strictly liable. Had a cow trespassed, or had it instead bitten a neighbor; had a tiger mangled somebody, or had it simply chewed grass; had a bomb exploded, or had it just rolled and crushed somebody's foot?[40] The second limit was usually put in terms of whether the victim had done something which, though not necessarily *negligent,* had especially exposed him to the risk. Had the victim engaged in an "unnatural" use of his land; had the victim, a zoologist, gone into the tiger's cage to study the family habits of large cats; had the victim gone where no blasting company could expect humans to be?[41] In setting out these limits, the courts were in effect expressing judgments as to whether the injurer or the victim could better decide the advantages of avoidance as against accident costs. Both limits suggest questions such as who has the greater knowledge of the risk involved and who is better able to choose to avoid that risk by altering behavior should the risk appear too great. In discussing both these limits, moreover, the courts seemed to consider irrelevant the question of whether a third-party decider would approve of the decision made or not, and concentrated instead on who could best make the decision. The issue was not, in other words, whether the owner of the land *ought* to build a reservoir or keep tigers as he did. Neither was it whether the victim acted "reasonably" in engaging in an unnatural use of *his* land or in entering the tiger's cage. Instead it was whether his situation made him better suited than the owner to compare the benefits and the costs of the risk he took.[42]

To say this, though, is to remain at much too simple a level. We have so far assumed simply an injurer and a victim, when in fact each be-

39. Fletcher v. Rylands, 3 H & C 774, 159 Eng. Rep. 737 (1865), *rev'd* Fletcher v. Rylands, L.R. 1 Exch. 265 (1866), *aff'd* Rylands v. Fletcher, L.R. 3 H.L. 330 (1868).
40. *See, e.g.,* Hartford v. Brady, 114 Mass. 466 (1874); Wiggins v. Industrial Accident Bd., 170 P. 9 (Mont., 1918); Scribner v. Kelley, 38 Barb. 14 (N.Y. 1862); Troth v. Wills, 8 Pa. Super. 1 (1897) (Wickham, J., dissenting).
41. *See, e.g.,* Rozewski v. Simpson, 9 Cal.2d 515, 71 P.2d 72 (1937); Oklahoma City v. Hudson, 405 P.2d 178 (Okla. 1965); Harder v. Maloney, 250 Wis. 233, 26 N.W.2d 830 (1947).
42. *See, e.g.,* Rozewski v. Simpson, 9 Cal. 2d 515, 71 P.2d 72 (1937).

longs to a category of blasters, factory owners, product users, workers, and so forth.[43] We have assumed that the costs of paying for accidents or avoiding them rest on the individual, and therefore that the cost-benefit decision under a strict liability rule is made at a totally decentralized level. Furthermore, we have ignored the problems which arise when the victim is neither the blaster nor the blastee, but a third party rescuer, neither the lawn mower manufacturer nor the user who rides it on the highway, but a pedestrian who is hit when it goes out of control. Such problems obviously cannot be ignored under either a fault or a strict liability standard.[44] Similarly, we have avoided the problem of who is to decide which category is in the best position to make the cost-benefit analysis and act on it, and how generalized this decision is to be. That is, we have ignored (a) who decides whether blasters are generally better suited than blastees to balance costs and benefits, (b) how many exceptions to this general notion will be permitted, and (c) who will be permitted to find that a given situation is an exception. These problems do not alter the test; they require, however, somewhat more sophistication in its application.

IV. The Strict Liability Test Refined

A. *Level and Generality of Application*

The greatest differences among areas of strict liability go precisely to the question of the level of generality at which a decision is made with respect to the category or party best suited to make the appropriate cost-benefit analysis. In blasting and ultrahazardous activities generally, the court-made decision that the blaster is best suited to make the cost-benefit analysis is at a high level of generality. In many jurisdictions the decision contemplates virtually no exceptions so long as the injury arises out of the risk which makes the activity ultrahazardous.[45] The likelihood of foolish behavior by the victim or the unusual sensitivity of some victims are deemed to be best considered by the blaster. Some courts, it is true, have raised the question of whether there would be liability if a blaster blasted in what seemed to be a totally deserted place.[46] The victim, these courts have in effect said, is better suited to gauge the costs of making his presence in such an

---

43. See generally Costs, *supra* note 10, *passim*.
44. See Sills v. Massey-Ferguson, Inc., 296 F. Supp. 776 (N.D. Ind. 1969), and cases there cited.
45. See, *e.g.*, Bedell v. Goulter, 199 Ore. 344, 261 P.2d 842 (1953).
46. See, *e.g.*, Houghton v. Loma Prieta Lumber Co., 152 Cal. 500, 93 P. 82 (1901); Kendall v. Johnson, 51 Wash. 477, 99 P. 310 (1909).

unusual place known as against the costs of taking whatever risks may be attendant on being in a place unexpectedly. But some judges have in effect reasoned that such an exception, precisely because it would require more individualized judgments, might not be worth making.[47] Perhaps an occasional victim would be better suited to make the cost-benefit analysis, but the administrative cost of dealing with such instances would not be worthwhile, given their presumed rarity.

In strict products liability, instead, the judgment, again court-made, that by and large producers are better suited than users to make the cost-benefit analysis is deemed much less generally applicable, and the manufacturer is allowed to try to show in each specific case that the user was in the best position to make the analysis. The questions asked as to the adequacy of warning and the appropriateness of use, and, in some jurisdictions, the availability of the defense of contributory negligence, suggest how far from certain courts are that the generalized premise that the producer is the cheapest cost avoider will apply to the individual case.[48] As a result, a combination of judge and jury is allowed to find that given the availability of substitutes, the adequacy of warning and the capacity of an individual user to identify himself as being especially risky or especially safe, the general assumption as to who is better suited to compare the risks and benefits will not apply. That such determinations must be made in ways which are much more realistic than were analogous decisions in old assumption of risk cases, is the lesson of cases like *Henningsen* and *Sills*.[49] But this in no way detracts from the judgment that in determining who is better suited to make a cost-benefit analysis in products liability cases, a fair degree of case by case analysis is worthwhile.

Workmen's compensation differs from both ultrahazardous activities and products liability in that the original decision was legislatively made. It also differs in that it tends to divide the decision of who is better suited to evaluate costs and benefits according to the *type of damage* rather than *type of accident*. We are not here concerned with

---

47. The administrative costs of making such individualized judgments would presumably be too great. *See, e.g.*, Whitman Hotel Corp. v. Elliott & Watrous Engineering Co., 137 Conn. 562, 79 A.2d 591 (1951) (Baldwin, J., concurring), noting that such limitations on strict liability for blasting "add a needless and confusing qualification or condition." 137 Conn. at 576, 79 A.2d at 598.

48. New Jersey is one jurisdiction where contributory negligence remains a defense to strict liability. Maiorino v. Weco Products Co., 45 N.J. 570, 214 A.2d 18 (1965). *Cf.* Cintrone v. Hertz Truck Leasing & Rental Service, 45 N.J. 434, 212 A.2d 769 (1965). This may be in part the result of the abandonment of the defense of assumption of risk in New Jersey. *See* note 55 *infra*. *See generally* Supp. to 2 F. HARPER & F. JAMES, THE LAW OF TORTS § 22.7 (1968).

49. Henningsen v. Bloomfield Motors, Inc., 32 N.J. 358, 161 A.2d 69 (1960); Sills v. Massey-Ferguson, Inc., *supra* note 44.

the fact that workmen's compensation schedules are hopelessly out of date,[50] but instead with the very fact that they deal with damages on a scheduled basis. The result of this is that the measure of damages for dignitary losses and even wage losses is that of the ordinary worker doing that job. If a great violinist mangles his hand in a steel mill, causing him extreme suffering and economic loss, that is his burden. One may contrast this with cases involving ultrahazardous activities where, except in very unusual situations, one takes one's victim as one finds him. On the other hand, the fact that a worker is warned that a machine is especially dangerous, or must be used in a given way, will not negate the employer's liability, short of extremes like wanton and wilful behavior by the victim.[51]

Without going into further detail, one can discern a certain rationality in these cases as to the appropriate level of generality of the original liability decision and the exceptions made to it. This does not mean we agree with all of the cases, by any means. But it is not unreasonable to suppose that a violinist is the best evaluator of the relative advantages and costs of working in a steel mill, with regard to the suffering he will feel if he loses his hand, while he is not as likely to be in that position with respect to blasting injuries. Similarly, a user of a product may be well suited to evaluate whether he wishes to use a given product in a given way despite a warning of danger, whereas an employee using that same product on the job would not be so suited. If we add to the foregoing considerations the administrative costs inherent in allowing an attempt to show an exception to the general rule, it is easy to understand the levels of generality which have in fact emerged.[52]

B. *Categories of Injurers and Victims*

So far we have discussed the problems involved in minimizing primary accident costs as if either the injurer or the victim actually bore the losses which occurred. As has been amply discussed elsewhere, that is clearly not the case.[53] The existence of insurance and of other ways in which a cost is removed from its initial bearer and borne ultimately by others need not be reexamined here. The effect of factors such as insurance on the choice of the party to hold liable under a strict liability test must, however, be made explicit.

---

50. *See* U.S. Dep't of Labor, Bureau of Labor Standards, Bull. No. 161 State Workmen's Compensation Laws (1969).
51. *See* 1A A. Larson, Workmen's Compensation Law § 31 (1967).
52. The administrative costs include, of course, the likelihood of error which may result from a particularized approach, as well as the costs of adjudicating particular disputes. *See* Costs, *supra* note 10, at 251, 255-59.
53. See the discussion of externalization in Costs, *supra* note 10, at 144-50, 244-50.

It does no good to leave the accident cost on the victim in a products liability case, on the ground that he is in a better position than the injurer to make a cost-benefit analysis, if the victim will not bear the loss in any event. The issue must be whether, given the fact of this "externalization," the *actual* bearer of the loss is better suited to make the analysis than is the injurer (assuming, of course, that the injurer would bear the loss if he were held liable). The point is a simple one and need not be gone into at length. The crucial decision on who is best suited to make the appropriate cost-benefit analysis must be made among the *categories* which actually bear a loss and not among the individuals who only do so initially.[54]

This point is, of course, equally valid for the two Learned Hand type tests. Sophisticated application of those tests would require that the collective judgment as to whether costs are worth avoiding be made at the level of categories which would end up paying, and not at the level of the single injurer and single victim. The fact that in practice this is almost impossible under existing fault rules is one of the weaknesses of the fault-insurance system as a device for reducing primary accident costs.[55] In theory, however, it should be admitted that one could apply a Learned Hand test at a category level. Whether the language of fault with the stigma it implies would also be appropriate to such a test at a non-individual level may be quite another matter.

C. The Need for Realism in Applying the Test

It should come as no surprise that considerations of knowledge, alternatives, and category levels are implicit in the search for the cheapest cost avoider. The very fact that these factors *are only implicit* in the test, however, requires us to be extremely practical in gauging their existence in specific situations.[56]

54. This does not mean that there should be one liability rule for insured persons and another for the uninsured. It means instead that in devising a rule appropriate to a particular category, the availability of insurance and other means of externalizing costs should be taken into account. The resulting liability rule would thus reflect the general extent of externalization from the individual to the entire category, though the rule might well be applied to all those within the category, whether insured or not. *See, e.g.*, Darling v. Charleston Community Memorial Hospital, 33 Ill. 2d 326, 336-38, 211 N.E.2d 253, 259-60 (1965), *cert. denied* 383 U.S. 946, abrogating the doctrine of charitable immunity in Illinois; *cf.* Gelbman v. Gelbman, 23 N.Y.2d 434, 297 N.Y.S.2d 529, 245 N.E.2d 192 (1969).

55. *See* Costs, *supra* note 10, at 244-50. The current movement for reform in the treatment of automobile accidents can be explained in part by the tendency of the traditional system to incur considerable administrative costs as a result of focusing on specific accidents in allocating costs among the parties despite the fact that the costs allocated are externalized through liability insurance.

56. A recent opinion refusing to dismiss the complaint in an action seeking recovery from the entire blasting cap industry for injuries to children caused by blasting caps is a good example of the kind of approach which is required. Chance v. E.I. DuPont de Nemours & Co., 69 C-273 (E.D.N.Y., decided May 18, 1972).

In this regard, it is well to reemphasize the relational nature of the test. It does not matter that there is currently no way in which a manufacturer of a risky medicine can make it safer for users who have no realistic alternative to taking the medicine—even though the user can identify himself as an especially risky party. *Relatively,* the manufacturer is better suited to make the only cost-benefit analysis that matters, which is one between further research and current damages. The problem may be very different if the medicine has reasonably close substitutes which carry different risks for different groups of people. An example might be a birth control pill which carries some risks of thrombosis to a group which can readily identify itself (say, through a blood test), but which has substitutes—either another pill which avoids that risk but is slightly less than 100 per cent effective (and, therefore, carries a risk for another easily self-defining group, those who wish a baby under *no* circumstances and object to abortions even if legal), or other fully effective but cumbersome birth control devices. The existence of close substitutes in this case may make the user best able to conduct the appropriate cost-benefit analysis.

Similarly, the need to establish the relative ability to make a cost-benefit analysis requires us to look realistically at the ability of the parties to act upon a perception that they are in risky categories. If there are only two medicines available to combat a serious disease, one involving a .0001 per cent risk of losing a leg, and the other involving a .0001 per cent risk of losing an arm, it is not realistic to suggest that the user is well suited to act upon the findings of a cost-benefit analysis. True, violinists will tend to prefer one medicine and olympic runners the other, but for most people no meaningful choice is available, and the size of the risk involved is so small, that it seems likely that leaving the loss on the user will result in little incentive to research.[57] It seems to us preferable to make the producer liable and thereby create a situation where there is a meaningful incentive to research, even though this may somewhat increase pharmaceutical costs to people who value only their feet.[58]

Realism is especially necessary when third parties are involved. Then the question is not whether, for example, the category to which the seller belongs or the one to which the user belongs is in the best posi-

57. We are not suggesting that the basic purpose of strict liability necessarily is, or should be, the creation of additional incentives toward safety research. In the example in text, our proposed test imposes liability on the manufacturer because he is the party who can, by actions reasonably to be expected, reduce the risk. *See* note 29 *supra.*

58. It may be that the producer is not the cheapest cost avoider in the long run, and this needs to be kept in mind in deciding whether to impose liability. *See* note 29 *supra. Compare* Posner at 75-76, RESTATEMENT OF TORTS, SECOND, § 402A, Comment K, and McLeod v. W.S. Merrell Co., 174 So.2d 736, 739 (Fla. 1965).

tion to make the cost-benefit analysis; rather, it must be asked which category is in that position relative to the category to which the third-party victim belongs. Sometimes the third party's category is the cheapest cost avoider and then the problem is easy. At other times, however, things are not so simple. If both the manufacturer and the user are in a better position than the third party victim to make the cost-benefit analysis, the strict liability test would require, as a general rule, that the victim should recover, whether he sues the manufacturer or the user.[59] If the victim chose to sue the party other than the cheapest cost avoider, that defendant should be free to join the cheapest cost avoider as a defendant or to sue him subsequently for indemnity. In either case, the strict liability rule would make the cheapest cost avoider liable and optimization of primary accident costs would be achieved, at least if we ignore the administrative costs of joinder or of the indemnificatior suit. There may well be situations, however, in which the relative abil: ties of the manufacturer and the user to make the cost-benefit analys. are so clear, and the administrative costs of joinder or indemnification are so great, that we would deny liability if the victim made the "wrong" choice and sued a defendant other than the cheapest cost avoider. For in these cases the victim is in the best position to choose the optimal defendant and should be induced to do so. But courts may in some cases be misled into assuming that where the user is in a better position than the manufacturer to make the cost-benefit analysis, it follows that the manufacturer should not be liable to third parties.[60] This error may be compounded by a tendency to assume that in third party situations the user is in a better position merely because the manufacturer warned him.[61] Instead, the fact that a manufacturer has warned the user to avoid a particular use should serve to bar a third party victim from recovering from the manufacturer only if (a) the warning is so clearly adequate as to settle the issue between manufacturer and user and (b) this fact is sufficiently known to the victim after the accident as to put him in a good position to choose the proper

59. The trend is toward strict liability of the manufacturer for injuries to third-party bystanders. See Sills v. Massey-Ferguson, Inc., 296 F. Supp. 776 (N.D. Ind. 1969) and cases there cited.

60. Compare Sills v. Massey-Ferguson, Inc., 296 F. Supp. 776, 783 (N.D. Ind. 1969). An analogous assumption often made is that a drug manufacturer fulfills its duty to consumers ("third parties") by warning the medical profession ("the users") of possible side effects. See, e.g., Basko v. Sterling Drug, Inc., 416 F.2d 417, 426 (2d Cir. 1969).

61. Thus in the drug cases it may be assumed that if a manufacturer warns the doctor of a slight risk associated with a valuable drug, the doctor is thereby placed in a better position than the manufacturer to make the cost-benefit analysis. See, e.g., Davis v. Wyeth Laboratories, Inc., 399 F.2d 121, 130 (9th Cir. 1968). This will not necessarily be the case. See pp. 1062-63 supra.

defendant.[62] The point is not so much that the concepts are hard, but rather that they can quite easily be applied erroneously.

In this respect, the history of the doctrine of assumption of risk is instructive. The doctrine asked questions like whether the defendant had the "right" to impose the risk on the plaintiff, which frequently made it circular.[63] An emphasis instead on knowledge and appreciation of the risk and availability of alternatives, equally part of the doctrine, might easily have enabled it to serve to absolve defendants only in those situations where the plaintiff's category was the cheapest cost avoider—where, in other words, the cost-benefit analysis was better left to the plaintiff.[64] Instead, the doctrine came to be applied in cases where knowledge and appreciation of the risk and availability of alternatives were in no realistic sense present for the plaintiff.[65] This may well have been because goals other than primary cost reduction prevailed in those cases, and the circular elements in the language of assumption of risk were emphasized while non-existent knowledge and appreciation of risk were assumed in order to suit those goals.[66] Thus applied, the doctrine has been much attacked.[67] That it survived at all suggests that the

---

62. *Cf.* Eck v. E.I. DuPont de Nemours & Co., 393 F.2d 197 (7th Cir. 1968).

63. *See* F. HARPER & F. JAMES, THE LAW OF TORTS § 21.3 (1956).

64. There have been, of course, many assumption of risk cases where appreciation of the risk and the availability of alternatives have been emphasized. *See, e.g.,* Guerrero v. Westgate Lumber Co., 164 Cal. App. 2d 612, 331 P.2d 107 (1958); Ridgway v. Yenny, 223 Ind. 16, 57 N.E.2d 581 (1944); Rush v. Commercial Realty Co., 7 N.J. Misc. 337, 145 A. 476 (1929).

65. This was particularly true in industrial accident cases antedating the passage of workmen's compensation legislation. *See, e.g.,* Alabama G.S.R. Co. v. Carroll, 84 Fed. 772, 28 C.C.A. 207, 52 U.S. App. 442 (1898); Titus v. Bradford, B. & K. R.R. Co., 136 Pa. 618, 20 A. 517 (1890). *But see* Davidson v. Cornell, 132 N.Y. 234, 30 N.E. 573 (1892).

66. This suggestion is a familiar one. *See, e.g.,* Tiller v. Atlantic Coast Line R.R., 318 U.S. 54, 58-67 (1943).

Compare Posner's suggestion, Posner, *supra* note 9, at 45-46, that assumption of risk was "supported by economic logic," since it served to enable the risk preferring employee (a railroad brakeman employed on a train not equipped with standard safety appliances in Posner's example) to "market his taste for risk." Of course, the same objective could have been achieved without the assumption of risk doctrine by allowing the employer to "buy out" from liability. In theory, precisely the same wage differentials and safety precautions would result as are set forth in Posner's example. *See* Calabresi, *Fault, Accidents and the Wonderful World of Blum and Kalven,* 75 YALE L.J. 216, 225-28 (1965). In practice, however, the assumption of risk doctrine, by placing the risk on the employee in the first instance, may not have served adequately to inform the employee of the risk he was assuming, whereas a rule placing liability on the employer unless he could "buy out" (*i.e.,* persuade the employee to accept the risk) would presumably have served to inform the employee of the nature and magnitude of the risk. This assumes, of course, that during the period covered by Posner's study railroads were better informed about the hazards of operating without standard safety appliances than were brakemen.

67. *See, e.g.,* Bohlen, *Voluntary Assumption of Risk,* 20 HARV. L. REV. 14, 91 (1906); James, *Assumption of Risk,* 61 YALE L.J. 141 (1952); James, *Assumption of Risk: Unhappy Reincarnation,* 78 YALE L.J. 185 (1968).

The doctrine has been abandoned in some jurisdictions, in part because of the confusion which has prevailed in its application. *See, e.g.,* McGrath v. American Cyanamid Co., 41 N.J. 272, 196 A.2d 238 (1963).

kernel of truth it contains is quite real, not that its application was often correct. Concepts like "the cheapest cost avoider" or "the category best suited to make the cost-benefit analysis" can be as easily misapplied as assumption of risk. This does not, however, mean they are useless. It only means that courts and legal scholars should be assiduous in scrutinizing their use, in criticizing misapplications and in pointing out when they are being employed to serve goals other than those of primary accident cost reduction.[68]

V. The Learned Hand Test Versus the Strict Liability Test

If the strict liability test is often difficult to apply correctly, and if Learned Hand type tests might, *in theory*, be just as capable of accomplishing optimal primary accident cost reduction, why have such fault-based tests fallen increasingly into disfavor?[69] It is not likely that the answer lies simply in the existence of distributional goals which are better served by the strict liability test. That such goals are relevant we have no doubt, and we shall discuss their relevance later. But their relevance must be limited, since the two Learned Hand tests themselves accomplish diametrically different distributional results.[70] Thus if the aim of the current trend away from the fault system were simply to favor victims as a category, this could be done as well—indeed better— by shifting from the Learned Hand test to the *reverse* Learned Hand test than by shifting to a strict liability standard. The suspicion must remain that the shift to strict liability is based in part on other grounds.

It has already been noted that the Learned Hand type tests are more "interventionistic," more collective, than is the strict liability test. Under either of the Hand tests, an organ of the state decides whether an action is worthwhile or not, and imposes the costs on the actor if it deems the action *not* worthwhile. It is not hard to see that this involves a greater degree of state involvement than that implied in the strict liability test. The latter implies state intervention only to decide which category can best determine whether an action is worthwhile, and this in turn implies less risk that traditional kinds of collective considerations will come into play.[71] But this difference between the tests, though politically significant, hardly accounts for the decline in popularity of the fault tests. After all, we have also seen an increase in recent

---

68. We do not mean to suggest that other goals are irrelevant to accident law, but that courts, legislatures and scholars should try to avoid confusing primary accident cost reduction with other goals. *See* part VI, *infra,* for a discussion of other goals.
69. *See* notes 1, 2 & 3 *supra.*
70. *See* p. 1059 *supra.*
71. *See* note 20 *supra.*

years in direct criminal prohibitions aimed at conduct in the accident area deemed not worthwhile.[72] Such prohibitions surely involve greater state intervention than do even the Learned Hand tests.[73] That political preference for laissez faire has spurred the move toward strict liability therefore seems as unlikely as the explanation that the move has been solely influenced by distributional goals. We suspect that the move to strict liability today, no less than similar moves to respondent superior, ultrahazardous activity liability and workmen's compensation in the past, are based at least in part on a desire to accomplish better primary accident cost reduction.

Earlier we noted that it seems unlikely that either Learned Hand test could effectively be applied in practice at the category level. We questioned whether at the level where it really mattered, that is at the level of who actually pays, the rubric of "fault" is likely to be congenial. And yet it is clear that if the Learned Hand tests *are* to accomplish optimal primary accident cost reduction they must be applied at that level, and not at the arbitrary level of parties to an accident who do not ultimately bear the costs and who are not therefore given any incentive to choose avoidance even where it is worthwhile. The appropriate avoidance decisions *must* be made at a category level, and at that level the Learned Hand tests may seem unjust. Furthermore, the categories which end up bearing the losses as a result of an application of negligence tests on a case by case basis are not likely to be those which would be selected were such tests applied at a category level, nor is this technique likely to be the most efficient way available for selecting the categories which *are* chosen. All this has been discussed at length elsewhere, and need not be gone into further,[74] but it is important to note that the reluctance to apply the Learned Hand test to categories may be a significant underlying explanation for the current disfavor of "negligence" calculus type tests.

There is, however, another set of reasons which may explain the move away from Learned Hand tests. Hard though the strict liability

72. The prohibitions which have received the most attention have been those relating to automobile safety. See the Traffic and Motor Vehicle Safety Act, 15 U.S.C.A. §§ 1381-1431 (Supp. 1972).

73. For example, under either Hand type test, a party burdened with the costs because the collective deciders have deemed avoidance to be worthwhile may, at least in some cases, choose to omit safety measures and pay compensatory damages instead. In contrast, a collective prohibition is generally meant to be obeyed. See Costs, *supra* note 10, at 68-69.

74. See Costs, *supra* note 10, at 255-59. To summarize that discussion briefly: case-by-case determination entails substantial administrative costs, tends to focus on unusual rather than recurring causes and on accident avoidance rather than accident cost avoidance, and is a misleading way of compiling those statistics which are meaningful at the category level.

test may be to apply correctly, it is nonetheless easier to apply than is the calculus of fault. We have seen that it may well be difficult to know whether the category to which a seller, user or third party belongs can best make a cost-benefit analysis of risks involved and act on that analysis. But it is more difficult still to decide correctly not only who can most cheaply act on a cost-benefit analysis, but also what the result of that cost-benefit analysis must be. Yet this is precisely what the Learned Hand-type tests require of the governmental deciders if they are to achieve optimal primary accident cost avoidance. None of the significant difficulties involved in the strict liability test are avoided, and to them is added the danger that the governmental deciders will resolve the cost-benefit analysis incorrectly.

One cannot answer, moreover, that the Learned Hand-type tests avoid some of the difficulties inherent in the strict liability test by deciding collectively whether or not avoidance is worthwhile, whereas the strict liability test leaves such judgments to the individual categories. This answer is not available because the negligence tests result in compensatory damages rather than prohibitions. Individual categories are, therefore, allowed to decide that avoidance is *not* worthwhile despite a contrary determination by the collectivity (or vice versa).[75]

This may serve to explain the concomitant, seemingly paradoxical rise of collective prohibitions together with the less interventionistic strict liability test, at the expense of negligence type tests. Where a collective determination that an action is *not* worthwhile can be made with a modicum of assurance, prohibitions enforced criminally or through uninsurable fines seem appropriate. Where, instead, there is serious doubt that such a collective determination of utility is likely to be correct, the best solution is an individualistic one. This implies a decision limited to selecting the best decider, the cheapest cost avoider, among the relevant categories, and not extending to which particular acts or forebearances are appropriate. Viewed in this light, the rise of criminally enforced prohibitions in some areas, and strict liability in others, rather than being paradoxical, can be viewed as a quite sensible reaction to the same stimulus—that is, to the desire to minimize the sum of accident costs and the costs of avoiding accidents.

VI. Relationship to Other Goals

We have seen that there are a variety of devices which could in theory be used to accomplish primary accident cost reduction. Concep-

---

75. *See* note 73 *supra*. Of course, a party may also decide to ignore a collective prohibition, but in considering the likelihood and magnitude of the penalty he must take into account the stigma involved, and this results in a very different kind of calculus.

tually, they range from: (a) those in which the decision-maker is highly centralized and makes criminally enforceable determinations of which actions are worthwhile and which are not through (b) those in which negligence type calculi are employed to make the same decisions at a more decentralized but nonetheless state agency level, enforcing those decisions through compensatory damages; to (c) those in which collective decisions are made only to identify who is the cheapest cost avoider —the category best suited to determine if avoidance of accidents is worth its costs—allowing the chosen category to make the cost-benefit decision itself. We have also seen that these devices in practice imply different likelihoods of success in accomplishng primary cost avoidance. Finally, we have seen that these approaches will each have a different distributional effect. Far from being insignificant, distributional differences may well determine the approach chosen. Some discussion of distributional effects and goals is thus essential to an understanding of the two Learned Hand type tests and the strict liability alternative.

In discussing the distributional aspects of liability rules there are two problems which it is well to separate. The first relates to the types of effects that are lumped together in the concept of distribution, and the proper role of each of these effects in the choice of liability rules. The second goes to the quite different question of the appropriate role of juries and courts, as against legislatures, in selecting among liability rules in order to accomplish distributional effects.

That both problems are crucial can be seen through an example. The present Learned Hand test tends to make injurers richer at the expense of victims. The reverse Learned Hand test would have precisely the opposite effect. In choosing between them a society will presumably be influenced not only by which of the two tests is more likely to accomplish optimal primary accident cost reduction, but also, if it has such a preference, by which category it wishes to make wealthier. This choice may be affected by factors such as the initial relative wealth of the categories, but relative wealth is only a part of the choice implied. For one category may be better able to spread losses than the other, or one category may in some sense be viewed as being worthier. Sorting out the relevant effects lumped under the term distribution, therefore, is a necessary task for society in choosing among liability rules. But when that is done another series of questions remains: Which, if any, of the distributional considerations are appropriate to judicial decisions among liability rules, which are appropriate to ad hoc jury determinations, and which can only be properly settled by legislatures?

It should be plain that a full treatment of these questions cannot be attempted in this article. Nevertheless, some indications of relevant distributional considerations and some reflections on the historical role of courts and juries with respect to these can be offered.

For the purposes of this article, we are lumping together as distributional all those effects of liability rules which do not relate to minimizing (a) the sum of accident costs and avoidance costs, and (b) the administrative costs entailed by that minimization. Thus under a society's distributional goals we are including preferences of quite varied types. These preferences may reflect a desire to distribute or fractionize losses, often called spreading. They may reflect a preference for moving toward a given distribution of wealth, such as greater wealth equality, better treatment for higher castes, or better treatment for castes which in the past have been poorly treated. They may instead reflect a desire to further what might be viewed as dynamic efficiency goals—as might occur by favoring the doers, the entrepreneurs in a society. Finally, they may reflect a society's notion, if it has one or if it has many, of rewarding individuals' merits—of recognizing their just deserts.

All of these preferences are in fact relevant in some way to the choice of liability rules. Indeed, all of them, together with the pure efficiency notion reflected in the aim of minimizing the sum of accident and accident avoidance costs, are part of what is at times called justice.[76] They are relevant because there is no a priori reason why a legislature might not choose a liability rule solely because it tends to redistribute income from, say, rich to poor. Whether a legislature would be wise to employ liability rules for this purpose is, of course, another matter. That depends on, among other things, the availability of alternative devices for accomplishing the desired income redistribution and on the effect which this use of a liability rule might have on the achievement of other goals whose effectuation is tied to the operation of such rules. But there is no logical reason why a legislature's desires with respect to income equality or caste preference cannot be well served through the choice of one liability rule as against another. Similarly, and in practice even more commonly, a legislature's preference as to spreading, desert and long run efficiency can effectively be furthered by choosing one liability rule rather than another.

Recently Professor Fletcher has argued instead that the only distributional considerations which should be considered in choosing among

---

76. *See* F. HARPER, THE LAW OF TORTS §§ 1, 3 & 4 (1933). *See also* Bierman v. City of New York, 302 N.Y.S.2d 696, 60 Misc. 2d 497 (Civ. Ct. of the City of New York, 1969). *Cf.* Magrine v. Spector, 100 N.J. Super. 223, 238-41, 241 A.2d 637, 646-47 (Botter, J.S.C., dissenting).

liability rules are those which relate to an individual's just desert—those which decide who is to be richer or poorer on the basis of what people have done rather than what they are or where they start out.[77] Indeed the argument goes further, and suggests that such considerations should determine the choice of liability rules regardless of any "instrumentalist" goals like the reduction of the sum of accident costs and the costs of avoiding accidents.

In one sense, it is very easy to agree with Professor Fletcher. If a society has a sufficiently well-developed theory of deserts such that all the other considerations of efficiency and distributional equity we have mentioned are reflected in that theory, then "desert" tautologically will determine the appropriate liability rules for that society. Unfortunately, we do not find ourselves able to define, let alone find, such an all encompassing theory of deserts in our society.[78] Indeed, we often find that what pass for statements of desert, of who ought to be richer or poorer on the basis of merit, can quite readily be seen as judgments based on the desire to accomplish either efficient accident avoidance or some other of the distributional preferences mentioned previously.

Nor does Professor Fletcher's test for deserts help us very much. He argues that losses ought to lie where they fall unless the victim did not create a risk "reciprocal" to the one which resulted in his being injured. Examining examples of reciprocity and non-reciprocity, we are struck by three things. The first is that frequently reciprocity is simply an approximation of the result which would be required by that most instrumentalist of tests, the strict liability test described in this article.[79] The second observation is that when reciprocity and the test we propose seem to deviate, the strict liability result appears to be more desirable.[80]

---

77. Fletcher, *Fairness and Utility in Tort Theory*, 85 HARV. L. REV. 537, 547 n.40 (1972).

78. A recent book by Professor Rawls may be thought to be an attempt to formulate such a theory. J. RAWLS, A THEORY OF JUSTICE (1972). *But see* Hampshire, *A New Philosophy of the Just Society*, THE N.Y. REV. BOOKS, Feb. 24, 1972, at 34 (Vol. XVIII, No. 3) questioning whether the formulation of a complete theory of deserts is possible. *See also* Feinberg, Review, 81 YALE L.J. 1004 (1972).

79. The examples of liability set out by Fletcher, *supra* note 77, at 547-48, illustrate this point rather well. Liability for crop dusting as between neighbors is, we think, unrelated to whatever risks happen to be imposed upon the duster by those neighbors who breathe his dust. It is based instead on the relative ability of the duster to calculate the costs and benefits of dusting in the particular situation involved and act upon that calculation.

80. Returning to Fletcher's crop dusting example, suppose instead that the parties are a farmer who dusts his 500 acres of irrigated reclaimed desert and a homesteader who, with knowledge of the farmer's agricultural methods, chooses out of 500,000 acres of available (and equally beautiful, accessible and desirable, but undusted) desert one acre adjacent to the farmer's land for a homestead. Suppose also, to give reciprocity more than its due, that the homesteader in no way benefits from the farmer's presence, that is, he uses none of the farmer's produce. The homesteader imposes no risks on

The third observation is that when we do not approve (in terms of who is made richer and who is poorer) of a result dictated by the efficiency test, it is often in cases where reciprocity would lead to the same undesirable result.[81]

None of these observations should be especially surprising. Justice notions do attach to efficiency considerations such as those served by the strict liability test, and this is sufficient to explain why approximations of that test should seem just. They also attach to distributional preferences like "favor spreading," "further wealth equality," and "benefit a particular ethnic group," which go to what people are rather than what they do. This explains why that which is preferable, given a society's desire to further wealth equalization or a caste preference, may seem more desirable than the result which either a strict liability test or a reciprocity test would impose. Justice notions attach to other societal preferences which can only with difficulty be explained in terms of either efficiency or wealth distributional preferences designed to make some groups richer because of what they are. These other justice notions, which we are unable to describe in general terms, are, of course, crucial to the choice of liability rules.[82] Indeed, we have elsewhere left room for a veto of liability rules which violate such non-generalized justice imperatives,[83] because to date these imperatives have not been put together in a way which would enable us to talk about them other than as constraints within which other, more generalized goals can be seen to operate. Professor Fletcher instead offers reciprocity as a way of putting these imperatives together in the field of accidents.

It is with this in mind then, that one must examine reciprocity. Is there anything about reciprocity which should make it justify making someone richer or poorer apart from efficiency and apart from distributional preferences based on what people are? When the question is

the farmer, and reciprocity would therefore seem to require holding the farmer liable for the results of dust breathing by the homesteader, regardless of the availability and cost to the farmer of alternative methods of crop protection. The strict liability test, taking into account the relative abilities of the parties to compare the costs of dust breathing by the homesteader with the costs of avoidance, and to act on the basis of such a calculation, would not impose liability on the farmer. Professor Fletcher might respond that the homesteader "creates" the risk by moving, but that response would reduce the reciprocity test to a tautology. That is, reciprocity would give no guidance for decision, but would simply be a label attached to a result reached on other grounds.

81. If the farmers were a preferred group, such as disabled veterans, whose crop dusting was essential to their livelihood, we might disapprove of a liability rule (whether based on reciprocity or efficiency) which, in effect, prevented crop dusting.

82. See Calabresi & Melamed, *Property Rules, Liability Rules, and Inalienability: One View of the Cathedral*, 85 HARV. L. REV. 1089, 1104-05 (1972).

83. COSTS, *supra* note 10, at 24-26, 291-308.

thus posed, when reciprocity is viewed not as an approximation of efficiency but as an approximation of a generalized theory of desert, it turns out to be philosophically very meager.[84]

If income equality, dynamic efficiency, and spreading are all relevant to a society's choice of liability rules, it does not follow that all are equally suited to being considered by courts or juries. Obviously, those which are deemed suited to judicial considerations will depend on one's view of the nature of adjudication and the role of courts and juries in a legal process. We cannot possibly begin to resolve these issues in this article. We can, however, point out some solutions which are transparently too simple, both in themselves and in terms of what courts and juries have done historically.

One cannot write off distributional considerations based on ability to spread, or on wealth or caste, as Professor Fletcher has done, with a reference to Aristotle and a comment that taxation is for legislatures and not for courts.[85] When courts chose a Learned Hand test rather than a reverse Learned Hand test, they did not simply toss a coin, given that the tests were equally efficient in theory.[86] Distributive consequences may not have been the dominant or even a conscious motive for the decisions, but it is difficult to argue that historically these consequences were irrelevant to the choice.[87] Similarly, too many courts have explicitly considered the ability to spread losses in torts cases as a factor in choosing one liability rule instead of another to allow us to dismiss its relevance to judicial decisions out of hand.[88] One can, of

84. The examples discussed by Fletcher, *supra* note 77, at 547-48 seem to indicate that the reciprocity test is temporally bound. That is, the risk imposer who does not recover is usually the party who creates an "unusual" risk. An unusual risk may mean a risk which can be cheaply avoided, but that is the strict liability test. Fletcher seems to be looking instead to which risks are new. If this is what is meant, reciprocity, without more, is incapable of serving as a philosophical theory of desert. For it would amount basically to saying only that those who take new risks are less deserving than those who take customary risks.

85. *See* Fletcher, *supra* note 77, at 547, n.40.

86. Here we are assuming, with Professor Posner, that historically the courts did "choose" a Learned Hand test. Posner, *supra* note 9, *passim*. Certainly they did not choose the reverse.

If for some reason the tests in practice would not equally yield optimizing solutions, if, for example, victims in practice proved far less able to alter their behavior than injurers (notwithstanding that the value of their activity was less than the resultant accident costs), then the choice of the Learned Hand test rather than the reverse would imply a distributional effect *in spite of* efficiency considerations.

87. *Cf.* the explanation usually given for the development of the fellow servant rule. *See, e.g.,* W. Prosser, Torts 529 (4th ed. 1971). *Cf.* also note 66 *supra*.

88. These decisions in recent years have been an outgrowth of the concurring opinion of Justice Traynor in Escola v. Coca Cola Bottling Co., 24 Cal.2d 453, 461, 750 P.2d 436 (1944). *See* W. Prosser, Torts § 5 at 22 (4th ed. 1971).

course, question the wisdom of such decisions.[89] One might further suggest that courts should consider such distributive effects only when they reflect reasonably explicit societal goals. Alternatively, one might maintain that courts should be free to follow their own distributional preferences so long as they do not conflict with well defined societal goals (such as, perhaps, efficiency), provided that the legislature has the power to reverse the court's judgment. Finally, one might support the position that because of the way judges are picked, they are suited to balance other goals, like efficiency, with explicitly distributional ones in choosing liability rules for a society. All these are possible approaches worth considering. What one cannot do, we would suggest, is to act as if distributional considerations did not historically play a role in judicial choice of liability rules, and must not do so today regardless of the strength and clarity of a society's commitment to specific distributional preferences.[90]

Having said this, we do not here need to argue with Professor Posner over whether the particular choice of Learned Hand test made and applied between 1895 and 1905 was based, as many have said,[91] on distributional considerations or was, as he maintains, essentially an efficiency choice.[92] It is perfectly clear *at the very least* that that choice, both when made well before 1895 and as applied for many years, had distributional effects which are very different from those produced by alternative tests which were as, or more, likely to accomplish primary accident cost avoidance. That these different distributional goals seem to be in the ascendancy today may again help to explain the move away from the classical Learned Hand test. They do not, however, suffice to explain why the move has been to strict liability rather than to a reverse Learned Hand test, which would seem to serve the currently dominant distributional goals of spreading and distribution in favor of victims more fully than does the strict liability test.[93]

89. *See, e.g.*, the dissenting opinions of Chief Justice Taft in Lonzrick v. Republic Steel Corp., 6 Ohio St. 2d, 227, 218 N.E.2d 185 (1966), and of Judge Burke in Goldberg v. Kollsman Instrument Corp., 12 N.Y.2d 432, 191 N.E.2d 81 (1963). *See also* Wights v. Staff Jennings, Inc., 241 Ore. 301, 309, 405 P.2d 624, 628-29 (1965), where the court refused to adopt strict products liability based on a "risk spreading" rationale, stating that such a theory "proves too much."

90. Other institutions may do a better job of dealing with distributional considerations, but this need not mean that courts are compelled to ignore them.

91. *See, e.g.*, Horwitz, Did the Legal System Subsidize Economic Growth in Ante-Bellum America? (unpublished paper delivered at the annual meeting of the American Historical Association, Boston, 1970).

92. Posner, *supra* note 9, at 32.

93. There have been numerous suggestions that a strict liability test serves the goal of spreading; *see, e.g.*, James, *Accident Liability Reconsidered: The Impact of Liability Insurance*, 57 YALE L.J. 549 (1948).

It would require another article to go into all of the distributional ramifications of

One more consideration remains in discussing the relationship to the test chosen of goals other than efficiency. Not only does the choice of test have substantial distributive effects, but its application in specific or doubtful cases does also. Thus the issue is not simply whether a society opts for a direct prohibition, a Learned Hand test, a reverse Learned Hand test or a strict liability test. Whatever goals are sought will also be at the mercy of applications of the chosen test. It is here, of course, that Fletcher's caveat about the role of courts seems more directly in point, though even here we would not be as ready as he is dogmatically to exclude considerations of distributive justice from the purview of courts and juries. The issue is a nice one and reasonable men may differ as to whether distributive considerations should apply (1) at all, or (2) only in cases where primary cost avoidance considerations do not provide a clear outcome, or (3) whether they ought to dominate over efficiency considerations even when the latter would imply a clear result.

As a practical matter, we would suggest that in applications of the traditional Learned Hand test, distributive considerations have very frequently at least played the second role and not infrequently the third. Unlike Posner, we find some support for this point of view in his admirable collection of appellate decisions.[94] Many dubious and some clearly "inefficient" decisions can be thus explained.[95] Without doing a similar study in more recent times, we would suggest that the change in the application of the fault standard since 1905 which has seemed so obvious to so many writers, may well reflect a similar kind of interplay between new distributional goals and the efficiency implications of the traditional Learned Hand test.

This kind of interplay is unlikely to stop merely because a change is made to a strict liability test which combines better primary accident cost avoidance with distributional goals which seem more congenial to the current age. Even within a regime of strict liability, courts and juries deciding which category is the cheapest cost avoider will in unclear cases most likely continue to consider whether some distributional goals are not best served by one decision rather than the other.

the strict liability test. We believe that this test would tend to favor victims as a category, because in practice they are, *inter alia*, generally less well informed than injurers, but it would not do so to the same extent as a reverse Learned Hand test, which would put the cost of all accidents not worth avoiding on injurers.

94. Posner, *supra* note 9, at 52-96.

95. We find it difficult to agree, for example, that application of the principle of respondent superior to employers but not to families was based entirely on efficiency grounds. Posner, *supra* note 9, at 43. It seems more likely that distributional considerations were relevant to that determination.

Nor would we be surprised if distributional goals will fairly frequently lead to liability results under a strict liability test which are pretty clearly wrong if one considers primary cost avoidance alone. Sometimes this will be the effect of legislative determinations, but at other times it will be the result of decisions by judge and jury—as it has been in the past. To say that this is wrong would be to conclude that once a liability test is chosen the role of the courts is to give effect only to efficiency. It may well be that this conclusion is appropriate, given the nature of courts and the lack of consensus for particular distributional preferences like spreading, greater wealth equality, or compensation of maltreated castes. This conclusion is not, however, a necessary one. Indeed, many years ago, Professor Clarence Morris argued that courts were very well suited to make just this kind of distributional decision, though only when whole *classes* of cases were affected.[96] Similarly, the ability and suitability of the jury to do the same in *individual* cases has been frequently argued.[97]

As a practical matter, introducing such distributional considerations, whether at the legislative or the judicial level, does make application of the strict liability test easier, just as in the past it made application of the Learned Hand test easier. For often a hard issue of whether the victim's category or the injurer's category is best suited to make a cost-benefit analysis between avoidance and compensation becomes easy if one choice serves distributional goals while the other undercuts them. In practice it will also be as hard to tell just what the roles of efficiency and distribution were in making the choice as it is for Professor Posner and us to agree on what the roles of the two sets of goals were in his 1895-1905 cases. Analytical frameworks, and the distinctions made therein, serve to elucidate; they rarely tell us what judges and juries did in individual cases.

VII. Conclusion

We have tried, in this article, to describe a framework, a test, which might help to put into place the factors that seem to be central to defining the limits of strict liability in the areas of the law where it has come to dominate. We contrasted this test with the classical negligence calculus and its mirror image. We noted that this strict liability test seems more likely than either of the others to accomplish a minimization of the sum of accident costs and of accident avoidance costs. We

96. Morris, *Hazardous Enterprises and Risk Bearing Capacity,* 61 YALE L.J. 1172 (1952).
97. *See, e.g.,* F. JAMES, CIVIL PROCEDURE § 7.4 at 240 (1965).

then discussed why we believe the move toward such a test cannot be explained solely in terms of distributional goals, though we readily admitted that such goals might also be served by the move. Finally, we expressed the view that even though such a test is very well suited to accomplishing an optimal reduction of primary accident costs, we would expect that in its application goals other than efficiency will often predominate.

Because Fleming James, through his writing, teaching, and warm colleagueship, first guided and then sustained our earliest as well as our more recent work in this field, we gratefully dedicate this piece to him. May retirement for him, as it was for his teacher, Arthur Corbin, simply be an opportunity to push the quest further.

TOWARD AN ECONOMIC THEORY OF LIABILITY

JOHN PRATHER BROWN*

R ECENTLY there have appeared a number of important articles by both lawyers and economists analyzing the economic effects of liability rules.[1] This
paper formalizes the analysis of these effects. When two parties, the injurer
and the victim, can both take measures to reduce the likelihood of accidents,
and the measures are costly for both, the standard theory of production with
two inputs and one output yields the conditions for the socially optimal amount
of each accident avoidance measure. The effects of decentralizing the problem
and using only liability rules to solve it can then be analyzed in terms of a
two-person noncooperative game. I first show that there is a complete symmetry within each of the following pairs of liability rules: no liability and
strict liability; the negligence rule and strict liability with contributory negligence; and the negligence rule with contributory negligence and strict
liability with what I call dual contributory negligence. An analysis of the
legal standards for negligence follows. I show that there is an important
ambiguity in the so-called "Learned Hand Rule" for determining the level of
avoidance effort below which a party is adjudged negligent. Two of the formu-
lations of the rule lead to inefficient results.

Next the main results of the paper are presented. First, given the negligence
rule with contributory negligence and what I call the Incremental Standard
of care, the social optimum is shown to be the unique equilibrium for the
noncooperative game. A corollary is that the same results hold when the
negligence standard is replaced by strict liability with contributory negligence. When the Incremental Standard is replaced by the Limited Information

* Assistant Professor of Economics, Brown University; Fellow in Law and Economics,
University of Chicago Law School. The author would like to thank William Brock,
Harry Kalven, Jr., J. Huston McCulloch, John L. Peterman, Lester Telser, John Ver
Steeg, and the members of the Industrial Organization Workshop at the University of
Chicago for helpful comments and criticism.

[1] See Guido Calabresi, The Costs of Accidents: A Legal and Economic Analysis (1970),
and (with Jon T. Hirschoff), Toward a Test for Strict Liability in Torts, 81 Yale L.J.
1055 (1972); R. H. Coase, The Problem of Social Cost, 3 J. Law & Econ. 1 (1960);
Harold Demsetz, When Does the Rule of Liability Matter?, 1 J. Leg. Studies 13 (1972);
Roland N. McKean, Products Liability: Trends and Implications, in Symposium on
Products Liability, 38 U. Chi. L. Rev. 3 (1970); Richard A. Posner, A Theory of Negligence, 1 J. Leg. Studies 29 (1972), and Strict Liability: A Comment, 2 J. Leg. Studies
205 (1973).

Incremental Standard the identity between equilibrium and optimality is destroyed. In an appendix the Coase Theorem is restated in our framework and compared with our results.

I. THE MODEL

Consider a small device, a black box, which is attached to some otherwise useful object such as a railway crossing, an airplane, or a sidewalk. The only function of the device is to emit a bill for a large amount of money from time to time, so we shall call it a liability generator. That large amount of money is fixed at A.

On the liability generator are two controls, X and Y. Each of these controls is continuously variable. Increasing either or both increases the probability that the accident will be avoided, but at a decreasing rate. The probability that an accident is avoided in a given time interval is denoted $P(X, Y)$, so the probability that an accident occurs in that interval is $1 - P(X, Y)$.[2] Figure 1 shows the relationship between X, Y and $P(X, Y)$. Examples of what will be meant here by controls are built-in safety devices and careful driving in the railway crossing case, defect-free radar and careful flying in the airplane case, and shoveling snow and careful walking in the sidewalk case.

By this description of accident avoidance we have constructed an almost exact analogue of the neoclassical production function, familiar to economists, where there are two inputs, X and Y, producing one output, $P(X, Y)$, which in our case is the probability that an accident will be avoided.[3] Just as the inputs to production are costly and should be economized on, so the accident avoidance controls X and Y are costly. Let the cost per unit of X be W_x and the cost per unit of Y be W_y. The total cost for a given level of X and Y is then

[2] The time interval is chosen small enough that the probability of more than one accident in the interval is negligible.

[3] I say an almost exact analogue because we must take explicit account of the possibility that the accident can be completely avoided and further amounts of accident avoidance contribute nothing. Formally, we assume (1) that $P(X, Y)$ is continuous and twice differentiable in X and Y, (2) that the marginal products of both inputs are non-negative, and (3) marginal products do not increase. The possibility of complete avoidance admits the possibility that marginal products and their rate of change are zero. Our final assumption about $P(X, Y)$ is (4) that $P_{xy}(X, Y) \equiv \dfrac{\partial P^2(X, Y)}{\partial X \partial Y} < 0$. We shall discuss this assumption later in the analysis.

I have chosen to have two controls to concentrate on the necessity in most accident contexts of having more than one party take costly measures to avoid accidents. Formally, it is a trivial extension to have more than two parties, but the legal implications of explicitly recognizing that there are more than two parties with responsibilities to avoid accidents should be explored carefully. The occasional cases where only one party can avoid the accident are special cases of this analysis where the equiprobability curves of Figure 1 would be either horizontal or vertical straight lines.

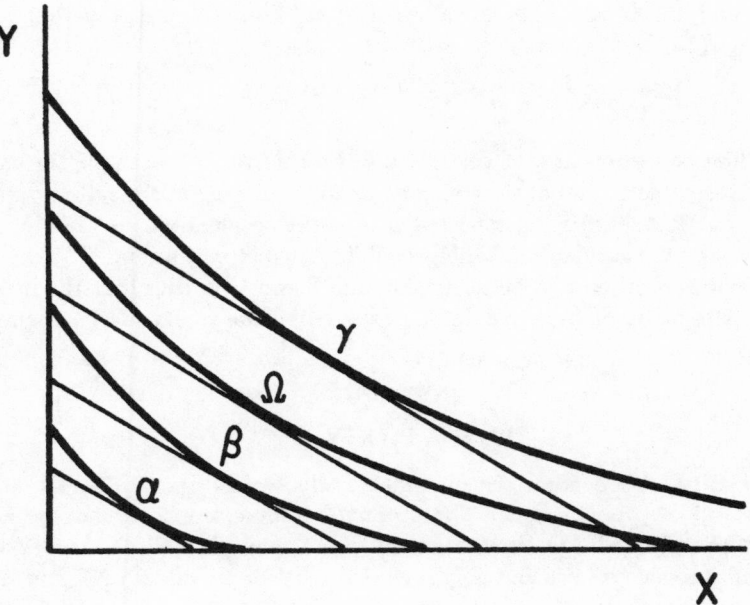

FIGURE 1

$W_xX + W_yY$. The straight lines in Figure 1 are all of the combinations of X and Y having the same total cost. This completes the transformation of the accident avoidance problem into the standard production theory format. To find the least cost combination to X and Y which will yield a given probability of accident avoidance one need only find the point on the equiprobability curve just tangent to a cost line. Examples are drawn in Figure 1 at α, β, γ and Ω.

Which combination of avoidance measures X and Y and the resulting probability of accident $P(X, Y)$ is the most preferred? To answer that question we consider the case where both X and Y are under the control of the same party. In the simple case first before us, all quantities are measured in terms of money, so it makes no difference who makes the decision. The outcome we shall call the social optimum, and we shall use it to evaluate outcomes when X and Y are controlled by different people, which is of course the most interesting problem.

The social optimum we shall define as that combination of avoidance measures which minimizes the sum of the costs of the controls and the expected cost of the accident. With the apparatus that we have developed it is now a simple matter to write down the problem and to characterize the solution.

Formally, the socially optimal values of X and Y are those that minimize social cost, $C_S(X, Y)$. Thus

$$\min_{X, Y} C_S(X, Y) = W_x X + W_y Y + A[1 - P(X, Y)]. \qquad (1)$$

The first two terms are the costs of the two controls, for example the costs of the crossing gates and of slower, more cautious driving in the railway crossing case. The last term is the expected cost of the accident and is the product of the cost of the accident and the probability that it will occur.

For the social cost to be at a minimum it must be true that the marginal cost of each input be equal to the expected value of its marginal product. That is

$$W_x = A P_x(X, Y) \qquad \text{and} \qquad (2)$$

$$W_y = A P_y(X, Y) \qquad (3)$$

where $P_x(X, Y)$ denotes the marginal product of X and $P_y(X, Y)$ denotes the marginal product of Y. The optimal solution can be found by solving equations (2) and (3) simultaneously for X and Y. Call the values which minimize social cost X_Ω and Y_Ω. Then it is true for all values of X and Y that

$$C_S(X_\Omega, Y_\Omega) \leqslant C_S(X, Y) \qquad \text{for all X and Y.} \qquad (4)$$

The optimal values are those that would be chosen if both X and Y were under common control. The problem that interests us here is where X and Y are controlled by different people.

Before proceeding further it will be helpful to deal with two misleading concepts, one used by lawyers and the other used by economists. The first is the notion that liability ought to be placed on whoever caused the accident. In the scheme we have described, who caused the accident, the victim or the injurer? They both did. The problem is exactly analogous to the futile arguments among economists in the nineteenth century about whether capital or labor causes production. They both do. We must go on to further considerations to decide how the fruits of production should be divided; similarly we have to decide who should bear the liability for accidents when they are jointly caused. The only role for discussions of causation is to exonerate a party completely by proving that he is a stranger to the accident.

A similar issue arises with the notion of "least cost avoider." A number of writers, among them Calabresi and Demsetz, have recommended placing liability on the best cost avoider. For example, Demsetz states: "It is difficult to suggest any criterion for deciding liability other than placing it on the party able to avoid the costly interaction most easily."[4] Looking back at

4 Harold Demsetz, *supra* note 1, at 28.

Figure 1, how can we identify the best cost avoider? One possible meaning would be to compare the cost of the victim's completely avoiding the accident (*i.e.*, setting $P(0, Y) = 0$, with the cost of the injurer's completely avoiding the accident $P(X, 0) = 0$). The party with the lowest cost would be the cheapest cost avoider. Another possible interpretation of the phrase "least cost avoider" is that it is a local notion depending on (X, Y), that is, on what the parties in fact chose to do. This leaves unanswered how liability should be assigned in order to induce the parties to take the optimal amount of avoidance action. The notion of least cost avoider is thus likely to confuse rather than to clarify matters.

II. DECENTRALIZATION USING A LIABILITY RULE

When the two avoidance mechanisms are in the hands of different people, for example the manufacturer and the driver when the liability generator is attached to an automobile, or the manufacturer and patient in the case of a drug, the question arises as to how the bill shall be paid when an accident takes place. The question is answered by the court. Since this paper is concerned with how injurer and victims can be expected to respond under different liability rules I have chosen to provide only the simplest abstraction of the court and its functioning. For our purposes the only function of the legal system is the impeccable administration of whatever liability rule is in force. In order to concentrate on what is our major concern, the parties' behavior, we ignore the distinction between judge and jury, the problems of proof and burden of proof, the uncertainty of the outcome, the mistakes that the court can make, and the expense of operating the legal system.

To fix ideas for the rest of the discussion, let X be controlled by Xavier the Injurer, and Y by Yvonne the Victim. The rule that determines which party must pay the bill emitted by the liability generator is called a liability rule. The liability rule will in general be a function of the level of avoidance chosen by each party and will be expressed as the fraction of the bill, A, owed by each party. Let $L_x(X, Y)$ and $L_y(X, Y)$ be the liabilities of Xavier and Yvonne, respectively. Then

$$L_x(X, Y) \geqslant 0, \; L_y(X, Y) \geqslant 0 \qquad \text{for all X, Y} \qquad (5)$$

$$L_x(X, Y) + L_y(X, Y) = 1 \qquad \text{for all X, Y.} \qquad (6)$$

The amount that must be paid by Xavier when an accident takes place is $A L_x(X, Y)$ and the amount to be paid by Yvonne is $A L_y(X, Y)$.

A number of different liability rules have been discussed in the recent literature.[5] They are simple to put into the framework we propose but for some

[5] See Calabresi, Calabresi and Hirschoff, and Posner works cited in note 1 *supra*.

of them we require one further notion, that of a legal standard of negligence. Let (X^*, Y^*) be the legal standard of negligence. If X is less than X^* then the injurer will be found legally negligent. Similarly, if Y is less than Y^*, the victim will be found negligent. Now we are ready to describe the liability rules.

1. *No liability*. The victim is liable under all circumstances.

$$L_x(X, Y) = 0 \qquad L_y(X, Y) = 1 \qquad \text{for all X, Y.} \qquad (7)$$

2. *Strict liability*. The injurer is liable under all circumstances.

$$L_x(X, Y) = 1 \qquad L_y(X, Y) = 0 \qquad \text{for all X, Y.} \qquad (8)$$

3. *The negligence rule*. The victim is liable unless the injurer is found negligent.

$$L_x(X, Y) = \begin{cases} 0 \\ 1 \end{cases} \quad L_y(X, Y) = \begin{cases} 1 & \text{if } X \geqslant X^* \\ 0 & \text{if } X < X^* \end{cases} \qquad (9)$$

4. *Strict liability with contributory negligence*. The injurer is liable unless the victim is found negligent.

$$L_x(X, Y) = \begin{cases} 1 \\ 0 \end{cases} \quad L_y(X, Y) = \begin{cases} 0 & \text{if } Y \geqslant Y^* \\ 1 & \text{if } Y < Y^* \end{cases} \qquad (10)$$

5. *The negligence rule with contributory negligence*. The injurer is liable if he is negligent *and* the victim is not. The victim is liable otherwise.

$$L_x(X, Y) = \begin{cases} 1 \\ 0 \end{cases} \quad L_y(X, Y) = \begin{cases} 0 & \text{if } X < X^* \text{ and } Y \geqslant Y^* \\ 1 & \text{otherwise} \end{cases} \qquad (11)$$

The negligence rule with contributory negligence has been the dominant rule in tort law since *Brown v. Kendall*.[6] In that landmark case the defendant (the injurer) took up a stick to separate fighting dogs belonging to the plaintiff (the victim) and the defendant. In the course of beating the dogs the defendant accidentally hit the plaintiff in the eye, injuring him severely. Chief Justice Shaw laid down the rule: ". . . if both plaintiff and defendant at the time of the blow were using ordinary care, or if at that time the defendant was using ordinary care, and the plaintiff was not, or if at that time, both the defendant and the plaintiff were not using ordinary care, then the plaintiff could not recover."[7]

Notice that there is complete symmetry in our model between no liability and strict liability on the one hand and between the negligence rule on the

---

[6] 60 Mass. (6 Cush.) 292 (1850).
[7] *Id*. at 296.

one hand and strict liability with contributory negligence on the other. The strict liability rule that would be symmetrical to the negligence rule with contributory negligence has been mentioned only by Calabresi and Hirschoff in the recent literature. It might be called:

6. *Strict liability with dual contributory negligence.* The victim is liable if he is negligent *and* the injurer is not. The injurer is liable otherwise.

$$L_x(X, Y) = \begin{cases} 0 \\ 1 \end{cases} \quad L_y(X, Y = \begin{cases} 1 & \text{if } Y < Y^* \text{ and } X \geqslant X^* \\ 0 & \text{otherwise} \end{cases}. \quad (12)$$

The six liability rules are displayed graphically in Figure 2.

There are two further liability rules that are somewhat outside the tradition encompassed in the six rules presented here in that the standard of care for one party is the level of care exercised by the other party. They are relative negligence and comparative negligence.

7. *Relative negligence.* The injurer is liable if the increment to accident avoidance per dollar of avoidance by him is greater than that per dollar of avoidance by the victim, *i.e.,* if a dollar spent by the injurer could have bought more avoidance than a dollar spent by the victim.

In our notation the liability rule for the injurer is

$$L_x(X, Y) = \begin{cases} 1 & \text{if } \dfrac{P_x(X, Y)}{W_x} > \dfrac{P_y(X, Y)}{W_y} \\ 0 & \text{otherwise} \end{cases} \quad (13)$$

$L_y(X, Y)$ is, as usual, the complement of $L_x(X, Y)$, that is,

$$L_y(X, Y) = 1 - L_x(X, Y) \quad (14)$$

Graphically, there is a very simple interpretation of the relative negligence rule. The slope of the equiprobability lines (isoquants) is $-\dfrac{P_x(X, Y)}{P_y(X, Y)}$ and the slope of the equal cost lines is $-\dfrac{W_x}{W_y}$. Therefore the injurer is negligent at (X, Y) if the equiprobability line is steeper than the equal cost line at (X, Y). Notice that at any (X, Y) either the injurer or the victim is relatively negligent. In case of ties we have arbitrarily assumed that the victim is liable. The negligence boundary is the locus of least cost combinations for different probabilities. See Figure 3.

8. *Comparative negligence.* The doctrine of comparative negligence apportions the liability according to the relative liability of the two parties. This doctrine is established in admiralty law, but otherwise it is not recognized

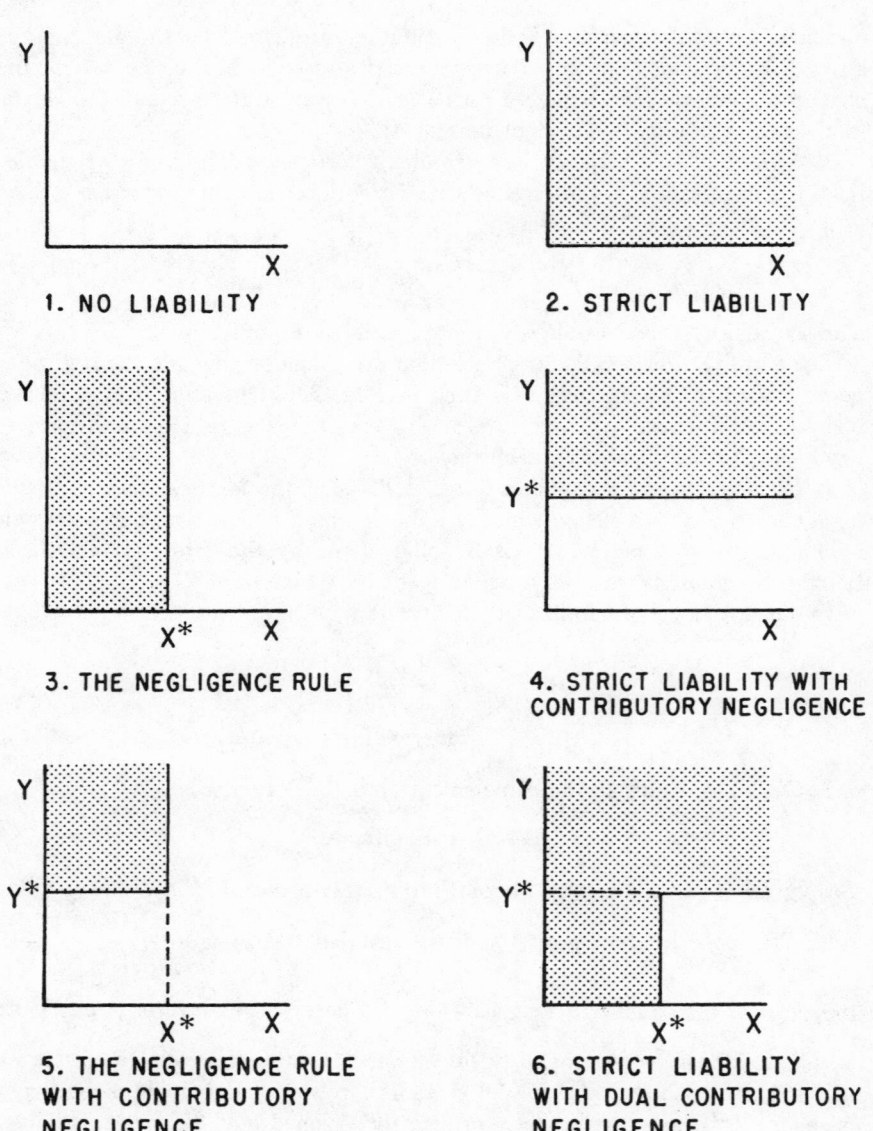

FIGURE 2 (INJURER LIABLE IN SHADED AREA)

in any state except where it is established by statute, *e.g.*, in Wisconsin, Georgia, and Mississippi.[8] It is not clear whether negligence is defined as a

---

[8] See Charles O. Gregory & Harry Kalven, Jr., Cases and Materials on Torts 250-54 (2d ed. 1969).

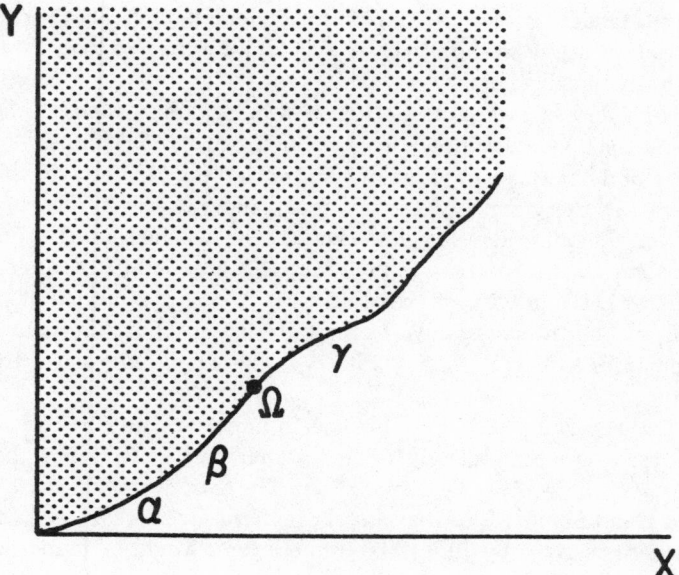

RELATIVE NEGLIGENCE

FIGURE 3 (INJURER LIABLE IN SHADED AREA)

marginal concept or an average one. If a marginal negligence concept is used, then, if n_x is the negligence of the injurer and n_y the negligence of the victim,

$$n_x = \frac{P_x(X, Y)}{W_x} \quad \text{and} \quad n_y = \frac{P_y(X, Y)}{W_y} \qquad (15)$$

Negligence is the incremental reduction in accident probability per dollar spent, and the liability of the injurer is his negligence divided by the negligence of both parties:

$$L_x(X, Y) = \frac{n_x}{n_x + n_y} \qquad (16)$$

The liability of the victim is $1 - L_x(X, Y)$.

III. THE LEGAL STANDARD OF NEGLIGENCE

We noted above that some of the liability rules require a legal determination of negligence by one party or the other. Call the legal standard of negligence for the injurer X^* and for the victim Y^*. In legal discussions this is often called the standard of care. If X is found to be less than X* then the injurer will be judged negligent. Similarly, if Y is found to be less than Y* the victim will be judged negligent.

The negligence standard most often cited in legal discussions of the problem is the so-called Learned Hand Rule,[9] which can be paraphrased as follows. The duty of a party is a function of three variables: (1) the probability of an accident; (2) the gravity of the accident; and (3) the burden of adequate precaution. Liability depends on whether the product of the first two is greater than the third. In our notation, the probability of an accident is $1 - P(X, Y)$, the gravity of the accident is A, and the burden of precaution is W_xX for the injurer and W_yY for the victim. Thus, the Learned Hand Rule compares $A(1 - P(X, Y))$ with W_xX for the injurer and with W_yY for the victim.

The Learned Hand Rule is ambiguous in important ways, as we shall show. In fact there are three closely related standards of negligence that can be derived from Judge Hand's formulation. The first we shall call the Literal Learned Hand Standard, or the Literal Standard for short. If we take literally the standard as given by Judge Hand, the injurer would be found negligent if

$$W_xX < A(1 - P(X, Y)) \qquad (17)$$

and the victim would be found negligent if

$$W_yY < A(1 - P(X, Y)). \qquad (18)$$

This standard compares the total cost to a party with the expected cost of the accident.

There is one question for which the Literal Standard unambiguously gives the correct answer, but it is typically the wrong question, and might well suggest the wrong answer to the right question. Consider Figure 4. As drawn, the expected benefits are greater than the costs to the injurer for every level of X. The question that the Literal Standard answers correctly is this: Is it better to provide complete protection, $X = T$, rather than no protection at all, $X = 0$? Then we need only compare the product of the probability of an accident and the gravity of the accident, TC, with the burden of adequate precaution, TB. In the case described in the figure, because TC is greater than TB, it is better to provide complete protection than no protection at all. Should it be the duty of the injurer to provide complete protection in this case? Clearly the answer is no. Although it is better to provide full protection than none at all, the optimal amount of protection from an overall point of view is Ω, where the marginal cost of protection is equal to the marginal expected benefit from the protection. By moving from

[9] United States v. Carroll Towing Co., 159 F.2d 169 (2d Cir. 1947)

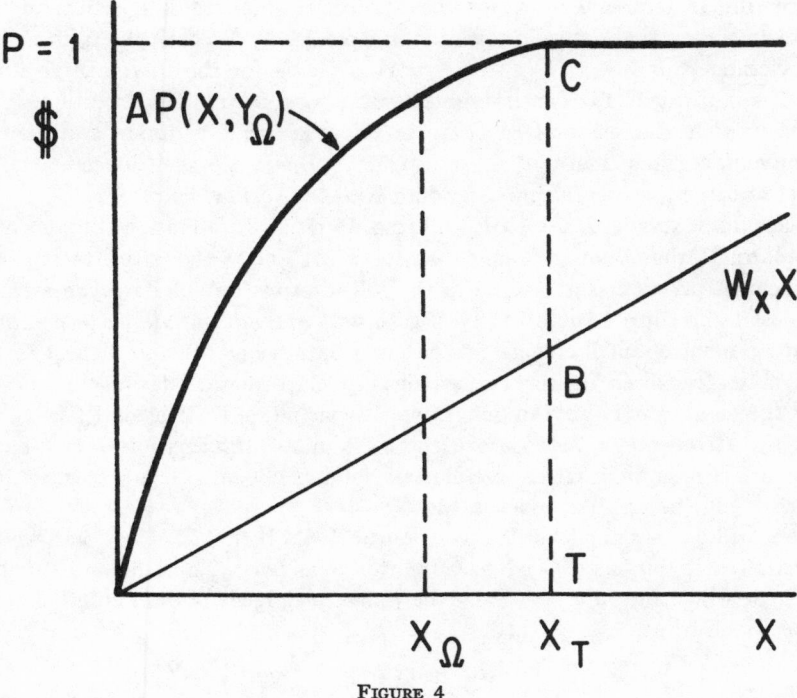

FIGURE 4

X_T to X_Ω costs would decrease more than benefits. Clearly, we need a better negligence standard.[10]

The second standard derivable from Judge Hand's formulation is the Incremental Standard. Here we assume that the judicial system can ferret out complete information about the underlying technology of accident prevention so that negligence for one party is determined on the *assumption that the other party is already acting in an optimal manner.* Thus the negligence standard for the injurer, X^*, is that value of X such that

$$W_x = A P_x(X^*, Y_\Omega) \qquad (19)$$

and for the victim is Y^*, that value of Y such that

$$W_y = A P_y(X_\Omega, Y^*). \qquad (20)$$

[10] Calabresi and Hirschoff seem to have been misled by a literal reading of the Learned Hand rule. They say, for example (*supra* note 1, at 1057), "If the cost to the defendant of avoiding the accident would have been less than the cost of the accident, discounted by the probability of its occurrence, the defendant's failure to avoid the accident is termed negligence." This is the Learned Hand Literal Standard, in our terminology.

Under the Incremental Standard the negligence standard is identical to the conditions for social cost minimization independently for both the injurer and the victim. Thus $X^* = X_\Omega$ and $Y^* = Y_\Omega$. Solving for the Incremental Standard is equivalent to identifying the social cost minimizing solution. The court uses the Incremental Standard to find the social optimum and defines any avoidance less than optimal as negligent. Below we shall investigate the effect of using the Incremental Standard with the various liability rules.

The third standard we shall call the Limited Information Incremental Standard. Rather than assuming that the court knows the entire technology of accident prevention as we did in the full information standard, we assume here that the court is able to investigate only the effects on the probability of an accident of small changes in the immediate neighborhood of the (X, Y) pair actually chosen by the two parties. In mathematical terms this means that the court is only able to determine the partial derivatives of $P(X, Y)$ at (X, Y). In effect, if the court uses the Limited Information Incremental Standard it is saying that an avoidance level is negligent if it is less than that which would be optimal *given what the other party has in fact done*. The injurer will be held negligent at some point (X, Y) if that X is less than would be required to minimize social cost, treating Y as fixed. Thus the lowest value of X for which the injurer will not be judged negligent is the minimum with respect to X of

$$C_S(X, Y) = W_x X + W_y Y + A(1 - P(X, Y))$$

The necessary marginal conditions for a minimum imply that the injurer will be found negligent at (X, Y) if

$$W_x < A P_x(X, Y) \qquad (21)$$

and the victim will be found negligent at (X, Y) if

$$W_y < A P_y(X, Y). \qquad (22)$$

To emphasize that the level of X that just allows the injurer to avoid being found negligent, X^*, depends on the avoidance actions taken by the victim, we shall use the functional notation $X^*(Y)$. Similarly, since the level of Y that just allows the victim to avoid being found negligent depends on the actions taken by the injurer, we write $Y^*(X)$.

The Incremental Standards are a good approximation, I think, of the way that courts actually proceed. The attorney for the plaintiff will try to find some act which, if the defendant had taken it, would have significantly reduced the probability of the accident at low cost. But that is precisely the statement that the increment in the expected loss was greater than the cost of avoidance, which is the definition of the Incremental Standards of negligence. The defendant will try to respond that the expected benefits of the proposed act were, in fact, less than the costs of undertaking it. When the court is asked to decide between the two points of view it is being asked to compare the incremental expected benefits with the incremental costs. Thus it is not peculiar that the outcome of large, important cases often seems to turn on the value of small changes in the behavior of one party or the other.

IV. A NONCOOPERATIVE GAME PLAYED ACCORDING TO LIABILITY RULES

What are the equilibrium values of X and Y when they are chosen by different people independently? How will Xavier and Yvonne behave when their only communication with each other will be in court after an accident occurs? All other transactions are assumed to be so costly that they do not take place.

We shall assume that the goal of Xavier is to choose X to minimize his expected private costs, that is:

$$\min_{X} C_x(X, Y) = W_x X + A L_x(X, Y)(1 - P(X, Y)) \qquad (23)$$

and Yvonne minimizes her private costs:

$$\min_{Y} C_y(X, Y) = W_y Y + A L_y(X, Y)(1 - P(X, Y)). \qquad (24)$$

These are simply the sum of the cost of their own preventive efforts and their expected liability when an accident occurs.

Both parties are assumed to know A, W_x, W_y, and $P(X, Y)$ as well as the liability rule in force and that the other party is interested only in private costs. Our problem is to try to find equilibria for the games and determine whether they are unique. An equilibrium for a game is a pair of values (X, Y) chosen by the two players such that, given the choice by the opponent, neither party has an incentive to change his own choice.

Before analyzing the various rules it will be useful to describe two response functions for each party. They are called response functions because, like the response functions in Cournot's analysis of duopoly, they show what response a party would choose, given the choice of the opponent.

The first response function we call $X^f(Y)$. The superscript f denotes full cost. It is defined as the injurer's preferred value of X given Y, assuming that the injurer must pay in full for any damages. That is, $X^f(Y)$ is that X for which $W_x X + A(1 - P(X, Y))$ is at a minimum. Alternatively, $X^f(Y)$ is the value of X which minimizes social cost when Y is fixed, since the only difference between private and social costs is the constant $W_y Y$, since Y is considered fixed. It is a necessary condition of minimization that at each value of $X^f(Y)$

$$W_x = A\, P_x(X^t, Y). \qquad (25)$$

We take the total differential of this condition

$$A\, P_{xx}\, dX^t + A\, P_{xy}\, dY = 0 \qquad (26)$$

and solve it for $\dfrac{dX^t}{dY}$

$$\frac{dX^t}{dY} = -\frac{P_{xy}}{P_{xx}}. \qquad (27)$$

This gives us the change in the optimal X for a change in Y. Convexity implies that $P_{xx} < 0$. Therefore if $P_{xy} < 0$ as we assume, then

$$\frac{dX^t}{dY} < 0 \qquad (28)$$

that is, a decrease in Y will call forth an increase in X.

Throughout the rest of our analysis we shall employ one slightly restrictive assumption about the technology of accident avoidance, namely that $P_{xy} < 0$. The technical effect of the assumption is to insure that the full cost response functions X^t and Y^t are both downward sloping. If they were upward sloping there could be a second intersection on one axis or the other and hence a second equilibrium. Assuming $P_{xy} < 0$ is equivalent to assuming that a decrease in accident avoidance by one party ought to call forth an increase in accident avoidance by the other. For example, if cars drive faster on one residential street than on another we would expect mothers to take greater care that their children do not stray onto the first street than onto the second, or as trains approach a crossing more rapidly we would expect cars to approach more slowly. Only in the bizarre case where the technology of accident prevention were such that the appropriate response to faster trains would be *less* caution on the part of drivers would the assumption of $P_{xy} < 0$ be inappropriate.

Correspondingly, there is, of course, the response function for the victim, $Y^t(X)$, which is the victim's preferred value of Y given X, assuming that the victim must pay in full for any damages. Therefore $Y^t(X)$ is the value of X which minimizes $W_y Y + A[1 - P(X, Y)]$. Figure 5 shows $X^t(Y)$ and $Y^t(X)$.

The second response function we shall consider gives the party's preferred strategy, given the opponent's strategy, for the actual expected private costs, $C_x(X, Y)$ or $C_y(X, Y)$, which depend on the liability rule in force. This response function is denoted $X^e(Y)$ for the injurer and $Y^e(X)$ for the victim. The superscript e signifies equilibrium. $X^e(Y)$ is that value of X for each Y

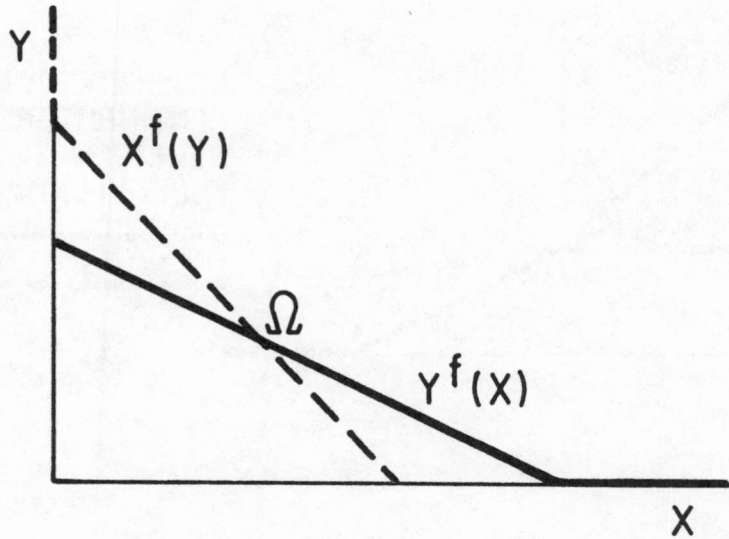

FIGURE 5

that minimizes $C_x(X, Y)$. For example, if the liability rule is the negligence rule with contributory negligence and the negligence standard is the Incremental Standard,

$$C_x(X, Y) = \begin{cases} W_x X + A[1 - P(X, Y)] & \text{if } X < X_\Omega \text{ and } Y \geqslant Y_\Omega \\ W_x X & \text{otherwise.} \end{cases} \quad (29)$$

In the same case $Y^e(X)$ is that value of Y which minimizes the victim's expected private costs, which are

$$C_y(X, Y) = \begin{cases} W_y Y & \text{if } X < X_\Omega \text{ and } Y \geqslant Y_\Omega \\ W_y Y + A[1 - P(X, Y)] & \text{otherwise.} \end{cases}$$

$X^e(Y)$ and $Y^e(X)$ are plotted in Figure 6. The shaded area is the area where the injurer is liable.

V. EQUILIBRIUM UNDER THE VARIOUS LIABILITY RULES

1. *No Liability*

First consider the rule of no liability. All bills emitted by the liability generator are to be paid by the victim, Yvonne, without regard to any measures either she or the injurer took. Then the costs paid by the injurer are only the costs of his own avoidance measures, so his problem is to

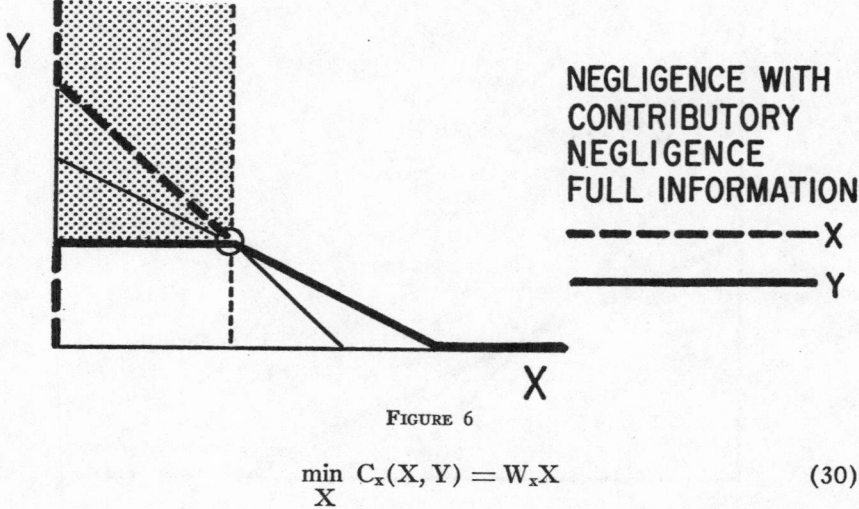

FIGURE 6

$$\min_{X} C_x(X, Y) = W_x X \tag{30}$$

It is obvious that he will choose $X = 0$; there are no benefits to him from avoiding accidents. In other words $x^e(Y) = 0$ for all Y.

For the victim the task is to

$$\min_{Y} C_y(0, Y) = W_y Y + A(1 - P(0, Y)) \tag{31}$$

that is, minimize the sum of his avoidance costs and expected losses given that the injurer will do nothing. This sum will be at a minimum when

$$W_y = A P_y(0, Y) \tag{32}$$

that is, at $Y^f(0)$. The equilibrium values of the game are $X = 0$ and $Y = Y^f(0)$, rather than the social optimum (X_Ω, Y_Ω). It is obvious that the equilibrium is unique. See Figure 7a.

2. Strict Liability

Next consider the rule of strict liability. The injurer is responsible for all accidents. The argument is identical to that for the rule of no liability except that the roles of injurer and victim, X and Y, are reversed. The victim will have no incentive to take any precautions: the injurer will choose the best level of precaution given that the victim takes none. The equilibrium is $(X^f(0), 0)$. Again, it is obvious that the equilibrium is unique. See Figure 7b.

The situation changes radically when we move on to liability rules that apply negligence standards to one or both parties.

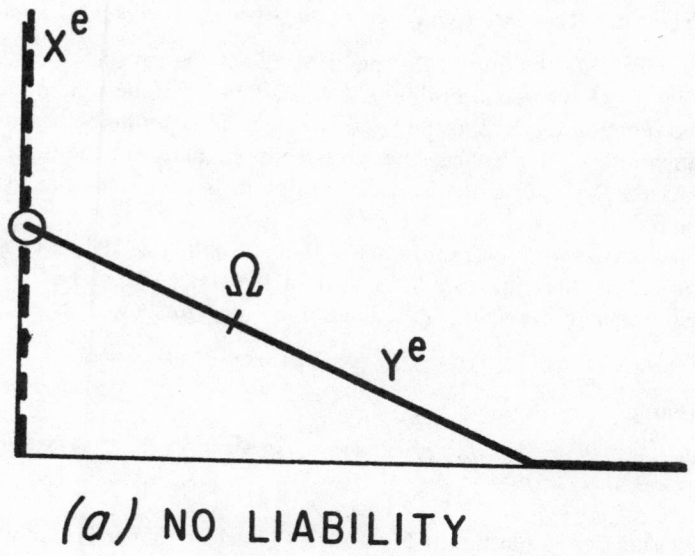

(a) NO LIABILITY

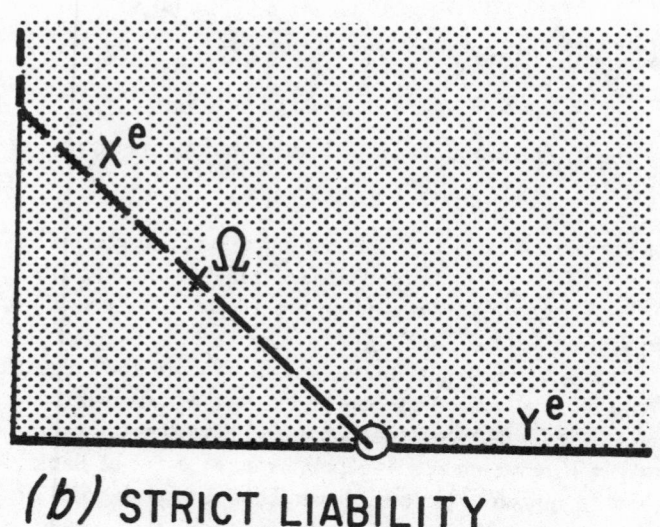

(b) STRICT LIABILITY

FIGURE 7

3. *Negligence Rule with Contributory Negligence, Incremental Standard*

We can now state the first of the major results of the paper.

Theorem 1: If the social optimum (X_Ω, Y_Ω) is a unique minimum of the social cost function $C_S(X, Y)$, the liability rule in force is the Negligence Rule with Contributory Negligence, the negligence standard is the Incremental Standard, and $P_{xy} < 0$, then the social optimum is a unique noncooperative equilibrium.

Proof of Theorem 1: First we show that (X_Ω, Y_Ω) is a non-cooperative equilibrium. For the injurer we have to show that his costs, given Y_Ω, are less at X_Ω than at any other value of X. That is, we have to show that

$$C_x(X_\Omega, Y_\Omega) \leqslant C_x(X, Y_\Omega) \qquad \text{for all X.} \tag{33}$$

Recall that

$$C_x(X, Y_\Omega) = \begin{cases} W_x X + A[1 - P(X, Y_\Omega)] & \text{if } X < X_\Omega \\ W_x X & \text{if } X \geqslant X_\Omega \end{cases} \tag{34}$$

This cost function is plotted in Figure 8a. It is clear that it is a minimum at X_Ω.

In analogous fashion we must show that given the injurer's choice of X_Ω, the victim can do no better than Y_Ω. See Figure 8b. That is, we must show that

$$C_y(X_\Omega, Y_\Omega) \leqslant C_y(X_\Omega, Y) \qquad \text{for all Y.} \tag{35}$$

This we do by writing out $C_y(X_\Omega, Y)$

$$C_y(X, Y) = W_y Y + A[1 - P(X_\Omega, Y)] \tag{36}$$

and minimizing it. The condition for its being a minimum is

$$W_y = A P_y(X_\Omega, Y) \tag{37}$$

which is identically a condition for the minimization of social cost at (X_Ω, Y_Ω). Therefore $C_y(X_\Omega, Y)$ is minimized at Y_Ω, which completes the proof that (X_Ω, Y_Ω) is a noncooperative equilibrium. What has been shown is that $X^e(Y_\Omega) = X_\Omega$ and $Y^e(X_\Omega) = Y_\Omega$.

To show that (X_Ω, Y_Ω) is a unique equilibrium we show that X^e and Y^e intersect only once, at (X_Ω, Y_Ω). See Figure 9a. A party will never choose a point where he is liable other than on the full cost equilibrium, X^f or Y^f. Also a party will never choose any point where he is not liable other than the one which requires him to do the least. Therefore, each party's equilibrium will be either on the full cost equilibrium X^f or Y^f or the lowest cost point where he is not liable. Thus in the figure X^e crosses the shaded area on X^f and then drops to zero as soon as the injurer is not liable. Similarly, Y^e stays

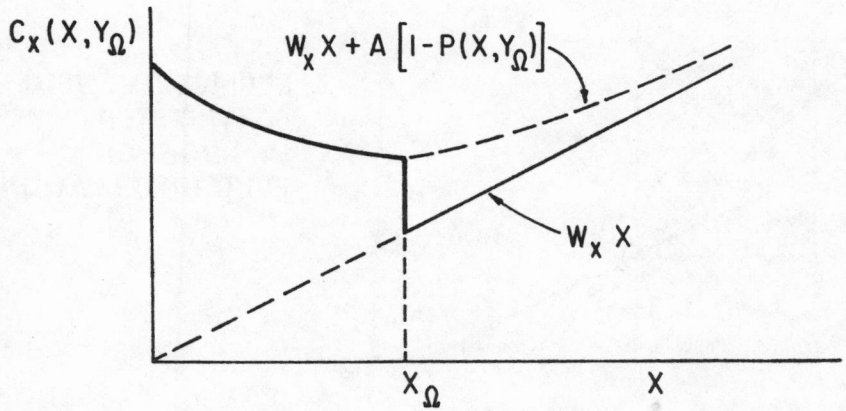

INJURER'S COSTS WHEN VICTIM HAS CHOSEN Y_Ω

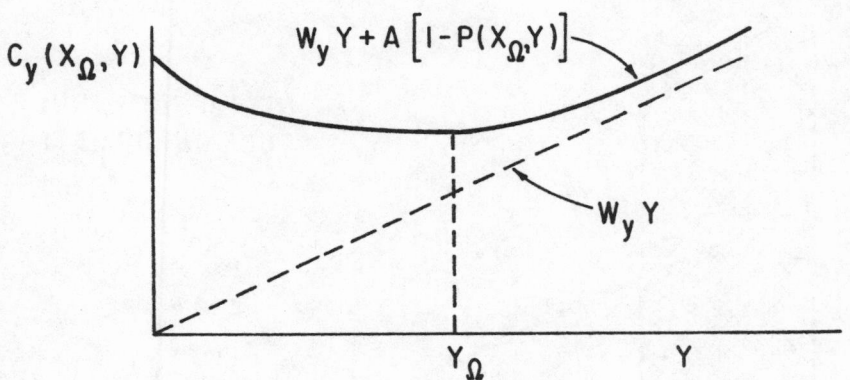

VICTIM'S COSTS WHEN INJURER HAS CHOSEN X_Ω

FIGURE 8

at the lowest part of the shaded area, where the victim is not liable, and then crosses the unshaded area, where she is liable, on Y^f. The only intersection of X^e and Y^e is at (X_Ω, Y_Ω); hence (X_Ω, Y_Ω) is a unique non-cooperative equilibrium, because both parties are in equilibrium there and only there.

4. *The Negligence Rule, Incremental Standard*

Corollary 1: The results of Theorem 1 hold if the liability rule is changed from the negligence rule with contributory negligence to the negligence rule.

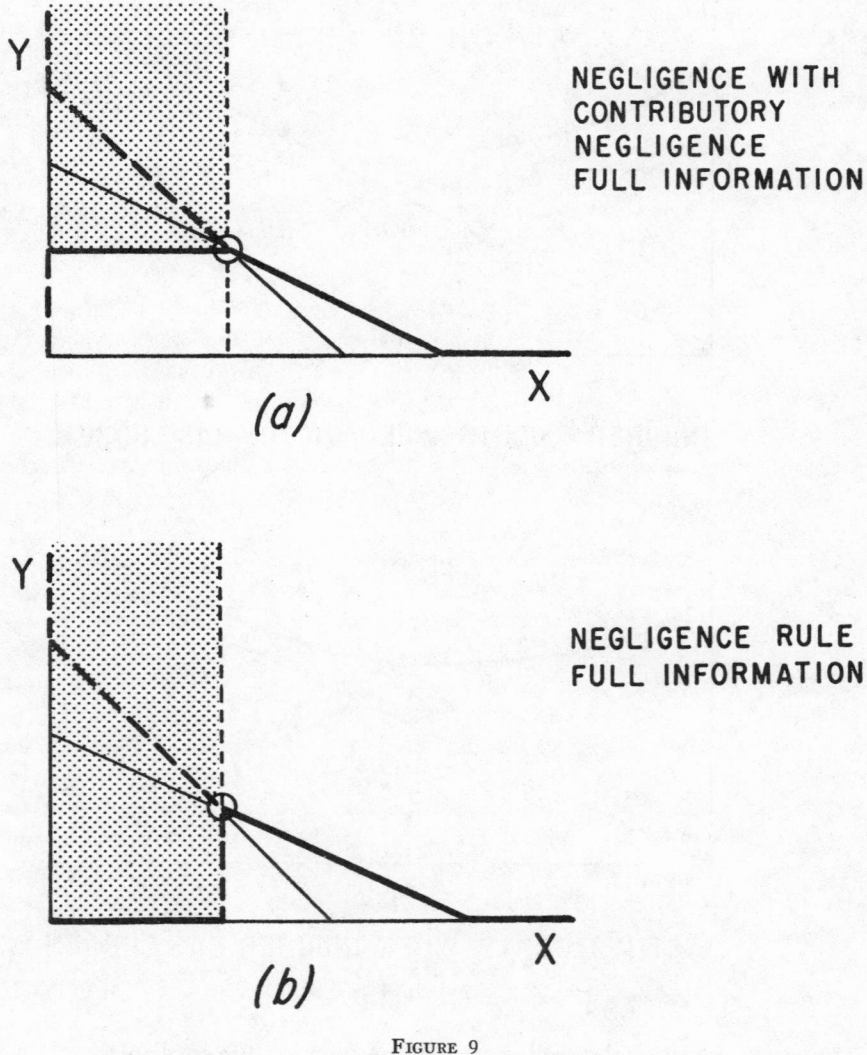

(a)

NEGLIGENCE WITH
CONTRIBUTORY
NEGLIGENCE
FULL INFORMATION

(b)

NEGLIGENCE RULE
FULL INFORMATION

FIGURE 9

Proof: The equilibrium reaction functions $X^e(Y)$ and $Y^e(X)$ are plotted in Figure 9b for the case of the negligence rule and the Incremental Standard. The changes in the functions resulting from the change in liability rule are inconsequential from the point of view of the proof of the theorem. The reaction functions still only intersect at the social optimum, (X_Ω, Y_Ω).

5. *Strict Liability with Contributory Negligence and with Dual Contributory Negligence*

Corollary 2: The results of Theorem 1 hold if the liability rule is changed to either strict liability with contributory negligence or strict liability with dual contributory negligence.

Proof: To obtain the results for strict liability with contributory negligence we merely exchange the roles of X and Y in the proof of Corollary 1. To obtain the results for strict liability with dual contributory negligence we exchange X and Y in the argument of the theorem.

One can summarize the results on decentralized games with liability rules so far as follows: with either no liability or strict liability rules in effect the incentives on the party without liability are perverse so the resulting equilibrium will not be the optimal one. For all four remaining rules, which are based on negligence of one or both parties, given the Incremental Standard the game will have a unique equilibrium and that equilibrium is the social optimum. Within the framework of our analysis there is no preferred choice among any of the four rules.

Perhaps it would be useful to point out here what the analysis does not say. It does not say that there is no basis for choice among the four rules; only that the factors that we have chosen to analyze do not lead us to choose any one of the negligence rules. If the cost of using the courts to transfer liability is very high, then the negligence rule with contributory negligence becomes more attractive because it transfers liability least often. Within the scope of our analysis any of the negligence rules is preferable to either the no liability rule or strict liability. That preference could, of course, be overthrown by factors outside the analysis. One could construct an argument for no liability (as in the case of "no-fault" insurance schemes) by showing that the costs of administering the negligence system far outweigh the losses caused by the incorrect incentives which are inherent in no-fault schemes. Also our analysis assumes a completely informed court system that does not have difficulty in producing accurate evidence. There are no evidentiary problems and who has the burden of proof is irrelevant.

VI. THE LIMITED INFORMATION INCREMENTAL STANDARD

Now we turn to the case where the court no longer knows what the social optimum is and only judges each party's behavior on the basis of small changes from where the parties actually were when the accident occurred. That is, we shall assume that the courts use the Limited Information Incremental Standard as the standard of care. The boundary between the injurer being negligent and not, $X^*(Y)$, is no longer a vertical line at X_Ω but rather is identical with $X^f(Y)$ passing through (X_Ω, X_Ω). Similarly, $Y^*(X) = Y^f(X)$.

1. *The Negligence Rule with Contributory Negligence*

Theorem 2: The results of Theorem 1 are destroyed when the Incremental Standard of negligence is replaced by the Limited Information Incremental Standard. The social optimum is not an equilibrium; in fact there is no equilibrium.

Proof: First we shall show that the social optimum, (X_Ω, Y_Ω), is not an equilibrium. To do so we need only consider the cost function of the injurer when the victim is at the social optimum $C_x(X, Y_\Omega)$.

$$C_x(X, Y_\Omega) = W_x X \tag{38}$$

That is, at no value of X is the injurer liable when $Y = Y_\Omega$; therefore the injurer will have no incentive to provide any accident avoidance measures at all. His costs will be at a minimum if $X = 0$. Therefore (X_Ω, Y_Ω) is not an equilibrium.

X^e and Y^e are plotted in Figure 10a for the case of the Limited Information Incremental Standard. The argument for the shape of the curves is the same as in Theorem I and does not need to be repeated. What appears to be an intersection at $(0, Y^f(0))$ is not. $X^e(Y^f(0))$ is not zero. (Only for $Y^f(0) - \epsilon$, where ϵ is arbitrarily small, is X^e zero.) Hence there is no equilibrium and the parties will cycle about as shown in Figure 10a.

Corollary 1: When the liability rule is changed from the negligence rule with contributory negligence to the negligence rule, the social optimum is again not an equilibrium.

Proof: Refer to Figure 10b. The logic of the proof is to confirm that X^e and Y^e are as drawn.

Corollary 2: Symmetrical results hold for strict liability with contributory negligence when the standard of care is the Limited Information Incremental Standard.

Proof: Merely exchange the roles of X and Y in Corollary 1.

Corollary 3: Symmetrical results hold for strict liability with dual contributory negligence when the standard of care is the Limited Information Incremental Standard.

Proof: Exchange the roles of X and Y in Theorem 2.

2. *Relative Negligence*

Theorem 3: If the liability rule in force is the relative negligence rule, then the social optimum is a unique noncooperative equilibrium.

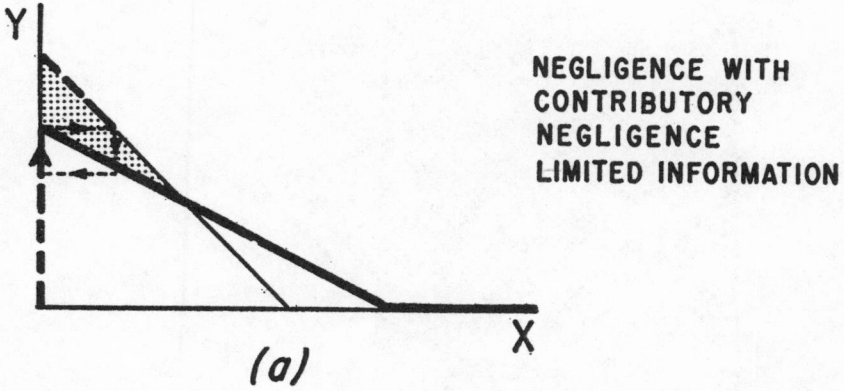

**NEGLIGENCE WITH
CONTRIBUTORY
NEGLIGENCE
LIMITED INFORMATION**

(a)

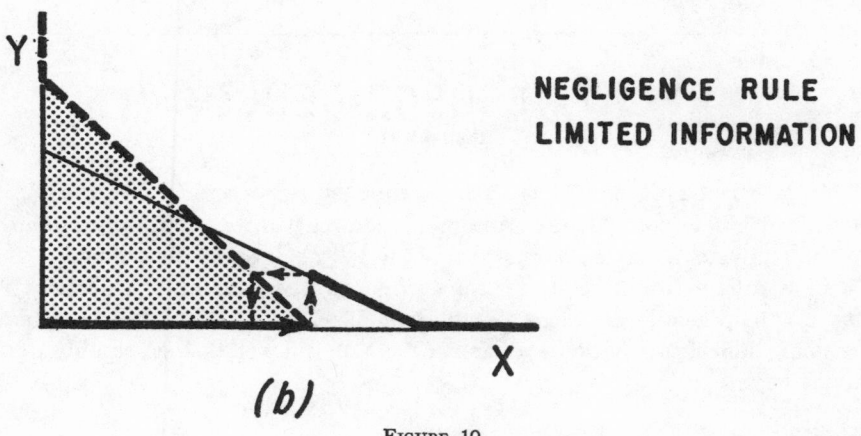

**NEGLIGENCE RULE
LIMITED INFORMATION**

(b)

FIGURE 10

Proof: X^e and Y^e are plotted in Figure 11. The shaded area is the area where the injurer is liable. In the unshaded area, the victim is liable. As before, the injurer will choose the least costly place where he is not liable unless X^f lies to the left, *i.e.*, is less expensive. Then he will choose X^f. Similarly, the victim will choose a strategy of the least costly place where she is not liable unless Y^f lies below that point, in which case she will choose Y^f. X^e and Y^e intersect at (X_Ω, Y_Ω). The two equilibria are adjacent from zero to (X_Ω, Y_Ω). In that range the injurer's strategy will be to follow exactly the relative negligence boundary (the expansion path in conventional economic production theory parlance) because by our convention the victim is

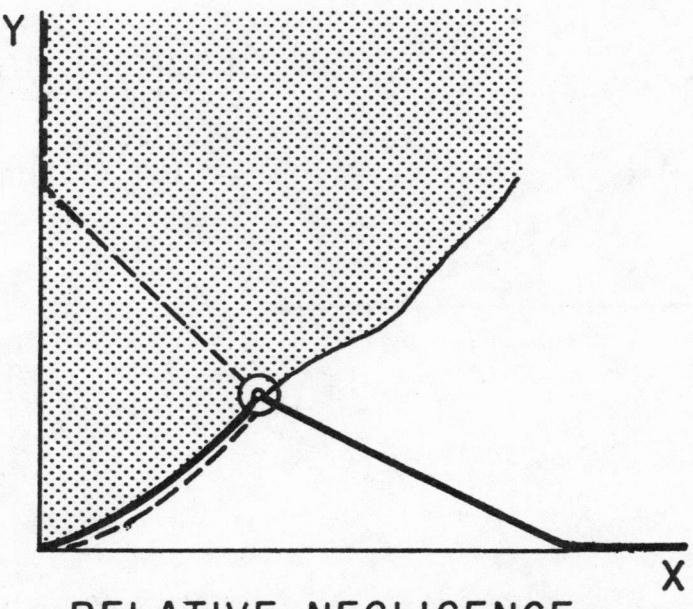

RELATIVE NEGLIGENCE
FIGURE 11

liable exactly on the boundary. The victim's strategy here is, in principle, undefined. There does not exist an optimal strategy in this area, only a limit to the strategy. What she wants to do is to get as close to the boundary as possible without touching it. For any given strategy not on the boundary one can in principle get closer to the boundary, *e.g.*, half as far, but this technical difficulty is not critical since (X_Ω, Y_Ω) is a well-defined equilibrium in any case.

3. *Comparative Negligence*

Rather than analyze completely the comparative negligence rule, I shall simply show that the social optimum is *not* an equilibrium under the comparative negligence rule. At (X_Ω, Y_Ω), $L_x(X, Y) = \frac{1}{2}$ since both parties are equally "negligent." Let Y be fixed at Y_Ω. The injurer will choose X_Ω only if his expected cost is at a minimum there. Now

$$C_x(X_\Omega, Y_\Omega) = W_x X + \frac{1}{2} A[1 - P(X, Y)] \tag{39}$$

which will be the minimum over X only if

$$W_x = \frac{1}{2} A P_x(X_\Omega, Y_\Omega). \tag{40}$$

But by the definition of (X_Ω, Y_Ω),

$$W_x = A P_x(X_\Omega, Y_\Omega) \tag{41}$$

so (X_Ω, Y_Ω) cannot be an equilibrium.[11]

CONCLUSIONS

In this paper economic analysis has been used to subject a variety of liability rules and standards of care to scrutiny in an abstract setting. It is my contention, which I hope the paper supports, that economic analysis is a useful method of organizing legal questions. It brings out similarities among apparently different legal doctrines, and it allows one to bring a large body of analysis to bear.

The paper first described accident avoidance by two parties in such a way that we could exploit the analogy with the economic theory of production. We used the model thus developed to characterize eight different liability rules discussed in the legal literature, and three variants of the Learned Hand formulation of the standard of care. The literal variant of Judge Hand's formulation we rejected immediately because it was not an incremental standard. Then we analyzed each of the liability rules, using (where appropriate) both of the remaining standards of care, the Incremental Standard and the Limited Information Incremental Standard. The analysis consisted of considering the victim and the injurer as noncommunicating parties in a game played according to liability rules. We identified the noncooperative equilibrium point as the solution for the game and in each case compared it with the social optimum.

To summarize the results, equilibrium for the simple no-liability rule as well as for the simple strict-liability rule did not coincide with the social optimum, nor did equilibrium for the comparative-negligence rule. When the standard of care was the Incremental Standard the social optimum was identical with the equilibrium for the relative-negligence rule, as well as with the equilibrium for all four of the common law negligence-based rules. The standard of care is critical, for, when it was changed to the Limited Information Incremental Standard, the identity between equilibrium and optimality was destroyed.

[11] This argument is not strictly true. We have left out the effect of changing X on the liability rule. It is possible, for particular values of the first and second derivatives, that the neglected effect will exactly cancel out the difference we point to in the text. Though it is possible, in general we cannot expect it to happen.

STRICT LIABILITY VERSUS NEGLIGENCE

STEVEN SHAVELL*

I. Introduction and Discussion

T HE aim of this article is to compare strict liability and negligence rules on the basis of the incentives they provide to "appropriately" reduce accident losses. It will therefore be both convenient and clarifying to abstract from other issues in respect to which the rules could be evaluated. In particular, there will be no concern with the bearing of risk—for parties will be presumed risk neutral—nor with the size of "administrative costs"—for the legal system will be assumed to operate free of such costs—nor with distributional equity—for the welfare criterion will be taken to be the following aggregate: the benefits derived by parties from engaging in activities less total accident losses less total accident prevention costs.

Because the analysis of the rules will employ a mathematical model, it seems desirable to consider first in an informal way the points to be made and the logic behind them. Since this discussion will not serve as a complete summary, readers will probably also want to at least look at the statements of the propositions in the later parts of the paper and will almost certainly wish to read the concluding comments (which are not focused on the details of the model).

Accidents will be conceived of as involving two types of parties, "injurers" and "victims," only the latter of which are assumed to suffer direct losses. The category of accidents that will be examined initially are *unilateral* in nature, by which is meant that the actions of injurers but not of victims are assumed to affect the probability or severity of losses. The unilateral case is studied for two reasons. First, it is descriptive of situations in which whatever changes in the behavior of victims that could reasonably be expected to result from changes in liability rules would have only a small influence on accident losses.[1] The second reason is pedagogical; it is easier to understand the general *bilateral* case after having studied the unilateral case.

* Associate Professor of Economics, Harvard University, and Visiting Professor, Harvard Law School. I wish to thank the National Science Foundation (NSF grant SOC-76-20862) for financial support and Peter Diamond, Douglas Ginsburg, Henry Hansmann, Duncan Kennedy, and, especially, A. Mitchell Polinsky and Richard Posner for comments.

[1] Examples of accidents occurring in such situations and which therefore might be considered

Unilateral Case

This case (as well as the bilateral case) will be considered in each of several situations distinguished by the nature of the relationship between injurers and victims.

Accidents between strangers (see Proposition 1): In this subcase it is supposed that injurers and victims are strangers, that neither are sellers of a product, and that injurers may choose to engage in an activity which puts victims at risk.

By definition, under the negligence rule all that an injurer needs to do to avoid the possibility of liability is to make sure to exercise due care if he engages in his activity.[2] Consequently *he will not be motivated to consider the effect on accident losses of his choice of whether to engage in his activity or, more generally, of the level at which to engage in his activity;* he will choose his level of activity in accordance only with the personal benefits so derived. But surely any increase in his level of activity will typically raise expected accident losses (holding constant the level of care). Thus he will be led to choose too high a level of activity;[3] the negligence rule is not "efficient."

Consider by way of illustration the problem of pedestrian-automobile accidents (and, as we are now discussing the unilateral case, let us imagine the behavior of pedestrians to be fixed). Suppose that drivers of automobiles find it in their interest to adhere to the standard of due care but that the possibility of accidents is not thereby eliminated. Then, in deciding how much to drive, they will contemplate only the enjoyment they get from doing so. Because (as they exercise due care) they will not be liable for harm suffered by pedestrians, drivers will not take into account that going more miles will mean a higher expected number of accidents. Hence, there will be too much driving; an individual will, for example, decide to go for a drive on a mere whim despite the imposition of a positive expected cost to pedestrians.

However, under a rule of strict liability, the situation is different. Because

---

unilateral are not hard to imagine: a water main breaks and floods the basement of a home; a plane crashes into a house; a surgeon performs the wrong procedure on an anaesthetized patient. Concededly, even in these examples the victim could have taken *some* protective action (the surgeon's patient could have hired another surgeon to watch over the operation), but, we may plausibly assume, not at a cost nearly low enough to make it worthwhile.

[2] It is assumed for ease of exposition that courts have no difficulty in determining if a party did in fact exercise due care; the reader will have no trouble in appropriately modifying the arguments to be made so as to take into account relaxation of such simplifications as this.

[3] Specifically, while he will choose to engage in the activity just up to the level at which the personal benefit from a marginal increase would equal zero, it would be best from society's viewpoint for him to engage in the activity only up to the level at which his benefit from a marginal increase would equal the (positive) social marginal cost in terms of accident losses.

an injurer must pay for losses whenever he is involved in an accident,[4] he will be induced to consider the effect on accident losses of both his level of care *and* his level of activity. His decisions will therefore be efficient. Because drivers will be liable for losses sustained by pedestrians, they will decide not only to exercise due care in driving but also to drive only when the utility gained from it outweighs expected liability payments to pedestrians.

Accidents between sellers and strangers (see Proposition 2): In this subcase it is assumed that injurers are sellers of a product or service and that they conduct their business in a competitive market. (The assumption of competition allows us to ignore monopoly power, which is for the purposes of this article a logically tangential issue.) Moreover, it is assumed that victims are strangers; they have no market relationship with sellers either as their customers or as their employees.

Under the negligence rule the outcome is inefficient, but the reasoning is slightly different from that of the last subcase. While it is still true that all a seller must do to avoid liability is to take due care, why this results in too high a level of activity has to do with market forces. Because the seller will choose to avoid liability, the price of his product will not reflect the accident losses associated with production. This means that buyers of the product will face too low a price and will purchase too much, which is to say that the seller's level of activity will be too high. Imagine that the drivers are engaged in some business activity—let us say that they are taxi drivers. Then, given that they take due care, the taxi drivers will not have liability expenses, will set rates equal to "production" cost (competition among taxi drivers is assumed), will experience a greater demand than if rates were appropriately higher, and will therefore carry too many fares and cause too many accidents.

Under strict liability, the outcome is efficient, and again the reasoning is a little different from that in the last subcase. Since sellers have to pay for accident losses, they will be led to take the right level of care. And since the product price will reflect accident losses, customers will face the "socially correct" price for the product; purchases will therefore be appropriately lower than what they would be if the product price did not reflect accident losses. Taxi drivers will now increase rates by an amount equal to expected accident losses suffered by pedestrians, and the demand for rides in taxis will fall.

Accidents between sellers and customers—or employees (see Proposition 3 and Part III. B (iii)): It is presumed here that victims have a market relationship with sellers as either their customers or their employees; and since both situations are essentially the same, it will suffice to discuss only that when victims are customers. In order to understand the role (which is important)

---

[4] Causal or other reasons for limiting the scope of liability are ignored.

of customers' knowledge of risk, three alternative assumptions will be considered: customers know the risk presented by each seller; they do not know the risk presented by each seller but they do know the average seller's risk;[5] they misperceive even this average risk.

Under the negligence rule, the outcome is efficient only if customers correctly perceive risks. As before, when the victims were strangers, sellers will take due care in order to avoid liability, so that the product price will not reflect accident losses. However, now the accident losses are borne by the customers. Thus, the "full" price in the eyes of customers is the market price plus imputed perceived accident losses. Therefore, if risks are correctly perceived, the full price equals the socially correct price, and the quantity purchased will be appropriate. But if risks are not correctly perceived, the quantity purchased will be inappropriate; if customers underestimate risks, what they regard as the full price is less than the true full price and they will buy too much of the product, and conversely if they overestimate risks.[6]

Think, for example, of the risk of food poisoning from eating at restaurants. Under the negligence rule, restaurants will decide to avoid liability by taking appropriate precautions to prepare meals under sanitary conditions. Therefore, the price of meals will not reflect the expected losses due to the (remaining) risk of food poisoning. If customers know this risk, they will correctly consider it in their decisions over the purchase of meals. But if they underestimate the risk, they will purchase too many meals; and if they overestimate it, too few.

Under strict liability, the outcome is efficient regardless of whether customers misperceive risks. As in the last subcase, because sellers have to pay for accident losses, they will decide to take appropriate care and will sell the product at a price reflecting accident losses. Thus customers will face the socially correct price and will purchase the correct amount. Their perception of the risk is irrelevant since it will not influence their purchases; as they will be compensated under strict liability for any losses, the likelihood of losses will not matter to them. Restaurant-goers will face a price that reflects expected losses due to food poisoning when meals are prepared under sanitary conditions; they will buy the same—and appropriate—number of meals whether they think the probability of food poisoning is low or high, for they will be compensated for any losses suffered.[7]

---

[5] If sellers are assumed to be identical (as they are in the formal model) and therefore to act identically, the average risk will in fact be the risk presented by each seller. But it will be seen from the discussion of the situation when sellers are not liable that the first and second assumptions are nevertheless different.

[6] It may be instructive to mention the parallel situation in regard to employee victims. If employees correctly perceive risks at the workplace, then they will (appropriately) choose to work for a firm only if the "net" wage—the market wage less the expected accident losses they bear—is at least equal to their opportunity elsewhere. But if, say, they underestimate risks, they might choose to work for a firm when the net wage is in fact below their opportunity elsewhere.

[7] However, it is worthwhile noticing that if they could not possibly be compensated for a kind

When sellers are simply not liable for accident losses, then the outcome is efficient only if customers know the risk presented by each seller. For, given this assumption, because customers will seek to buy products with the lowest full price (market price plus expected accident losses), sellers will be induced to take appropriate care (since this will lower the accident-loss component of the full price). While it is true that if a restaurant took inadequate precautions to prevent food poisoning, it could offer lower-priced meals, it is also true that customers would respond not just to the market price of meals but also to the likelihood of food poisoning—which they are presumed to know. Therefore customers would decide against giving the restaurant their business. Consequently, restaurants will be led to take adequate precautions and to charge accordingly. Moreover, because customers will base purchases on the correctly perceived full price, they will buy the correct amount.

If, however, customers do not know the risk presented by individual sellers, there are two sources of inefficiency when sellers are not liable. The first is that, given the risk of loss, the quantity purchased by customers may not be correct; of course, this will be true if customers misperceive the risk. The second source of inefficiency is that sellers will not be motivated by market forces to appropriately reduce risks. To understand why, consider the situation when customers do correctly perceive the average risk (when they do not correctly perceive this risk, an explanation similar to the one given here could be supplied). That is, assume that customers know the risk presented by sellers as a group but do not have the ability to "observe" the risk presented by sellers on an individual basis. Then sellers would have no inducement to exercise adequate care. Suppose that restaurant-goers know the risk of food poisoning at restaurants in general and it is, say, inappropriately high. Then if a *particular* restaurant were to take sufficient precautions to lower the risk, customers would not recognize this (except insofar as it eventually affected the average risk—but under the assumption that there are many competing restaurants, this effect would be negligible). Thus the restaurant could not charge a higher price for its meals—customers would have no reason not to go to the cheaper restaurants. In consequence, a situation in which sellers take inadequate care to reduce risks would persist; and similar reasoning shows that a situation in which they take adequate care would not persist. (Notice, however, that since customers are assumed to correctly perceive the average risk, at least they will purchase the correct number of meals—correct, given the high risk.)

---

of loss from food poisoning, then misperception of risk certainly would matter. For instance, if there were a risk of death from food poisoning and if restaurant-goers underestimated it, then they would expose themselves to a higher risk of death by eating restaurant meals than they would truly want to bear. Thus, the conclusion of this paragraph that misperception of risk does not matter under strict liability holds only in respect to risks compensable by payment of money damages.

Finally, it should be observed that the discussion of liability in the present subcase bears on the role of tort law in a contractual setting. When customers make purchases, they are willingly entering into a kind of contract—in which they agree to a price and pay it, receive goods, and expose themselves to a risk (in the absence of liability).[8] Therefore, our conclusions may be generally expressed by the statement that, when customers' knowledge of risks is perfect, the rule of liability does not matter; the "contractual" arrangement arrived at in the market is appropriate. But when the knowledge is not perfect, there is generally scope for the use of liability, and the relative performance of liability rules depends on the precise nature of the imperfection in knowledge. The force of this point, and the fact that it is not always an obvious one, is perhaps well illustrated by the situation described in the previous paragraph. In that situation, customers did correctly perceive average risk, so that there was "assumption of risk," but this did not lead to a desirable result. The situation was one therefore in which, under our assumptions, courts ought not to allow the defense of assumption of risk to be successfully asserted.

Bilateral Case

In this case, account is taken of the possibility that potential victims as well as injurers may influence the probability or magnitude of accident losses by their choices of both level of care and of level of activity.

Accidents between strangers (see Propositions 4 and 5):[9] Under the negligence rule,[10] the outcome is not efficient. As was true in the unilateral case, since all that an injurer needs to do to avoid liability is to exercise due care,

[8] It should be remarked that the possibility of contractual arrangements that go beyond mere agreement on price is not considered here; for example, the possibility that sellers might give customers some form of guarantee is not allowed for in the discussion or in the analysis. However, our conclusions do have some relevance to what contractual arrangements might be made. This is because what is "efficient" is, by definition, what maximizes benefits minus costs, which is in turn what is in the mutual interest of the sellers and customers to do. (To illustrate, if customers *realize* that they do not know the risk of loss, then they might wish for, and insist on, a blanket guarantee, in effect making the seller strictly liable, and thereby giving him an incentive to reduce the risk of loss.) Of course, the reason this is not considered here is that a satisfactory treatment would require us to study at the least the value of explicit arrangements over the arrangements that inhere in the applicable tort and contract law, the costs of making explicit arrangements as opposed to the expected costs of reliance on the applicable law, and the willingness of courts to enforce what is at variance with the applicable law.

[9] The explanation given in this and in the next subcase for why neither strict liability with a defense of contributory negligence nor the negligence rule results in an efficient outcome is in its essence that given by Richard Posner, Economic Analysis of Law 139-40 (2d ed. 1977). See also Duncan Kennedy, A History of Law and Economics or the Fetishism of Commodities (1979) (unpublished mimeographed paper at Harvard University) which makes related points at 54-63.

[10] In the present discussion, it will make no difference whether or not the reader thinks of this rule as incorporating the defense of contributory negligence.

he will choose too high a level of activity. In regard to victims, however, the situation is different. Since a victim bears his accident losses, he will choose an appropriate level of care *and* an appropriate level of his activity, given the (inefficient) behavior of injurers. The drivers will exercise due care but will go too many miles. And the pedestrians, knowing that they must bear accident losses, will exercise due care (in crossing streets and so forth) and they will also reduce the number of miles they walk in accordance with expected accident losses per mile.

Under strict liability with a defense of contributory negligence, the outcome is symmetrical to the last—and again inefficient.[11] Because all that a victim needs to do to avoid bearing accident losses is to take due care, he will have no motive to appropriately reduce *his* level of activity; this is the inefficiency. However, because injurers now bear accident losses, they will take the appropriate amount of care and choose the right level of activity, given the inefficient behavior of victims. Drivers will exercise due care and go the correct number of miles. Pedestrians will also exercise due care but will walk too many miles.

From this discussion it is apparent that the choice between strict liability with a defense of contributory negligence and the negligence rule is a choice between the lesser of two evils. Strict liability with the defense will be superior to the negligence rule when it is more important that injurers be given an incentive through a liability rule to reduce their activity level than that victims be given a similar incentive; that is to say, when it is more important that drivers go fewer miles than that pedestrians walk fewer miles.

Because neither of the familiar liability rules induces efficient behavior, the question arises, *"Is there any conceivable liability rule depending on parties' levels of care and harm done that induces efficient behavior?"* It is proved below (Proposition 5) that the answer is *"No."* The problem in essence is that for injurers to be induced to choose the correct level of activity, they must bear all accident losses; and for victims to choose the correct level of their activity, they also must bear all accident losses. Yet it is in the nature of a liability rule that both conditions cannot hold simultaneously; clearly, injurers and victims cannot each bear all accident losses.[12]

Accidents between sellers and strangers (see Proposition 6): Because the reader will be able to appeal to arguments analogous to those already made and in order to avoid tedious repetition, explanation of the results stated in this and the next subcase will be abbreviated or will be omitted.

[11] It is of course clear that under strict liability without the defense the outcome is inefficient, for victims would have no motive to take care.

[12] However, when other means of social control are also employed, it is possible to achieve an efficient outcome. For example, if use of the negligence rule were supplemented by imposition of a tax on the level of injurer activity, an efficient outcome could be achieved.

Under both the negligence rule and strict liability with a defense of contributory negligence, the outcome is inefficient, as was true in the last subcase. Under the negligence rule, sellers will take appropriate care, but since the product price will not reflect accident losses, too much will be purchased by customers. Also, since victims bear accident losses, they will take appropriate care and choose the right level of activity. Under strict liability with the defense, sellers will take appropriate care and the product price will reflect accident losses, so the right amount will be purchased. Victims will exercise due care but will choose too high a level of activity. In addition, as in the last subcase, there does not exist any liability rule that induces efficient behavior.

Accidents between sellers and customers—or employees (see Propositions 7a and 7b and Part IV.B (iii)): As before it will be enough to discuss here only the situation when victims are customers. If customers have perfect knowledge of the risk presented by each seller, then the outcome is efficient under strict liability with a defense of contributory negligence or the negligence rule or if sellers are not subject to liability at all. For instance, in the latter situation, since customers wish to buy at the lowest full price, sellers will be led to take appropriate care; and since customers will make their purchases with the full price in mind, the quantity they buy will be correct; and since they bear their losses, they will take appropriate care.

There is, however, a qualification that needs to be made concerning the way in which it is imagined that customers influence accident losses. If one assumes that customers influence losses only by their choice of level of care and of the amount purchased, then what was stated in the previous paragraph is correct; and in regard to services and nondurables (such as meals at restaurants) this assumption seems entirely natural. But in regard to durable goods, it might well be thought that customers influence accident losses not only by their choice of level of care and of purchases, but also by their decision as to frequency of use per unit purchased. The expected number of accidents that a man will have when using a power lawn mower would seem to be influenced not only by whether he in fact purchases one (rather than, say, a hand mower) and by how carefully he mows his lawn with it, but also by how frequently he chooses to mow his lawn. In order for customers to be led to efficiently decide the frequency of use, they must bear their own accident losses. Thus, in regard to durables, the outcome is efficient under the negligence rule or if sellers are not liable, but the outcome is inefficient under strict liability with a defense of contributory negligence; for then if the man buys a power lawn mower, he will have no motive to appropriately reduce the number of times he mows his lawn.

Now suppose that customers correctly perceive only average risks. Then, subject again to a qualification concerning durables, the results are as follows. The outcome is efficient under strict liability with a defense of contributory negligence or under the negligence rule, but the outcome is not efficient if sellers are not liable, for then they will not take sufficient care. The qualification is that if the sellers produce durables, strict liability with the defense is inefficient, leaving the negligence rule as the only efficient rule.

Last, suppose that customers misperceive risks. Then the outcome is efficient only under strict liability with a defense of contributory negligence; and the qualification to this is that, if sellers produce durables, even strict liability with the defense is inefficient, so that there does not exist a liability rule which is efficient.

II. THE MODEL

The assumptions here are much as described in the introduction. There is a single physical good, called "income." The utility (or disutility) of any action which a party takes is assumed to have a well-defined equivalent in terms of income; and, henceforth, when reference is made to income, what will be meant is the amount of literal income plus income equivalents. The (von Neumann-Morgenstern) utility of income is assumed to be equal to income. Thus, parties are risk-neutral; expected utility is expected income. Since the social-welfare function is taken to be the sum of expected utilities, social welfare is the sum of expected incomes.

Accidents are assumed to involve two types of parties, injurers and victims. The number of injurers is assumed equal to the number of victims (and equal to the number of customers in the market case described below); this assumption is inessential and could obviously be modified. In the absence of liability rules, all accident losses fall on victims. The class of injurers and the class of victims are themselves each comprised of identical parties.

Injurers either engage in a nonmarket activity—the "nonmarket" case—or are sellers of a product or service—the "market" case. In the market case, sellers are expected to be profit-maximizing price takers and to face constant production costs per unit. Thus, they earn zero profits in competitive equilibrium. Victims are either strangers, customers, or employees. If victims are customers or employees, three alternative assumptions (which were discussed in the introduction) are made about their knowledge of accident risks.

Parties take liability rules as given; they do not circumvent the rules by contractual arrangement.[13] They also take the behavior of others as given.

---

[13] The justification is the familiar one, that some "transaction cost" stands in the way. In the nonmarket case and the market case involving strangers, it is that it would be very difficult for each potential injurer to get together with and make a contractual arrangement with each of his potential victims. In the market case, the assumption is that the costs of

Under these assumptions, the (Nash) equilibrium associated with the use of a liability rule can be determined.

An analysis of equilibrium outcomes under liability rules for the nonmarket and market cases is made both in the part of the paper concerned with unilateral accidents and in the one dealing with bilateral accidents. In the nonmarket case, victims are assumed to engage in their activity at a fixed level and to exercise a fixed level of care. Their only role in the market case is, if they are customers, to decide how much to buy or, if they are employees, to decide where to work. The liability rules examined are no liability, strict liability, and the negligence rule. In the bilateral case, two additional liability rules are considered, strict liability with a defense of contributory negligence and the negligence rule with that defense.

If a liability rule results in the outcome that maximizes social welfare, it will be called efficient. The efficient values of variables will be denoted with an "*".

Because the notation used changes somewhat in the different cases analyzed, it will be easiest to present it and to modify it as needed.

III. Unilateral Accidents

Define the following variables,

$x \geqq 0$ care level of an injurer.
$y \geqq 0$ activity level of an injurer,
$l(x)$ expected accident losses per
unit of injurer activity level.[14]

Expected accident losses are assumed to fall with care, so $l' < 0$, but at a decreasing rate, so $l'' > 0$. Notice that the model allows for the possibility that injurers may choose not to engage in their activity at all; this corresponds to $y = 0$.

Under strict liability, an injurer is assumed to pay for all accident losses suffered by victims of accidents in which he is involved. Under the negligence rule an injurer has to pay for accident losses only if his care level is less than a due care level. Define

$\bar{x}$ = injurer's due care level.

---

bargaining and perhaps of recording an agreement make it easier for the involved parties to rely on a liability rule.

[14] We are implicitly assuming that increasing the activity level corresponds to a physical repetition of an activity and causes a proportional rise in expected accident losses. For example, doubling the activity level would double expected accident losses (the level of care held constant). This assumption often seems to be the natural one to make, but it will be clear that the qualitative nature of our results would not be altered if expected accident losses were a more general function of x and y.

Thus, as emphasized in the introduction, y does not enter into a determination about negligence.

A. *The Nonmarket Case: Accidents between Strangers*

Recall that in this case, injurers are not sellers of a product or service but they may decide to engage in an activity which puts victims at risk. Define

$$a(x,y) = \text{income equivalent of the utility to}$$
$$\text{an injurer of engaging in his activity at}$$
$$\text{level } y \text{ and exercising care } x. [15]$$

Assume that taking more care reduces this, so $a_x < 0$.[16] Assume also that, given the care level, increases in the activity level up to some point result in increases in utility; beyond that point, however, utility falls with increases in the activity level. Specifically, for any x, $a_y(x,y) > 0$ for $y < y(x)$ and $a_y(x,y) < 0$ for $y > y(x)$. Here $y(x)$ is (uniquely) defined by either $a_y(x,y) = 0$ or, if this never holds, by $y(x) = 0$.

Social welfare W is given by[17]

$$W(x,y) = a(x,y) - yl(x). \tag{1}$$

Note that what enters into W is not only expected accident losses (through yl) and prevention costs (through a_x), but also the benefits of participating in the activity (through a_y). The efficient values x^* and y^* maximize W.

Since under strict liability an injurer must pay for accident losses to possible victims, an injurer's position is

$$a(x,y) - yl(x). \tag{2}$$

The injurer's problem, maximizing (2) over x and y, is the social problem. Strict liability is therefore efficient.

Under the negligence rule, assume that the due care level $\bar{x}$ is sufficiently low so that injurers decide to act in a nonnegligent way, that is, to choose $x = \bar{x}$.[18] Thus, the injurer's problem becomes one of choosing y to maximize

---

[15] The reader might find it convenient to think about the case $a(x,y) = z(y) - v(x)y$, where $z(y)$ is the benefit of engaging in the activity at level y and $v(x)$ is the cost of taking care x per unit of activity.

[16] Subscripts denote partial derivatives. The arguments of derivatives will frequently be suppressed in the notation.

[17] We need only consider social welfare for a "representative" injurer and victim pair—recall that we have assumed for simplicity that their numbers are equal. An injurer's expected income is $a(x,y)$ − expected liability payments, and a victim's is expected liability payments − $yl(x)$. Adding these gives W.

[18] If $\bar{x}$ were so high that injurers decided to be negligent, they would be, in effect, strictly liable. It does not seem natural to analyze this possibility as one having to do with the negligence rule.

$$a(\bar{x}, y). \tag{3}$$

The injurer therefore increases y to the point at which it yields no marginal benefit; in other words, he selects $y(\bar{x})$. Let $y^*(\bar{x})$ be the efficient y given $\bar{x}$ (that is, $y^*(\bar{x})$ maximizes W over y given $\bar{x}$). Then the injurer's activity level is excessive in the sense that $y(\bar{x}) > y^*(\bar{x})$, and for this reason one can immediately conclude that the negligence rule is not efficient.[19] The socially optimal due care level, say $\bar{x}^*$, is determined by maximizing

$$W(\bar{x}, y(\bar{x})) = a(\bar{x}, y(\bar{x})) - y(\bar{x})l(\bar{x}) \tag{4}$$

over $\bar{x}$ (where $\bar{x}$ must be in the range low enough so that injurers decide to set $x = \bar{x}$). Under fairly weak assumptions, it is true that $\bar{x}^* > x^*$.[20] The optimal due care standard exceeds the efficient care level because it is socially desirable to compensate for inability to control the activity level by forcing injurers to exercise special care (and because this in itself reduces the value of the activity, inducing injurers to lower the activity level).

If there is no liability, the outcome is generally worse than that under the negligence rule (with $\bar{x}^*$ as the due care standard), since injurers exercise no care. That is, $x = 0$ and $y = y(0)$ is the outcome.[21]

The conclusions about the welfare comparison of liability rules may be summarized as follows.

PROPOSITION 1. *Suppose that injurers and victims are strangers. Then strict liability is efficient and is superior to the negligence rule, which is superior to not having liability at all.*

B. *The Market Case: Accidents between Sellers and Victims*

Injurers are now assumed to be sellers of a product or service. The precise interpretation of care x will be explained in the various subcases, which are distinguished by whether the victims are strangers, customers, or employees. The activity level y will be interpreted as the seller's output.

---

[19] Assume that W is concave in y, that $\bar{x} > 0$, and that $y(\bar{x}) > 0$. Then $y(\bar{x})$ is identified by the first-order condition $a_y = 0$. But $y^*(\bar{x})$ is determined by $a_y = l$. Since $l > 0$ and W is concave, $y^*(\bar{x}) < y(\bar{x})$. Note, however, that the concavity assumption is not needed to show that the negligence rule is not efficient; without it we can still conclude that $y^*(\bar{x}) \neq \bar{y}(\bar{x})$.

[20] Let $[0, \hat{x}]$ be the range of $\bar{x}$ such that injurers would choose $x = \bar{x}$. It is easy to show that $\hat{x} > x^*$. Thus, assuming concavity of (4) in $\bar{x}$, we need only argue that $dW/d\bar{x} > 0$ when evaluated at x^*. But $dW/D\bar{x} = W_x - y'l$ and it is plausible that both terms should be positive at x^*. Assuming that W is concave in x and that the optimal x given $\bar{y}(x^*)$ exceeds x^*, we have $W_x > 0$. Also, assuming that $y' < 0$, $-y'l > 0$.

[21] To show that the negligence rule would be better, we need only demonstrate that $\bar{x}^* > 0$ (for $\bar{x} = 0$ corresponds to no liability). This is plausible for the reasons given in the previous footnote: A sufficient condition for $dW/d\bar{x} > 0$ at $\bar{x} = 0$ is that $W_x(0, y(0)) > 0$ and $y'(0) < 0$.

Before considering the subcases, additional notation is needed, as is a description of competitive market equilibrium. Define

$$c(x) = \text{production cost per unit given } x,$$
$$p = \text{product price,}$$

and assume that $c' > 0$ and $c'' > 0$. The seller's full cost per unit produced and sold is

$$c(x) + \text{expected liability payments per unit.} \tag{5}$$

Since sellers maximize expected profits and are price takers,

$$x \text{ is chosen by sellers to minimize } c(x) + \text{expected}$$
$$\text{liability payments per unit.} \tag{6}$$

Also, in equilibrium, price must equal full cost,

$$p = c(x) + \text{expected liability payments per unit.} \tag{7}$$

(However, (6) and (7) will be slightly modified when the victims are customers and can observe x.) Now define

$$b(y) = \text{income equivalent of gross benefits enjoyed by}$$
$$\text{a customer who purchases } y.$$

These benefits are gross of any expected accident losses he has to bear. We assume $b' > 0$ and $b'' < 0$. The customer's position u is

$$u(y) = b(y) - py - \text{any expected accident losses he}$$
$$\text{has to bear.} \tag{8}$$

The customer's demand is therefore determined by

$$u(y) \text{ is maximized over } y. \tag{9}$$

Equilibrium p, x, and y are determined by (6), (7), and (9).
Social welfare W is given by

$$W = b(y) - yc(x) - yl(x), \tag{10}$$

the gross value of output to customers minus production costs—note that the increase in c with x corresponds to prevention costs—minus expected accident losses. As in the nonmarket case, maximizing W requires taking into account the benefits of y as well as accident costs and prevention costs. From (10), it is clear that the efficient value x^* is determined by

$$\text{minimize } c(x) + l(x) \text{ over } x \tag{11}$$

and that y^* is then determined by

$$\text{maximize } b(y) - y(c(x^*) + l(x^*)) \text{ over } y. \tag{12}$$

(i) *Victims are strangers.* Here x is interpreted as the care the seller exercises in the conduct of his operations.

Under strict liability sellers are induced to choose the care level that minimizes production costs plus accident losses. Moreover because customers pay a price that reflects production costs plus accident losses, they are induced to purchase the socially correct output. To prove this, note that full cost per unit is $c(x) + l(x)$, which (see (6)) sellers minimize. Hence (see (11)), x^* is the care level. Therefore (see (7)), price p equals $c(x^*) + l(x^*)$. Hence (see (8) and (9)), consumers maximize $b(y) - py = b(y) - (c(x^*) + l(x^*))y$. This implies (see (12)) that y^* is chosen. Consequently, strict liability is efficient.

Under the negligence rule, an efficient outcome is not achieved. This is because sellers escape liability by acting nonnegligently. Hence the price charged customers reflects production costs but not accident losses. Since customers face too low a price, output is too high. To demonstrate this, assume (for the reason given in the nonmarket case) that $\bar{x}$ is low enough so that sellers decide to be nonnegligent. Then production cost and price must be $c(\bar{x})$. Consequently, customers choose y to maximize $b(y) - py = b(y) - c(\bar{x})y$. Let $y(\bar{x})$ be the customers' choice and $y^*(\bar{x})$ the efficient y given $\bar{x}$. Then $y(\bar{x}) > y^*(\bar{x})$, output is excessive, which also implies that the negligence rule cannot be efficient. The optimal due care level $\bar{x}^*$ is determined by maximizing

$$W(\bar{x}, y(\bar{x})) = b(y(\bar{x})) - c(\bar{x}) - y(\bar{x})l(\bar{x}) \tag{13}$$

over $\bar{x}$ (in the range such that sellers choose to be nonnegligent). As in the nonmarket case, it can be shown that $\bar{x}^* > x^*$, and for analogous reasons.[22]

If there is no liability, sellers have no motive to prevent accidents nor do customers have a motive to buy a socially appropriate quantity, since price does not reflect accident losses. Therefore, the outcome is worse than under the negligence rule. Specifically, production cost and price are $c(0)$ and customers choose $y(0)$.[23]

In summary, the conclusions are just as in the nonmarket case.

PROPOSITION 2. *Suppose that injurers are sellers and that victims are strangers. Then strict liability is efficient and is superior to the negligence rule, which is superior to not having liability at all.*

(ii) *Victims are customers.* In this subcase x might still be interpreted as the care the seller exercises in the conduct of his operations. This would be

[22] This and other claims made in this paragraph can be proved using arguments analogous to those in notes 19 & 20 *supra*.

[23] That no liability is inferior to the negligence rule can be shown by establishing, as in note 21 *supra*, that $\bar{x}^* > 0$.

appropriate if one is thinking about accidents which occur at the time and place of sale of a product or service. On the other hand, if one is considering accidents which occur after the time of purchase and involve a product that the customer takes away with him (a car, a piece of industrial machinery), then x should be interpreted as an index of the safety and reliability of the product.

Under strict liability, an argument virtually identical to that given in (i) shows that the efficient outcome results. Sellers again choose x in accord with (11). Thus price is $c(x^*) + l(x^*)$, and as customers do not bear accident losses, they select y in accord with (12). Note that this argument in no way depends on customers' knowledge of the risk of accident losses.

However, under the negligence rule, the analysis changes. Assume first that customers know what expected accident losses are either for particular sellers or only on average. Then the efficient outcome results if the due care level $\bar{x}$ is set equal to the efficient level x^*. To prove this, suppose that sellers choose x^*. Then, as they are nonnegligent, price equals $c(x^*)$. Since customers bear losses $l(x^*)$ per unit and know their magnitude, they maximize over y their utility position, $b(y) - py - l(x^*)y = b(y) - (c(x^*) + l(x^*))y$. Thus, they choose y^*. Therefore, to complete the proof, we need only show that sellers would choose x^* or, more precisely, that no seller would have a motive to choose an x other than x^* if there were an equilibrium in which x^* was the commonly chosen care level. To show this, suppose, on the contrary, that some seller chooses $x > x^*$. If customers can't observe *his x*, then he gets no benefit in the price from raising x but does incur greater production costs. On the other hand, if customers can observe his x, it is easy to show they wouldn't purchase from him if he charged his cost of production. If he did that, a customer's utility position would be the maximum over y of $b(y) - (c(x) + l(x))y$ which (since $x \neq x^*$) must be less than $b(y^*) - (c(x^*) + l(x^*))y^*$, the utility position of the customer if he buys from a seller who chooses x^*. Now assume that some seller chooses $x < x^*$. Then, as he will be liable for accident losses, his problem is to minimize full unit costs, namely $c(x) + l(x)$. But this implies that he chooses x^*, a contradiction.

Consider now the outcome under the negligence rule given the assumption that customers misperceive risks. Specifically, suppose that if expected accident losses are really $l(x)$, customers think they are $(1 + \lambda)l(x)$. Thus $\lambda > 0$ means that customers overestimate risk and $\lambda < 0$ that they underestimate risk. Assume that $\bar{x}$ is such that sellers choose $x = \bar{x}$. The price is therefore $c(\bar{x})$ and customer purchases are determined by maximizing over y the perceived utility position $b(y) - py - (1 + \lambda)l(\bar{x}) = b(y) - (c(\bar{x}) + (1 + \lambda)l(\bar{x}))y$. Therefore customers buy too little (less than $y^*(\bar{x})$) if they overestimate risk and too much if they underestimate risk. In particular, an efficient outcome cannot result.

Finally, consider the situation if there is no liability. Assume initially that customers can identify expected accident losses for particular sellers. Then competitive forces would induce sellers to choose an efficient care level and customers' purchases would be efficient. To show this we demonstrate that a situation in which sellers choose x^* is an equilibrium which results in an efficient outcome. Assuming that x^* is chosen by sellers, price must equal $c(x^*)$. Thus, customers (recognizing that they bear $l(x^*)$) choose y to maximize $b(y) - py - l(x^*)y = b(y) - (c(x^*) + l(x^*))y$. Consequently, they choose y^*. If a seller chose $x \neq x^*$, no customer would choose to buy from him. For if the customer were charged the production cost, his utility would be the maximum over y of $b(y) - (c(x) + l(x))y$. Since $x \neq x^*$, this must be less than $b(y^*) - (c(x^*) + l(x^*))y^*$, which is the customer's alternative.

If there is no liability and customers know expected accident losses only on average, then an efficient outcome would not result, for sellers would have no motive to take care. That is, $x = 0$ would hold. Also price would equal $c(0)$. Since they would realize that they bear $l(0)$, customer purchases would be determined by maximizing $b(y) - py - l(0)y = b(y) - (c(0) + l(0))y$. Thus, at least purchases would be efficient given the inefficiently low care level.

When there is no liability and customers misperceive average risks, then, as in the last paragraph, sellers choose $x = 0$, but in this instance customers purchase the wrong amount given that $x = 0$. Thus the outcome is worse than in the previous paragraph.

These results are summarized below.

PROPOSITION 3. *Suppose that injurers are sellers and that victims are customers. Then the relative performance of liability rules depends on the knowledge customers have about risk.* (See Table 1.)

As for the ranking of the inefficient outcomes in Table 1, it was shown that (a) is superior to (c) and it can also be shown that (b) is superior to (c) (using the argument of note 21 *supra*); however there is no necessary relationship between (a) and (b).

(iii) *Victims are employees.* In this subcase the results and their proofs are exactly parallel to those in the last subcase (in Proposition 3 merely substitute the word "employee" for "customer"). Therefore, it will not be necessary to verify all the results. However, it will be described how the model changes and, to provide a pattern for the reader, a proof that strict liability is efficient will be given.

The variable x is interpreted as the care the seller exercises in his production process.

It is assumed that an employee's wage minus the expected accident losses that he has to bear must equal his "opportunity wage," which is set by economy-wide forces of supply and demand and is therefore taken as exogenous. Define

TABLE 1

Knowledge of risk of accident loss	Form of Liability		
	Strict Liability	Negligence	No Liability
Accurate knowledge about each seller's risk	efficient	efficient	efficient
Accurate knowledge only of the average risk	efficient	efficient	inefficient (a)
Misperception of average risk	efficient	inefficient (b)	inefficient (c)

$$w = \text{wage paid to employee,}$$
$$\bar{w} = \text{opportunity wage,}$$

so that[24]

$$\bar{w} = w - \text{expected accident losses borne.} \qquad (14)$$

The seller's unit cost of production is

$$c(x) = w + k(x), \qquad (15)$$

where $k(x)$ are nonlabor production costs given x.

Under strict liability the efficient outcome results because, on the one hand, firms are induced to choose a care level that minimizes nonlabor production costs plus expected accident losses and, on the other, because customers face a price that reflects total production costs plus expected accident losses. To see this, note that since employees do not bear accident losses, $\bar{w} = w$. Hence, firms minimize $c(x) + l(x) = \bar{w} + k(x) + l(x)$, which means that they choose x^*. Price therefore equals $c(x^*) + l(x^*)$ and customers choose y to maximize (12).

IV. Bilateral Accidents

Define the following additional notation,

$$s \geqq 0 \quad \text{care level of a victim,}$$
$$t \geqq 0 \quad \text{activity level of a victim.}$$

Expected accident losses are assumed to fall with victims' care and to rise with victims' activity levels. Also, if victims do not engage in their activity (t

---

[24] The wage is normalized so that it is the amount paid per unit of labor time necessary to produce one unit of output.

= 0), then losses are zero. More will be said later about how expected accident losses are related to s and t.

As previously noted, along with the liability rules examined in the last section, both strict liability and the negligence rule will be considered when there is a defense of contributory negligence. Therefore, define

$$\bar{s} = \text{due care level for victims.}$$

However, there will never be need to distinguish between the negligence rule with and without the defense. This is because in this model the two negligence rules are equivalent (as is true in most models which assume that injurers are identical).[25]

The results and proofs of this section closely parallel those of the last. Therefore, although formal statements of the results will be given, proofs will usually either be omitted or only sketched.

A. *The Nonmarket Case: Accidents between Strangers*

Define

$$h(s,t) = \text{income equivalent of the utility to a} \\ \text{victim of engaging in his activity at} \\ \text{level } t \text{ and exercising care } s$$

and assume that h has properties analogous to those of the function $a(x,y)$ (namely, assume that $h_s < 0$, $h_t(s,t) > 0$ for $t < t(s)$, etc.). Also define

$$l(x,s) = \text{expected accident losses per victim per} \\ \text{unit of injurer activity and of victim ac-} \\ \text{tivity,}$$

where $l_x < 0$ and $l_s < 0$. Thus, expected accident losses as a function of x, y, s, and t are $ytl(x,s)$.[26]

Social welfare is

$$W(x,y,s,t) = a(x,y) + h(s,t) - ytl(x,s), \tag{16}$$

the sum of the benefits of engaging in their activities for victim and injurer less the expected cost of accidents.

[25] While it is true that if an injurer is negligent, whether there is a defense of contributory negligence matters, it turns out that, in the situations which we consider, all injurers decide to act in a nonnegligent way. Therefore, whether there is a defense of contributory negligence is irrelevant.

[26] Expected accident losses have this form if we make the same assumption about the victim's activity level as we have made about the injurer's: an increase in the activity level is a physical repetition of an activity which causes a proportional rise in expected accident costs. This makes analysis easier (principally, the proof to Proposition 5), and it will be clear that the qualitative nature of the results would not change were expected accident costs to depend in a more general way on $x,y,s,$ and t.

Under strict liability with a defense of contributory negligence, an efficient outcome cannot be achieved, for assume otherwise. Then, in particular, it must be that $s = \bar{s} = s^*$. This means victims will never have to bear losses. Consequently they will have no motive to reduce accident losses by lowering their activity level, and t will exceed t^*.

An argument similar to this one (and to the basic argument made in the last part) shows that an efficient outcome cannot be achieved under the negligence rule. Under the negligence rule injurers are not given an incentive to reduce accident losses by lowering their activity level.

Thus, as stated before, the choice between strict liability with a defense of contributory negligence and the negligence rule is a choice in favor of the lesser of two evils.

However, a rule of strict liability without a defense of contributory negligence would never be desirable, as it would always be dominated by strict liability with the defense. (The argument showing this is essentially that of note 21 *supra*). Similarly, it would never be desirable not to have liability, for this would result in an outcome inferior to that under the negligence rule. No welfare comparison can be made between strict liability and not having liability without knowing whether it is more important to control victim or injurer behavior.

In summary,

PROPOSITION 4. *Suppose that injurers and victims are strangers. Then none of the usual liability rules is efficient. Strict liability with a defense of contributory negligence is superior to the negligence rule if it is sufficiently important to lower injurer activity levels. Strict liability without the defense and no liability are each inferior to whichever rule is better: either strict liability with the defense or the negligence rule.*

The next result states that there is no conceivable liability rule that induces parties to act efficiently.

PROPOSITION 5. *Suppose that injurers and victims are strangers and consider any liability rule which may depend on any or all of the following variables: the victim's losses, the care he exercises, the care the injurer exercises. Then the liability rule is not efficient.*

To prove this, note that under a liability rule of the type under consideration, expected payments by the injurer must be of the form $ytq(x,s)$. Now suppose that the rule is efficient. If the injurer is to select the efficient activity level, then y^* must be the solution to

$$\underset{y}{\text{maximize}} \; a(x^*,y) - yt^*q(x^*,s^*). \tag{17}$$

On the other hand, since y^* maximizes $W(x^*,y,s^*,t^*)$, y^* must be the solution to

$$\text{maximize } a(x^*,y) - yt^*l(x^*,s^*). \tag{18}$$
$$y$$

Consequently, it must be that $q(x^*,s^*) = l(x^*,s^*)$. Similarly, if the victim is to choose his efficient activity level, then t^* must solve

$$\text{maximize } h(s^*,t) + y^*t(q(x^*,s^*) - l(x^*,s^*)). \tag{19}$$
$$t$$

But since t^* must also solve

$$\text{maximize } h(s^*,t) - y^*tl(x^*,s^*), \tag{20}$$
$$t$$

it must be that $q(x^*,s^*) = 0$, which is a contradiction.

B. The Market Case: Accidents between Sellers and Victims

The same assumptions are made about the market as in Part III.B. However, victims now play a role in accidents.

(i) *Victims are strangers.* In this subcase, the results are just like those described in the nonmarket case, and for reasons which combine the arguments given there and in Part III.B(i). (See also the discussion in the introduction.)

PROPOSITION 6. *Suppose that injurers are sellers and that victims are strangers. Then the results are as given in Propositions 4 and 5.*

(ii) *Victims are customers.* In this subcase, the customer care level will have the usual interpretation. However, the customer activity level could be interpreted in several ways. First, think of it as the quantity of the good the customer purchases. This is the interpretation that will be made in regard to purchases of services or of products which are not durables. In this situation, then, the victim's activity level and the injurer's activity level are one and the same, namely, the level of output (so $t = y$); expected accident losses are given by $yl(x,s)$; and the following result holds.

PROPOSITION 7a. *Suppose that injurers are sellers of a nondurable good or service and that victims are customers. Then the relative performance of liability rules depends on the knowledge customers have about risks. (See Table 2.)*

Now consider the situation when customers buy durable goods—say lawn mowers or, if the customer is a firm, industrial machinery. In this situation,

TABLE 2

Knowledge of risk of accident loss	Form of Liability			
	Strict Liability with Defense of Contributory Negligence	Negligence	Strict Liability	No Liability
Accurate knowledge about each seller's risk	efficient	efficient	inefficient	efficient
Accurate knowledge only of the average risk	efficient	efficient	inefficient	inefficient
Misperception of average risk	efficient	inefficient	inefficient	inefficient

it is assumed that the customer contributes to expected accident losses not only through the choice of care level and quantity purchased but also by the rate of use, denoted by r, of each unit purchased (number of times a mower is used per week, the frequency of operation of a machine). Therefore, the income equivalent of the utility of use to the customer will be written $h(s,t,r)$ (with $h_r > 0$) and the expected accident losses, $yrl(x,s)$. The results must now be modified as follows.

PROPOSITION 7b. *Suppose that injurers are sellers of a durable good and that victims are customers. Then the relative performance of liability rules depends on the knowledge customers have about risks.* (See Table 3.)

The point to be noticed here is (as explained before) that strict liability with a defense of contributory negligence never leads to an efficient outcome. It is true that in order to avoid being contributorily negligent, customers exercise due care and, because price reflects accident losses, they purchase the socially correct amount. However, they have no motive to lower expected accident losses by reducing their frequency of use of the product they buy. In contrast, under the negligence rule, provided that customers have knowledge of accident risks, an efficient outcome is achieved. Sellers exercise due care to avoid being found negligent. Customers choose the socially desirable care level, quantity to purchase, *and* rate of use since they bear accident losses.

(iii) *Victims are employees.* In this subcase, there is some difficulty in interpreting what the activity level would mean. In many situations, there is no obvious aspect of the discretionary behavior of the employee that would not come under the rubric of care. If so, the results turn out to be identical to

TABLE 3

Knowledge of risk of accident loss	Form of Liability			
	Strict Liability with Defense of Contributory Negligence	Negligence	Strict Liability	No Liability
Accurate knowledge about each seller's risk	inefficient	efficient	inefficient	efficient
Accurate knowledge only of the average risk	inefficient	efficient	inefficient	inefficient
Misperception of average risk	inefficient	inefficient	inefficient	inefficient

those reported in Proposition 7a. However, in situations where there is a type of employee decision that fits the description of activity level given here, then the results are those of Proposition 7b.

V. Concluding Comments

1. A question which is in a sense logically prior to the analysis of this article must be mentioned, namely, *"Why isn't the level of activity usually considered in the formulation of a due care standard?"* After all, the inefficiencies discussed here were viewed in the main as deriving from the fact that in order to avoid being found negligent (or contributorily negligent), parties are not motivated to alter their level of activity.[27] The answer to the question appears to be that the courts would run into difficulty in trying to employ a standard of due care expanded in scope to include the level of activity. In formulating such a broadened due care standard, courts would, by definition, have to decide on the appropriate level of activity, and their competence to do this is problematic. How would courts decide the number of

[27] Were the level of activity included in the "due care" standard, a party would, by definition of due care, have to choose both the level of activity and the level of care appropriately in order to avoid liability; thus the inefficiencies analyzed in this article would be eliminated. However, A. Mitchell Polinsky, Strict Liability versus Negligence in a Market Setting (1979) (unpublished mimeographed paper, Stanford University) makes a point of qualification to this. He observes that in the market case it is not enough for the level of activity to be incorporated in the due care standard for each firm within the industry, for then too many firms would enter it; rather, the level of activity would somehow have to be made part of the due care standard for the industry as a whole. He also notes a similar point in respect to the nonmarket case.

miles an individual ought to drive or how far or how often a pedestrian ought to walk?[28] How would courts decide the level of output an industry—much less a firm within an industry—ought to produce? To decide such matters, courts would likely have to know much more than would normally have to be known to decide whether care, conventionally interpreted, was adequate.[29]

2. From the logic of the arguments presented here, it can be seen that what is important about the variable "level of activity" is only that it is not included in the due care standard. Any other variable omitted from the standard would also be inappropriately chosen in many of the circumstances in which we said the same of the level of activity. For example, in regard to accidents involving firms and strangers it has been noted that, if the scale of a firm's research in safety technology is not comprehended by the standard of due care, then under the negligence rule the firm would not be expected to invest sufficiently in such research.[30]

3. Commentators on tort law have in recent years frequently pointed to the reciprocal nature of harm, especially in the sense that the victim must be present in order to suffer harm. This has unfortunately engendered a misleading piece of folklore: that the very concept of harm is rendered ambiguous. While it is undeniable that for harm to occur there must be a victim, I can see no sense in which this truism leads to conceptual problems in instrumentalist analysis. Here, under the heading of bilateral accidents, the situation when victims as well as injurers could vary their level of activity (and of care) was studied; and one such possibility for victims was a level of activity of zero, which is to say, the "victims" are not around to be harmed. Thus, for example, the result (Proposition 4) concerning strict liability (with the defense of contributory negligence) versus negligence in regard to accidents between strangers might be expressed by saying that strict liability is preferable if it is more desirable to control whether injurers are present than it is to control whether victims are present; and the next result (Proposition 5) might be expressed by saying that there is no liability rule which generally induces both victims and injurers to make the efficient decision as to whether they should be present.[31]

---

[28] There might also be evidentiary problems. The courts might find it difficult to learn how many miles an individual drives or a pedestrian walks.

[29] On this argument, we would expect that when courts could easily discern what the level of activity ought to be, then it would be incorporated into the standard of due care. One legal doctrine which appears to confirm this is that of "coming to the nuisance," for the doctrine is applied in precisely those situations when the *activity* of coming to the nuisance—which is quite distinct from the level of *care* exercised once one is near the nuisance—may be seen as clearly socially undesirable.

[30] See Posner, *supra* note 9, at 139 & 140.

[31] It should be noted that Proposition 5 holds if one thinks of the level of activity as a binary variable (and/or if there is no variable "care"), for the proof does not depend on the level of activity being a continuous variable (nor on the existence of the variable care).

4. The analysis presented here does appear to help to explain certain features of tort law. A notable example is provided by the so-called pockets of strict liability: for ultrahazardous activities, ownership of wild animals, and so forth. These areas of strict liability seem to have two characteristics. First, they are such that injurer activity has a distinctive aspect (which makes the activity easy for the law to single out) and imposes nonnegligible risks on victims (which make the activity worthwhile controlling). And, second, they are such that victim activity is usually not at all special—on the contrary, it is typically entirely routine in nature, part of what it is to carry on a normal life—and is therefore activity that cannot and ought not be controlled. Consequently, it is appealing to explain the pockets of strict liability by the idea (expressed in Propositions 4 and 6) that strict liability is preferable if it is more desirable to control injurers' activity than victims'.[32]

However, there are many features of tort law which the analysis by itself does not seem to satisfactorily explain. And this is not unexpected, for it is in the nature of the formal approach to isolate selected factors of interest by ignoring others; the formal approach aims for a particular kind of insight, not for true balance or comprehensiveness.[33] Two examples will illustrate various limitations in our ability to employ in a direct way the results of this article. The first concerns the trend in decisions in product-liability cases toward expansion of manufacturer's liability. If this trend can be likened to one toward holding manufacturers strictly liable, we may be tempted to explain it as broadly rational given some of our results (Propositions 2, 3, 6,

---

[32] Posner, *supra* note 9, at 140-41, makes essentially this point. Also George P. Fletcher, Fairness and Utility in Tort Theory, 85 Harv. L. Rev. 537 (1972), explains the pockets of strict liability (at 547-49) by appeal to the notion that strict liability is imposed when parties create "nonreciprocal" risks. Our discussion might be viewed as helping to explain why it is that when parties create nonreciprocal risks, they should be strictly liable (but Fletcher would probably not welcome this interpretation).

[33] Of course, the informal instrumentalist approach is more flexible, aims for, and achieves greater balance and generality. But, whether formal or informal, the instrumentalist approach has been subject to the limitation that it does not refer to "moralist" argument or explanation— that which sounds in terms of what is "right" or "fair" or "just" to do in the particular situation at hand. (Fletcher, *supra* note 32, is a recent and valuable discussion of the contrast between the instrumentalist and moralist approaches. See also Richard Epstein, A Theory of Strict Liability, 2 J. Legal Stud. 151 (1973).) Perhaps a few tentative remarks about this will not be out of order. Given that (i) we believe that to an important extent legal institutions are/should be shaped by moralist notions and that legal decisions are/should be made in consideration of them; and that (ii) the instrumentalist approach has some merit (I am not saying how much) in descriptive and normative analysis of law, it seems plausible (by implicit reasoning) that (iii) moralist notions must encapsulate instrumentalist goals (and, of course, there are explicit arguments for this, such as those of the utilitarian ethical theorists). Yet it also seems that (iv) to an important extent the moralist notions (or many of them) must be viewed as having a life of their own—cannot be fruitfully, or at least naturally, viewed as embodying what would normally be conceived of as instrumentalist goals. One would hope that discussion of such issues in the future might help to clarify the extent to which the division between instrumentalists and moralists merely reflects use of a different mode of discourse, and is therefore not "real," and the extent to which the division is in fact substantive.

7a). However, realism requires us to look at other, complementary explana-
tions of the trend, such as that strict liability may provide a better means of
risk sharing than the negligence rule, or that strict liability may be easier to
apply than the negligence rule. Moreover, realism requires us to ask wheth-
,er there even is an explanation of the trend based on its social rationality—
whether in fact the trend might be socially undesirable, say on the ground
that the expansion in the scope of liability has led to an excessively costly
volume of disputes. Similar questions may be asked in respect to the second
example, which concerns the fact that the negligence rule is the dominant
form of tort liability in Anglo-American and in Western European legal
systems today. Our analysis certainly does not suggest why this should be so,
since, at least as often as otherwise, strict liability (with a defense of contributory negligence) is superior to the negligence rule. We are therefore led
to ask again about such matters as risk sharing, administrative simplicity,
and (especially) the social costs of expansion of the scope of liability.

5. Many of the points made in this article have been discussed before, and
doubtless numerous times.[34] For example, the literature on enterprise liability virtually always considers the effect of such liability on product price,
and the influence of this on purchases. The contribution made here would
therefore seem to lie principally in the attention given to context—to the
specifics of the relationship obtaining between injurers and victims—and in
the unified way in which the variety of problems is viewed.

[34] But it is hard to find the points stated in explicit and general form. However, the reader
should certainly refer to "Strict Liability vs. Negligence" in Posner *supra* note 9, at 137-42,
which is the clearest discussion of our subject of which I am aware, and on which this article
may properly be regarded as building. The reader should also refer to Guido Calabresi, Optimal
Deterrence and Accidents, 84 Yale L. J. 656 (1975). And the reader might also want to look at
the following papers by economists: John Prather Brown, Toward an Economic Theory of
Liability, 2 J. Legal Stud. 323 (1973); Peter A. Diamond, Single Activity Accidents, 3 J. Legal
Stud. 107 (1974); Jerry Green, On the Optimal Structure of Liability Laws, 7 Bell J. Econ. 553
(1976); and Steven Shavell, Accidents, Liability, and Insurance (forthcoming in Am. Econ.
Rev.). In these papers liability rules are studied when parties can affect accident losses only by
altering their levels of care; levels of activity are implicitly regarded as fixed (but see Section 11
of Diamond's paper). The reader may also find relevant Michael Spence, Consumer Misperceptions, Product Failure, and Producer Liability, 44 Rev. Econ. Stud. 561 (1977). He studies the
use of strict liability and fines in the case of unilateral accidents; and he allows for sellers to offer
guarantees and for consumers to be risk averse and to misperceive risks.

On liability and insurance

Steven Shavell*

The question considered in this article is how liability rules and insurance affect incentives to reduce accident risks and the allocation of such risks. This question is examined when liability is strict or based on the negligence rule; and, if first-party and liability insurance are available, when insurers have information about insured parties' behavior and when they do not have such information. The conclusions are in essence that although both of the forms of liability create incentives to take care, they differ in respect to the allocation of risk; that, of course, the presence of insurance markets mitigates this difference and alters incentives to take care; and that despite the latter effect, the sale of insurance is socially desirable.

1. Introduction

■ This article is concerned with identifying how liability rules and insurance affect incentives to reduce accident risks and the allocation of such risks.[1] Two principal forms of liability will be examined: *strict liability*, under which a party who has caused a loss must pay damages whether or not he was negligent; and the *negligence rule*, under which a party who has caused a loss is required to pay damages only if he was negligent. The two major types of insurance coverage will also be considered: *first-party insurance*, that is, coverage against direct loss; and *liability insurance*, coverage against having to pay damages.

It is clear that liability rules influence accident avoidance as well as the allocation of accident risks. It is evident too that insurance has both effects, for by its nature insurance spreads losses; and it also alters incentives—in a way that depends on the extent of coverage and on the connection, if any, between the terms of a policy and actions taken by an insured party to reduce risk.

Moreover, the effects of liability rules and of insurance are mutually dependent. The allocation of risk associated with the use of a liability rule depends on insurance coverage, and the latter depends on the liability rule since the rule determines in part the risks parties face. Likewise, the incentives to avoid accidents created by liability rules influence and are influenced by insurance coverage; and this raises a question of interest, namely, could liability insurance be socially disadvantageous on account of its dulling the incentive to reduce accident risks?[2]

---

* Harvard Law School.

I wish to thank G. Calabresi, P. A. Diamond, A. Klevorick, A. M. Polinsky, and R. Posner for comments and the National Science Foundation (Grant nos. SOC-76-20862 and SES-80-14208) for financial support.

[1] The term "accident" is to be given the broadest interpretation. It will refer to instances of loss arising in most any type of situation in which the actions of a party (an individual or a firm) affect the probability distribution of loss suffered by others.

[2] This question was seriously discussed when liability insurance was first offered for sale in England and in the United States. As one commentator writes, "For a time . . . there was considerable uncertainty as to whether any contract by which an insured was to be protected against the consequences of his own negligence . . . was not void as contrary to public policy. . . . [But] when it became apparent that no dire consequences

In view of these remarks about the relationship between liability rules and insurance, the main features of the model and the analysis to be presented may be briefly indicated before proceeding.[3] In the model, accidents are assumed to involve two types of parties, "injurers" and "victims," only the former of which are assumed to be able to affect the likelihood of accidents, and only the latter of which are assumed to suffer direct losses in the event of accidents. Given this model, the following conclusions are reached.

(i) Strict liability and negligence both create incentives to reduce accident risk, but they differ with respect to the allocation of risk.[4] Under strict liability injurers bear risk and victims are protected against risk, whereas under the negligence rule injurers do not bear risk—if they are not negligent, they will not have to pay damages when involved in accidents—and victims do bear risk. In consequence, if insurance is unavailable, then strict liability will be attractive when injurers are risk neutral (or, more generally, are better able to bear risk than victims), and the negligence rule will be appealing in the reverse situation.[5]

(ii) The availability of insurance alters this conclusion and suggests that with respect to the bearing of risk, strict liability and negligence should be equally attractive; for victims can avoid the risk that they would bear under the negligence rule by purchasing first-party insurance, and injurers can shift the risk that they would bear under strict liability by purchasing liability insurance. However, matters are complicated if liability insurers cannot monitor injurer behavior, since problems of "moral hazard" would then result in injurers' purchasing only partial coverage.

(iii) The availability of liability insurance does not have an undesirable effect on the working of liability rules. Although the purchase of liability insurance changes the incentives created by liability rules, the terms of the insurance policies sold in a competitive setting would be such as to provide an appropriate substitute (but not necessarily

---

in fact resulted, these objections passed out of the picture . . . ." (Prosser, 1971, p. 543). However, it is worth noting that liability insurance is not sold in the Soviet Union, where the view is held that the insurance would interfere unduly with the role of liability as a deterrent (Tunc, 1973).

[3] The analysis builds in two important respects on Brown (1973), Diamond (1974), Green (1976), and Shavell (1980), which study accidents and liability when parties are risk neutral and thus when there are no insurance markets. The first respect in which the model of this article differs from those in the articles cited is in its portrayal of the functioning of liability rules. In the cited articles, a liable party pays any judgment rendered against him out of his own pocket, whereas in the model studied here—and as is usually the case in fact—a liable party pays little or none of a judgment against him; instead his liability insurer pays. This means that the way in which liability rules are envisioned here to create incentives to reduce accident risks is to a considerable degree indirect, being associated with the terms of liability insurance policies.

The second respect in which the present model differs from the others is simply that because account is taken of attitudes toward risk, the normative comparison of liability rules involves considerations of the allocation of risk as well as of reduction of accident losses. Indeed, this means that liability rules are sometimes not equivalent here when they would have been had parties been assumed risk neutral. Similarly, because this article considers the possibility of risk aversion and, therefore, the presence of insurance markets, the social desirability of liability insurance can be examined.

In addition to the articles cited above, the reader may wish to refer to Spence (1977) and to Epple and Raviv (1978), which study strict product liability but not the negligence rule and which, in any event, focus on different issues (Spence on warranties; Epple and Raviv on market structure). Finally, the reader should refer to Calabresi (1970) and to Posner (1977), which contain interesting and suggestive, informal analysis of accidents and liability.

[4] The model abstracts from considerations other than those of incentives and the allocation of risk. In particular, there is no account taken of administrative costs (but see the concluding comments).

[5] Moreover, it will be shown that were strict liability the form of liability in this situation, it would be best for the level of liability to be less than losses caused, as if to insure partially the risk averse injurers. In other words, when the generator of an externality is risk averse, "fully internalizing" the externality is not desirable.

equivalent) set of incentives to reduce accident risks. In other words, it is not socially beneficial for the government to intervene in the operation of competitive liability insurance markets (thus answering the question posed above).[6]

2. The model

■ It is assumed in the model that injurers are identical and act so as to maximize the expected utility of wealth, and the same is presumed about victims. Under one interpretation to be made, injurers are taken to be sellers of a product for which each victim has an inelastic demand for a single unit;[7] under the other interpretation, injurers are assumed to be engaged in a private, nonmarket activity.[8] Now define the following notation:

U = utility function of injurers—who are risk neutral or risk averse;
u = initial wealth of injurers; $0 < u$;
V = utility function of victims—who are risk neutral or risk averse;
v = initial wealth of victims; $0 < v$;
x = level of injurers' expenditures on accident prevention activity;
$p(x)$ = probability of an accident, given x; $0 < p < 1$ and p is decreasing and strictly convex[9] in x;
l = loss[9] sustained by a victim if there is an accident; $0 < l < u$[10];
r = under the first interpretation of the model, the price paid by victims for the product sold by injurers; under the other interpretation, a "lump sum" amount paid (before an accident might occur) by victims and received, as a lump sum, by injurers.

The problem to be solved using this model and notation is to choose "policy variables" in a Pareto efficient way, that is, in a way such that no alternative choice would raise the expected utility of both injurers and victims.[11] It is assumed that given the choice of policy variables, injurers select a level of prevention activity and a liability insurance policy (if available) to maximize their expected utility EU, while taking as fixed the behavior of victims and the value of r;[12] and victims select a first-party insurance policy (if available) to maximize their expected utility EV, while taking as fixed injurers' behavior and the value of r. Formally, then, the problem is:

to choose policy variables to maximize EV subject to the constraints: (1)

victims maximize EV (taking injurers' behavior and r as given);   (2)

---

[6] It will be seen that this fact cannot be interpreted as an application of the theorem of welfare economics stating that a competitive equilibrium with complete markets is Pareto efficient.

[7] Under this interpretation, victims may either be imagined to suffer a loss due to a production-related accident (oil spill ruins beach front property), or else to suffer a loss due to failure of the product purchased (explosion of purchased boiler causes damage to plant).

[8] We do not ask whether (or to what extent) the injurer would engage in his activity. That question is among those considered in Shavell (1980).

[9] The possibility of nonmonetary losses is not considered.

[10] In other words, it is assumed that injurers are able to pay for the losses they might cause.

[11] In the various versions of the problem that will be considered, the relevant policy variables will be obvious from context. They may include parameters of a liability rule, a choice among alternative liability rules, or, possibly, a decision about intervention in insurance markets.

[12] For the assumption that injurers take r as fixed to make sense under the interpretation that r is the price of the product they sell and that loss is caused by product failure, it must be assumed that victim/consumers of the product cannot determine the accident probabilities of sellers on an individual basis. (Otherwise, the level of prevention activity would affect the price r through its influence on the accident probability.)

injurers maximize EU (taking victims' behavior and r as given); $\quad\quad$ (3)

$$r \text{ satisfies } EU = \bar{U}; \quad\quad (4)$$

and, sometimes, subject also to the constraint that

competitive first party and liability insurance markets operate. $\quad\quad$ (5)

Under the interpretation whereby injurers are sellers of a product, the price r may be viewed as market determined: Suppose that there is free entry into the product market and that $\bar{U}$ is the injurers' "opportunity level" of utility (injurers may engage in an alternative activity that yields $\bar{U}$). Then, in equilibrium, r must be such that their expected utility is $\bar{U}$. Under the other interpretation, when injurers are not sellers of a product, the reference level of expected utility $\bar{U}$, and thus the amount r, may be regarded as reflecting a social decision about their welfare.

3. The first-best solution to the accident problem

■ Before considering liability rules and insurance, it will be of interest to know what an omniscient and benevolent dictator would do to solve the accident problem. The dictator would choose in a Pareto efficient way the level of injurers' prevention activity and the levels of wealth for both injurers and victims, contingent on accident involvement and subject to a resource constraint. More precisely, denoting by v_n the wealth of a victim if he is not involved in an accident, v_a his wealth if he is, and similarly for u_n and u_a, the dictator would

$$\maximize_{x, v_n, v_a, u_n, u_a} EV = (1 - p(x))V(v_n) + p(x)V(v_a) \quad\quad (6)$$

subject to:

$$EU = (1 - p(x))U(u_n) + p(x)U(u_a) = \bar{U}; \quad\quad (7)$$

$$[(1 - p(x))v_n + p(x)v_a] + [(1 - p(x))u_n + p(x)u_a] + [p(x)l + x] = u + v. \quad (8)$$

Note that equation (8) states that expected resource use equals the available resources.[13] We then have

Proposition 1. A first-best solution to the accident problem is achieved if and only if (a) the level of prevention activity minimizes expected accident losses plus the costs of prevention activity (i.e., $p(x)l + x$); and (b) risk averse parties (injurers or victims) are left with the same level of wealth regardless of whether an accident actually occurs.

Note: The explanation for this is, of course, that the dictator can fully insure risk averse parties and, thus, it becomes desirable to maximize total expected resources, which means minimizing expected accident losses plus prevention costs.

Proof: Note first that given any x, a necessary and sufficient condition for optimality of v_n, v_a, u_n, and u_a is that they satisfy (7) and (8), that $v_n = v_a$ if the victim is risk averse, and that $u_n = u_a$ if the injurer is risk averse.[14]

Consequently, we may set $\gamma = v_n = v_a$ and $\mu = u_n = u_a$. (If the victim is risk neutral, we may always take $v_n = v_a$; and similarly if the injurer is risk neutral, we may always take $u_n = u_a$.) Thus the problem (6)–(8) is equivalent to

$$\maximize_{\gamma, \mu, x} V(\gamma) \quad\quad (9)$$

---

[13] The justification for writing the resource constraint in terms of expected values is the conventional one, that accident risks are small and independent. Note that the constraint makes sense only if the number of injurers equals the number of victims, an assumption which would be easy to modify.

[14] This is a standard result in the theory of Pareto-efficient sharing of risk (see for example Borch (1962)) and can easily be verified from the Kuhn-Tucker conditions for the problem (6)–(8).

subject to:

$$U(\mu) = \bar{U}, \tag{10}$$

$$\gamma + \mu + p(x)l + x = u + v. \tag{11}$$

But (10) determines a value, say $\bar{\mu}$, of μ, so that the two constraints reduce to

$$\gamma = (u + v - \bar{\mu}) - (p(x)l + x). \tag{12}$$

Hence, the problem is simply to maximize over x the quantity $V(u + v - \bar{\mu} - (p(x)l + x))$, which is equivalent to minimizing $p(x)l + x$. Q.E.D.

Note that the first-best level of prevention activity, to be denoted x^*, must be unique (by strict convexity of $p(x)$). Since the situation of interest is where $x^* > 0$, this will be assumed to be true below.

4. The achievable solution to the accident problem

■ To determine the solution to the accident problem when liability rules are used—that is, to determine Pareto efficient solutions to the problem (1)–(5)—the rules must first be formally defined. Under strict liability, whenever an injurer is involved in an accident, he must pay the victim an amount in damages. Denote damages by d, and observe that in principle damages need not equal the victim's loss. Under the negligence rule, an injurer must pay damages to the victim only if the court determines that the injurer's prevention activity fell short of a *standard of due care*. Denote the standard of due care by $\bar{x}$. It will be assumed that the courts' information about the injurer's behavior is accurate, so that an injurer will be found negligent if and only if he was in fact negligent.[15]

The operation of liability rules will now be studied both when insurance is assumed to be available and when it is not. The latter case is of interest both because it will allow us to see more easily the difference that insurance makes and also because in reality insurance might be unavailable.

□ **Functioning of liability rules when insurance is not available.** Let us first show

Proposition 2. Under strict liability, suppose that injurers are risk neutral. Then, according to a Pareto efficient solution, (a) damages paid by an injurer equal a victim's losses (i.e., $d = l$) and (b) a first-best outcome is achieved. On the other hand, if injurers are risk averse, then under an efficient solution (c) damages paid are less than a victim's losses (i.e., $d < l$) and (d) a first-best outcome is not achieved.

Note: Parts (a) and (b) are true for familiar reasons: When $d = l$, the "externality" of accident losses is "fully internalized," so that the injurers choose an appropriate level of prevention activity. Also, since injurers are risk neutral, it does not matter that they bear risk. Finally, victims, who might be risk averse, bear no risk since they are compensated for accident losses.

With regard to (c), it is not surprising that when injurers are risk averse, the externality they generate should not be fully internalized. (Under the first interpretation of the model, this means that buyers of a risky product are better off if risk averse sellers are subject to less than full liability for harm done.) Were d set equal to l, injurers would be exposed to "excessive" risk, with the consequence that they would have to be compensated excessively for bearing the risk or for engaging in excessive accident prevention activity. (The actual magnitude of the efficient d would depend on the victims' attitude toward risk as well; presumably, the more risk averse the victims, the higher would be

---

[15] The importance of this assumption is noted in the concluding comments.

this d.) Part (d) is true because if the efficient d is positive (as one would expect), then injurers bear risk; and if the efficient d is 0,[16] then injurers will choose x equal to 0, which is not first-best (as $x^* > 0$).

Proof: Assume first that injurers are risk neutral. Then if a first-best outcome is achieved when $d = l$, certainly $d = l$ must be a Pareto efficient solution to the problem of concern. We shall therefore assume that $d = l$ and shall show that a first-best outcome would result. If $d = l$, injurers will select x to maximize[17]

$$EU = (1 - p(x))(u + r - x) + p(x)(u + r - x - l) = u + r - (x + p(x)l). \quad (13)$$

Therefore, they will select x to minimize $x + p(x)l$. Moreover, since victims (who might be risk averse) will receive l whenever there is an accident, their income will be constant. Thus, if r is such that $EU = \bar{U}$, the "if" part of Proposition 1 implies that the first-best solution (corresponding to $\bar{U}$) is achieved. This proves parts (a) and (b).

Assume now that injurers are risk averse, so that

$$EU = (1 - p(x))U(u + r - x) + p(x)U(u + r - x - d). \quad (14)$$

Victims' expected utility is then

$$EV = (1 - p(x))V(v - r) + p(x)V(v - r - l + d), \quad (15)$$

and the problem (1)–(5) reduces to

$$\underset{d,r,x}{\text{maximize } EV} \quad (16)$$

subject to:[18]

$$EU_x = 0 \quad (17)$$

$$EU = \bar{U}. \quad (18)$$

Since the constraints (17) and (18) determine (and, let us assume, uniquely) r and x as functions of d, the problem may be written as

$$\text{maximize } EV(d) = (1 - p(x(d)))V(v - r(d)) + p(x(d))V(v - r(d) - l + d). \quad (19)$$

Now observe that[19]

$$EV'(d) = -p'x'[V(v - r) - V(v - r - l + d)]$$
$$- r'(1 - p)V'(v - r) + p(1 - r')V'(v - r - l + d). \quad (20)$$

To show that $d < l$, we shall verify that $EV'(l) < 0$. (A similar series of steps will verify that $EV'(d) < 0$ for $d > l$.) From (20), we have that $EV'(l) = (p - r')V'(v - r)$, so that we need to verify that $r' > p$. To do this, differentiate (18) to get

$$EU_x x'(d) + EU_r r'(d) + EU_d = 0, \quad (21)$$

and using (17), solve for r',

$$r'(d) = \frac{-EU_d}{EU_r} = \frac{p(x)U'(u + r - x - d)}{(1 - p(x))U'(u + r - x) + p(x)U'(u + r - x - d)}$$
$$= p(x)/[(1 - p(x))\frac{U'(u + r - x)}{U'(u + r - x - d)} + p(x)]. \quad (22)$$

---

[16] Examples can be constructed in which the efficient d is 0.

[17] Since the injurer is risk neutral, we may assume that the utility function is just $U(w) = w$ for any wealth w.

[18] It will be assumed that the first-order condition (17) determines the injurer's choice of x for the values of r and d to be considered.

[19] In the next expression and several later ones, certain functions will for convenience be written without their arguments (e.g., p' rather than $p'(x(d))$).

It is clear from (22) that $r' > p$ for any $d > 0$ (and thus for $d = l$). This establishes part (c), and part (d) is clear from the Note. $Q.E.D.$

The next result is

Proposition 3. Under the negligence rule, suppose that victims are risk neutral. Then, according to a Pareto efficient solution, (a) the standard of due care equals the first-best level (i.e., $\bar{x} = x^*$), and (b) a first-best outcome is achieved. However, if victims are risk averse, then under a Pareto efficient solution (c) the standard of due care is generally different from the first-best level, and (d) a first-best outcome is not achieved.

Note: Parts (a) and (b) are true because if $\bar{x} = x^*$, injurers will find it in their interest to choose $x = \bar{x}$, that is, to act in a nonnegligent way. Thus, the injurers, who might be risk averse, bear no risk. As victims are risk neutral, the fact that they bear risk does not matter. But, of course, when victims are risk averse, that they bear risk does matter, so that, as stated in (d), a first-best outcome would not be achieved. Moreover, in this case it will be seen that it would often be desirable that $\bar{x} > x^*$, so as to further reduce the likelihood of accidents.

Proof: To establish (a) and (b), let us show that when victims are risk neutral, a first-best outcome will result if $\bar{x} = x^*$ and $d = l$. To see this, consider first the possibility that injurers choose an $x \geq x^*$. Then, clearly, it must be that they choose $x = x^*$. On the other hand, if the injurers choose an $x < x^*$, then, since they would be found negligent if involved in accidents,

$$EU = (1 - p(x))U(u + r - x) + p(x)U(u + r - x - l)$$

$$\leq U(u + r - x - p(x)l) < U(u + r - x^* - p(x^*)l) < U(u + r - x^*). \quad (23)$$

(Use was made here of the fact that x^* minimizes $x + p(x)l$.) Thus injurers would choose x^*, would not be found negligent if involved in accidents, and would bear no risk. As victims are risk neutral, Proposition 1 then implies that a first-best outcome would be achieved.

Now assume that victims are risk averse and consider only $\bar{x}$ such that injurers would choose $x = \bar{x}$.[20] (Even if we restrict attention to the case when $d = l$, the set of such $\bar{x}$ properly includes $[0, x^*]$ since (23) is a strict inequality.) For such $\bar{x}$, $EV = (1 - p(\bar{x}))V(v - r) + p(\bar{x})V(v - r - l)$ and $EU = U(u + r - \bar{x})$. The problem of concern is therefore to maximize EV over r and $\bar{x}$ subject to $EU = \bar{U}$. But from the latter constraint, it follows that r and $\bar{x}$ are determined by $r = \bar{x} + k$, where k is an appropriate constant, so that the problem reduces to

$$\underset{\bar{x}}{\text{maximize}} \, (1 - p(\bar{x}))V(v - k - \bar{x}) + p(\bar{x})V(v - k - \bar{x} - l). \quad (24)$$

If V were linear, the solution to (24) would be $\bar{x} = x^*$, but since V is concave we would, as remarked, expect the solution to exceed x^*. It is possible, however, that the solution to (24) would be less than x^*.[21] In any event, since victims are risk averse and bear risk, Proposition 1 implies that a first-best outcome is not achieved. $Q.E.D.$

□ **Functioning of liability rules when insurance is available.** It will be assumed here that parties can purchase insurance at actuarially fair rates from a competitive insurance industry. Thus, if victims are risk averse, they will choose to buy full coverage against any risk they bear.

---

[20] Otherwise, the liability rule reduces to strict liability.

[21] The intuition is that even though a risk averse injurer has a greater motive to reduce the probability of a loss than does a risk neutral injurer, spending to reduce the probability exposes him to a larger risk (for if he loses l, his final income will be lower by l *plus* his expenditure).

In contrast, whether risk averse injurers will purchase full coverage depends on whether liability insurers can "observe" the levels of prevention activity of individual injurers. If liability insurers cannot do this, then, clearly, they cannot link the premium or terms of the policy to the level of prevention activity. Consequently, were injurers to purchase complete coverage, there would be a problem of moral hazard: Injurers would have no reason to avoid accidents, would therefore be involved in accidents with high probability, and would find themselves paying a high premium per dollar of coverage. But if injurers purchased policies with incomplete coverage, they would be exposed to some risk, would thus have some inducement to avoid accidents, would be involved in accidents with a lower probability than before, and would therefore pay a lower premium per dollar of coverage (though still an actuarially fair premium—given their altered behavior). Hence, it should seem plausible and can be shown under quite general assumptions that injurers would in fact purchase policies with incomplete coverage.[22]

On the other hand, if liability insurers can observe prevention activity, then they can make the premium or other policy terms depend on such activity, thereby giving injurers an incentive to avoid accidents even if they purchase full coverage. Hence, it should seem plausible in this case that risk averse injurers would purchase complete coverage and would be motivated to act so as to minimize expected damages plus prevention costs (i.e., $p(x)d + x$).[23]

The next result can now be stated and proved.

Proposition 4. Under strict liability, according to a Pareto efficient solution, (a) damages paid by an injurer equal a victim's losses (i.e., $d = l$), (b) government intervention in the liability insurance market is not desirable, and (c) a first-best outcome is achieved unless injurers are risk averse and liability insurers cannot observe their level of prevention activity.

Note: In the case when injurers are risk neutral and liability insurers cannot observe prevention activity, injurers would decide against purchase of liability insurance. The reason is that because of moral hazard, the cost of insurance coverage would exceed an injurer's expected cost were he not to purchase coverage; and since protection against risk is of no consequence to him, he would not buy coverage. Hence, the situation will be essentially that in the first part of Proposition 2, and a first-best outcome will be achieved. Note also that the issue of intervention in insurance markets is moot since no one buys insurance.

If injurers are risk neutral and liability insurers can observe prevention activity, then injurers will be indifferent as to whether and in what amount to purchase liability coverage and will, if $d = l$, be induced to choose x^* by their exposure to liability or by the terms of their insurance policy, should they have one. Also, since victims will bear no risk (although they could always purchase insurance if they needed it), Proposition 1 implies that a first-best outcome will be achieved and, thus, that government intervention in insurance markets could not be desirable.

---

[22] The formal problem that yields this result is

$$\max_{\pi, q} EU = (1 - p(x))U(u + r - \pi - x) + p(x)U(u + r - \pi - x + q - d)$$

subject to (i) EU is maximized over x and (ii) $\pi = p(x)q$, where π is the insurance premium and q is the level of coverage. Constraint (i) says that the insured chooses x in a personally optimal way, given his insurance policy, and constraint (ii) is the condition of actuarial fairness. Shavell (1979b) discusses conditions under which the solution has $q < d$, which we shall assume to be true; Arrow (1971) and Pauly (1974) also analyze the general problem of moral hazard.

[23] The formal problem that yields this result is $\max_{q,x} EU = (1 - p(x))U(u + r - p(x)q - x) + p(x)U(u + r - p(x)q - x + q - d)$. Note that in this problem the individual takes into account that his choice of x affects the premium he pays, whereas in the problem described in note 22 that was not true. It is well known and easy to verify that the solution to this problem is $q = d$ and the x that minimizes $p(x)d + x$.

If injurers are risk averse and liability insurers can observe prevention activity, injurers will purchase full coverage against damages, will therefore not bear risk and, if $d = l$, will be induced by the terms of their policy to choose x^*. Thus, Proposition 1 again implies our result.

In the last case (which is complex), when liability insurers cannot observe the prevention activity of risk averse injurers, the injurers will purchase incomplete coverage against damages (as explained in the paragraph preceding the Proposition). If we let q denote their level of coverage, this means that the injurers will bear a positive residual risk of $d - q$, so that a first-best outcome will not be achieved. Moreover, it becomes obvious that the argument that liability insurance eliminates the incentive to avoid accidents is mistaken. Because injurers will still bear a risk after purchase of liability coverage, they will make some effort to avoid accidents. But, of course, what is asserted in the Proposition is a stronger claim than that liability insurance does not eliminate incentives. What is asserted is that if $d = l$ and injurers purchase liability coverage, there are no measures the government can take to improve welfare. Why this should be so may be put informally as follows. One supposes that there would be scope for beneficial government intervention in the liability insurance market only if the sale of liability coverage were to worsen the welfare of victims. But if $d = l$, the welfare of victims is unaffected by the occurrence of accidents because the victims are fully compensated for losses. Thus there is no apparent opportunity for beneficial intervention in the insurance market.[24]

At the same time, it is important to point out (and will be shown at the end of the proof) that in this last case under discussion an efficient solution could also be achieved by the government's banning liability insurance and reducing liability from l to $l - q$, leaving risk averse victims to purchase first-party coverage of q.[25] (Note that this does not contradict the Proposition, for the banning of liability insurance and reduction of liability do not raise welfare; they leave it unchanged.)

Proof: If injurers are risk neutral and liability insurers cannot observe x, suppose that injurers were to purchase coverage $q > 0$. Then they would select x to maximize $u + r - \pi - x - p(x)(d - q)$, where π is the actuarially fair premium. If we denote the solution to this problem by x_1, then π must equal $p(x_1)q$, so that the expected wealth of injurers would be

$$u + r - p(x_1)q - x_1 - p(x_1)(d - q) = u + r - x_1 - p(x_1)d. \qquad (25)$$

On the other hand, if injurers do not purchase any coverage, they will select x to maximize $u + r - x - p(x)d$, so that denoting the solution to this by x_2, their expected wealth would be

$$u + r - x_2 - p(x_2)d. \qquad (26)$$

Since, as is easily verified, $x_1 < x_2$, and since x_2 maximizes $u + r - x - p(x)d$ and is unique (for $p(x)$ is strictly convex), the expression in (26) is larger than that in (25). Hence, the injurers will not purchase liability insurance coverage, and we may appeal to the argument proving Proposition 2 (a) and (b) to establish Proposition 4 in the present case.

If injurers are risk neutral, $d = l$, and liability insurers can observe x, then whatever level of coverage injurers select (they are in fact indifferent among all levels of coverage,

---

[24] But if there were a nonmonetary component to the loss suffered by victims for which compensation could not possibly be made (perhaps blindness or paralysis), then the victims' welfare would be affected by the occurrence of accidents. Thus, limiting the purchase of liability insurance might in principle be desirable.

[25] This describes a solution which resembles the situation in the Soviet Union. As mentioned in note 2, liability insurance is not available there.

including none), they will be induced to choose x^*. This follows because their premium for coverage $q \geqq 0$ will depend on x and equal $p(x)q$, so that they will choose x to maximize

$$u + r - p(x)q - x - p(x)(l - q) = u + r - x - p(x)l. \qquad (27)$$

Since if $d = l$, x^* will be chosen, and since victims will bear no risk, Proposition 1 implies our result.

If injurers are risk averse and liability insurers can observe x, the remark in the Note following the proposition supplies the argument for the result.

We shall use a two-part argument to establish (a) and (b) for the case in which injurers are risk averse and liability insurers cannot observe x. First, we shall consider what would be done by a benevolent dictator whose powers are limited only by inability to observe x and, therefore, by inability to set x directly. Then we shall show in a series of steps that under strict liability, with $d = l$, the operation of the liability insurance market leads to the same result that the dictator would have chosen. This will complete the argument establishing (a) and (b).

The problem of the benevolent dictator who cannot observe x is

$$\underset{v_n, v_a, u_n, u_a}{\text{maximize}} \, EV = (1 - p(x))V(v_n) + p(x)V(v_a) \qquad (28)$$

subject to

$$EU = (1 - p(x))U(u_n - x) + p(x)U(u_a - x) = \bar{U} \qquad (29)$$

$$EU \text{ is maximized over } x \qquad (30)$$

$$[(1 - p(x))v_n + p(x)v_a] + [(1 - p(x))u_n + p(x)u_a] + p(x)l = u + v. \qquad (31)$$

Here the variables are defined as in Section 3, except that now u_n and u_a are gross of the costs of prevention activity. Constraint (30) is introduced because injurers are free to select x. As in the proof of Proposition 1, it is easy to show that we may take $v_n = v_a$. Thus, setting $\gamma = v_n = v_a$, the dictator's problem becomes

$$\underset{\gamma, u_n, u_a}{\text{maximize}} \, EV = V(\gamma) \qquad (32)$$

subject to (29), (30), and to

$$\gamma + (1 - p(x))u_n + p(x)u_a + p(x)l = u + v. \qquad (33)$$

Now let us show that the above problem is equivalent to the following one: liability is strict, with $d = l$; liability insurance is sold at an actuarially fair price; but the government, rather than the competitive insurance market, determines the extent of coverage q. This latter problem is (where π, recall, is the premium for insurance)

$$\underset{q, \pi, r}{\text{maximize}} \, V(v - r) \qquad (34)$$

subject to

$$EU = (1 - p(x))U(u + r - \pi - x) + p(x)U(u + r - \pi - x + q - l) = \bar{U} \qquad (35)$$

$$EU \text{ is maximized over } x, \qquad (36)$$

$$\pi = p(x)q. \qquad (37)$$

Under the change of variables $\gamma = v - r$, $u_n = u + r - \pi$, $u_a = u + r - \pi + q - l$, direct substitution shows that the problem (34)–(37) is, as claimed, the same as the problem (32), (29), (30), (33).

Now write (34)–(37) in the equivalent form

$$\underset{q, \pi, r}{\text{maximize}} \, EU = (1 - p(x))U(u + r - \pi - x) + p(x)U(u + r - \pi - x + q - l) \qquad (38)$$

subject to

$$EU \text{ is maximized over } x, \tag{39}$$

$$\pi = p(x)q, \tag{40}$$

$$EV = V(v - r) = \bar{V}, \tag{41}$$

where $\bar{V}$ is the optimal value of V in (34)–(37). Observe that (41) alone determines r. Thus, (38)–(41) reduce to

$$\underset{q,\pi}{\text{maximize } EU} \tag{42}$$

subject to (39) and (40). But (see note 22) this is exactly the problem that is solved by the liability insurance market. Hence, we have completed our proof of (a) and (b) for the case in which injurers are risk averse and liability insurers cannot observe x. Part (c) also follows since liability coverage will be partial.

With regard to the claim made in the Note about the banning of liability insurance, suppose that such insurance cannot be purchased and let $\hat{d} = l - q$, and $\hat{r} = r - \pi$, where r, q, and π are the values from the efficient solution when liability insurance can be purchased. The reader may easily verify that the injurer would then select the same level of prevention activity and enjoy the same expected utility as in the efficient solution with the purchase of liability insurance allowed; the same is true of the victim, who, if risk averse, buys first party insurance, paying π for coverage of q. *Q.E.D.*

The last result is

Proposition 5. Under the negligence rule, a Pareto-efficient solution is such that: (a) the standard of due care equals the first-best level (i.e., $\bar{x} = x^*$); (b) a first-best outcome is achieved; and (c) government intervention in the liability insurance market is not desirable.

Note: As in Proposition 3, if $\bar{x} = x^*$, injurers will decide to be nonnegligent and will choose $x = x^*$, but now this is true despite their opportunity to act negligently and to protect themselves by purchase of liability insurance. And although this also means that victims will bear risk, they can purchase full coverage from first-party insurers. Thus a first-best solution will be achieved and, therefore, government intervention in insurance markets could not be desirable.

Proof: It will suffice to show that liability insurance would not be purchased, for then an argument virtually identical to that of parts (a) and (b) of Proposition 3 may be employed to show (a) and (b) here; and (c) follows from (b). Let us therefore assume that when $\bar{x} = x^*$, injurers purchase coverage, and show that this leads to a contradiction. If they purchase coverage, it must be that $x < x^*$ (for otherwise injurers would never be found negligent if involved in accidents and would have no reason to insure). Thus, the injurers' premium must be $p(x)q$, so that

$$EU = (1 - p(x))U(u + r - p(x)q - x) + p(x)U(u + r - p(x)q - x + q - l))$$

$$\leq U((1 - p(x))(u + r - p(x)q - x) + p(x)(u + r - p(x)q - x + q - l))$$

$$= U(u + r - x - p(x)l) < U(u + r - x^* - p(x^*)l)$$

$$< U(u + r - x^*). \tag{43}$$

But this is a contradiction, since it means that injurers would prefer to choose x^* and to be nonnegligent. *Q.E.D.*

4. Concluding comments

■ Because the object here was to isolate the roles of liability rules and of insurance in providing incentives and in allocating risk, it was of course necessary to exclude much from the analysis. Hence, we shall close with brief comments on several of the more important omissions, pointing out how, if at all, they affect our results.

Perhaps the most noticeable simplification of the model was the assumption that victims could not alter accident risks. Were that assumption relaxed, however, appropriate analogues to our results would remain true.[26] Consider, for instance, the situation under strict liability with a defense of contributory negligence (allowing the injurer to escape liability if the victim was shown to have acted negligently), when insurers can observe the level of prevention activity of risk averse insureds, be they injurers or victims. In this situation it can be demonstrated that a first-best outcome can be achieved (in Nash equilibrium). Victims are induced to act in a nonnegligent way despite their opportunity to purchase first-party insurance, and injurers, realizing that victims will not be found contributorily negligent, are induced under the terms of their liability policies to choose the socially optimal level of prevention activity. The arguments applied with respect to victims to show these and other results in the more general case are essentially those we presented with respect to injurers, for not only may victims alter accident risks, but also first-party coverage (like liability coverage) involves potential elements of moral hazard.

Another simplifying assumption of the model was that there were no "administrative" costs connected with the supply of insurance or with the operation of the legal system. Consideration of administrative costs would have made a difference to our study, especially with regard to the closely related issues of the type of insurance coverage offered by the market and the comparison of liability rules. Suppose, for example, that it would be very expensive to determine injurers' prevention activity. Then liability insurers would not do so, and therefore, as explained, the policies they sell would involve incomplete coverage. Consequently, as stated in Proposition 4, under strict liability risk averse injurers would be left bearing a risk, which is socially undesirable. On the other hand, according to Proposition 5, under the negligence rule the socially undesirable bearing of risk would be avoided, for the injurers would act in a nonnegligent way. Yet it should not be concluded from this that the negligence rule would be superior to strict liability, for the application of the negligence rule requires the courts to ascertain injurers' prevention activity—an undertaking that was assumed in the first place to have been sufficiently costly to make it less than worthwhile for liability insurers. This should illustrate both the complexities that would be involved in an analysis of our subject incorporating administrative costs and the need for caution in interpretation of results.

A third simplifying assumption of the model was that there were no errors or uncertainty as to legal outcomes. Thus, under strict liability, an injurer who caused a loss was always found liable, and under the negligence rule, an injurer's fault or lack of fault was always correctly determined. Were these assumptions altered, certain unnatural features of equilibrium in our model would disappear: under strict liability, victims would no longer be completely protected against risk, and, if risk averse, they would purchase first-party coverage; and under the negligence rule, nonnegligent injurers would no longer be sure that they would be found free of fault, and, if risk averse, they would purchase liability coverage. These new elements of uncertainty under the liability rules would generally mean that our results would hold only in an approximate sense.

References

ARROW, K. "Insurance, Risk, and Resource Allocation" in *Essays in the Theory of Risk-Bearing*, Chicago: Markham, 1971, pp. 134–143.

BORCH, K. "Equilibrium in a Reinsurance Market." *Econometrica*, Vol. 30 (1962), pp. 424–444.

BROWN, J. "Toward an Economic Theory of Liability." *Journal of Legal Studies*, Vol. 2 (1973), pp. 323–350.

---

[26] In Shavell (1979a), an earlier version of this article, the possibility that victims can alter accident risks is taken into account.

CALABRESI, G. *The Costs of Accidents*. New Haven: Yale University Press, 1970.

DIAMOND, P. "Single Activity Accidents." *Journal of Legal Studies*, Vol. 3 (1974), pp. 107–164.

EPPLE, D. AND RAVIV, A. "Product Safety: Liability Rules, Market Structure, and Imperfect Information." *American Economic Review*, Vol. 68 (1978), pp. 80–95.

GREEN, J. "On the Optimal Structure of Liability Laws." *Bell Journal of Economics*, Vol. 7 (1976), pp. 553–574.

PAULY, M. "Overinsurance and Public Provision of Insurance." *Quarterly Journal of Economics*, Vol. 87 (1974), pp. 44–62.

POSNER, R. *Economic Analysis of Law*, 2nd ed. Boston: Little, Brown & Co., 1977.

PROSSER, W. *Law of Torts*. St. Paul: West Publishing Co., 1971.

SHAVELL, S. "Accidents, Liability, and Insurance." Mimeographed, Harvard Institute of Economic Research, Discussion Paper No. 685, 1979a.

———. "On Moral Hazard and Insurance." *Quarterly Journal of Economics*, Vol. 93 (1979b), pp. 541–562.

———. "Strict Liability vs. Negligence." *Journal of Legal Studies*, Vol. 9 (1980), pp. 1–25.

SPENCE, A.M. "Consumer Misperceptions, Product Failure, and Product Liability." *Review of Economic Studies*. Vol. 64 (1977), pp. 561–572.

TUNC, A. *Torts*, Introduction to Volume XI, *International Encyclopedia of Comparative Law*. The Hague: Mouton, 1973.

FAIRNESS AND UTILITY IN TORT THEORY

George P. Fletcher *

Professor Fletcher challenges the traditional account of the development of tort doctrine as a shift from an unmoral standard of
strict liability for directly causing harm to a moral standard based
on fault. He then sets out two paradigms of liability to serve as constructs for understanding competing ideological viewpoints about the
proper role of tort sanctions. He asserts that the paradigm of reciprocity, which looks only to the degree of risk imposed by the
parties to a lawsuit on each other, and to the existence of possible
excusing conditions, provides greater protection of individual interests than the paradigm of reasonableness, which assigns liability
instrumentally on the basis of a utilitarian calculus. Finally, Professor Fletcher examines stylistic differences between the two paradigms which may explain the modern preference for the paradigm
of reasonableness.

I. Two Paradigms of Liability

TORT theory is suffering from declining expectations. Commentators still chronicle cases and expound doctrine for
practitioners. But the thrust of the academic literature is to
convert the tort system into something other than a mechanism for
determining the just distribution of accident losses. Some writers
seek to convert the set of discrete litigations into a makeshift medium of accident insurance or into a mechanism for maximizing
social utility by shifting·the costs of accidents (or accident prevention) to the party to whom it represents the least disutility.
Thus the journals cultivate the idiom of cost-spreading, risk-
distribution and cost-avoidance.[1] Discussed less and less are

* Professor of Law, University of California at Los Angeles. B.A. University
of California at Berkeley, 1960; J.D. University of Chicago, 1964; M. Comp. L.
University of Chicago, 1965.

[1] The leading work is G. CALABRESI, THE COSTS OF ACCIDENTS (1970) [herein-
after cited as CALABRESI]. See also A. EHRENZWEIG, NEGLIGENCE WITHOUT FAULT
(1951), reprinted in 54 CALIF. L. REV. 1422 (1966); J. FLEMING, THE LAW OF
TORTS 9–14 (3d ed. 1965); Calabresi, The Decision for Accidents: An Approach
to Nonfault Allocation of Costs, 78 HARV. L. REV. 713 (1965); Calabresi, Does
the Fault System Optimally Control Primary Accident Costs?, 33 LAW & CONTEMP.
PROB. 429 (1968); Calabresi, Some Thoughts on Risk Distribution and the Law
of Torts, 70 YALE L.J. 499 (1961); Keeton, Conditional Fault in the Law of
Torts, 72 HARV. L. REV. 401 (1959); Morris, Hazardous Enterprises and Risk
Bearing Capacity, 61 YALE L.J. 1172 (1952).

precisely those questions that make tort law a unique repository
of intuitions of corrective justice: What is the relevance of risk-
creating conduct to the just distribution of wealth? What is the
rationale for an individual's "right" to recover for his losses?
What are the criteria for justly singling out some people and making them, and not their neighbors, bear the costs of accidents?
These persistent normative questions are the stuff of tort theory,
but they are now too often ignored for the sake of inquiries about
insurance and the efficient allocation of resources.

The fashionable questions of the time are instrumentalist:[2]
What social value does the rule of liability further in this case?
Does it advance a desirable goal, such as compensation, deterrence, risk-distribution, or minimization of accident costs? True,
within this instrumentalist framework some writers are concerned
about the goal of vindicating the community's sense of fairness.[3]
But this approach generally makes the issue of fairness look like
the other goals of the tort system. Any other notion of fairness —
one that is not a goal, but a non-instrumentalist reason for redistributing losses [4] — strikes some contemporary writers as akin

---

[2] For a discussion of instrumentalism in legal reasoning, see Dworkin, *Morality and the Law*, N.Y. Rev. Books, May 22, 1969, at 29.

[3] *See* CALABRESI 291–308; 2 F. HARPER & F. JAMES, THE LAW OF TORTS 743 (1956) [hereinafter cited as HARPER & JAMES] ("[The law of torts] must satisfy the ethical or moral sense of the community, its feeling of what is fair and just."). Professors Keeton and O'Connell discuss the obligations of motorists with-out converting the issue into a question of community expectations. R. KEETON & J. O'CONNELL, BASIC PROTECTION FOR THE TRAFFIC VICTIM 256–72 (1965).

[4] This bias toward converting values which are ends in themselves into in-strumentalist goals is well illustrated by the history of the exclusionary rule in search and seizure cases. The leading modern decisions establishing the exclusion-ary rule relied on two prominent rationales for the rule: (1) the imperative of judicial integrity, and (2) the desirability of deterring unconstitutional police behavior. *See* Mapp v. Ohio, 367 U.S. 643, 659 (1961); Elkins v. United States, 364 U.S. 206, 222 (1960). Preserving judicial integrity is a non-instrumentalist value — like retribution, fairness, and justice. One preserves judicial integrity not because it will produce good in the future but because it is "imperative" — it is in the nature of the judicial process — to do so. This is not the kind of value with which most writers in recent years could feel comfortable. As a result, the litera-ture tended to tie the exclusionary rule almost exclusively to the goal of deterring improper police behavior. *See* Allen, *Due Process and State Criminal Procedures: Another Look*, 48 Nw. U.L. Rev. 16, 34 (1953); LaFave & Remington, *Controlling the Police: The Judge's Role in Making and Reviewing Law Enforcement Deci-sions*, 63 MICH. L. REV. 987, 1002–03 (1965); Oaks, *Studying the Exclusionary Rule in Search and Seizure*, 37 U. CHI. L. REV. 665, 668–71 (1970). The implica-tion of tying the exclusionary rule to the goal of deterrence is that if suppressing evidence does not in fact deter the police — and there is reason to believe that it does not, *see* L. TIFFANY, D. MCINTYRE, JR. & D. ROTENBERG, DETECTION OF CRIME 101, 183–99 (1967) — then the entire justification for the rule collapses. See the

to a nonrational community taboo.[5]

Reluctant as they are to assay issues of fairness, tort theorists tend to regard the existing doctrinal framework of fault and strict liability as sufficiently rich to express competing views about fairly shifting losses.[6] This conceptual framework accounts for a number of traditional beliefs about tort law history. One of these beliefs is that the ascendancy of fault in the late nineteenth century reflected the infusion of moral sensibility into the law of torts.[7] That new moral sensibility is expressed sometimes as the principle that wrongdoers ought to pay for their wrongs.[8] Another traditional view is that strict tort liability is the analogue of strict criminal liability, and that if the latter is suspect, so is the former.[9] The underlying assumption of both these tenets is that negligence and strict liability are antithetical rationales of liability. This assumed antithesis is readily invoked to explain the ebbs and flows of tort liability. Strict liability is said to have prevailed in early tort history, fault supposedly held sway in the late nineteenth century, with strict liability now gaining ground.[10]

These beliefs about tort history are ubiquitously held,[11] but to varying degrees they are all false or at best superficial. There has no doubt been a deep ideological struggle in the tort law of the last century and a half. But, as I shall argue, it is not the struggle between negligence and fault on the one hand, and strict liability on the other. Rather, the confrontation is between

---

portentous dissent of Chief Justice Burger in Bivens v. Six Unknown Named Agents of Federal Bureau of Narcotics, 403 U.S. 388, 411 (1971).

The distinctive characteristic of non-instrumentalist claims is that their validity does not depend on the consequences of the court's decision. Whether a court protects judicial integrity or achieves a fair result turns on an assessment of the facts of the dispute, not on a correct prediction of what may follow.

[5] Calabresi's analysis is instructive. He reasons that the issue of fairness must involve "moral attitudes," CALABRESI 294, and then considers the taboo against fornication as an example of "moral attitudes." Id. at 295.

[6] See, e.g., W. BLUM & H. KALVEN, PUBLIC LAW PERSPECTIVES ON A PRIVATE LAW PROBLEM: AUTO COMPENSATION PLANS (1965); Fleming, The Role of Negligence in Modern Tort Law, 53 VA. L. REV. 815 (1967).

[7] See O. HOLMES, THE COMMON LAW 79-80 (1881); Ames, Law and Morals, 22 HARV. L. REV. 97, 99 (1908); p. 564 infra.

[8] See, e.g., Lord Atkin's opinion in Donoghue v. Stevenson, [1932] A.C. 562, 579.

[9] See J. SALMOND, LAW OF TORTS 12-13 (6th ed. 1924); cf. Smith, Tort and Absolute Liability — Suggested Changes in Classification (pts. 1-3), 30 HARV. L. REV. 241, 319, 409 (1917).

[10] See Gregory, Trespass to Negligence to Absolute Liability, 37 VA. L. REV. 359 (1951).

[11] Most treatise writers agree with this outline, though they may no longer regard strict liability as aberrant. See FLEMING, supra note 1, at 289-90; HARPER & JAMES 785-88; W. PROSSER, THE LAW OF TORTS 16-19 (4th ed. 1971) [hereinafter cited as PROSSER].

two radically different paradigms for analyzing tort liability [12] — paradigms which represent a complex of views about (1) the appropriate standard of liability, (2) the appropriate style of legal reasoning, and (3) the relationship between the resolution of individual disputes and the community's welfare.

These paradigms of liability cut across traditional doctrinal lines,[13] creating a deep ideological cleavage between two ways of resolving tort disputes. The conflict is whether judges should look solely at the claims and interests of the parties before the court, or resolve seemingly private disputes in a way that serves the interests of the community as a whole. From this cleavage spring divergent ways of looking at concepts like fault, rights of recovery, and excuses from liability. Do these concepts provide a medium of doing justice between the parties, or are they a medium for serving the interests of the community? A stand on this threshhold question generates an interrelated set of views, including a characteristic style of legal rhetoric. In this essay I wish to explicate these two paradigms of liability, show their operation in the case law [14] and thus enrich the conceptual tools with which we analyze tort liability and the patterns of tort history.

Of the two paradigms, I shall call the first the paradigm of reciprocity. According to this view, the two central issues of tort law — whether the victim is entitled to recover and whether the defendant ought to pay — are distinct issues, each resolvable without looking beyond the case at hand. Whether the victim is so entitled depends exclusively on the nature of the victim's activity when he was injured and on the risk created by the defendant. The social costs and utility of the risk are irrelevant, as

---

[12] There is admittedly an element of fashion in using words like "paradigm" and "model." My usage is patterned after T. KUHN, THE STRUCTURE OF SCIENTIFIC REVOLUTIONS (2d ed. 1970), in which the concept of paradigmatic thinking is used to account for the varieties of scientific response to identical data. My underlying thought is that tort history is characterized by the same kind of conflict that marked the competition between the phlogiston and oxidation theories of burning, id. at 53–56, or the conflict between Ptolemaic and Copernican astronomy. This approach is useful when what one wants to know is why judges (or scientists) are curious about and responsive to particular facts at particular stages of history. Kuhn, himself, suggests the analogy between legal and scientific processes; in explaining his concept of paradigm, he likens it to "an accepted judicial decision in the common law." Id. at 23.

[13] See pp. 550–51 infra.

[14] The text has the limited concern of assessing problems of fairness within a litigation scheme. There is growing skepticism whether one-to-one litigation is the appropriate vehicle for optimizing accidents and compensating victims. See, e.g., CALABRESI 297–99; Franklin, Replacing the Negligence Lottery: Compensation and Selective Reimbursement, 53 VA. L. REV. 774 (1967).

is the impact of the judgment on socially desirable forms of behavior. Further, according to this paradigm, if the victim is entitled to recover by virtue of the risk to which he was exposed, there is an additional question of fairness in holding the risk-creator liable for the loss. This distinct [15] issue of fairness is expressed by asking whether the defendant's creating the relevant risk was excused on the ground, say, that the defendant could not have known of the risk latent in his conduct. To find that an act is excused is in effect to say that there is no rational, fair basis for distinguishing between the party causing harm and other people. Whether we can rationally single out the defendant as the loss-bearer depends on our expectations of when people ought to be able to avoid risks. As will become clear in the course of this discussion, these expectations should not always depend upon the social utility of taking risks; rather they should often depend on non-instrumentalist criteria for judging when men ought to be able to avoid excessive risks of harm. For example, the standard of uncommon "ultra-hazardous activities," introduced by the first *Restatement* [16] is apparently a non-instrumentalist standard: one looks only to the risk and not to its social utility to determine whether it is ultra-hazardous.[17] Yet it is never made clear by the *Restatement* why extra-hazardous risks warrant "strict liability" while ordinarily hazardous risks do not.

As part of the explication of the first paradigm of liability, I shall propose a specific standard of risk that makes sense of the *Restatement*'s emphasis on uncommon, extra-hazardous

---

[15] There might be many standards of liability that would distinguish between the question of the victim's right to recover and the fairness of the risk-creator's rendering compensation. The writ of Trespass recognized the distinction, answering the first by determining whether the injury was directly caused, *see* Scott v. Shepherd, 96 Eng. Rep. 525, 526 (C.P. 1773) (Blackstone, J.), and the second by assessing whether the risk-creating act was attributable to inevitable accident, *see* Cotterill v. Starkey, 173 Eng. Rep. 676 (Q.B. 1839) (inevitable accident); Goodman v. Taylor, 172 Eng. Rep. 1031 (K.B. 1832) (inevitable accident); Beckwith v. Shordike, 98 Eng. Rep. 91, 92 (K.B. 1767) (Ashton, J.) (defense of involuntary trespass approved in principle but rejected on the facts); Mitten v. Faudrye, 79 Eng. Rep. 1259 (K.B. 1625) (involuntary trespass). *See generally* 8 W. HOLDSWORTH, A HISTORY OF ENGLISH LAW 455–57 (2d ed. 1937). Common law courts began to abandon the test of "directness" in the mid-nineteenth century, *see* note 86 *infra*, and in this century there has been no widely accepted criterion of risk other than the standard of reasonableness. As I shall show below, *see* pp. 556–59 *infra*, reasonableness is a standard that merges the issues of the victim's right to recover with the fairness of the risk-creator's rendering compensation.

[16] RESTATEMENT OF TORTS §§ 519–20 (1938).

[17] *But cf.* RESTATEMENT (SECOND) OF TORTS § 520(f) (Tent. Draft No. 10, 1964) (recognizing "the value of an activity to the community" as a factor bearing on the classification of an activity as abnormally dangerous).

risks, but which shows that the *Restatement*'s theory is part of a larger rationale of liability that cuts across negligence, intentional torts, and numerous pockets of strict liability. The general principle expressed in all of these situations governed by diverse doctrinal standards is that a victim has a right to recover for injuries caused by a risk greater in degree and different in order from those created by the victim and imposed on the defendant — in short, for injuries resulting from nonreciprocal risks. Cases of liability are those in which the defendant generates a disproportionate, excessive risk of harm, relative to the victim's risk-creating activity. For example, a pilot or an airplane owner subjects those beneath the path of flight to nonreciprocal risks of harm. Conversely, cases of nonliability are those of reciprocal risks, namely those in which the victim and the defendant subject each other to roughly the same degree of risk. For example, two airplanes flying in the same vicinity subject each other to reciprocal risks of a mid-air collision. Of course, there are significant problems in determining when risks are nonreciprocal, and we shall turn to these difficulties later.[18] For now, it is sufficient to note that the paradigm of reciprocity represents (1) a bifurcation of the questions of who is entitled to compensation and who ought to pay, (2) a commitment to resolving both of those issues by looking only to the activity of the victim and the risk-creator, and (3) a specific criterion for determining who is entitled to recover for loss, namely all those injured by nonreciprocal risks.

The conflicting paradigm of liability — which I shall call the paradigm of reasonableness — represents a rejection of noninstrumentalist values and a commitment to the community's welfare as the criterion for determining both who is entitled to receive and who ought to pay compensation. Questions that are distinct under the paradigm of reciprocity — namely, is the risk nonreciprocal and was it unexcused — are collapsed in this paradigm into a single test: was the risk unreasonable? The reasonableness of the risk thus determines both whether the victim is entitled to compensation and whether the defendant ought to be held liable. Reasonableness is determined by a straightforward balancing of costs and benefits. If the risk yields a net social utility (benefit), the victim is not entitled to recover from the risk-creator; if the risk yields a net social disutility (cost), the victim is entitled to recover.[19] The premises of this paradigm are

---

[18] *See* pp. 571–72 *infra.*

[19] This is a simpler statement of the blancing test known as the "Learned Hand formula," defined in United States v. Carroll Towing Co., 159 F.2d 169 (2d Cir. 1947). The same inquiry has been used to define the defense of necessity to in-

that reasonableness provides a test of activities that ought to be encouraged and that tort judgments are an appropriate medium for encouraging them.

The function of both of these paradigms is to distinguish between those risks that represent a violation of individual interests and those that are the background risks that must be borne as part of group living. The difference between the two paradigms is captured by the test provided by each for filtering out background risks. The paradigm of reciprocity holds that we may be expected to bear, without indemnification, those risks we all impose reciprocally on each other. If we all drive, we must suffer the costs of ordinary driving. The paradigm of reasonableness, on the other hand, holds that victims must absorb the costs of reasonable risks, for these risks maximize the composite utility of the group, even though they may not be mutually created background risks.

The paradigm of reasonableness bears some resemblance to present-day negligence, but it would be a mistake to associate the two paradigms, respectively, with strict liability and negligence. As I shall argue, the paradigm of reciprocity cuts across strict liability, negligence and intentional torts, and the paradigm of reasonableness accounts for only a subset of negligence cases. A large number of negligence cases lend themselves to analysis under both paradigms. Suppose there is a collision between two drivers on the highway, neither of whom has done anything out of the ordinary. Neither would be liable to the other. That result might be explained on the ground that the risks are reciprocal; each endangers the other as much as he is endangered. Or nonliability might be explained on the ground that ordinary driving is a socially beneficial activity. As my exposition develops, I will account for this overlap and explain why some cases of negligence liability fit only under the paradigm of reasonableness.

II. THE PARADIGM OF RECIPROCITY

A. The Victim's Right to Recover

Our first task is to demonstrate the pervasive reliance of the common law on the paradigm of reciprocity. The area that most consistently reveals this paradigm is the one that now most lacks doctrinal unity — namely, the disparate pockets of strict liability. We speak of strict liability or "liability without fault" in cases

---

tentional torts and crimes. *See* Mouse's Case, 77 Eng. Rep. 1341 (K.B. 1609) (justifying the jettisoning of ferry cargo to save the passengers); MODEL PENAL CODE § 3.02 (Proposed Official Draft, 1962).

ranging from crashing airplanes [20] to suffering cattle to graze on another's land.[21] Yet the law of torts has never recognized a general principle underlying these atomistic pockets of liability. The *Restatement*'s standard of ultra-hazardous activity speaks only to a subclass of cases. In general, the diverse pockets of strict liability represent cases in which the risk is reasonable and legally immune to injunction. They are therefore all cases of liability without fault in the limited sense in which fault means taking an unreasonable risk.[22] Beyond these characteristics distinguishing strict liability from negligence, there is no consensus of criteria for attaching strict liability to some risks and not to others.[23]

I shall attempt to show that the paradigm of reciprocity accounts for the typical cases of strict liability [24] — crashing airplanes,[25] damage done by wild animals,[26] and the more common cases of blasting, fumigating and crop dusting.[27] To do this, I shall consider in detail two leading, but seemingly diverse instances of liability for reasonable risk-taking — *Rylands v. Fletcher* [28] and *Vincent v. Lake Erie Transportation Co.*[29] The point of focusing on these two cases is to generate a foundation

---

[20] RESTATEMENT (SECOND) OF TORTS § 520A (Tent. Draft No. 12, 1966).

[21] McKee v. Trisler, 311 Ill. 536, 143 N.E. 69 (1924).

[22] The word "fault" is also used to refer to the absence of excusing conditions, *see* pp. 551, 556–57 *infra*, and in this sense strict liability is not liability without fault.

[23] In Keeton, *Is There a Place for Negligence in Modern Tort Law?*, 53 VA. L. REV. 886, 894–96 (1967), the author synthesizes strict liability under the principle that every activity should be liable for its "distinctive risks."

[24] It is important to distinguish the cases of strict liability discussed here from strict products liability, a necessary element of which is an unreasonably dangerous defect in the product. *See* Davis v. Wyeth Laboratories, Inc., 399 F.2d 121 (9th Cir. 1968). *See generally* Traynor, *The Ways and Meanings of Defective Products and Strict Liability*, 32 TENN. L. REV. 363 (1965). Because of the market relationship between the manufacturer and the consumer, loss-shifting in products-liability cases becomes a mechanism of insurance, changing the question of fairness posed by imposing liability. *See* BLUM & KALVEN, *supra* note 6, at 58–61.

[25] *See* p. 548 *infra* and note 20 *supra*; PROSSER 514–16.

[26] *E.g.*, Collins v. Otto, 149 Colo. 489, 369 P.2d 564 (1962) (coyote bite); Filburn v. People's Palace & Aquarium Co., 25 Q.B.D. 258 (1890) (escaped circus elephant). *See generally* PROSSER 496–503.

[27] *E.g.*, Exner v. Sherman Power Constr. Co., 54 F.2d 510 (2d Cir. 1931) (storing explosives); Western Geophysical Co. of America v. Mason, 240 Ark. 767, 402 S.W.2d 657 (1966) (blasting); Luthringer v. Moore, 31 Cal. 2d 489, 190 P.2d 1 (1948) (fumigating); Young v. Darter, 363 P.2d 829 (Okla. 1961) (crop dusting).

[28] 159 Eng. Rep. 737 (Ex. 1865), *rev'd*, L.R. 1 Ex. 265 (1866), *aff'd*, L.R. 3 H.L. 330 (1868).

[29] 109 Minn. 456, 124 N.W. 221 (1910).

for inducing the claim that unexcused nonreciprocity of risk is the unifying feature of a broad spectrum of cases imposing liability under rubrics of both negligence and strict liability.

In *Rylands v. Fletcher* the plaintiff, a coal mine operator, had suffered the flooding of his mine by water that the defendant had pumped into a newly-erected reservoir on his own land. The water broke through to an abandoned mine shaft under the defendant's land and thus found its way to the plaintiff's adjoining mine. The engineers and contractors were negligent in not providing stronger supports for the reservoir; yet because they were independent contractors, the defendant was not liable for their negligence. Though the defendant's erecting and maintaining the reservoir was legally permissible, the Exchequer Chamber found for the plaintiff,[30] and the House of Lords affirmed.[31] Blackburn's opinion in the Exchequer Chamber focused on the defendant's bringing on to his land, for his own purposes, "something which, though harmless whilst it remain there, will naturally do mischief if it escape." [32] Lord Cairns, writing in the House of Lords, reasoned that the defendant's activity rendered his use of the land "non-natural"; accordingly, "that which the Defendants were doing they were doing at their own peril." [33]

Neither Blackburn's nor Cairns' account provides an adequate rationale for liability. It may be that a body of water will "naturally do mischief if it escapes," but so may many other things, like water in a pipe, oil in a furnace tank, and fire in a fireplace. It is unlikely that Blackburn would favor liability for the harmful consequences of all these risky practices. Cairns' rationale of non-natural use, for all its metaphysical pretensions, may be closer to the policy issue at stake in the dispute. The fact was that the defendant sought to use his land for a purpose at odds with the use of land then prevailing in the community. He thereby subjected the neighboring miners to a risk to which they were not accustomed and which they would not regard as a tolerable risk entailed by their way of life. Creating a risk different from the prevailing risks in the community might be what Lord Cairns had in mind in speaking of a non-natural use of the land. A better term might have been "abnormal" or "inappropriate" use. Indeed these are the adjectives used in the proposed revision of the *Restatement* to provide a more faithful rendition of the case law tradition of strict liability.[34]

---

[30] L.R. 1 Ex. 265 (1866).
[31] L.R. 3 H.L. 330 (1868).
[32] L.R. 1 Ex. at 279.
[33] L.R. 3 H.L. at 339.
[34] RESTATEMENT (SECOND) OF TORTS § 520 (Tent. Draft No. 10, 1964).

A seemingly unrelated example of the same case law tradition is *Vincent v. Lake Erie Transporation Co.*, a 1910 decision of the Minnesota Supreme Court.[35] The dispute arose from a ship captain's keeping his vessel lashed to the plaintiff's dock during a two-day storm when it would have been unreasonable, indeed foolhardy, for him to set out to sea. The storm battered the ship against the dock, causing damages assessed at five hundred dollars. The court affirmed a judgment for the plaintiff even though a prior case had recognized a ship captain's right to take shelter from a storm by mooring his vessel to another's dock, even without consent.[36] The court's opinion conceded that keeping the ship at dockside was justified and reasonable, yet it characterized the defendant's damaging the dock as "prudently and advisedly [availing]" himself of the plaintiff's property.[37] Because the incident impressed the court as an implicit transfer of wealth, the defendant was bound to rectify the transfer by compensating the dock owner for his loss.[38]

The rationales of *Rylands* and *Vincent* are obviously not interchangeable. Building a reservoir is not availing oneself of a neighbor's property. And mooring a ship to a wharf is not an abnormal or "non-natural" use of either the ship or the wharf. Yet by stripping the two cases of their rhetoric and by focusing on the risks each defendant took, one can bring the two cases within the same general principle. The critical feature of both cases is that the defendant created a risk of harm to the plaintiff that was of an order different from the risks that the plaintiff imposed on the defendant.

Without the factor of nonreciprocal risk-creation, both cases would have been decided differently. Suppose that Rylands had built his reservoir in textile country, where there were numerous mills, dams, and reservoirs, or suppose that two sailors secured their ships in rough weather to a single buoy. In these situations each party would subject the other to a risk, respectively, of

[35] 109 Minn. 456, 124 N.W. 221 (1910).

[36] *See* Ploof v. Putnam, 81 Vt. 471, 71 A. 188 (1908) (defendant dock owner, whose servant unmoored the plaintiff's ship during a storm, held liable for the ensuing damage to the ship and passengers).

[37] 109 Minn. at 460, 124 N.W. at 222.

[38] This case is not entirely apt for my theory. The existence of a bargaining relationship between the defendant and the plaintiff poses the market adjustment problems raised in note 24 *supra*. *See* Calabresi, *The Decision for Accidents: An Approach to Nonfault Allocation of Costs*, 78 HARV. L. REV. 713, 726 (1965) (arguing the irrelevance of the result in *Vincent* as to *both* the efficient allocation of resources and the welfare of the parties). Accordingly, I treat the case as though the defendant were a type of ship owner who never had to enter into bargains with wharf owners. The case is also a seductive one for Professor Keeton. *See* Keeton, *supra* note 1, at 410–18; Keeton, *supra* note 23, at 895.

inundation and abrasion. Where the risks are reciprocal among the relevant parties, as they would be in these variations of *Rylands* and *Vincent*, a rule of strict liability does no more than substitute one form of risk for another — the risk of liability for the risk of personal loss.[39] Accordingly, it would make little sense to extend strict liability to cases of reciprocal risk-taking, unless one reasoned that in the short run some individuals might suffer more than others and that these losses should be shifted to other members of the community.[40]

Expressing the standard of strict liability as unexcused, nonreciprocal risk-taking provides an account not only of the *Rylands* and *Vincent* decisions, but of strict liability in general. It is apparent, for example, that the uncommon, ultra-hazardous activities pinpointed by the *Restatement* are readily subsumed under the rationale of nonreciprocal risk-taking. If uncommon activities are those with few participants, they are likely to be activities generating nonreciprocal risks. Similarly, dangerous activities like blasting, fumigating, and crop dusting stand out as distinct, nonreciprocal risks in the community. They represent threats of harm that exceed the level of risk to which all members of the community contribute in roughly equal shares.

The rationale of nonreciprocal risk-taking accounts as well for pockets of strict liability outside the coverage of the *Restatement*'s sections on extra-hazardous activities. For example, an individual is strictly liable for damage done by a wild animal in his charge, but not for damage committed by his domesticated pet.[41] Most people have pets, children, or friends whose presence

---

[39] A student note nicely develops this point in the context of ultra-hazardous activities. Note, *Absolute Liability for Dangerous Things*, 61 HARV. L. REV. 515, 520 (1948).

[40] One argument for so shifting losses would be that some individuals have better access to insurance or are in a position (as are manufacturers) to invoke market mechanisms to distribute losses over a large class of individuals. This argument assumes that distributing a loss "creates" utility by shifting units of the loss to those who may bear them with less disutility. The premise is the increasing marginal utility of cumulative losses, which is the inverse of the decreasing marginal utility of the dollar — the premise that underlies progressive income taxation. *See* Calabresi, *Some Thoughts on Risk Distribution and the Law of Torts*, 70 YALE L.J. 499, 517–19 (1961); Blum & Kalven, *The Uneasy Case for Progressive Taxation*, 19 U. CHI. L. REV. 417, 455–79 (1952). This is an argument of distributive rather than corrective justice, for it turns on the defendant's wealth and status, rather than his conduct. Using the tort system to redistribute negative wealth (accident losses) violates the premise of corrective justice, namely that liability should turn on what the defendant has done, rather than on who he is. *See* THE NICOMACHEAN ETHICS OF ARISTOTLE, Book V, ch. 4, at 114–15 (Ross transl. World's Classics ed. 1954). What is at stake is keeping the institution of taxation distinct from the institution of tort litigation.

[41] *See, e.g.*, Fowler v. Helck, 278 Ky. 361, 128 S.W.2d 564 (1939); Warrick v. Farley, 95 Neb. 565, 145 N.W. 1020 (1914).

creates some risk to neighbors and their property. These are risks that offset each other; they are, as a class, reciprocal risks. Yet bringing an unruly horse into the city goes beyond the accepted and shared level of risks in having pets, children, and friends in one's household. If the defendant creates a risk that exceeds those to which he is reciprocally subject, it seems fair to hold him liable for the results of his aberrant indulgence. Similarly, according to the latest version of the *Restatement*, airplane owners and pilots are strictly liable for ground damage, but not for mid-air collisions.[42] Risk of ground damage is nonreciprocal; homeowners do not create risks to airplanes flying overhead. The risks of mid-air collisions, on the other hand, are generated reciprocally by all those who fly the air lanes. Accordingly, the threshold of liability for damage resulting from mid-air collisions is higher than mere involvement in the activity of flying. To be liable for collision damage to another flyer, the pilot must fly negligently or the owner must maintain the plane negligently; they must generate abnormal risks of collision to the other planes aflight.

Negligently and intentionally caused harm also lend themselves to analysis as nonreciprocal risks. As a general matter, principles of negligence liability apply in the context of activities, like motoring and sporting ventures, in which the participants all normally create and expose themselves to the same order of risk.[43] These are all pockets of reciprocal risk-taking. Sometimes the risks are grave, as among motorists; sometimes they are minimal, as among ballplayers. Whatever the magnitude of risk, each participant contributes as much to the community of risk as he suffers from exposure to other participants. To establish liability for harm resulting from these activities, one must show that the harm derives from a specific risk negligently engendered in the course of the activity. Yet a negligent risk, an "unreasonable" risk, is but one that unduly exceeds the bounds of reciprocity. Thus, negligently created risks are nonreciprocal relative to the risks generated by the drivers and ballplayers who engage in the same activity in the customary way.

If a victim also creates a risk that unduly exceeds the reciprocal norm, we say that he is contributorily negligent and deny

---

[42] *See* note 20 *supra.*

[43] Negligence is, of course, prominent as well in the analysis of liability of physicians to patients and occupiers of land to persons injured on the premises. *See* Cohen, *Fault and the Automobile Accident: The Lost Issue in California,* 12 U.C.L.A.L. Rev. 164, 179 (1964). These are cases of injuries in the course of consensual, bargaining relationships and therefore pose special problems. *Cf.* note 24 *supra.*

recovery.[44] The paradigm of reciprocity accounts for the denial
of recovery when the victim imposes excessive risks on the defendant, for the effect of contributory negligence is to render the
risks again reciprocal, and the defendant's risk-taking does not
subject the victim to a relative deprivation of security.[45]

Thus, both strict liability and negligence express the rationale
of liability for unexcused, nonreciprocal risk-taking. The only
difference is that reciprocity in strict liability cases is analyzed
relative to the background of innocuous risks in the community,
while reciprocity in the types of negligence cases discussed above
is measured against the background of risk generated in specific
activities like motoring and skiing. To clarify the kinship of
negligence to strict liability, one should distinguish between two
different levels of risk-creation, each level associated with a defined community of risks. Keeping domestic pets is a reciprocal
risk relative to the community as a whole; driving is a reciprocal
risk relative to the community of those driving normally; and
driving negligently might be reciprocal relative to the even narrower community of those driving negligently. The paradigm
of reciprocity holds that in all communities of reciprocal risks,
those who cause damage ought not to be held liable.[46]

---

[44] E.g., Butterfield v. Forrester, 103 Eng. Rep. 926 (K.B. 1809) (defendant
put a bar across the highway; plaintiff was riding without looking where he was
going). In many cases of contributory negligence the risk is self-regarding and
does not impose risks on the defendant. RESTATEMENT (SECOND) OF TORTS § 463
(1965); PROSSER 418–20. In these cases the rationale for denying recovery is
unrelated to the paradigm of reciprocity. There is considerable dispute about what
the rationale may be. Id. at 417–18; HARPER & JAMES 1193–1209.

[45] If the "last clear chance" doctrine is available, however, the victim may
recover despite his contributory negligence. Peterson v. Burkhalter, 38 Cal. 2d
107, 237 P.2d 977 (1951) (motorist's last clear chance vis-a-vis a negligent motor
scooter driver); RESTATEMENT (SECOND) OF TORTS §§ 479–80 (1965). A rationale
for this doctrine might be that the defendant's risk is nonreciprocal even as to the
class of victims taking negligent risks.

[46] Suppose a motorist runs down a pedestrian on the way to his parked car.
Or suppose that an ambulance injures a pedestrian while speeding through the
streets to rescue another injured pedestrian. These hypothetical problems pose
puzzles at the fringes of the paradigm of reciprocity. The first is the question
whether reciprocity must be temporal; the second, whether the interests of the
victim or of the class he represents ought to bear on the analysis of reciprocity.
These problems require further thought. Cf. Professor Fried's theory of the risk
pool, which treats risks occurring at different times as offsetting. C. FRIED, AN
ANATOMY OF VALUES 177–93 (1970).

Problems in defining communities of risks may account for the attractiveness
of the reasonableness paradigm today. The increased complexity and interdepend-
ence of modern society renders legal analysis based upon a concept of community
that presupposes clear lines of membership, relatively little overlapping, and a
fair degree of uniformity in the activities carried on, exceedingly difficult in many
cases. Cf. pp. 571–72 infra.

To complete our account of the paradigm of reciprocity, we should turn to one of its primary expressions: intentional torts, particularly the torts of battery and assault. Several features of the landlord's behavior in *Carnes v. Thompson* [47] in lunging at the plaintiff and her husband with a pair of pliers make it stand out from any of the risks that the plaintiff might then have been creating in return. An intentional assault or battery represents a rapid acceleration of risk, directed at a specific victim. These features readily distinguish the intentional blow from the background of risk. Perceiving intentional blows as a form of nonreciprocal risk helps us understand why the defendant's malice or animosity toward the victim eventually became unnecessary to ground intentional torts.[48] The nonreciprocity of risk, and the deprivation of security it represents, render irrelevant the attitudes of the risk-creator.[49]

All of these manifestations of the paradigm of reciprocity — strict liability, negligence and intentional battery — express the same principle of fairness: all individuals in society have the right to roughly the same degree of security from risk. By analogy to John Rawls' first principle of justice,[50] the principle might read: we all have the right to the maximum amount of security compatible with a like security for everyone else. This means that we are subject to harm, without compensation, from background risks, but that no one may suffer harm from additional risks without recourse for damages against the risk-creator. Compensation is a surrogate for the individual's right to the same security as enjoyed by others. But the violation of the right to equal security does not mean that one should be able to enjoin the risk-creating activity or impose criminal penalties against the risk-creator. The interests of society may often require a disproportionate distribution of risk. Yet, according to the paradigm of reciprocity, the interests of the individual require us to grant compensation whenever this disproportionate distribu-

---

[47] 48 S.W.2d 903 (Mo. 1932).

[48] *See* Vosburg v. Putney, 80 Wis. 523, 50 N.W. 403 (1891). Animosity would obviously be relevant to the issue of punitive damages, *see* PROSSER 9–10, the formal rationales for which are retribution and deterrence, not compensation.

[49] This account of battery also explains the softening of the intent requirement to permit recovery when the defendant "knew to a substantial certainty" that his act would result in the victim's falling. Garratt v. Dailey, 46 Wash. 2d. 197, 279 P.2d 1091 (1955) (defendant, a young boy, pulled a chair out from the spot where the victim was about to sit down).

[50] Rawls, *Justice as Fairness*, 67 PHILOSOPHICAL REV. 164, 165 (1958) ("[E]ach person participating in a practice, or affected by it, has an equal right to the most extensive liberty compatible with a like liberty for all."). The ideas expressed in *Justice as Fairness* are elaborated in J. RAWLS, A THEORY OF JUSTICE (1971)

tion of risk injures someone subject to more than his fair share of risk.[51]

B. Excusing Nonreciprocal Risks

If the victim's injury results from a nonreciprocal risk of harm, the paradigm of reciprocity tells us that the victim is entitled to compensation. Should not the defendant then be under a duty to pay? Not always. For the paradigm also holds that nonreciprocal risk-creation may sometimes be excused, and we must inquire further, into the fairness of requiring the defendant to render compensation. We must determine whether there may be factors in a particular situation which would excuse this defendant from paying compensation.

Though the King's Bench favored liability in its 1616 decision of *Weaver v. Ward*,[52] it digressed to list some hypothetical examples where directly causing harm would be excused and therefore exempt from liability. One kind of excuse would be the defendant being physically compelled to act, as if someone took his hand and struck a third person.[53] Another kind would be the defendant's accidentally causing harm, as when the plaintiff suddenly appeared in the path of his musket fire.[54] The rationale for denying liability in these cases, as the court put it, is that the defendant acted "utterly without . . . fault." [55]

If a man trespasses against another, why should it matter whether he acts with "fault" or not? What the King's Bench must have been saying is that if a man injures another without fault on his part, there is no rational and fair basis for charging the costs of the accident to him rather than to an arbitrary third person. The inquiry about fault and excusability is an inquiry about rationally singling out the party immediately causing harm as the bearer of liability. Absent an excuse, the trespassory, risk-creating act provides a sufficient basis for imputing liability. Finding that the act is excused, however, is tantamount to per-

---

[51] It might be that requiring the risk-creator to render compensation would be economically tantamount to enjoining the risk-creating activity. *See* note 115 *infra*. If imposing a private duty of compensation for injuries resulting from nonreciprocal risk-taking has an undesirable economic impact on the defendant, the just solution would not be to deny compensation, but either to subsidize the defendant or institute a public compensation scheme.

[52] 80 Eng. Rep. 284 (K.B. 1616).

[53] *Id.*

[54] *Id.*

[55] "[T]herefore no man shall be excused of a trespass (for this is the nature of an excuse, and not of a justification, prout ei bene licuit) except it may be judged utterly without his fault." *Id.*

ceiving that the act is not a factor fairly distinguishing the trespassing party from all other possible candidates for liability.

It is important to note that the inquiry whether the act sets the actor apart and makes him a fit candidate for liability was originally a non-instrumentalist inquiry. The King's Bench in 1616 did not ask: what good will follow from holding that physical compulsion and unavoidable accident constitute good excuses? [56] The question was rather: How should we perceive an act done under compulsion? Is it the same as no act at all? Or does it set the actor off from his fellow men? Thus, excusing is not an assessment of consequences, but a perception of moral equivalence. It is a judgment that an act causing harm ought to be treated as no act at all.

The hypotheticals of *Weaver v. Ward* correspond to the Aristotelian excusing categories of compulsion and unavoidable ignorance.[57] Each of these has spawned a line of cases denying liability in cases of inordinate risk-creation. The excuse of compulsion has found expression in the emergency doctrine, which excuses excessive risks created in cases in which the defendant is caught in an unexpected, personally dangerous situation.[58] In *Cordas v. Peerless Transportation Co.*,[59] for example, it was thought excusable for a cab driver to jump from his moving cab in order to escape from a threatening gunman on the running board. In view of the crowd of pedestrians nearby, the driver clearly took a risk that generated a net danger to human life. It was thus an unreasonable, excessive, and unjustified risk. Yet the overwhelmingly coercive circumstances meant that he, personally, was excused from fleeing the moving cab.[60] An example

---

[56] This is not to say that utilitarians have not attempted to devise an account of excuse based on the beneficial consequences to society of recognizing excuses. *See* J. BENTHAM, AN INTRODUCTION TO THE PRINCIPLES OF MORALS AND LEGISLATION 173 (1907). For an effective critique of Bentham, see H.L.A. Hart, *Prolegomenon to the Principles of Punishment*, 60 ARISTOTELIAN SOC'Y PROCEEDINGS 1 (1959), in H.L.A. HART, PUNISHMENT AND RESPONSIBILITY (1968).

[57] THE NICOMACHEAN ETHICS OF ARISTOTLE, *supra* note 40, Book III, ch. 1, at 48 ("Those things, then, are thought involuntary, which take place under compulsion or owing to ignorance.").

[58] *See e.g.*, St. Johnsbury Trucking Co. v. Rollins, 145 Me. 217, 74 A.2d 465 (1950); Majure v. Herrington, 243 Miss. 692, 139 So. 2d 635 (1962). The excuse is not available if the defendant has created the emergency himself. *See* Whicher v. Phinney, 124 F.2d 929 (1st Cir. 1942). *See generally* PROSSER 168–69.

[59] 27 N.Y.S.2d 198 (N.Y. City Ct. 1941).

[60] The rhetoric of reasonableness obscures the difference between assessing the risk and excusing the defendant on the ground that pressures were too great to permit the right decision. *Cf.* p. 560 *infra*. Yet it is clear that the emergency doctrine functions as a personal excuse, for the defense is applicable even if the actor made the wrong choice, *i.e.*, took an objectively unreasonable risk. *See* St. Johnsbury Trucking Co. v. Rollins, 145 Me. 217, 222, 74 A.2d 465, 468 (1950)

of unavoidable ignorance excusing risk-creation is *Smith v. Lampe*,[61] in which the defendant honked his horn in an effort to warn a tug that seemed to be heading toward shore in a dense fog. As it happened, the honking coincided with a signal that the tug captain expected would assist him in making port. Accordingly the captain steered his tug toward the honking rather than away from it. That the defendant did not know of the prearranged signal excused his contributing to the tug's going aground. Under the facts of the case, the honking surely created an unreasonable risk of harm. If instantaneous injunctions were possible, one would no doubt wish to enjoin the honking as an excessive, illegal risk. Yet the defendant's ignorance of that risk was also excusable. Under the circumstances he could not fairly have been expected to inform himself of all possible interpretations of honking in a dense fog.

As expanded in these cases, the excuses of compulsion and unavoidable ignorance added dimension to the hypotheticals put in *Weaver v. Ward*. In *Cordas* and *Smith* we have to ask: What can we fairly expect of the defendant under the circumstances? Can we ask of a man that he remain in a car with a gun pointed at him? Can we require that a man inform himself of all local customs before honking his horn? Thus the question of rationally singling out a party to bear liability becomes a question of what we can fairly demand of an individual under unusual circumstances. Assessing the excusability of ignorance or of yielding to compulsion can be an instrumentalist inquiry. As we increase or decrease our demands, we accordingly stimulate future behavior. Thus, setting the level of excusability could function as a level of social control. Yet one can also think of excuses as expressions of compassion for human failings in times of stress — expressions that are thought proper regardless of the impact on other potential risk-creators.

Despite this tension between thinking of excusing conditions in an instrumentalist or non-instrumentalist way, we can formulate two significant claims about the role of excuses in cases decided under the paradigm of reciprocity. First, excusing the risk-creator does not, in principle, undercut the victim's right to recover. In most cases, it is operationally irrelevant to posit a right to recovery when the victim cannot in fact recover from the excused risk-creator. Yet it may be important to distinguish between victims of reciprocal, background risks and victims of

---

(admonishing against assessing the risk with hindsight); Kane v. Worcester Consol. St. Ry., 182 Mass. 201, 65 N.E. 54 (1902) (Holmes, C.J.) (the choice "may be mistaken and yet prudent").

[61] 64 F.2d 201 (6th Cir.), *cert. denied*, 289 U.S. 751 (1933).

nonreciprocal risks. The latter class of victims — those who have been deprived of their equal share of security from risk — might have a claim of priority in a social insurance scheme. Further, for a variety of reasons, one might wish in certain classes of cases to deny the availability of particular excuses, such as insanity in general or immaturity for teenage drivers.[62] Insanity has always been a disfavored excuse; even the King's Bench in *Weaver v. Ward* rejected lunacy as a defense.[63] However, it is important to perceive that to reject the excuse is not to provide a rationale for recovery. It is not being injured by an insane man that grounds a right to recovery, but being injured by a nonreciprocal risk — as in every other case applying the paradigm of reciprocity. Rejecting the excuse merely permits the independently established, but previously unenforceable right to prevail.

Secondly, an even more significant claim is that these excuses — compulsion and unavoidable ignorance — are available in all cases in which the right to recovery springs from being subjected to a nonreciprocal risk of harm. We have already pointed out the applicability of these excuses in negligence cases like *Cordas* and *Smith v. Lampe*. What is surprising is to find them applicable in cases of strict liability as well; strict liability is usually thought of as an area where courts are insensitive to questions of fairness to defendants. Admittedly, the excuses of compulsion and unavoidable ignorance do not often arise in strict liability cases, for men who engage in activities like blasting, fumigating, and crop dusting typically do so voluntarily and with knowledge of the risks characteristic of the activity. Yet there have been cases in which strict liability for keeping a vicious dog was denied on the ground that the defendant did not know, and had no reason to know, that his pet was dangerous.[64] And doctrines of proximate cause provide a rubric for considering the excuse of unavoidable ignorance under another name.[65] In *Madsen v. East Jordan*

---

[62] Daniels v. Evans, 107 N.H. 407, 224 A.2d 63 (1966) rejected the defense of immaturity in motoring cases and thus limited Charbonneau v. MacRury, 84 N.H. 501, 153 A. 457 (1931) to cases in which the activity is "appropriate to [the minor's] age, experience and wisdom." 107 N.H. at 408, 224 A.2d at 64.

[63] "[T]herefore if a lunatick hurt a man, he shall be answerable in trespass . . . ." 80 Eng. Rep. at 284. *See* Alexander & Szasz, *Mental Illness as an Excuse for Civil Wrongs*, 43 NOTRE DAME LAW. 24 (1967).

[64] *See* Fowler v. Helck, 278 Ky. 361, 128 S.W.2d 564 (1939); Warrick v. Farley, 95 Neb. 565, 145 N.W. 1020 (1914).

[65] In Fletcher v. Rylands, L.R. 1 Ex. 265, 279–80 (1866), Blackburn, J., acknowledges the defenses of vis major and act of God. Both of these sound in a theory of excuse. Vis major corresponds to the excuse of physical compulsion recognized in Weaver v. Ward, 80 Eng. Rep. 284 (K.B. 1616), and acts of God are risks of which the defendant is presumably excusably ignorant.

Irrigation Co.,[66] for example, the defendant's blasting operations frightened the mother mink on the plaintiff's farm, causing them to kill 230 of their offspring. The Utah Supreme Court affirmed a demurrer to the complaint. In the court's judgment, the reaction of the mother mink "was not within the realm of matters to be anticipated." [67] This is precisely the factual judgment that would warrant saying that the company's ignorance of this possible result was excused,[68] yet the rubric of proximate cause provided a doctrinally acceptable heading for dismissing the complaint.[69]

It is hard to find a case of strict liability raising the issue of compulsion as an excuse. Yet if a pilot could flee a dangerous situation only by taking off in his plane, as the cab driver in *Cordas* escaped danger by leaping from his moving cab, would there be rational grounds for distinguishing damage caused by the airplane crash from damage caused by *Cordas'* cab? One would think not. Both are cases of nonreciprocal risk-taking, and both are cases in which unusual circumstances render it unfair to expect the defendant to avoid the risk he creates.

The analysis of excuses in cases of strict liability would apply as well in cases of intentional torts. Yet there are some intentional torts, like trespass to land, where the excuse of unavoidable ignorance is unavailable.[70] Where the tort fulfills subsidiary noncompensatory purposes, such as testing the title to land, these divergent purposes might render excuses unavailable.[71]

---

[66] 101 Utah 552, 125 P.2d 794 (1942).

[67] *Id.* at 555, 125 P.2d at 795.

[68] *Madsen* is somewhat different from *Smith v. Lampe*, discussed at p. 553 *supra*. In *Smith* the driver was ignorant that honking could have any harmful result. Here it is just the particular harm of which the defendant was unaware.

[69] There seem to be two different types of proximate cause cases: (1) those that function as a way of raising the excuse of unavoidable ignorance and (2) those that hold that the damage is so atypical of the activity that even if the actor knew the result would occur, he would not be liable. If there were a replay of the facts in *Madsen*, with the defendant knowing of the risk to the mink, one would be surprised if the result would be the same; on the other hand, if the oil company in Mauney v. Gulf Refining Co., 193 Miss. 421, 9 So. 2d 780 (1942) knew of the risk that negligently starting a fire might startle a woman across the street, causing her to fall over a chair and suffer a miscarriage, the court would probably still find for the defendant. If this distinction is sound, it suggests that foreseeability is an appropriate test of proximate cause only in the first category, namely when the issue is really the excusability of the defendant's ignorance of the risk. *Cf.* pp. 571-73 *infra*.

[70] *See, e.g.*, Maye v. Tappan, 23 Cal. 306 (1863) (mistake of miner as to boundary between mines); Blatt v. McBarron, 161 Mass. 21, 36 N.E. 468 (1894) (mistake of process server as to right of entry); RESTATEMENT (SECOND) OF TORTS § 164 (1965).

[71] If the defendant could prevail by showing that his mistake was reasonable, the court would not have to resolve the conflicting claims of title to the land. Similarly, if the defendant in a defamation action could prevail by showing that

Where compensation is the primary issue, however, one may
fairly conclude that the basic excuses acknowledged in *Weaver
v. Ward* — compulsion and unavoidable ignorance — transcend
doctrinal barriers and apply in all cases of nonreciprocal risk-
taking.

Recognizing the pervasiveness of nonreciprocity as a standard
of liability, as limited by the availability of excuses, should provide a new perspective on tort doctrine and demonstrate that
strict liability and negligence as applied in the cases discussed
above are not contrary theories of liability. Rather, strict liability and negligence appear to be complementary expressions of
the same paradigm of liability.

III. THE PARADIGM OF REASONABLENESS

Until the mid-nineteenth century, the paradigm of reciprocity
dominated the law of personal injury. It accounted for cases of
strict liability and of intentional torts and for the distinction
implicit in the common law writ system between background
risks and risks directly violating the interests of others.[72] In the
course of the nineteenth century, however, the concepts underlying the paradigm of reciprocity gradually assumed new contours. A new paradigm emerged, which challenged all traditional
ideas of tort theory. The new paradigm challenged the assumption that the issue of liability could be decided on grounds of
fairness to both victim and defendant without considering the
impact of the decisions on the society at large. It further challenged the assumption that the victim's right to recovery was
distinguishable from the defendant's duty to pay. In short, the
new paradigm of reasonableness represented a new style of thinking about tort disputes.

The core of this revolutionary change was a shift in the
meaning of the word "fault." At its origins in the common law
of torts, the concept of fault served to unify the medley of excuses available to defendants who would otherwise be liable in
trespass for directly causing harm.[73] As the new paradigm
emerged, fault came to be an inquiry about the context and the

---

he was reasonably mistaken about the truth of the defamatory statement, the court
would never reach the truth or falsity of the statement. To permit litigation of the
truth of the charge, the law of defamation rejects reasonable mistake as an excuse.
See Corrigan v. Bobbs-Merrill Co., 228 N.Y. 58, 126 N.E. 260 (1920); Hulton &
Co. v. Jones, [1909] 2 K.B. 444, *aff'd*, [1910] A.C. 20. In both of these cases,
it was held irrelevant that the defendant did not intend his remarks to refer to
the plaintiff.

[72] *See* notes 15 *supra* and 86 *infra.*

[73] *See* pp. 551–52 *supra.*

reasonableness of the defendant's risk-creating conduct.[74] Recasting fault from an inquiry about excuses into an inquiry about the reasonableness of risk-taking laid the foundation for the new paradigm of liability. It provided the medium for tying the determination of liability to maximization of social utility, and it led to the conceptual connection between the issue of fault and the victim's right to recover. The essence of the shift is that the claim of faultlessness ceased being an excuse and became a justification. The significance of this transformation is difficult to appreciate today, for the concepts of excuse and justification have themselves become obscure in our moral and legal thinking.[75] To clarify the conceptual metamorphosis of the fault concept, I must pause to explicate the difference between justifying and excusing conduct.

---

[74] Unreasonable risk-taking — doing that which a reasonable man would not do — is now the standard measure of negligence. *See, e.g.*, PROSSER 145–51; RESTATEMENT (SECOND) OF TORTS §§ 282–83 (1965). *But cf.* MODEL PENAL CODE § 2.02(2)(d) (Proposed Official Draft, 1962) (defining negligence as the taking of a "substantial and unjustified risk" and invoking the reasonable man only to account for the blameworthiness of the negligent conduct).

[75] Inadequate appreciation for the distinction between excuse and justification is clearly seen today in negligence per se cases. Courts and commentators use the terms "justification" and "excuse" interchangeably to refer to the criteria defeating the statutory norm. *See, e.g.*, Alarid v. Vanier, 50 Cal. 2d 617, 327 P.2d 897 (1958); HARPER & JAMES 1007–10. As a consequence, they are unable to satisfactorily rationalize giving conclusive effect to the legislature's determination of safe conduct while at the same time permitting the jury to make the final determination of the defendant's negligence. If excuse and justification are just two different labels for a univocal concept, these goals do appear incompatible; the statute cannot be conclusive on the issue of negligence if the jury also decides the same issue. Recognizing that the concept of fault is dualistic, that excusability is a separate dimension of fault, would enable courts to regard the violation of a statute as conclusive on negligence, but inconclusive on the excusability of the negligent conduct. Thus, the legislature would be given its due without sacrificing justice to the individual defendant who can show, for example, that he was compelled to run the illegal risk or prevented from perceiving its magnitude.

The distinction between excuse and justification in these cases was not always so obscure. *See* Martin v. Herzog, 228 N.Y. 164, 168, 126 N.E. 814, 815 (1920) (Cardozo, J.) (defining "the *unexcused* omission of the statutory signals" as negligence per se) (emphasis added).

The MODEL PENAL CODE §§ 3.04(1), 3.11(1) (Proposed Official Draft, 1962) (excused force is nevertheless unlawful force, but privileged or justified force is not), maintained a distinction between excuse and justification in formulating a definition of unlawful force for the purpose of delimiting the scope of self-defense. But this distinction did not survive adoptation of the CODE in Illinois and Wisconsin. ILL. REV. STAT. ch. 38, § 7 (1969); WIS. STAT. § 939.42–.49 (1969). *See also* GA. CODE § 26–1011 (1933) ("There being no rational distinction between excusable and justifiable homicide, it shall no longer exist."), *as amended* § 26–901. The distinction is very much alive among philosophers, *see, e.g.*, Austin, *A Plea for Excuses*, 57 ARISTOTELIAN SOC'Y PROCEEDINGS 1 (1956–57), in FREEDOM AND RESPONSIBILITY 6 (H. Morris ed. 1961).

The difference between justifying and excusing conditions is most readily seen in the case of intentional conduct, particularly intentional crimes. Typical cases of justified intentional conduct are self-defense [76] and the use of force to effect an arrest.[77] These justificatory claims assess the reasonableness of using force under the circumstances. The questions asked in seeking to justify an intentional battery as self-defense relate to the social costs and the social benefits of using force and to the wrongfulness of the initial aggressor's conduct in attacking the defendant. The resolution of this cost-benefit analysis speaks to the legal permissibility and sometimes to the commendability of the *act* of using force under the circumstances. Excuses, in contrast, focus not on the costs and benefits of the *act*, but on the degree of the *actor*'s choice in engaging in it. Insanity and duress are raised as excuses even to concededly wrongful acts.[78] To resolve a claim of insanity, we are led to inquire about the *actor*'s personality, his capacities under stress and the pressures under which he was acting. Finding that the *actor* is excused by reason of insanity is not to say that the *act* was right or even permissible, but merely that the actor's freedom of choice was so impaired that he cannot be held accountable for his wrongful deed.

Justifying and excusing claims bear different relationships to the rule of liability. To justify conduct is to say that in the future, conduct under similar circumstances will not be regarded as wrongful or illegal. Excusing conduct, however, leaves intact the imperative not to engage in the excused act. Acquitting a

---

[76] Self-defense is routinely referred to today as an instance of justification. *See, e.g.,* MODEL PENAL CODE § 3.04 (Proposed Official Draft, 1962) (including self-defense in article 3 of the CODE, which is titled "General Principles of Justification"); CAL. PENAL CODE § 197 (West 1970) ("justifiable homicide"); note 75 *supra.* In contrast, Blackstone described *se defendendo* as an instance of excusable homicide. 4 W. BLACKSTONE, COMMENTARIES *183–84. In Blackstone's day, the rubric of excusable homicide applied to those cases in which the defendant suffered only forfeiture of goods, but not execution or other punishment. *See* R. PERKINS, CRIMINAL LAW 892 (1957).

[77] The clearest case of common law justification was that of a legal official acting under authority of law. *See* 4 W. BLACKSTONE, COMMENTARIES *178–79.

[78] The MODEL PENAL CODE (Proposed Official Draft, 1962) acknowledges that claims of insanity and duress are distinguishable from claims of justification and does not include them within article 3's "General Principles of Justification." Rather, they appear in §§ 4.01 and 2.09 respectively.

The common law is ambivalent on the status of duress. The defense is not recognized in homicide cases, State v. Nargashian, 26 R.I. 299, 58 A. 953 (1904), thus suggesting that the focus of the defense may be the rightness of the defendant's act, rather than the involuntariness of the actor's response to external coercion. German law unequivocally acknowledges that duress is an excuse and that it applies even in homicide cases. StGB § 52 (C.H. Beck 1970); A. SCHÖNKE & H. SCHRÖDER, STRATGESETZBUCH: KOMMENTAR 457 (15th ed. 1970).

man by reason of insanity does not change the norm prohibiting murder. Rather, it represents a judgment that a particular person, acting under particular pressures at a particular time, cannot be held accountable for violating that norm. The difference between changing the rule and finding in a particular case that it does not apply is best captured by asking whether in finding for the defendant the court recognizes a right to engage in the activity. To justify conduct as self-defense is to recognize a right to use force, but to excuse homicide under duress is not to acknowledge a right to kill. It is rather to recognize that an actor cannot be fairly blamed for having succumbed to pressures requiring him to kill.[79]

The distinction between justifying and excusing conduct applies with equal coherence in analyzing risk-creating behavior. Questions about the excusability of risk-creation focus on the actor's personal circumstances and his capacity to avoid the risk. Could he have resisted the intimidations of a gunman in his car? Could he have found out about the risks latent in his conduct? Questions about justification, on the other hand, look solely to the risk, abstracted from the personality of the risk-creator. What are the benefits of the risk? What are the costs? Does the risk maximize utility? As the inquiry shifts from excusing to justifying risks, the actor and his traits become irrelevant. At the level of justification, the only relevant question is whether the risk, on balance, is socially desirable. Excusing a risk, as a personal judgment about the actor, leaves the right of the victim intact; but justifying a risk recognizes the defendant's right to run that risk vis-à-vis the victim. If the risk is justified in this sense, the victim could hardly have a claim against the risk-creator. The right of the risk-creator supplants the right of the victim to recover.[80]

That the fault requirement shifted its orientation from ex-

---

[79] This is fairly clear in the law of *se defendendo*, which is the one instance in which the common law recognized an excuse to a homicide charge based on external pressure rather than the propriety of the act. *See* E. COKE, THIRD INSTITUTE *55; note 78 *supra*. For the defense to be available, the defedant had to first retreat to the wall if he could do so without risking his life and had to have no other means than the use of force for preserving his own life. Coke speaks of the killing in these cases as "being done upon inevitable cause." COKE, THIRD INSTITUTE *55.

These issues are more thoroughly discussed in Fletcher, *The Theory of Criminal Negligence: A Comparative Analysis*, 119 U. PA. L. REV. 401 (1971). For a general account of the deficiencies in the common law approach to excusing conditions, see G. Fletcher, The Individualization of Excusing Conditions, 1971 (unpublished manuscript on file at the Harvard Law School Library).

[80] T. COOLEY, A TREATISE ON THE LAW OF TORTS 81 (1879) ("That which it is right and lawful for one man to do cannot furnish the foundation for an action in favor of another.").

cusing to justifying risks had the following consequences: (1) fault became a judgment about the risk, rather than about the responsibility of the individual who created the risk; (2) fault was no longer a question of fairness to the individual, but an inquiry about the relative costs and benefits of particular risks; (3) fault became a condition for recognizing the right of the victim to recover. These three postures of the fault requirement diverged radically from the paradigm of reciprocity. Together, they provided the foundation for the paradigm of reasonableness, a way of thinking that was to become a powerful ideological force in tort thinking of the late nineteenth and twentieth centuries.[81]

The reasonable man became a central, almost indispensable figure in the paradigm of reasonableness.[82] By asking what a reasonable man would do under the circumstances, judges could assay the issues both of justifying and excusing risks. Reasonable men, presumably, seek to maximize utility; therefore, to ask what a reasonable man would do is to inquire into the justifiability of the risk.[83] If the risk-running might be excused, say by reason of the emergency doctrine or a particular defect like blindness or immaturity, the jury instruction might specify the excusing condition as one of the "circumstances" under which the conduct of the reasonable man is to be assessed. If the court wished to include or exclude a teenage driver's immaturity as a possible excusing condition, it could define the relevant "circumstances" accordingly.[84] Because the "reasonable man" test so adeptly encompasses both issues of justification and excuse, it is not surprising that the paradigm of reasonableness has led to the blurring of that distinction in tort theory.[85]

[81] The impact of the paradigm is not so much that negligence emerged as a rationale of liability, for many cases of negligence are compatible with the paradigm of reciprocity. See pp. 548–49 supra. The ideological change was the conversion of each tort dispute into a medium for furthering social goals. See Prosser's discussion of "social engineering," PROSSER 14–16. This reorientation of the process led eventually to the blurring of the issues of corrective justice and distributive justice discussed at note 40 supra.

[82] For early references to "reasonableness" as the standard of negligence, see Blyth v. Birmingham Waterworks Co., 156 Eng. Rep. 1047 (Ex. 1856); COOLEY, supra note 80, at 662. But cf. Vaughan v. Menlove, 132 Eng. Rep. 490, 493 (C.P. 1837) ("a man of ordinary prudence"). Notions of "ordinary" and "normal" men are compatible with the paradigm of reciprocity; reciprocal risks are those that ordinary men normally impose on each other. The shift to the "reasonable" man was significant, for it foreshadowed the normative balancing of the interests implicit in the concept of reasonableness as an objective standard.

[83] See pp. 558–59 supra.

[84] See note 62 supra.

[85] It is especially surprising that courts and commentators have not explicitly perceived that the emergency doctrine functions to excuse unreasonable risks. See cases cited note 58 supra; HARPER & JAMES 938–40; PROSSER 168–70.

No single appellate decision ushered in the paradigm of reasonableness. It derived from a variety of sources.[86] If there was a pivotal case, however, it was *Brown v. Kendall*,[87] decided by the Massachusetts Supreme Judicial Court in 1850. The facts of the case were well-suited to blurring the distinction between excusing the defendant's ignorance and assessing the utility of the risk that he took. In an effort to separate two fighting dogs, Kendall began beating them with a stick. Brown was standing nearby, which Kendall presumably knew; and both he and Brown moved about with the fighting dogs. At one point, when he had just backed up to a position in front of Brown, Kendall raised his stick, hitting Brown in the eye and causing serious injury. Brown sought to recover on the writ of trespass, whereby traditionally a plaintiff could establish a prima facie case simply by proving that his injuries were the direct result of the defendant's act — a relationship which clearly existed in the case.

In order for the defendant to invoke the defense of inevitable accident, he would have had to show that he neither knew nor could have been expected to know Brown's whereabouts at the

---

[86] One can distinguish among the following strains that converged in the course of the nineteenth century:

(1) the tendency to regard more and more affirmative conduct as equivalent to passive, background activity. The English courts took this view of activities that one had a right to engage in. *See* Tillett v. Ward, 10 Q.B.D. 17 (1882) (right to drive oxen on highway; no liability for damage to ironmonger's shop); Goodwyn v. Cheveley, 28 L.J. Ex. (n.s.) 298 (1859) (right to drive cattle on highway; no liability to neighboring property). The American courts started with the suggestion in Vincent v. Stinehour, 7 Vt. 62, 65 (1835), that duty-bound acts were to be treated like background risks. Brown v. Kendall, 60 Mass. (6 Cush.) 292, 296 (1850), extended this category to include all acts "lawful and proper to do," thus obliterating the distinction between background risks and assertive conduct.

(2) the judgment that those who go near dangerous areas, like highways, "[take] upon themselves the risk of injury from that inevitable danger . . . ." Fletcher v. Rylands, 65 L.R. 1 Ex. 265, 286 (1866) (Blackburn, J.).

(3) the indulgence by courts in a fallacious reinterpretation of older decisions, such as Gibbons v. Pepper, 87 Eng. Rep. 469 (K.B. 1695), to stand for the proposition that if the act is "not imputable to the neglect of the party by whom it is done, or to his want of caution, an action of trespass does not lie . . . ." Harvey v. Dunlop, Hill & Denio Supp. 193, 194 (N.Y. 1843); *cf.* Vincent v. Stinehour, 7 Vt. at 64 (If "no degree of blame can be imputed to the defendant, the conduct of the defendant was not unlawful."). The fallacy of this reasoning is the assumption that recognizing faultlessness as an excuse entailed an affirmative requirement of proving fault as a condition of recovery (fallacy of the excluded middle).

(4) the positivist view that tort liability was functionally equivalent to criminal liability. I J. AUSTIN, LECTURES ON JURISPRUDENCE 416, 516–20 (3d ed. R. Campbell 1869); J. SALMOND, LAW OF TORTS 12 (3d ed. 1912). According to this view, requiring an activity to pay its way is to impose a sanction for unlawful activity.

[87] 60 Mass. (6 Cush.) 292 (1850).

moment he last raised the stick. Thus, to argue that he should be excused on the ground of ignorance, he would have had to show that the situation was such that it was expectable and blameless for him not to inform himself better of Brown's position before the fateful blow. But an inquiry about the acceptability of the defendant's ignorance as an excuse leads to a broader assessment of the defendant's conduct in putting himself in a position where he unwittingly created a risk of harm to Brown. There is an important difference between (1) looking at the narrower context to determine whether at the moment of heightened risk — when Kendall raised the stick — his ignorance was excusable and (2) broadening the context and thereby leveling the risk by shifting the inquiry from the moment of the stick-raising to the general activity of separating the dogs. Observing that distinction was essential to retaining faultlessness as a question of excusing, rather than justifying trespassory conduct. Yet it was a distinction that had lost its conceptual force. The trial judge and Chief Justice Shaw, writing for the Supreme Judicial Court, agreed that the defense of inevitable accident went to the adequacy of the defendant's care under the circumstances.[88] But the two judges disagreed on the conceptual status of the issue of the required care. The trial judge, in line with several centuries of case authority, saw the issue as an exception to liability, to be proven by the defendant.[89] Shaw converted the issue of the defendant's failure to exercise ordinary care into a new premise of liability, to be proven by the plaintiff, thus signaling and end to direct causation as a rationale for prima facie liability.[90]

Admittedly, *Brown v. Kendall* could be read as a revision of the standard for excusing unwitting risk-creation: instead of extraordinary care, ordinary care should suffice to admit ignorance as an excuse; and it should be up to the plaintiff to prove the issue. Though the case might have yielded this minor modification of the law, Chief Justice Shaw's opinion created possibilities for an entirely new and powerful use of the fault standard, and the judges and writers of the late nineteenth and early twentieth centuries responded sympathetically.[91]

---

[88] Their difference was one of degree. The trial judge thought the issue was whether the defendant had exercised extraordinary care, *id.* at 293; Judge Shaw saw the issue as one of ordinary care, *id.* at 296.

[89] *Id.* at 294.

[90] *Id.* at 297.

[91] American authorities readily came to the conclusion that fault-based negligence and intentional battery exhausted the possibilities for recovery for personal injury. *See* Cooley, *supra* note 80, at 80, 164; *cf.* 3 S. Greenleaf, Evidence 74 (2d ed. 1848) (pre-*Brown v. Kendall*). Trespass survived much longer in the English literature. *See* Goodhart & Winfield, *Trespass and Negligence*, 49 L.Q.

Shaw's revision of tort doctrine made its impact in cases in which the issue was not one of excusing inadvertent risk-creation, but one of justifying risks of harm that were voluntarily and knowingly generated. Consider the following cases of risk-creation: (1) the defendant operates a streetcar, knowing that the trains occasionally jump the tracks;[92] (2) the defendant police officer shoots at a fleeing felon, knowing that he thereby risks hitting a bystander;[93] (3) the defendant undertakes to float logs downriver to a mill, knowing that flooding might occur which could injure crops downstream.[94] All of these victims could receive compensation for their injuries under the paradigm of reciprocity, as incorporated in the doctrine of trespassory liability; the defendant or his employees directly and without excuse caused the harm in each case. Yet as *Brown v. Kendall* was received into the tort law, the threshold of liability became whether, under all the circumstances, the defendant acted with ordinary, prudent care. But more importantly, the test of ordinary care transcended its origins as a standard for determining the acceptability of ignorance as an excuse, and became a rationale for determining when individuals could knowingly and voluntarily create risks without responsibility for the harm they might cause. The test for justifying risks became a straightforward utilitarian comparison of the benefits and costs of the defendant's risk-creating activity.[95] The assumption emerged that reasonable men do what

---

REV. 359 (1933); Roberts, *Negligence: Blackstone to Shaw to ? An Intellectual Escapade in a Tory Vein*, 50 CORNELL L. REV. 191 (1965). However, Roberts argued that trespass died among English practitioners well before the academic commentators wrote its obituary. *Id.* at 207–08.

[92] *See* Felske v. Detroit United Ry., 166 Mich. 367, 371–72, 130 N.W. 676, 678 (1911); Kelly v. United Traction Co., 88 App. Div. 234, 235–36, 85 N.Y.S. 433, 434 (1903). *But cf.* Chicago Union Traction Co. v. Giese, 229 Ill. 260, 82 N.E. 232 (1907) (applying res ipsa loquitur). Some of the earlier cases exonerating transportation interests were Beatty v. Central Iowa Ry., 58 Iowa 242, 12 N.W. 332 (1882) (employing cost-benefit analysis to hold railroad need not eliminate all risk when designing a grade crossing); Bielenberg v. Montana Union Ry., 8 Mont. 271, 20 P. 314 (1889) (statute making railroads absolutely liable for injury to livestock held unconstitutional; liability had to be based on negligence); Steffen v. Chicago & N.W. Ry., 46 Wis. 259, 50 N.W. 348 (1879) (train caused rock to shoot up and hit employee standing nearby; judgment for plaintiff reversed).

[93] *Brown v. Kendall* had an immediate impact in Morris v. Platt, 32 Conn. 75, 79–80 (1864) (liability for gun shot wound to bystander only if firing was negligent as to bystander); *see* Paxton v. Boyer, 67 Ill. 132 (1873); Shaw v. Lord, 41 Okla. 347, 137 P. 885 (1914).

[94] *See* Hopkins v. Butte & M. Commercial Co., 13 Mont. 223, 33 P. 817 (1893) (defendant's floating logs caused stream to dam, flooding plaintiff's land and destroying crops; no liability in the absence of negligence).

[95] The utilitarian calculus did not become explicit until Terry explicated the courts' thinking in his classic article, Terry, *Negligence*, 29 HARV. L. REV. 40 (1915).

is justified by a utilitarian calculus, that justified activity is lawful, and that lawful activities should be exempt from tort liability.

In the cases mentioned above, the arguments are readily at hand for maximizing utility by optimizing accidents: (1) the expense of providing rails to prevent streetcars from leaving the tracks would require a substantial increase in streetcar fares — it is better that occasional accidents occur; (2) capturing fleeing felons is sufficiently important to warrant a few risks to onlookers; (3) transporting logs sufficiently furthers the social good to justify some risks to farmers. More generally, if promoting the general welfare is the criterion of rights and duties of compensation, then a few individuals must suffer. One might fairly wonder, however, why streetcar passengers, law enforcement, and the lumber industry should prosper at the expense of innocent victims.

IV. Utility and the Interests of the Individual

The accepted reading of tort history is that the rise of the fault standard in the nineteenth century manifested a newly found sensitivity to the morality of legal rules. James Barr Ames captured orthodox sentiments with his conclusion that "[t]he ethical standard of reasonable conduct has replaced the unmoral standard of acting at one's peril." [96] This reading of the case law development finds its source in Holmes' dichotomy between acting at one's peril and liability based on fault.[97] The assumption of Holmes' influential analysis is that there are only two doctrinal possibilities: the fault standard, particularly as expressed in *Brown v. Kendall*,[98] and strict or absolute liability. The latter is dubbed unmoral; therefore, the only option open to morally sensitive theorists would appear to be liability for fault alone.

The mistake in this reading of legal history is the unanalyzed assumption that every departure from the fault standard partakes of the strict liability expressed in the maxim "a man acts at his peril." There are in fact at least four distinct points on the continuum from strict liability to the limitation on liability introduced by *Brown v. Kendall*. In resolving a routine trespass dispute for bodily injury, a common law court might, among other things:

(1) reject the relevance of excuses in principle and rule for the plaintiff;

---

[96] Ames, *Law and Morals, supra* note 7, at 99.

[97] *See* Holmes, *supra* note 7, at 79–80.

[98] *See* pp. 561–62 *supra*.

(2) recognize the principle of excusing trespassory conduct, but find under the facts of the case that the defendant's conduct was unexcused;

(3) find that the defendant's conduct was excused and therefore exempt from liability;

(4) recognize reasonableness as a justification for directly causing harm to another.

If the maxim "acting at one's peril" connotes a standard that is "unmoral" — a standard that is insensitive to the fairness of imposing liability — then the charge properly attaches only to the first of the above four categories. It is only in this situation that authoring harm is conclusive on liability. Yet there are few, if any, unequivocal examples of this form of decision in the common law tradition.[99] After *Weaver v. Ward*,[100] one can hardly speak of the common law courts maintaining, as a principle, that excusing conditions are irrelevant to liability.[101]

Cases of the second type did abound at the time of Holmes' writing.[102] They represent victories for injured plaintiffs, but they affirm, at least implicitly, the traditional requirement that the act directly causing harm be unexcused. Yet Holmes treats these cases as instances of absolute liability, of "acting at one's peril."[103] In so doing, he ignores the distinction between reject-

---

[99] Even in The Thorns Case, Y.B. Mich. 6 Edw. 4, f.7, pl. 18 (1466), reprinted in C. FIFOOT, HISTORY AND SOURCES OF THE COMMON LAW 195 (1949), where the defendant was liable in trespass for entering on plaintiff's land to pick up thorns he had cut, Choke, C.J., said the defendant would have a good plea if "he [had done . . . all that was in his power to keep them out]." *Id.* at 196.

[100] 80 Eng. Rep. 284 (K.B. 1616); *see* pp. 551–52 *supra*.

[101] *See generally* Wigmore, *Responsibility for Tortious Acts: Its History*, 7 HARV. L. REV. 441 (1894); Winfield, *The Myth of Absolute Liability*, 42 L.Q. REV. 37 (1926).

[102] In some cases, the unexcused nature of the defendant's risk-taking was obvious on the facts. *See* Leame v. Bray, 102 Eng. Rep. 724 (K.B. 1803) (defendant was driving on the wrong side of the highway; issue was whether trespass would lie); Underwood v. Hewson, 93 Eng. Rep. 722 (K.B. 1724) (defendant cocked gun and it fired; court held trespass would lie). In Dickenson v. Watson, 84 Eng. Rep. 1218 (K.B. 1682) the court said that the claim of "unavoidable necessity" was not adequately shown. In a third type of case, plaintiffs received verdicts despite instructions requiring the jury to assess the excusability of the defendant's act. *See* Goodman v. Taylor, 172 Eng. Rep. 1031 (K.B. 1832); *cf.* Castle v. Duryee, 2 Keyes 169, 174 (N.Y. 1865) (suggesting that the instructions were too favorable to the defendant).

[103] HOLMES, *supra* note 7, at 87–89. Holmes relies heavily on a quote from Grose, J., in Leame v. Bray, 102 Eng. Rep. 724, 727 (K.B. 1803): "[I]f . . . the act of the party . . . be the immediate cause of [the injury], though it happen accidentally or by misfortune, . . . he is answerable in trespass." Yet Grose, J., relies on Underwood v. Hewson, 93 Eng. Rep. 722 (K.B. 1724), and Weaver v. Ward, 80 Eng. Rep. 284 (K.B. 1616), *see* pp. 551–52, both of which at least implicitly recognize excusing conditions. Holmes supposed that if one were liable

ing excuses in principle (type one) and rejecting an alleged excuse on the facts of the case (type two). There is an obvious difference between finding for the plaintiff regardless of fault and finding for the plaintiff because the defendant fails to convince the trier of fact that he acted "utterly without fault." By ignoring this difference, as well as the distinction between denying fault by claiming an excuse and urging reasonableness as a justification, Holmes could generate a dichotomy that made *Brown v. Kendall* seem like an admirable infusion of ethical sensitivity into tort doctrine.

But the issue in the nineteenth century was not the choice between strict liability on the one hand and liability based on fault on the other. Nor was it a simplistic choice between an "unmoral" standard and an ethical one. Rather, the question of the time was the shape that the fault standard would take. Should the absence of fault function as an excuse within a paradigm of reciprocity? Or should it function as a standard for exempting from liability risks that maximize utility? That was the moral and policy question that underlay the nineteenth century revolution in tort thinking. The question posed by the conflict of paradigms was whether traditional notions of individual autonomy would survive increasing concern for the public welfare. If the courts of the time had clearly perceived and stated the issue, they would have been shaken by its proportions.

The same fundamental conflict between the public interest and individual autonomy arose even more sharply in criminal cases that reached the courts in the late nineteenth century. The public interest found expression in tort disputes by decisions protecting activities thought to be socially useful, and in criminal cases by decisions designed to deter activities thought to be socially pernicious. Just as one goal of social policy might require some innocent accident *plaintiffs* to suffer their injuries without compensation, the other might require some morally innocent *defendants* to suffer criminal sanctions. Indeed, both matters received decisive judicial action in the same decade. Shortly before Chief Justice Shaw laid the groundwork in *Brown v. Kendall*[104] for exempting socially useful risks from tort liability,[105] he expressed the same preference for group welfare over individual autonomy in criminal cases. In *Commonwealth v. Mash*[106] he

---

for an "accidental" injury, then liability, in some sense, violated principles of fairness; but the terms "accident" and "misfortune" are perfectly compatible with unexcused risk-taking.

[104] 60 Mass. (6 Cush.) 292 (1850).

[105] *See* pp. 561–62 *supra.*

[106] 48 Mass. (7 Met.) 472 (1844).

generated a rationale for a bigamy conviction against a woman who sincerely regarded her absent husband as dead. Shaw tacitly conceded that Mrs. Mash was not blameworthy for entering into the second marriage.[107] Yet that mattered little, he argued, for preventing bigamy was "essential to the peace of families and the good order of society. . . ."[108] Thus, in Shaw's mind, the social interest in deterring bigamy justified convicting a morally innocent woman.[109] Shaw's decision in *Mash* was of the same ideological frame as his rewriting of tort doctrine in *Brown v. Kendall*. If a judge is inclined to sacrifice morally innocent offenders for the sake of social control, he is also likely to require the victims of socially useful activities to bear their injuries without compensation.[110] It is not at all surprising, then, that the rise of strict liability in criminal cases parallels the emergence of the paradigm of reasonableness in the law of negligent torts.[111] If it is unorthodox to equate strict liability in criminal cases with a species of negligence in tort disputes, it is only because we are the victims of the labels we use. If we shift our focus from the magic of legal rubrics to the policy struggle underlying tort and criminal liability, then it is quite clear that the appropriate analogy is between strict criminal liability and the limitation imposed by the rule of reasonableness in tort doctrine.

---

[107] Shaw acknowledged the distinction between the "criminal intent" that rendered an actor blameworthy and the "criminal intent" that could be imputed to someone who voluntarily did the act prohibited by the legislature. *Id.* at 474. It was only in the latter sense, Shaw conceded, that Mrs. Mash acted with "criminal intent." *Id.*

[108] *Id.* at 473.

[109] Before sentence was pronounced, Mrs. Mash received a full pardon from the Governor. *Id.* at 475.

[110] Recent decisions of the California courts express the opposite position. The California Supreme Court has sought to protect morally innocent criminal defendants, People v. Hernandez, 61 Cal. 2d 529, 393 P.2d 673, 39 Cal. Rptr. 361 (1964) (recognizing reasonable mistake as to girl's age as a defense in statutory rape cases); People v. Vogel, 46 Cal. 2d 798, 299 P.2d 850 (1956) (recognizing reasonable mistake of marital status as a defense in bigamy cases), and at the same time it has extended protection to innocent accident victims, Elmore v. American Motors Corp., 70 Cal. 2d 578, 451 P.2d 84, 75 Cal. Rptr. 652 (1969) (strict products liability extended to bystanders).

[111] If this thesis is correct, it suggests that the change in judicial orientation in the late nineteenth century was both beneficial and harmful to large business enterprises. Limiting tort liability to negligence was obviously helpful in reducing the costs of doing business; but imposing strict liability on corporate officers raised the nonmonetary costs of production and marketing. *See, e.g.,* People v. Roby, 52 Mich. 577, 18 N.W. 365 (1884) (proprietor held strictly liable for Sunday sale of liquor by his clerk without proprietor's knowledge or intent); Regina v. Stephens, [1866] L.R. 1 Q.B. 702 (quarry owner held strictly liable for his workmen's dumping refuse).

Not surprisingly, then, the contemporary arguments against the utilitarianism expressed in strict criminal liability [112] yield a critique of the rule of reasonableness in tort doctrine. As applied in assessing strict criminal liability, the utilitarian calculus treats the liberty of the morally innocent individual as an interest to be measured against the social interest in deterring criminal conduct; it is a matter of judgment whether to favor the interests of the individual or the interests of society. But there are some sacrifices of individual liberty that persons cannot be expected to make for the welfare of their neighbors. In criminal cases, the claim of those opposing strict liability is that no man should be forced to suffer a condemnatory sanction just because his conduct happens to cause harm or happens to contravene a statute. Something more is required to warrant singling out a particular defendant and subjecting him to sanctions in the interest of deterring would-be offenders. There must be a rationale for overcoming his prima facie right to be left alone. That rationale is provided in the contemporary critical literature by the insistence that only culpable offenders be subject to sanctions designed to deter others.[113] Culpability serves as a standard of moral forfeiture.[114] It provides a standard for assessing when, by virtue of his illegal conduct, the defendant should be treated as having forfeited his freedom from sanctions.

Just as an individual cannot be expected to suffer criminal sanctions for the sake of the common good, he cannot fairly be expected to suffer other deprivations in the name of a utilitarian calculus. His life, bodily integrity, reputation, privacy, liberty and property — all are interests that might claim insulation from deprivations designed to further other interests. Insulation might take the form of criminal or injunctive prohibitions against conduct causing undesired deprivations. But criminal and injunctive sanctions are questionable where the activity is reasonable in the sense that it maximizes utility and thus serves the interests of the community as a whole. Protecting the autonomy of the individual does not require that the community forego activities that serve its interests. In the case of socially useful activities, then, insulation can take the form of damage awards shifting the cost of the deprivation from the individual to the agency unexcusably

---

[112] See, e.g., H. PACKER, THE LIMITS OF THE CRIMINAL SANCTION 62–135 (1968); Dubin, Mens Rea Reconsidered: A Plea for A Due Process Concept of Criminal Responsibility, 18 STAN. L. REV. 322 (1966); Griffiths, Book Review, 79 YALE L.J. 1388 (1970).

[113] See PACKER, supra note 112, at 62–70; Dubin, supra note 112, at 365–66.

[114] Culpability may also function as a standard of moral desert. I have attempted to clarify the difference between these two functions in Fletcher, supra note 79, at 417–18.

causing it. The burden should fall on the wealth-shifting mechanism of the tort system to insulate individual interests against community demands. By providing compensation for injuries exacted in the public interest, the tort system can protect individual autonomy by taxing, but not prohibiting, socially useful activities.[115]

V. The Interplay of Substance and Style

The conflict between the paradigm of reasonableness and the paradigm of reciprocity is, in the end, a struggle between two strategies for justifying the distribution of burdens in a legal system. The strategy of utility proceeds on the assumption that burdens are fairly imposed if the distribution optimizes the interests of the community as a whole. The paradigm of reciprocity, on the other hand, is based on a strategy of waiver. It takes as its starting point the personal rights of individuals in society to enjoy roughly the same degree of security, and appeals to the conduct of the victims themselves to determine the scope of the right to equal security. By interpreting the risk-creating activities of the defendant and of the victim as reciprocal and thus offsetting, courts may tie the denial of liability to the victim to his own waiver of a degree of security in favor of the pursuit of an activity of higher risk.

These two paradigms, and their accompanying strategies for distributing burdens, overlap in every case in which an activity endangers outsiders not participating in the creation of the risk. Where the courts deny liability, say, for leaving a golf club where a child might pick it up and swing it,[116] they must decide whether to appeal either to the paradigm of reciprocity and argue that the risk is an ordinary, reciprocal risk of group living, or to the paradigm of reasonableness and argue that the activity is socially beneficent and warrants encouragement. They must decide, in short, whether to focus on the parties and their relationship or on the society and its needs. In these cases where the paradigms overlap, both ways of thinking may yield the same result. Yet the rhetoric of these decisions creates a pattern that influences reasoning in cases in which the paradigms diverge.

The major divergence is the set of cases in which a socially useful activity imposes nonreciprocal risks on those around it.

---

[115] *But cf.* New York Times v. Sullivan, 376 U.S. 254 (1964), expressing the view that in some situations tort liability impermissibly inhibits the exercise of freedom of the press. If the liberty to create risks were conceived as analogous to free speech, the same criticism would apply to the argument of the text.

[116] *See* Lubitz v. Wells, 19 Conn. Supp. 322, 113 A.2d 147 (Super. Ct. 1955).

These are the cases of motoring, airplane overflights, air pollution, oil spillage, sonic booms — in short, the recurrent threats of modern life.[117] In resolving conflict between those who benefit from these activities and those who suffer from them, the courts must decide how much weight to give to the net social value of the activity. In *Boomer v. Atlantic Cement Co.*,[118] the New York Court of Appeals reflected the paradigm of reciprocity by defining the issue of holding a cement company liable for air pollution as a question of the "rights of the parties," [119] rather than the "promotion of the general public welfare." [120] Similarly, in its recent debate over the liability of airplane owners and operators for damage to ground structures, the American Law Institute faced the same conflict. It too opted for the paradigm of reciprocity.[121]

A variation on this conflict of paradigms emerges when a bystander, injured by a motorist, sues the manufacturer of the vehicle on the theory that a defect in the vehicle caused the accident. In these cases, the ultimate issue is whether the motoring public as a whole should pay a higher price for automobiles in order to compensate manufacturers for their liability costs to pedestrians. The rationale for putting the costs on the motoring public is that motoring, as a whole, imposes a nonreciprocal risk on pedestrians and other bystanders. In addressing itself to this issue in *Elmore v. American Motors Corp.*,[122] the California Supreme Court stressed the inability of bystanders to protect themselves against the risk of defective automobiles. Though it grouped pedestrians together with other drivers in extending strict products liability, the *Elmore* opinion appears to be more oriented to questions of risk and of who subjects whom to an excessive risk than it is to the reasonableness and utility of motoring.

---

[117] There is considerable support among commentators for classifying many of these activities as ultra-hazardous in order to impose liability regardless of their social value. *See, e.g.*, Avins, *Absolute Liability for Oil Spillage*, 36 BROOKLYN L. REV. 359 (1970); Baxter, *The SST: From Watts to Harlem in Two Hours*, 21 STAN. L. REV. 1, 50–53 (1968).

[118] 26 N.Y.2d 219, 257 N.E.2d 870, 309 N.Y.S.2d 312 (1970).

[119] 26 N.Y.2d at 222, 257 N.E.2d at 871, 309 N.Y.S.2d at 314.

[120] *Id.* In deciding whether to grant an injunction in addition to imposing liability for damages, however, the court did consider the economic impact of closing down the cement factory. 26 N.Y.2d at 225, 257 N.E.2d at 873, 309 N.Y.S.2d at 316.

[121] The Institute initially took the position that only abnormal aviation risks should generate liability for ground damage, *see* RESTATEMENT (SECOND) OF TORTS § 520A (Tent. Draft No. 11, 1965), and then, reversing itself the following session, voted to encompass all aviation risks to ground structure within the rule of strict liability, *see* RESTATEMENT (SECOND) OF TORTS § 520A, Note to Institute at 1 (Tent. Draft No. 12, 1966).

[122] 70 Cal. 2d 615, 451 P.2d 84, 75 Cal. Rptr. 652 (1969).

Thus, this opinion, too, hints at a reawakening of sensitivity to the paradigm of reciprocity.

On the whole, however, the paradigm of reasonableness still holds sway over the thinking of American courts. The reasonable man is too popular a figure to be abandoned. The use of litigation to pursue social goals is well entrenched. Yet the appeal to the paradigm might well be more one of style than of substance.

In assessing the reasonableness of risks, lawyers ask many seemingly precise questions: What are the consequences of the risk, its social costs and social benefits? What specific risks are included in the "ambit of the risk"? One can speak of formulae, like the Learned Hand formula,[123] and argue in detail about questions of costs, benefits and trade-offs. This style of thinking is attractive to the legal mind. Its tracings in proximate cause cases are the formulae for defining the scope of the risk. Thus *Palsgraf* enthrones the "eye of reasonable vigilance" to rule over "the orbit of the duty." [124] And the standard of "foreseeability" has become the dominant test of proximate cause.[125] With close examination one sees that these formulae are merely tautological constructs designed to support an aura of utilitarian precision. Only if remote consequences are defined out of existence can one total up the benefits and the costs of all (known) consequences. The test of "foreseeability" permits balancing by restrictively defining the contours of the scales. Unforeseeable risks cannot be counted as part of the costs and benefits of the risk; for, after all, they are unforeseeable and therefore unknowable.[126] There may be much work to be done in explaining why this composite mode of thought — the idiom of balancing, orbits of risk and foreseeability — has captured the contemporary legal mind. But there is little doubt that it has, and this fashionable style of thought buttresses the substantive claims of the paradigm of reasonableness.

The paradigm of reciprocity, on the other hand, for all its substantive and moral appeal, puts questions that are hardly

---

[123] *See* note 19 *supra*.

[124] Palsgraf v. Long Island R.R., 248 N.Y. 339, 343, 162 N.E. 99, 100 (1928).

[125] PROSSER 267; WINFIELD ON TORT 91–92 (8th ed. J. Jolowicz & T. Lewis 1967). The case adopting the test for the Commonwealth is Overseas Tankship (U.K.) Ltd. v. Morts Dock & Engineering Co. Ltd. (The Wagon Mound), [1961] A.C. 388. *But cf.* RESTATEMENT (SECOND) OF TORTS § 435 (no liability for "highly extraordinary" consequences).

[126] Though this aspect of the test is only dimly perceived in the literature, many scholars favor the test of "foreseeability" (or its equivalent) on the ground that it renders the issue of proximate cause symmetrical with the issue of negligence. *See* R. KEETON, LEGAL CAUSE IN THE LAW OF TORTS 18–20 (1963); Pollack, *Liability for Consequences*, 38 L.Q. REV. 165, 167 (1922).

likely to engage the contemporary legal mind: When is a risk so excessive that it counts as a nonreciprocal risk? When are two risks of the same category and thus reciprocally offsetting? It is easy to assert that risks of owning a dog offset those of barbecuing in one's backyard, but what if the matter should be disputed? There are at least two kinds of difficulties that arise in assessing the relationship among risks. The first is that of protecting minorities. Does everyone have to engage in crop dusting for the risk to be reciprocal, or just half the community? A tempting solution to the problem is to say that as to someone not engaged in the activity, the risks are per se nonreciprocal. But the gains of this simplifying stroke are undercut by the assumption necessarily implicit in the concept of reciprocity that risks are fungible with others of the same "kind." Yet how does one determine when risks are counterpoised as species of the same genus? If one man owns a dog, and his neighbor a cat, the risks presumably offset each other. But if one man drives a car, and the other rides a bicycle? Or if one plays baseball in the street and the other hunts quail in the woods behind his house? No two people do exactly the same things. To classify risks as reciprocal risks, one must perceive their unifying features. Thus, risks of owning domestic animals may be thought to be of the same kind. And, theoretically, one might argue with equal vigor that all sporting activities requiring the projection of objects through the air create risks of the same order, whether the objects be baseballs, arrows, or bullets. Determining the appropriate level of abstraction is patently a matter of judgment; yet the judgments require use of metaphors and images — a way of thinking that hardly commends itself as precise and scientific.

In proximate cause disputes the analogue to this style of thinking is the now rejected emphasis on the directness and immediacy of causal links, as well expressed in the *Polemis* case [127] and Judge Andrews' dissent in *Palsgraf*.[128] As Hart and Honore have recognized,[129] we rely on causal imagery in solving problems of causal connection in ordinary, nonlegal discourse. Why, then, does the standard of "direct causation" strike many today as arbitrary and irrational? [130] Why does metaphoric thinking command so little respect among lawyers? [131] Why not agree

[127] *In re* Polemis, [1921] 3 K.B. 560.

[128] Palsgraf v. Long Island R.R., 248 N.Y. 339, 347, 162 N.E. 99, 101 (1928).

[129] H.L.A. HART & A. HONORE, CAUSATION IN THE LAW 24–57, 64–76 (1959).

[130] *See, e.g.*, PROSSER 264 ("this approach [*i.e.* direct causation] is obviously an arbitrary one"); Seavey, *Mr. Justice Cardozo and the Law of Torts*, 39 COLUM. L. REV. 20, 37, 52 HARV. L. REV. 372, 389, 48 YALE L.J. 390, 407 (1939) ("those using the test of directness are merely playing with a metaphor").

[131] Part of the reaction against writers like Beale, *The Proximate Consequences*

with Judge Andrews that the issue of proximate cause is akin to assessing when a stream merges with waters of another source? [132]

Metaphors and causal imagery may represent a mode of thought that appears insufficiently rational in an era dominated by technological processes. Yet why should the rhetoric of reasonableness and foreseeability appeal to lawyers as a more scientific or precise way of thinking? The answer might lie in the scientific image associated with passing through several stages of argument before reaching a conclusion. The paradigm of reasonableness requires several stages of analysis: defining the risk, assessing its consequences, balancing costs and benefits. The paradigm of reciprocity requires a single conclusion, based on perceptions of similarities, of excessiveness, and of directness. If an argument requires several steps, it basks in the respectability of precision and rationality. Yet associating rationality with multistaged argumentation may be but a spectacular lawyerly fallacy — akin to the social scientists' fallacy of misplaced concreteness (thinking that numbers make a claim more accurate).

Whether or not multistaged argumentation is more rational than a perception of directness or excessiveness, one cannot but be impressed with the interplay of substantive and stylistic criteria in the conflict between the two paradigms of tort liability. Protecting innocent victims from socially useful risks is one issue. The relative rationality of defining risks and balancing consequences is quite another. That there are these two levels of tension helps explain the ongoing vitality of both paradigms of tort liability.

The courts face the choice. Should they surrender the individual to the demands of maximizing utility? Or should they continue to protect individual interests in the face of community needs? To do the latter, courts and lawyers may well have to perceive the link between achieving their substantive goals and explicating their value choices in a simpler, sometimes metaphoric style of reasoning.

---

of an Act, 33 HARV. L. REV. 633 (1920), is that metaphoric thinking is "mechanical" and insensitive to issues of "policy." PROSSER 264. Legal realism made it unfashionable to try to solve policy problems with verbal formulae and common sense rules. See HART & HONORE, supra note 129, at 92–93.

[132] 248 N.Y. at 352, 162 N.E. at 103.

About the editors: Mark Kuperberg is assistant professor of economics at Swarthmore College. Charles R. Beitz is associate professor of political science at Swarthmore College.